AF387485

INDIA – A FEDERAL UNION OF STATES

BOOKS BY DR MADHAV GODBOLE

1. *India's Governance: An Incisive Commentary on Some Burning Issues*, Konark Publishers, New Delhi, 2019

2. *The Babri Masjid-Ram Mandir Dilemma: An Acid Test for India's Constitution*, Konark Publishers, New Delhi, 2019

3. *Indira Gandhi: An Era of Constitutional Dictatorship*, Manas Publications, New Delhi, 2018

4. *Secularism: India At A Crossroads*, Rupa & Co., New Delhi, 2016

5. *The God Who Failed: An Assessment of Jawaharlal Nehru's Leadership*, Rupa & Co., New Delhi, 2014

6. *Good Governance: Never on India's Radar*, Rupa & Co., New Delhi, 2014

7. *India's Parliamentary Democracy on Trial*, Rupa & Co., New Delhi, 2011

8. *The Judiciary and Governance in India*, Rupa & Co., New Delhi, 2008

9. *The Holocaust of Indian Partition: An Inquest*, Rupa & Co., New Delhi, 2006

10. *Public Accountability and Transparency: The Imperatives of Good Governance*, Orient Longman, New Delhi, 2003

11. *The Changing Times: A Commentary on Current Affairs*, Orient Longman, New Delhi, 2000

12. *Unfinished Innings: Recollections and Reflections of a Civil Servant*, Orient Longman, New Delhi, 1996

13. *Rural Employment Strategy: A Quest in the Wilderness*, Himalaya Publishing House, Mumbai, 1990

14. *Public Expenditures in Maharashtra: A Case For Expenditure Strategy*, Himalaya Publishing House, Mumbai, 1989

15. *Industrial Dispersal Policies: A Case Study of Maharashtra*, Himalaya Publishing House, Mumbai, 1978.

INDIA – A FEDERAL UNION OF STATES

Fault Lines, Challenges and Opportunities

MADHAV GODBOLE

Konark Publishers Pvt Ltd
New Delhi • Seattle

Konark Publishers Pvt Ltd
206, First Floor,
Peacock Lane, Shahpur Jat,
New Delhi - 110 049
Tel : +91-11-4105 5065
e-mail : india@konarkpublishers.com
website : www.konarkpublishers.com

Konark Publishers International
8615, 13th Ave SW,
Seattle, WA 98106
Phone : (415) 409-9988
e-mail : us@konarkpublishers.com

ISBN No.: 978-81-949286-1-4
Edited by Ranjana Narayan
Cover jacket by Misha Oberoi
Cover image©Shutterstock
Printed and bound at Thomson Press (India) Ltd

For
My wife Sujata, as we celebrate 57 years
of cherished companionship
&
my grandchildren
Aditi, Manan, Gaayatri, and Taarini

Contents

Advance Praise

“

This is an erudite and timely study. India is a Union of States and the founding fathers drafted the Constitution in the light of their knowledge, experience and foresight; they also anticipated certain contingencies. The experience of over seven decades, and demands of realpolitik, have shed light on its limitations and Shri Godbole has rightly emphasized the need for putting in place correctives to bring about a structure of *cooperative federalism* that would 'require a complete change in the mindset of the Centre and the states'. An essential ingredient of this has to be the Rajya Sabha for whose more effective functioning in a federal arrangement a number of suggestions have been made by the author.

—Mohammad Hamid Ansari
Former Vice President of India

Shri Madhav Godbole belongs to the vanishing tribe of civil servants who, in the words of Sardar Patel, represented the 'steel frame' of administration. His rich experience in governance and proximity to the power centres during his long and distinguished career make him eminently suitable to raise several critical issues confronting the country today, many of which have been ignored or insufficiently deliberated upon. He is a prolific writer on these and allied matters and his latest offering to the discerning readers, *India – A Federal Union of States: Fault Lines, Challenges and Opportunities,* is thought-provoking, and impels right minded members of the public to seriously introspect about the several issues discussed therein.

The fault lines disturbing the fine balance of power envisaged by the Constitution and the multifarious factors responsible for it have been aptly identified and critically examined. Drawing upon the fund of accumulated experience and knowledge of the author, the book puts forward several out-of-the-box ideas for stemming the downslide. One may agree or disagree with some or many of the ideas articulated as the way forward, but one is compelled to think, debate and come up with one's own optimal solutions to the issues highlighted. Hopefully, the book generates widespread national debate on the seminal issues, as envisaged by the author, snowballing into the 'way forward' as visualised by the author, or otherwise, compatibly with the country's constitutional credentials as a sovereign, socialist, secular, democratic republic. Kudos to the author on his latest book with the expectation of many more to follow from his pen.

—Justice B. N. Srikrishna
Former Judge of the Supreme Court of India

Madhav Godbole has written an extremely valuable book on the federal structure under which the Centre and states in India operate. It is a comprehensive study touching on both political and economic dimensions of the structure as it has evolved. He is highly critical of some of the decisions of the Centre. He also offers several interesting suggestions to make the structure truly federal. A must-read book by all policymakers, political parties and political analysts.

—Dr C. Rangarajan
Former Chairman, Economic Advisory Council
to the Prime Minister & Former Governor, RBI

An issue as urgent as fire rushing towards us. An author, both by his experience and erudition, uniquely able to guide us through treacherous pitfalls. Solutions that are as practical as they are suited to our immense diversity. A must for our times.

—**Arun Shourie**
Former editor, *The Indian Express;*
Former Minister, GOI; and
a leading intellectual

Deeply thought-provoking and insightful. India's federalism decoded—a must-read for every citizen who believes in a better future for India.

—**Deepak Parekh**
Chairman, HDFC Bank, and
a leading financial expert

99

Preface

Will India be a Commonwealth of States, United Nations of India, or some other term denoting a loose federation, or will it continue to be a Federal Union of States, as at present? This question must not be evaded. It has to be faced squarely.

Meghnad Desai bemoans that 'Indians are uneasy about the idea of many "nations" within India. There is deep insecurity about admitting diversity without attributing a lack of patriotism. The United Kingdom has begun to admit for the last fifty years that it is a collection of nations.... Not all nations within India have been treated well' (*The Indian Express*, 24 April 2016, p. 12).

As far back as 1969, Durga Das, in his book, *India: From Curzon to Nehru and After*, had stated, 'In the final analysis, any government at the Centre will, *as of today*, be judged in terms of how it tackles the two issues on whose solution depends the stability of the Indian Union. These are: the Centre-state relations and Kashmir' (Das 1969, p. 410). Though 50 years have elapsed since Durga Das wrote this, these two issues continue to dominate the national discourse. Both these are comprehensively dealt with in this book.

India is not a federation but a Union of States, as the Constitution puts it. India's model of federalism has been bewilderingly and variously described as: quasi-federalism, administrative federalism, pragmatic federalism, asymmetrical federalism, amphibian federalism, competitive federalism, cooperative federalism, creative federalism, collaborative federalism, paramountcy federation, bargaining federalism, flexible federalism, coercive federalism, dual federalism, new federalism, and so on. I have preferred to call it a Federal Union of States, i.e., a union of states organised on a federal basis.

There are several difficulties in writing about India's federalism. One is India's size and diversity. As Atul Kohli puts it in *Democracy and Discontent: India's Growing Crisis of Governability*, 'The country has nearly as many people as all of Africa and Latin America combined, and has probably as much ethnic diversity as is seen in all of Western Europe' (Kohli 1991, p. 11).

The other difficulty is the vast difference in the constituent units of the Union. India has 28 states and eight union territories. Their area, geography, natural endowments, population, financial resources, problems, and perceptions differ a great deal. Their representation in the Rajya Sabha ranges from one member to 80 members. M. Govinda Rao and Nirvikar Singh have stated: In terms of area, Rajasthan is 90 times larger than the smallest state, Goa. In terms of population, Uttar Pradesh, the state with the largest population, is 308 times bigger than the smallest state, Sikkim. The density of population varies from 13 in Arunachal Pradesh to 901 in West Bengal. Maharashtra has the highest net state domestic product (NSDP) which is 284 times that of the state with the lowest NSDP, Sikkim. In 2000-01, Goa, a small state, had a per capita NSDP of Rs 44,613, which was almost nine times that of Bihar with Rs 4,813. The high income states with about 18-19 per cent area and population generated 29 per cent of the NSDP whereas the low income states, with 43-45 per cent of geographic area and population, accounted for only 28 per cent of income (Rao and Singh 2005, pp. 73-74).

Economic viability has never been a consideration in granting statehood. In such a situation, giving equal representation to all states in the Rajya

Sabha is not feasible. Keeping these features in view, the discussion in the book is confined to issues and grievances common to all states.

Importantly, the problem is no longer limited merely to Centre-state relations. It is also an inter-state problem between richer and poorer states. While poorer states have been pressing the Union government to ensure for them a greater share of the national pie, the richer states have begun asking for more powers so as to be able to protect their share of the pie. These issues have surfaced in the controversy regarding the terms of reference of the Fifteenth Finance Commission and the reference year population to be taken into account for devolution of resources.

In addition are the North-South regional connotations evident in the official language policy, which continue to rise from time to time. All these issues and concerns need to be addressed to safeguard the stability of the federation. Clearly, India must evolve its own model of federalism to suit its unique requirements.

Punjab, the richest state in the country in terms of per capita income till 2002-03, has slipped to the 13th position. Even in agriculture, Punjab is falling behind with just 2 per cent annual growth in agriculture.

Mention must be made of the difficulties in writing about J&K. One difficulty is that most of the official records on the subject are still treated as secret. Y.D. Gundevia, former Foreign Secretary, could not access them and his book was titled *Outside the Archives*. Although letters from Nehru are published in the *Selected Works of Jawaharlal Nehru*, letters written by others to Nehru are not accessible, except for copies retained by them. In his memoirs (*Flames of the Chinar*, p. 126), Sheikh Abdullah complained that he had requested Nehru for permission to publish his letters to him [Nehru], Maulana Azad and Rafi Ahmed Kidwai, after [Ghulam Mohammad] Bakshi had referred to them, but 'to no avail. The ban remains' (Ajit Bhattacharjea 2008, p. 168, footnote 2). A.G. Noorani has stated that the texts of Sheikh Abdullah's letters of 12 and 15 October, 1949 [when Article 370 was under finalisation] are not available, whereas those of Ayyangar (N. Gopalaswami Ayyangar – a Cabinet minister without portfolio and former Dewan of Kashmir) and Sardar Patel's letters to him [Ayyangar] and to each other, are (Noorani 2014, pp. 423-4). The other difficulty is that misconceptions about many issues—and particularly the special status of J&K, which have persisted and have been perpetuated over the years—make any rational discussion impossible. I have tried to remedy this by putting together relevant material, available in the public domain, to enable a more informed debate on the issues.

Former Governor of Reserve Bank of India, D. Subbarao, in his article, 'Over to the States' (*The Indian Express*, 18 November 2019) has rightly stated that with the economic centre of gravity shifting to states, India's growth hinges on cooperative federalism. The changing dynamics of the fiscal federalism is brought out by ballpark estimates that the Centre collects about 60 per cent of the combined revenue (Centre and states), but gets to spend only about 40 per cent of the combined expenditure. This asymmetry is mirrored on the states' side. Together they collect 40 per cent of the combined revenue, but spend as much a 60 per cent of the combined expenditure. And how the states manage their public finances matters much more than before. The quality of expenditure at the state level has a multiplier effect on overall development outcomes. The other most important element is their critical role in creating a conducive investment climate in the country.... *If ever there was an opportune moment for a big push on cooperative federalism, it is now* (Subbarao 2019, p. 8). This is underlined by the latest data which showed that in 'ease of doing business', UP, one of the BIMARU (sick) states[1] had jumped from 16th rank in 2016 to 2nd rank in 2019, in the all-India ranking of states.

The slogan 'One Nation, One Election' has serious implications for India's federalism. Currently, even the electoral rolls for elections at all levels are not the same.[2] The Law Commission of India has highlighted the changes which simultaneous elections will entail in the Constitution

---

1. Bihar, Madhya Pradesh, Rajasthan and Uttar Pradesh.

2. The electoral rolls maintained by the Election Commission of India are used for the Lok Sabha and the state assembly elections while the rolls maintained by the State Election Commissions are used for local body elections.

and the Representation of the People Act, 1951. But more important are the political implications which will call for a national debate on the subject.

The same is true of the concept of 'One Nation, One Market' which will require a fresh look at the division of legislative powers laid down in the Seventh Schedule of the Constitution and several other provisions of the Constitution.

The situation, which prevailed during 1947-49 when India's Constitution was under discussion, needs to be noted. The most important was the hegemony of the Congress Party at the time. There were no Opposition parties with much mass following. The Constituent Assembly had not visualised that in a few decades the Congress Party would be decimated by demands for 'Congress-*mukt* Bharat' (nation free of Congress) and a real national alternative to the Congress Party would emerge, and a multi-party democracy with sharp ascendance of regional parties would prevail in the country.

It was often argued that during the hegemony of the Congress Party, Centre-state issues could be resolved by discussions at the party level. But, this was not always true. The Belgaum-Karwar border issue has been pending resolution since 1958. For the first nearly 40 years, the Congress Party was in power in both Karnataka and Maharashtra. Prime Minister Indira Gandhi had promised to find an amicable solution to the dispute during the Emergency. I had written in my memoirs, *Unfinished Innings*:

> The suggested solution of dividing Belgaum city along the railway line did not make any sense to me. After all, Belgaum was still a part of India. Dividing cities and putting up Berlin walls was not an answer to the problem. I explained this point of view to Chief Minister [S.B. Chavan] when I was asked to rush with all the papers and maps to Chandigarh towards the end of December 1975[3] where

---

3. I was Secretary to Chief Minister of Maharashtra at the time. This subject was handled directly in the Chief Minister's office.

> the All India Congress Committee (AICC) session was being held. The Prime Minister proposed to discuss the issue with the Chief Ministers of Maharashtra and Karnataka at the session but nothing came of these discussions. (Godbole 1996, p. 117)

Since then, the issue has defied any solution even when there was a Congress or BJP government in power *at the same time* in both the states. Finally, the government of Maharashtra filed Original Suit No. 4 of 2004 in the Supreme Court, which is still pending. This has also been true of the river water dispute between Punjab and Haryana in respect of the SYL canal; and Odisha and Chhattisgarh in regard to Mahanadi river, to give just a few instances. There is thus no alternative to providing institutional mechanisms for resolving inter-state issues.

Majoritarianism is the curse of democracy. With massive majority in Parliament and in the states, Indira Gandhi undertook a series of amendments which effectively rewrote the Constitution on several major points, including its 'basic structure'. As K.V. Raghunatha Reddy, Minister in her Cabinet, said, 'A party with two-thirds majority, using a three-line whip, could change the Constitution in twenty-four hours' (Austin 1999, pp. 426-7, footnote 54).

It will be recalled that the fear of Hindu majoritarianism led to the Partition of India. With the BJP's rise to commanding heights of power and its objective to strive for a Hindu *Rashtra* (nation), the threat of Hindu majoritarianism is now real. This is underlined by ludicrous demands such as for the disenfranchisement of Muslims; amendment of the Places of Worship (Special Provisions) Act, 1991, to permit reconversion of Muslim places of worship in Mathura and Varanasi (to begin with); permitting government servants to become members of the RSS; and declaring Himachal Pradesh a Hindu state as non-Hindus account for just 5 per cent of its total population. But it is forgotten that the Hindus are a minority in a number of states, and also union territories. Based on the above logic, should J&K be declared a Muslim union territory,

Punjab a Sikh state, and Nagaland, Arunachal Pradesh, and Meghalaya Christian states? The Supreme Court itself had observed in 2015 that it had doubts about how long India would remain secular (*The Indian Express*, 10 February 2015, p. 1). Religious majoritarianism is likely to be a major fault line in the coming years but India seems to be least inclined to address the existential issue of separation of religion from politics.

Equally worrisome are the linguistic, sectarian, racial and provincial connotations of majoritarianism. It is high time these are recognised in public discourse and their ill effects openly debated. The rise of sub-nationalism is another highly disturbing phenomenon which is undercutting the fundamental rights of citizens by legalising discrimination based on language and place of birth, *and* denying equality of opportunity in matters of public employment.

With several states headed by non-BJP political parties and the BJP heading the Central government and intense political polarisation, Centre-state relations are under severe strain, reminiscent of the Indira Gandhi years. There seems to be a lack of even common civilities and courtesies in interpersonal relations. The Chief Minister of Kerala, Pinarayi Vijayan, was not given an appointment to meet Prime Minister Narendra Modi in June 2018 and was asked to meet the Central ministers concerned instead. The Kerala Chief Minister's strong stand against Prime Minister Modi, for the latter's refusal to meet him to discuss the state's pending issues, developed into a full-scale political stand-off, going beyond Centre-state issues, though the Prime Minister did meet the CM in July 2018. Kerala has approached the Supreme Court against the passage of three agricultural reform bills by Parliament in September 2020. The Kerala legislative assembly has also passed a resolution against the three Central enactments. Prakash Javadekar, the then Union Environment Minister, called the Chief Minister of Delhi, Arvind Kejriwal, a 'terrorist' (*The Indian Express*, 4 February, 2020, p. 1). However, the minister later denied having called Kejriwal a 'terrorist'. The Chief Minister of West Bengal, Mamata Banerjee, did not show the courtesy of receiving Prime

Minister Modi on his visit to her state.

Inevitably, such strained relations are reflected in the manner in which Centre-state issues are addressed. A case in point is how the question of holding the national competitive examinations, NEET and JEE, has become politically controversial, even after the decision of the Supreme Court. Seven Opposition Chief Ministers ganging up against the Centre on this question made no sense, when delaying these examinations any further would have meant students losing a whole year. Several states such as Andhra Pradesh, Chhattisgarh, Kerala, Maharashtra, Punjab, Rajasthan and West Bengal have revoked 'general consent' given by them to the CBI under Section 6 of the Delhi Special Police Establishment Act, 1946, to conduct investigation of cases in their state. This process started in 2018 and has continued till the writing of this book in 2020. As a result, the CBI will now have to seek prior permission of the state governments on a case-by-case basis. Rather than realising the seriousness of the situation arising from the increasing distrust of the Centre, when this process started with Andhra, the GOI dismissed the development as an 'alliance of corrupt' (*The Indian Express*, 17 November 2018, p. 1). In such an atmosphere, working a quasi-federal Constitution will become increasingly difficult.

The controversy regarding the manner in which the states were to be compensated for the loss of revenue under the GST was most unfortunate. To put it bluntly, the initial decision of the Central government asking the states to borrow through the RBI was clerical and short-sighted. The larger national objective of sustaining the trust of the states in the commitment given by the Centre was more important. The approach of the Modi government in this regard was most unfortunate and counterproductive to the cause of cooperative federalism. Fortunately, after unsavoury controversy, the Centre has agreed to borrow the sums itself and to lend them to the states.

Serious doubts have been expressed over the years about the need for the second chamber (Rajya Sabha) of Parliament. It is no longer a 'House of

Elders', as was envisaged earlier. It no longer works as a sobering influence on the Lok Sabha, and can, in fact, be as noisy and disorderly as the Lok Sabha. I had in my book, *India's Parliamentary Democracy on Trial*, raised the question whether we needed the second chamber and had concluded: 'With the dominance of the political party system and the party discipline strengthened by the Anti-Defection Act, the role of the Rajya Sabha has lost its significance. If the Rajya Sabha is to be a mere replica of the Lok Sabha in terms of its composition, calibre, and functioning, one can ask why is such a second chamber necessary?' (Godbole 2011, p. 242). The only justification for its continuance is that *it is supposed to represent the states*. But, *it has now ceased to represent the states*. The Supreme Court has declared that the federal structure is a part of the basic structure of the Constitution but after the 95th amendment of the Constitution, effected by the Vajpayee government, the residential requirement for election to the Rajya Sabha has been done away with. The Supreme Court held in *Kuldip Nayar v. Union of India & Ors.* (AIR SCW 17 September 2006) that residence was never a constitutional requirement. It was never treated as an essential ingredient of the Council of States (Godbole 2011, p. 225). This makes a mockery of the federal structure. Rajya Sabha membership has now become a matter of patronage by the leadership of political parties. A member transplanted from outside the state can hardly be expected to safeguard the interests of the state he is supposed to represent. This needs to be rectified by effecting an amendment of the Constitution to lay down the requirement of residence in the given state for a minimum period as a qualification for membership of the Rajya Sabha. If the federal structure is to be strengthened, the role of the Upper House will have to be strengthened first.

Dr Rajendra Prasad, President of the Constituent Assembly, while speaking on the motion for adoption of the Constitution in November 1949, had, with great foresight, said: '*Whatever the Constitution may or may not provide, the welfare of the country will depend upon the way in which the country is administered. That will depend upon the men who administer it.... After all, a Constitution like a machine is a lifeless thing. It acquires life because of the men who control it and operate it...'* (LSS 1985, p. 5).

Dr B.R. Ambedkar, Chairman of the Drafting Committee of the Constitution, in his closing speech in the Constituent Assembly in November 1949, had spoken in the same vein:

> The working of the Constitution does not depend wholly upon the nature of the Constitution. The Constitution can provide only the organs of state such as the legislature, the executive and the judiciary. The factors on which the working of those organs of the state depend are the people and the political parties they will set up as their instruments to carry out their wishes and their politics. *Who can say how the people of India and their parties will behave?.... It is, therefore, futile to pass any judgment upon the Constitution without reference to the part which the people and their parties are likely to play.* (Mukherjee 2007, p. 211)

The experience of the last 70 years since the adoption of the Constitution shows that as far as Centre-state relations are concerned, it made no difference which political party was in power at the Centre, and the relations remained strained with the states ruled by political parties opposed to the Centre. This does not mean that they were smooth for the states ruled by the ruling party at the Centre. However, due to the party discipline, these differences did not come out in the open. Elections to the Lok Sabha becoming 'Presidential' and the emergence of a national leader with a larger than life image have added a new facet to Centre-state relations. This is seen in the comparisons made in the functioning of Prime Ministers Indira Gandhi and Narendra Modi. These changes have an important bearing on devising a sustainable federal structure for the future. Leaving matters to political discretion or hopes of developing healthy conventions is not workable. Making requisite constitutional changes and providing suitable institutional arrangements is the only viable option. Such major changes will require two-thirds majority in both Houses of Parliament. They would also have to be ratified by at least half of the state legislatures. Looking to the likely political scenario in the foreseeable future, this will require developing a broad consensus among national *and* regional political parties. For this to happen, the complex issues pertaining to federalism will *first* have to be understood and debated in a non-partisan, non-political manner. It is fervently hoped that this book will serve that purpose and set the ball rolling.

The canvas of federalism is vast. There are limitations of time and space on what a book can cover. Therefore, the discussion in this book is kept confined to the most troubling fault lines which are clamouring for attention. It does not cover a number of other issues such as inter-state water disputes. It also does not deal with the question of neglect by the states of the local self-governing institutions in the municipal and *panchayati raj* fields. Their empowerment as contemplated in the 73rd and 74th Amendments of the Constitution has remained unimplemented. While the states have been clamouring for larger devolution of powers and resources from the Centre, they are not prepared to devolve these on local bodies. Cooperative federalism can be a reality only if the process is carried through all the way to the village panchayat level.

Some portions of the text have been italicised to invite pointed attention of the readers.

Reference to the source is given at the end of the quotation in bracket with the name(s) of the author of the book, year of publication, and page number(s).

Madhav Godbole
Pune

Acknowledgements

I must acknowledge my debt, at least partially, to those who have helped me in writing this book. At the outset, credit must be given to my wife Sujata for her loving care and constant encouragement.

My daughter, Meera Godbole-Krishnamurthy, author and editor, took keen interest in the book, offered to edit it and shouldered the burden most diligently. She would not like my thanking her formally but I must note her contribution.

I must also place on record the immense help I received from the libraries in Pune of the Gokhale Institute of Politics and Economics, and the Indian School of Political Economy. I am grateful to Atul Suresh More, Technical Assistant in the Indian Law Society's Law College library, Pune, for taking personal interest and making books and reference material available to me.

I am obliged to Shri K.P.R. Nair, Managing Director, Konark Publishers, for getting the book published expeditiously. He has always taken keen interest in following up on my books and writings. I am grateful to Ranjana Narayan, Commissioning Editor, for editing the book so promptly, efficiently and with such meticulous care, and taking personal interest in its production. She was ably assisted by Jiza Joy, Coordinating Editor. Without their commitment, it would not have been possible to place the book in the hands of the readers in a timely manner.

My grandchildren—Aditi, Manan, Gaayatri and Taarini—kept me on my toes with their searching enquiries about the progress of the book. I have dedicated the book to them, since they and their generation have a stake in the success of India's federalism.

I

Indian Federalism – Emerging Fault Lines

Introduction

In this chapter we shall discuss the evolution of federalism during the British regime, starting with the modest beginnings culminating in the Government of India Act, 1935, followed after Independence, by integration of the princely states leading to the emergence of a united India and making of the Constitution. This will be followed by the analysis of the experience of the working of the federation so far, with reference to the Union-state relations, division of legislative powers between the Union and the states, misuse of Article 356 of the Constitution, and the institution of Governor of the state. The concluding section will discuss the slow, but a perceptible transition, over the years, towards a true federation with the increasing assertiveness of the states, and growing concerns about the sustainability of the present federal structure laid down by the Constitution.

Evolution

Modest Beginnings

The movement towards federalism during the British rule was gradual. On 20 August 1917 the government announced the policy of 'the gradual development of self-governing institutions with a view to progressive realisation of responsible government as an integral part of the Empire'. The GOI Act, 1919 created Governors' provinces, demarcated certain subjects as 'provincial subjects', and further divided these into 'reserved subjects' and 'transferred subjects'. The system of diarchy introduced by the Act was confined to the provincial sphere, and the Act made hardly any change in the structure of the Central government. Even in the provincial sphere, it was limited to certain subjects—namely, the 'transferred subjects'. Even in respect of these subjects, the ministers were responsible to the legislature which was not wholly elected and contained a section comprising officials.

The commission to review the implementation of the GOI Act 1919 was appointed in 1927 and recommended in its report three years later in 1930 that full responsible government should be established in the provincial sphere in place of diarchy, but no substantial change was proposed at the Centre. Rulers of some Indian states, outside British India, expressed their readiness to enter into a federation of British Indian provinces and Indian states. These matters were discussed at the Round Table Conference in London and finally led to the enactment of the GOI Act, 1935.

The 1935 Act extended, with certain qualifications, to the whole of the provincial sphere and to a part of the Central sphere. The number of Governors' provinces was increased from nine to 11 by the separation of Sind and Orissa. Full responsible government of the British parliamentary type was provided in each Governor's province. The Governor was to be appointed by His Majesty and he was to be aided and advised by a Council of Ministers. There were, however, certain matters in respect of which the Governor was required to act in his discretion without having to consult his ministers and certain other matters in respect of which he was required to exercise his individual judgment, though he was bound to consult his ministers.

B.N. Rau, Constitutional Advisor, has stated:

> One of the main difficulties in the introduction of full responsible government at the Centre had been that of reconciling Hindu and Muslim interests. A single central government with a single central legislature would ordinarily have meant the predominance of the majority community, both in the legislature and in the Cabinet; and this the Muslims, who formed a minority of less than one-third of the entire population of India, were not prepared to accept. (Rau 1960, pp. 320-8)

During the freedom movement, the Congress Party was initially ambivalent about federalism since the objective of the Congress was to provide an alternative to centralized British power. But to accommodate the Muslim concerns about Hindu majoritarianism, the Lucknow Pact (1916) between the Congress and the Muslim League and the subsequent negotiations over the next two or three decades were based on the federal concept. At the Nagpur Session (1920) the Congress also resolved that the federal structure would be based on the principle of language.

The Union Powers Committee of the Constituent Assembly, in its report submitted on 20 August 1947, stressed, 'There are many matters in which authority must be solely with the units and to frame a Constitution on the basis of a unitary state would be a retrograde step both politically and administratively.' The committee, agreeing with the Union Constitution Committee, had concluded that the soundest framework for our Constitution was a federation with a strong Centre (Chaube 2000, p. 182).

The day following the announcement of the Partition of the country on 3 June 1947, the Union Constitution Committee arrived at the following decisions: (i) the Constitution should be a federal structure with a strong

Centre; (ii) there should be three exhaustive lists, lists—namely, provincial and concurrent, with the residuary powers being retained by the Centre; and (iii) the Indian [princely] states should be on par with the provinces as regards the federal legislative list (Dhavan and Thomas 1992, p. 201). And this is what the Constitution finally provided for.

Government of India Act, 1935

The Congress was opposed to this Act for several reasons. *First*, the Act had not only not given Dominion status to India, but had also denied a responsible government at the Centre. The Congress Party considered it to be a 'new charter of slavery'. *Second*, the special powers given to the Governors and the Governor-General to overrule the decisions of the elected governments were not acceptable. The Congress wanted the Governors and the Governor-General to be constitutional heads. It was only after the Governor-General gave the requisite assurance that the popular ministries began to function.

In his Presidential address to the Indian National Congress in 1936, Jawaharlal Nehru said:

> Under the circumstances, we have no choice but to contest elections to the new provincial legislatures...while we [should] use the platform of the legislatures to press that programme [with our demand for Constituent Assembly in the forefront], *we seek to end these imperialist bodies by creating deadlock in them....* These deadlocks should preferably take place on these programmes so that the masses might learn how ineffective for their purpose are those legislatures. *I am convinced that for the Congress to favour the acceptance of office, or even to hesitate and waver about it, would be a vital error. It will be a pit from which it would be difficult for us to come out.* (J.B. Kripalani 2004, pp. 263-4)

The legislators taking their seats in the assemblies were required, as the law then stood, to take an oath of allegiance to the British sovereign. Many Congressmen had a conscientious objection to taking the oath in this form. The Congress Working Committee decided that taking such an oath 'in no way lessens or varies the demand for Independence.... The primary allegiance of all Congressmen as well as all other Indians is to the Indian people.' As there were conflicting opinions regarding the advisability of accepting office under the limitations mentioned, it was decided to hold a special convention of legislators and the AICC members in Delhi on 19 and 20 March 1937. Doubts having been raised regarding the propriety of legislators taking an oath of allegiance to the British sovereign, the first thing that the convention did was to administer to them an oath of loyalty to the nation, prior to the one they would take in the legislatures. However, the Congress allowed the Delhi Convention to pass a resolution which, inter alia, stated that the Congress Party in legislature may accept office if it was satisfied and was able to state publicly that the Governor would not use his special powers of interference or set aside the advice of ministers in regard to constitutional activities[1](Kripalani 2004, pp. 300-1).

But, in spite of Nehru's opposition, 'Patel took the earliest opportunity to bring Congress back to constitutionalism. He personally organized the elections held under the Act, formed Congress cabinets in eight provinces and directed their activities in a manner which leaves little room for doubt that Patel believed that India's goal of Independence could be achieved by "widening the scope of the Constitution [the GOI Act, 1935]"' (Tahmankar 1970, pp. 262-3).

The first elections under this Act were held in 1937 in which only 35 million people or 11.5 per cent of the total population were eligible to vote. In five out of the 11 provinces—Bihar, Central Provinces, Madras, Orissa and the United Provinces—the Congress was returned with a clear majority. In Assam, Bengal, Bombay and the North-West Frontier Province, it emerged as the single largest party. Only in Punjab and Sind,

---

1. In fact, this led to section 93 of the GOI Act, 1935, pertaining to Governor's powers becoming a dead letter.

predominantly Muslim provinces, it was in the minority. There was a massive increase in the Congress membership from about 650,000 in 1936 to over three million in 1937 and to 4.5 million in 1938 (Vohra 1997, p. 166).

Mountbatten, in his *Oral History Transcript* in NMML (p. 13), has mentioned that 'the partition of the country could have been avoided if the GOI Act, 1935, had been accepted [by Congress wholeheartedly]. According to Mountbatten, Gandhi had admitted to Wavell, after his release from prison in about 1944, that he got time to read the Act carefully only when he was in prison. Had he had time to study it earlier... he would have recommended acceptance.' Mountbatten has hailed the GOI Act, 1935 as 'perhaps the greatest single legislative achievement of the British in India' (Carter 2003, p. 287).

Lord Butler, in his *Oral History Transcript* in NMML, stated that Nehru made some rather extreme remarks about the GOI Act, 1935, by saying, 'It was a charter of slavery'. Later, delivering the Nehru Memorial Lecture on 10 November 1966, Butler said: 'But, later in his life Nehru told me that it proved to be an organic link between the old and the new.' As the *Oxford History of Ind*ia says, 'The mists of contemporary uncertainty and patriotic impatience shrouded the merits of the Government of India Act when it was passed; but twelve years later, the new Independence Act was seen to be, in large measure, the conception of 1935 developed and completed' (Grigg 1992, p. 14).

Hodson stated, 'this was the same Act under which, with relatively few amendments, power was transferred entirely from British to Indian hands; and as thus amended, it *served as the working constitution of independent India for three years...*' (Hodson 1969, p. 47).

Though Congress was so vehemently opposed to the GOI Act, 1935, large portions of it were incorporated in the new Constitution adopted by India. S.S. Gill has noted: 'The Constitution of India cannibalized the much maligned GOI Act of 1935 to the extent of incorporating 235 of its sections. The entire judicial and administrative framework of old rules, regulations and procedures were also adopted wholesale' (Gill 1996, p. 30). This is amply evident from Appendix 1.

Integration of the Princely States

Simultaneously with the drafting of the Constitution, the enormous and highly complex operation of integration of princely states was carried out with remarkable speed and statesmanship. V.P. Menon has stated that out of 554 states, Hyderabad and Mysore were left territorially untouched. Two hundred and sixteen states were merged in the Provinces in which they were situated, and to which they were contiguous. Five states were taken over individually as Chief Commissioners' Provinces under the direct control of the Government of India, besides 21 Punjab Hill States which formed Himachal Pradesh. Three hundred and ten states were consolidated into six unions, of which Vindhya Pradesh was subsequently converted into a Chief Commissioner's Province. Thus, as a result of integration, in the place of 554 states, 14 administrative units emerged. Speaking before the Constituent Assembly, Vallabhbhai Patel emphasised: 'The fact that the new Constitution specifies only nine states in Part III of Schedule I is an index of the phenomenal progress made by the policy of integration pursued by the GOI' (Shiva Rao 1968, p. 551).

The next step was to fit these units into a common administrative mould. The task was not an easy one. Administration in the erstwhile states was in varying stages of development and generally, barring a few exceptions, it was both personal and primitive.... Except for one or two states, the system of responsible government was unknown. In some there were legislatures with elected majorities, but in others, the legislatures were composed predominantly of nominated members. In either case, it was the ruler who retained the final veto in all respects of legislation and administration. Though the All India States Peoples' Conference had been in existence since 1927, it had made little headway in most of the states, as the rulers had severely curbed its activities (Menon 1956, pp. 435-6).

The White Paper on Indian States presented in 1950 showed that there were dramatic changes in the territorial scene in India following Independence. The main features thereof were the following:

> Apart from Hyderabad and Mysore, 216 states having a population of a little over 19 million were merged in the Provinces; 61 states having a population of about 7 million were constituted into new Centrally-administered units; and 275 states with a population of about 35 million were integrated to create new administrative units, namely, Rajasthan, Madhya Bharat, Travancore-Cochin, Saurashtra and PEPSU. (GOI 1955, p. 5)

The gigantic task of administrative integration was completed before the Constitution of India came into being. Incorporation of the states' forces into the Indian Army was another complicated task but was carried out smoothly. The third crucial aspect was financial integration. Menon has stressed that during the negotiations on federal structure prior to Independence, the rulers insisted on the maintenance of the *status quo* in fiscal matters and refused to surrender any financial powers to the federal government. This was the rock on which the federation had foundered in 1939.

Many of the princely states had been getting a substantial portion of their revenues by the levy of indirect taxes, particularly excise and inter-state customs duties. The maritime states of Kathiawar had levied customs duties of their own and this had resulted in a customs cordon being set up by the Government of India at the frontiers between these states and the province of Bombay. Thus, within the country there were a large number of tariff walls.

Menon has quoted the advantages of financial integration, as brought out by the V.T. Krishnamachari Committee on the Indian States Finances, which stated:

> *Firstly*, their people and governments will take their place in the polity

of India alongside of the people and the governments in the rest of India and share in its wider life with equal rights and obligations. *Secondly*, administrative standards and efficiency will increase by closer contacts with the administration of the Central government and especially by the uniform accounting and audit system which will result from the supervision of the Auditor General of India, recruitment to the higher services on an all India basis, a unified judicial system and access to technical advice and assistance furnished by the central government. *Thirdly*, states will have their share of such federal revenues as may be made divisible from time to time and of the grants, loans and other forms of financial assistance given by the centre, on the same basis as Provinces; and impetus will thus be given to development programmes in these areas.... There will then emerge uniformity of laws, rates, interpretation and administration of all federal fiscal measures resulting in uniform policies, principles and practices in the levy, assessment and collection of central taxes and duties. And tax evasion, always a serious evil, will be more effectively checked. The abolition of internal customs duties will result in freedom of trade within the country. A coordinated trade and tariff policy will have a uniform impact throughout the country. Ports and other important links in the country's system of communications and transport will be free to serve their natural hinterlands. National and regional economic planning on an all India basis will become possible. In this, as in all other respects, the states will play their part, and they will become entitled to all the benefits which accrue from the execution of such plans as require the aid of central resources and technical assistance. India will thus have an opportunity to emerge as a well-knit unit, fully integrated in all spheres, political, constitutional and economic. Its essential fundamental unity will be reinforced. (Menon 1956, pp. 461-2)

Menon, the architect of the scheme of integration of states, stated that out of the 554 states, over 450 had an annual revenue of less than Rs 15 lakh. He wrote:

> We cannot strike a balance sheet without juxtaposing the assets against the liabilities. For this purpose, we may ignore the consummation of the great ideal of a united and integrated India, which has affected the destinies of millions of people; the federal sources of income including the railway system of about 12,000 miles which the states surrendered to the centre without any compensation; and the abolition of the internal customs as a result of integration, which has greatly benefitted trade and commerce in the country. But we should certainly take into account the assets we have received from the states in the shape of immense cash balances and investments amounting to Rs 77 crores, as well as buildings and palaces. If these are weighed against the total amount of the privy purses, the latter would seem insignificant.

Vallabhbhai Patel, while speaking on adoption of Article 291[privy purse sums of rulers][2] of the Constitution, said:

> The privy purse settlements are therefore in the nature of consideration for the surrender by the rulers of all their ruling powers and also for the dissolution of the states as separate units. We would do well to remember that the British government spent enormous amounts in respect of the Mahratta settlements alone. We are ourselves honouring the commitments of the British government in respect of the pensions of those rulers who helped them to consolidate their empire. Need we cavil then at the small—I purposely use the word small—price we have paid for the bloodless revolution which has affected the destinies of millions of our people? (Shankar 1977, p. 663)

---

2. Repealed in 1971.

In his above speech, Patel highlighted:

> The capacity for mischief and trouble on the part of the rulers if the settlement with them would not have been reached on a negotiated basis was far greater than could be imagined at this stage.[3] Let us do justice to them; let us place ourselves in their position and then assess the value of their sacrifice. The rulers have now discharged their part of the obligations by transferring all ruling powers and by agreeing to the integration of their states. The main part of our obligation under these agreements is to ensure that the guarantees given by us in respect of privy purses are fully implemented. Our failure to do so would be a breach of faith and seriously prejudice the stabilisation of the new order. (Shankar 1977, p. 663)

If Patel had lived longer, perhaps privy purses would not have been abolished.

Speaking in September 1948, Nehru confessed:

> Even I, who have been rather intimately connected with the states' peoples movement for many years, had been asked six months ago what the course of developments would be in the next six months since then, I would have hesitated to say that such rapid changes would take place.... The historian who looks back will no doubt consider this integration of the states into India as one of the dominant phases of India's history. (V. P. Menon 2014, p. 442)

This was putting it too modestly; it was in fact an unbelievable

---

3. For example, the Communists in Telangana had emerged as allies of Razakars in Hyderabad. The Nizam had approached the President of the United States to arbitrate but the request was turned down. The Nizam had declared that he was willing to die a martyr and he and 200,000 Muslims were willing to be killed rather than be subjects of India. Arms and ammunition were being smuggled from Pakistan by an Australian adventurer, Sydney Cotton.

achievement, accomplished peacefully.

Menon emphasised: 'By the partition, India had lost an area of 364,737 square miles and a population of 81.5 million. By the integration of the states, we brought in an area of nearly 500,000 square miles with a population of 86.5 million (not including J&K)' (Menon 1956, pp. 487-90).

Gandhi appropriately wrote: 'The task of dealing with the princes was truly formidable, but I am convinced that Sardar was the only man who could have coped with it' (Tahmankar 1970, p. 237).

Special reference may be made to the integration of Hyderabad state which was of crucial importance. By the beginning of 1948, the Hyderabad issue had started causing serious anxiety. On 31 March 1948, Kasim Razvi of *Ittehadul-Muslimeen* declared that Hyderabad was an Islamic state and the Razakars were fully armed to defend their freedom and fight the 'Hindu Kafirs'. On 10 April, he said that Hyderabad would recover the ceded districts and 'the day was not far off when the waves of the Bay of Bengal would be washing the feet of our sovereign (Nizam)'.

Nehru had noted that some of the big states which were continued as separate units had responsible governments. The only exception was Hyderabad. The situation in Hyderabad was deteriorating rapidly. Patel thought the time had come to strike, but Nehru hesitated. Perhaps he was afraid his image abroad might be tarnished if force was used. It was also true that the Nizam had an army of 42,000 men, in addition to the fanatical force of Razakars estimated at 20,000. Aware of Nehru's intellectual doubts and concerns about international reaction to any military move against Hyderabad, Patel decided to handle the affair on his own. It was arranged that the Indian army should march into Hyderabad state in the early hours of 13th [September 1948]. But just at this crucial moment Jinnah died on 12 September. Patel was advised by the British Commander-in-Chief, General Roy Bucher, to postpone the operation lest India's enemies linked the operation with Jinnah's death. Patel did not agree and 'Operation Polo', as it was called, started as scheduled on the

13th. C. Rajagopalachari, who had succeeded Mountbatten as Governor-General, held a hastily summoned Cabinet meeting on the suggestion of Patel—ostensibly to hear about the progress of the operation—but really to put the record straight so that no one could say the action had been taken without the sanction of the Cabinet. Nehru gracefully agreed to all that was being done by Patel and the Defence Ministry.... Patel went to Hyderabad on 8 October 1950 and was welcomed by the Nizam personally when the plane arrived at the Begum Airport. That his Exalted Highness should go to receive the guest became a topic of much discussion in Hyderabad society. It did not escape the attention of political observers that he had excused himself for not going to welcome Prime Minister Nehru when he had visited the city a few weeks earlier (Tahmankar 1970, pp. 232-3).

The account given by Dharma Vira, the then Joint Secretary to the Cabinet, differs somewhat as compared to Tahmankar's above version. Vira has stated:

> Patel felt that if Hyderabad was allowed to remain independent, with its bias in favour of Pakistan, it will become a "tumour in the stomach of India", the poison of which might endanger the very health of the whole of India.... The whole issue was discussed threadbare at a number of Cabinet meetings. On many occasions the discussions were hot, disclosing divergent and diametrically opposed views. The Prime Minister ultimately had to agree to the police action proposed by Sardar Patel when he found himself in a minority in the Cabinet. (Dharma Vira 1975, p. 39)

Speaking in the Constituent Assembly, Patel said: 'The so-called lapse of paramountcy cannot alter the organic inter-relation of Hyderabad and India, and the mutual obligations of the one to the other.... We feel that internal security and a sense of confidence can only be secured at this stage if our troops are stationed at Secunderabad as they used to be before

August 1947' (Das 1973, pp. 236-7).

I have given this detailed account to show what a formidable task it was to integrate 553 states (excluding J&K, which is dealt with separately in Chapters 2 and 3) and build a unified country. Particular reference may be made to the provision of the Constitution by which the President of India (the Centre) could give directions to Part B states, over a period of 10 years, to bring their administration to the level of the Provinces which were classified as Part A states. The control exercised by the President expired with the reorganisation of states in 1956 when the distinction between Part A states and Part B states was done away with.

Winston Churchill had once said that India was a 'geographical expression', a land that was 'no more a single country than the Equator'. Just within two years of getting Independence, India had completed the impossible task of peacefully uniting India as one country. No one could say any longer that India was just a geographical entity.

It is important to note that the states were essentially created as a part of the integration of princely states and the reorganisation of states on linguistic basis discussed in Chapter 4. This process has continued thereafter with Parliament enacting legislations for creation of new states, and even downgrading a state (J&K) into two union territories.

Making of the Constitution

The elections to the Constituent Assembly held in 1946 were indirect. The Congress accommodated eminent jurists, lawyers and professionals who belonged to no political party or belonged to other parties. Subhash Kashyap, former Secretary General of the Lok Sabha, has written of the composition:

> The Congress was anxious that the Assembly should be as truly representative as possible of all elements in India's national life. Therefore, the Congress nominations were not confined to its own party members. Of the two hundred and five members elected to

the Assembly from the Governors' Provinces on the Congress vote, as many as thirty were from outside the Party. The concern of the Congress in regard to minorities was evident from the liberal representation given to them. From the minorities, the Scheduled Castes accounted for 29; the Indian Christians 6; Anglo-Indians 3; Parsees 3 and Tribals 4. The Congress leaders had recognised the need to bring together a body of experts regardless of party affiliations in formulating the principles and working out details. Mahatma Gandhi gave the lead in commending to the Congress executive 16 eminent persons to be elected on the Congress ticket so that they could participate in the work of Constitution-making. The presence of such persons like Alladi Krishnaswami Ayyar (an eminent advocate), N. Gopalaswami Ayyangar (a former civil servant), H.C. Mookherjee (an educationist), S. Radhakrishnan (a philosopher and educationist), H.N. Kunzru (president of Servants of India Society) and others enhanced the prestige and authority of the Constituent Assembly. (Kashyap 1990, p. 30)

Arun Shourie has pointed out, 'of the seven members who were selected for the Drafting Committee, only one was a Congressman. Ambedkar, who had all along opposed the Congress and denounced the leaders who were now in control, was elected chairman of the committee' (Shourie 1997, p. 448).

In regard to the criticism that the Constituent Assembly comprised of indirectly elected or nominated members and had, therefore, no popular mandate, Ambedkar had forcefully argued in the Assembly:

Sir, it may be true that this Assembly is not a representative Assembly in the sense that Members of this Assembly have not been elected on the basis of adult suffrage. I am prepared to accept that argument. But the further inference which is being drawn that if the Assembly had been elected on the basis of adult suffrage, it was then bound to possess greater wisdom and greater political knowledge is an inference which I utterly repudiate.... It might easily have been worse. *Power and knowledge do not go together. Oftentimes they are dissociated,* and I am quite frank enough to say that this House, such as it is, has probably a greater modicum and quantum of knowledge and information than the future Parliament is likely to have. (Palkhivala 1974, p. 4)

In his speech in the Constituent Assembly in November 1949, before it formally finished its work, Ambedkar underlined that the Assembly had sat for 141 days. The total number of amendments to the draft Constitution tabled was approximately 7,635. Of these, the total number of amendments actually moved in the House was 2,473 (Mukherjee 2007, pp. 206, 214).

A scholar records that of the original text of the Constitution, 220 Articles had been completely replaced and the wording of another 120 had been materially altered.... Many provisions were altered in the most basic ways by the interventions of persons whose names few of us would even have heard of since (Shourie 1997, p. 449).

It would be pertinent to take note of a few special aspects brought out in Ambedkar's speech. The condemnation of the Constitution largely came from two quarters, the Communist Party and the Socialist Party. The Communist Party wanted a Constitution based upon the *principle of the dictatorship of the proletariat.* They condemned the Constitution because it was based on parliamentary democracy. The Socialists, inter alia, wanted *freedom to nationalise or socialise all private property without payment of compensation.* Nehru and Vallabhbhai Patel had to contend with these preposterous demands. India is fortunate that these suggestions were not accepted.

There is another point on which the situation has changed radically since the time the Constitution was adopted. This is in regard to the role of the judiciary. Ambedkar had appreciatively quoted the principle that 'Courts may modify, they cannot replace. They can revise earlier interpretations as new arguments, new points of view are presented, they can shift the dividing line in marginal cases, but *there are barriers they cannot pass*, definite assignments of power they cannot reallocate. They can give a broadening construction of existing powers, but *they cannot assign to one authority powers explicitly granted to another*' (B. Shiva Rao vol. IV, 1968, p. 941). The role of the judiciary has expanded unbelievably since then and it has emerged as the most powerful organ of the state.

Anxieties were expressed in the Constituent Assembly about the extensive powers given to the Centre to override the states. Ambedkar was frank enough to admit the charge. He did , however, stress that '*these overriding powers do not form the normal feature of the Constitution. Their use and operation are expressly confined to emergencies only.* The second consideration is: Could we avoid giving overriding powers to the Centre when an emergency has arisen? Those who do not admit the justification for such overriding powers to the Centre even in an emergency, do not seem to have a clear idea of the problem which lies at the root of the matter' (Mukherjee 2007, p. 214).

Dealing with the criticism of over-centralisation in the Constitution, Ambedkar observed that a serious complaint was made on the ground that the states had been reduced to municipalities.... It was necessary to bear in mind the fundamental principle...of federalism that the legislative and executive authority was partitioned between the Centre and the states not by any law to be made by the Centre but by the Constitution itself. This was what the Constitution did. The states under our Constitution were in no way dependent upon the Centre for their legislative or executive authority. The Centre and the states were co-equal in the matter (Chatterjee 1980, p. 331).

As the discussion in this book shows, the concerns expressed in the Constituent Assembly regarding excessive powers given to the Centre have been fully borne out in practice during the last seven decades, bringing the federal structure under strain.

Interestingly, the Constituent Assembly rejected a motion to call India a 'federation of states'. Elaborating on the alternate term, 'Union of states', Ambedkar said:

> The use of the term "union" is deliberate. I tell you why the Drafting Committee has used it. The Drafting Committee wanted to make it clear that though India was to be a federation, the federation was not the result of an agreement by the states to join a federation and that the federation not being the result of an agreement, no state has the right to secede from it.... The draft Constitution has sought to forge means and methods whereby India will have a federation and at the same time will have uniformity in all basic matters, which are essential to maintain the unity of the country. (B. Shiva Rao, *The Framing of India's Constitution: A Study* 1968, p. 140)

Underlining the futility of discussion on the subject, Rajendra Prasad, President of the Constituent Assembly, said: 'Personally, I do not attach much importance to the label which may be attached to it—whether you call it a federal Constitution or a unitary Constitution or by any other name. It makes no difference so long as the Constitution serves the purpose' (B. Shiva Rao vol. IV, 1968, p. 950). While this may be partly true, as can be seen from the discussion in this book, it has made a great deal of difference to how the structure is operationalised.

Experience

Union-State Relations

After non-Congress governments came to power in several states, the overbearing attitude adopted by the Union government, particularly since the time of Indira Gandhi's prime ministership, led to strained relations between the Central government and the states, and these have become even more acrimonious over the years. As a result, the term 'confidence-building measures', which is generally used in the context of improving relations between countries, is equally apt for use in mending relations between the Union government and the states.

The cordiality of Union-state relations is the acid test of federalism. Looked at from this point of view, Indian federalism faces a number of problems. *First*, and most important, is the concept of a strong Centre underlying the Constitution. This was understandable against the backdrop of the Partition of the country through which India had become independent, but now it needs to be interpreted flexibly. *Second*, is the excessive reliance on the erstwhile colonial governance structure with which the ruling elite was familiar and which was replicated in the Constitution. *Third*, the division of powers between the Union and the states was aimed at assisting in the Central planning of the economy which was the crux of Nehru's economic policies at the time. *Fourth*, and equally importantly, though the Constituent Assembly provided the framework for a robust parliamentary democracy, it failed to visualise a future in which multiple political parties would be functioning in the country. It took for granted that the hegemony of the Congress Party would continue, for ever. *Fifth*, the two main national parties—namely, the BJP and the Congress, ideologically believe in ensuring a strong Centre and are disinclined to permit the states to have a larger say or leverage in national affairs.[4]

Durga Das has written:

> Three Chief Justices of the Supreme Court felt it necessary to express themselves strongly in favour of a unitary form of government as best suited to Indian conditions. Mehr Chand Mahajan virtually carried on a crusade in this regard after his term as Chief Justice. S.R. Das expressed similar view following his retirement. The succeeding Chief Justice of India, M. Hidayatullah, pleaded in favour of a

---

4. The AICC(I) in its memorandum submitted to the Sarkaria Commission had stated that from the eighties onward, Central power should increase to deal with 'disruptive forces' in the country (Austin 1999, p. 564, footnote 26).

unitary form of government in a Feroz Gandhi Memorial lecture. Echoing the growing feeling of the intelligentsia, he said that a unitary form of government at the Centre was essential *to prevent disintegration and balkanisation of the country through regional pulls and pressures*.... Indira Gandhi had told a group of editors in March 1969: The Marxists may clamour for greater autonomy for the states today. Should they come to power at the Centre, there would be no scope for such demands. *The Centre has clearly to be strong.* (Das 1969, p. 413)

Against this background, it is not surprising that the issues pertaining to Centre-state relations have remained frozen in time. This subject has been comprehensively examined by successive commissions starting with the Sarkaria Commission (1986), followed by the Commission to Review the Working of the Constitution (2002), the Second Administrative Reforms Commission (2004-2008 over which its 15 reports were submitted), and the Punchhi Commission (2010). Of these, the Sarkaria Commission report is the most exhaustive, forward-looking, thorough and balanced.[5] The acceptance of the recommendations of these commissions would have gone a long way in reducing the strains in Centre-state relations. But, successive Central governments of coalitions of political parties, and particularly the NDA and the UPA headed by the BJP and the Congress, respectively, continued to neglect the recommendations of these commissions.

C. Rajagopalachari, former Governor-General of India, thought that the solution to 'centrifugal interests' was to concede greater autonomy to the states. The Punjab state's memorandum to the Sarkaria Commission stated: 'At present, the main threat to India's unity and integrity comes not from outside [the country].... The present relentless centralisation drive... may alienate millions.... An authoritative and coercive approach...will

---

5. It had Justice R.S. Sarkaria as chairman, and B. Sivaraman and S. R. Sen as members.

inevitably erode political democracy' (Austin 1999, pp. 561, 629).

Significantly, the provisions of the Constitution, based on the GOI Act, 1935 (hereafter referred to as the Act), have become controversial. This is not surprising as those provisions were meant to help the colonial power keep a firm grip on administration and were not suited for an independent country with underpinning of parliamentary democracy, strong judiciary, freedom of the press and autonomous constitutional institutions. The whole administrative structure based on the 1935 Act therefore calls for a review. It is time the issues are examined afresh, jettisoning the baggage of the past. Three major concerns—division of legislative powers, misuse of powers by the Union government, and the institution of Governors of states—are discussed hereafter.

Division of Legislative Powers

The federal structure implies a clear-cut division of powers between the Centre and the federating units. Several versions of this are seen in operation in major federations around the world. India is avowedly a Union of States and not a federation. But, it has some very strong federal features. One of them is the very detailed division of legislative powers between the Union and the states, laid out in the Constitution itself.

The Seventh Schedule of the Constitution provides for three lists—the Union List (97 entries), the State List (66 entries) and the Concurrent List (47 entries). The residuary subjects, not listed in any of these lists, vest in the Union (except in the case of J&K, until the abrogation of Article 370). K.C. Wheare noted, 'Here is an enumeration more complete than anything attempted in the four federations [United States, Switzerland, Canada and Australia] (Wheare 1956, p. 81).

When the report of the Union Powers Committee was taken up for consideration in the Constituent Assembly, K. Santhanam, an erudite member, was highly critical and said: 'They have tried to take the GOI Act as their basis and considered what items can be transferred from the provincial list to the concurrent list and the provincial list to the federal list.' Alladi Krishnaswami Ayyar had repudiated the charge and said: 'While a good number of items in the central list can be brought under the heads of defence, foreign affairs and communications, the three main heads envisaged by the Cabinet Mission scheme, the other items such as bills of exchange, banking, corporate law, interunit trade bear upon the general welfare of the country.... We have been crying about a strong centre. If you look at the provincial list, very few (subjects) if at all [in] the provincial list have been taken up and transferred to the federal list.' N. Gopalaswami Ayyangar added: 'There is hardly a single item in the present provincial list in the GOI Act which this much-criticized committee, the Union Powers Committee, has transferred to the federal list' (Chaube 2000, pp. 183-4).

The defence of the country is clearly the responsibility of the Centre. However, the Central government has suggested to the Fifteenth Finance Commission that while considering the devolution of resources between the Centre and the states, the Commission should make the states bear a portion of this burden. The Centre has also proposed a new levy by way of a tax or cess to meet the increasing expenditure on internal security. To me, these proposals seem totally illogical. If conceded, the states will inevitably ask for a larger say in these matters.

These lists are drawn from the Act but have been further expanded a great deal. Some distinguishing features may be noted. *First*, the Union List is much larger than that under the Act. Since the adoption of the Constitution, not a single of these entries has been transferred to the State List or the Concurrent List. *Second*, the Concurrent List has been enlarged to give jurisdiction to both the Union and the states in respect of several subjects. Over the years, a number of entries from the State List have been transferred to the Concurrent List. These include administration of justice; constitution and organisation of all courts (except the Supreme Court and High Courts which were always in the Union List); education, including technical education, medical education and universities; trade and commerce; forests, protection of wild animals and birds; and weights and measures (Diwan 1978, pp. 187-8).

The Constitution provides that in the case of conflict in the provisions of the state and Central laws, the Central law would prevail, unless prior approval had been obtained by the state from the President of India before passing the law.

The Constituent Assembly debates on the subject bring out some prominent features. The GOI had taken the Prime Ministers of Provinces (as they were known at the time) into confidence before the proposals for the division of powers were placed before the Assembly. Hundreds of amendments moved by the members showed that, by and large, they were based on the distrust of the Provincial governments or their capacity to do justice to the subjects. Most amendments suggested transfer of subjects from the State List to the Union List or the Concurrent List. In very few cases, it was proposed that the entry be transferred from the Union or Concurrent List to the State List. The response of the government was based strictly on what was agreed to by the Prime Ministers of Provinces. Interestingly, on matters which are causing concern now—namely, the subjects of 'police' and 'public order' remaining exclusively in the State List, there was hardly any discussion in the Constituent Assembly. It was taken for granted that logically these subjects should remain with the states. However, the same did not hold good even in respect of subjects such as agriculture, forests or even primary education. These entries were in the State List but amendments were moved to transfer them to the Concurrent List.

Appropriately, the subject of higher education has been put in the Union List. Though 'education' (in the abstract) finds place in the Concurrent List, the power is expressly made subject to the power of the Union under various legislative entries assigned in the Union List. Thus the Union List contains the entry: 'Coordination and determination of standards in institutions of higher education or research and scientific and technical institutions'. According to the Supreme Court, 'powers of the state to legislate in respect of education, including universities, must to the extent to which it is entrusted to the Union Parliament be deemed to be restricted' (Bakshi 1987, pp. 425-6). The importance of these issues has come to the fore in the stand taken by some state governments against holding the all-India entrance examinations for medical colleges and final year examinations of colleges and universities due to the Covid-19 pandemic situation. These matters had to be finally decided by the Supreme Court.

At the outset, it needs to be stated that the Concurrent List includes, among others, items of common concern for the states and the Centre such as civil and criminal laws and procedures, education, administration of justice and electricity. The importance of having a common, nation-wide approach on several subjects can be readily appreciated. Pooling the resources of the states and the Centre can go a long way in meeting the ever-rising requirements of people. This is amply brought out by the sizeable investments made by the Central Government in the electricity sector to supplement the efforts of the states. To transfer all entries in the Concurrent List to the State List, as is being suggested by some chief ministers, will retard the progress of the country.

The Sarkaria Commission has rightly cautioned that ordinarily, the Union should occupy only that much field of a Concurrent subject on which uniformity of policies and action is essential in the larger interest of the nation, leaving the rest and the details for state action within the broad framework of the policy laid down in the Union law. Further, whenever the Union proposes to undertake legislation with respect to a matter in the Concurrent List, there should be prior consultation not only with the state governments individually, but also collectively, with the Inter-Governmental Council (IGC) which should be established under Article 263.[6] A resume of the views of the state governments and the comments of the IGC should accompany the bill when it is introduced in Parliament (GOI 1988, p. 89).

---

6. The Sarkaria Commission preferred to call it the Inter-Governmental Council, instead of Inter-State Council.

The entries 'police' and 'public order' figure in the State List. This has severely restricted the charter of the Union government. It is imperative that these entries are transferred to the Concurrent List. In this continental-size country with its multifarious problems of internal security, there is no provision for federal civil police. What we have are only the Central para-military police. The complex challenges of internal security, including of national and international terror organisations, drug cartels, secessionist movements like Khalistan and in the North-East, and Naxalism, require that the Central government is entrusted with the responsibility for police and public order on a concurrent basis. But while doing so, the experience of the United States in 'Operation Legend' launched by President Trump in July 2020 to deal with violent agitations in several cities must be noted as it turned into a confrontation between the Republican and Democratic Parties. New York Governor, Andrew Cuomo, and Chicago Mayor, Lori Lightfoot, among others, objected to the intervention of the federal forces. Sufficient safeguards will have to be provided to ensure that the decision to deploy Central police will not be taken by the GOI on political considerations and the concerned state government will be invariably consulted.

This subject came up for close examination in the review of the national security system following the Kargil War. The GOI had appointed four Task Forces to examine the diverse, complex issues. I was the chairman of the Task Forces on Border Management. After considering the recommendations of the Task Force on internal security, the government had come to the conclusion that the *Union government's ability to deal with situations caused by grave threats to internal security had eroded over the years and needed to be strengthened.* Importantly, this capability should flow from the Constitution. It decided that one way to do this would be to strengthen the provisions under Article 352 [proclamation of Emergency] and 359 [suspension of the enforcement of the rights conferred by Part III during emergencies]. It was also felt that it would be both appropriate and timely if the provisions of Article 355 [duty of the Union to protect states against external aggression and internal disturbance] are made use of proactively. To do so, supporting legislation will have to be enacted to, inter alia, cover the following:

(a) Suo moto deployment of Central forces, if the situation prevailing in the states so demands; the legislation will spell out situations in which such deployment may take place.

(b) Defining powers, jurisdiction, privileges and liabilities of the members of the Central forces while deployed in the states, in accordance with Entry 2A of the Union List.

(c) Specifying situations construed as failures/breakdown of the constitutional machinery in a state, in which the Central government can intervene to advise or direct, as the case may be, a state government and violations of these advisories /directions would invite action under Article 365/352.

Accordingly, the following action was to be taken with regard to the proposed legislation under Article 355:

(a) The matter be taken to the ISC (Inter-State Council) and a small group of members of the Council be constituted to examine the issues.

(b) The matter be discussed with the leadership of all political parties to generate consensus (GOI 2001, pp. 43-4).

This was way back in 2001. The GOI has still not placed it before the ISC. Of these years, UPA was in power for 10 years (2004-2014) when it did not call even one meeting of the ISC. But the BJP was in power from 2001 to 2004 and later from 2014 onwards till the writing of this book (2021). The BJP also did not pursue this matter. It must have been because of its apprehension that the proposal would be strongly opposed by the non-BJP state governments.

The question of the Centre's jurisdiction to pass laws pertaining to terrorist activities needs to be settled once and for all. Why should this subject not be in the Concurrent List? The National Investigation Agency Act (NIA) passed in 2008 after the terrorist attack on Mumbai was amended in 2019 to widen its scope. It has been challenged by the Congress Party government in Chhattisgarh on the ground of NIA's parallel police structure and the amended Act going against the federal structure of the Constitution (*The Indian Express*, 18 January 2020, p. 6). The power given to the Centre to define a terrorist or a terrorist organisation under the Unlawful Activities (Prevention) Amendment Act, 2019, has also become controversial on the ground that it impinges on the powers of the states. It will be recalled that the law for the creation of the National Counter Terrorism Centre (NCTC), which was proposed as an umbrella organisation of security agencies, could not be passed due to opposition by the states.

Corruption has become a major bane afflicting the system.[7] Governments at the Centre and in the states have been announcing a policy of zero tolerance for corruption but this has largely remained on paper. Rampant corruption is a national problem and there is no reason why there should not be a national policy on eradication of corruption. In my book, *Good Governance Never on India's Radar*, I had suggested a 26-point programme for nationwide adoption (Godbole 2014, pp. 213-7). Central enactments such as the Whistleblowers Act should be applicable all over the country, rather than each state enacting its own law.

It is imperative to authorise the Centre to *deploy* the Central paramilitary forces in the states, as opposed to the freedom of merely stationing them anywhere in the country. Such a provision was made during the Emergency, in the Forty-second Amendment of the Constitution in 1976, but when the Janata Government came to power, this amendment,

---

7. References to the need for eradication of corruption appear in the fortnightly letters of Nehru to chief ministers even in 1948 and 1949 (Parthasarathi 1985, pp. 391, 398, 420).

along with most other amendments made therein, was repealed by the Constitution (Forty-fourth Amendment) Act, 1978. In the recent past, this has become a huge handicap for the Centre in dealing with law and order situations leading to major communal clashes such as Ahmedabad riots (1968), Godhra riots (2002), the riots following the demolition of the Babri Masjid (1992) and the series of bomb blasts in Mumbai thereafter (1993). It needs to be understood that, strictly speaking, India is not a federation. Article 1 of the Constitution clearly states that 'India shall be a Union of states', though it has consciously adopted a number of federal features. These should not, however, be permitted to undermine its basic tenet—namely, that it is a Union of states. Therefore to argue that Indian federalism will be adversely affected by sharing the responsibilities of 'police' and 'public order' between the Union and the states is a gross misrepresentation.

It is time to review the three lists in the Seventh Schedule rationally. For example, Bibek Debroy has argued that the Boilers Act, which comes in the Union List, needs to be removed therefrom (*The Indian Express*, 10 October 2019, p. 11).

P. Chidambaram has expressed the view that school education must be transferred to the states, as it was in the original Constitution. And it should be followed by transferring more subjects from the Concurrent List to the State List. However, the NDA government has assumed greater role for the Centre in school and college education. Chidambaram feels that 'the RBI, [the] Competition Commission of India, and [the] CBDT [Central Board of Direct Taxes], [the] CBIC [Central Board of Indirect Taxes and Customs] have turned into controllers [thereby extending the Central control]' (*The Indian Express*, 7 July 2019, p. 13).

Ajay S. Shriram, Chairman and Senior Managing Director of DCM Shriram Ltd., feels that it is only now when 'farmer income' and not 'output' has taken centre stage that the 'market' is receiving due attention. He argues that moving agriculture from the State List to the Concurrent List can produce gains similar to those from the GST. There is no reason why a similar framework cannot be created for a crucial area impinging the livelihood of nearly half of the country's population (*The Indian Express*, 4 July 2019, p. 9). If Indian agriculture is to be made sustainable, then several issues will have to be examined afresh to increase the size of land holdings and to make amendments in the laws pertaining to sale and purchase of agricultural land. It is also pertinent to note that the Green Revolution would not have come about without the intervention of the GOI in importing high-yielding wheat varieties.

Currently, public health appears as entry 6 in the State List. However, the late Dr K.K. Aggarwal, Indian physician and cardiologist, had suggested that public health should be added to the Concurrent List. The Central government's initiative of launching a national health identity card is considered a big milestone in public healthcare. 'This will work as a health account for every Indian. It will bring a revolution in India's health sector and it can help reduce problems in getting treatment with the help of technology,' said Prime Minister Modi (*India Today*, 12 October 2020, p. 42). This is just an example of how the perceptions regarding division of responsibilities between the Centre and the states are undergoing changes. These varying viewpoints will have to be given due consideration while reviewing this matter afresh.

In this discussion, at one extreme are the demands that the Concurrent List should be abolished altogether and the entries be transferred to the State List. K. Chandrashekar Rao, Chief Minister of Telangana, has made such a demand. At the other extreme is the view that subjects which are of national importance must be put in the Concurrent List. When the issue of powers of the Dominion government to legislate on matters falling in the state's concerns was raised by the State of Ontario in Canada, the Privy Council applying the test of 'national concerns' had held that if the subject matter of the legislation goes beyond local or provincial concerns or interests…it must be treated as affecting the peace, order and good governance of Canada [*Ontario (AG) v. Canada Temperance Federation*].

As I had written in my article, 'Concurrent List: The Nation Comes

First', in *India Legal*, 6 January 2019:

> In a number of countries, the trend is towards greater centralisation of powers, rather than decentralisation. The decisions of the highest courts in these countries, too, have contributed to this development. The forces of globalisation and the compulsions of increasing international competition, too, have underlined the importance of adopting national policies on a number of subjects. An article by Dr K.K. Aggarwal titled "One India-One Health Policy?" in the *India Legal* issue of December 24, 2018, for example, makes a plea for adoption of a national health policy on the lines of the national eligibility-cum-entrance test. It has been gratifying to see that the initial resistance of some states such as Tamil Nadu to the entrance test for admission to medical colleges in the country has disappeared completely. There are indications of greater acceptance of the proposal for setting up more all-India services such as for the subordinate judicial service. Laying down all-India standards for various subjects, institutions and services is the only way in which the productivity, efficiency and quality of life can be improved. Thus, universally, the tendency is to look at issues in the larger national perspective. In the case of India too, in the light of experience so far, the Concurrent List needs to be enlarged, rather than curtailed, leave aside abolishing it. (Godbole 2020, pp. 186-7)

The political sagacity requires that these matters are discussed in the larger national interest, keeping aside the narrow concerns of federalism.

Misuse of Article 356

The repeated misuse of Article 356 of the Constitution to dismiss state governments belonging to the Opposition parties, on the ground of breakdown of the constitutional machinery, has been a source of major friction between the states and the Centre. Noted constitutional expert

A.G. Noorani has stated: 'Article 356 is based on the notorious section 93 of the Government of India Act, 1935, which provided for "Governor's rule" in the Provinces just as section 45 provided for the Governor-General's rule at the Centre.... In India, Article 356 is a weapon of first resort [rather than being the last]' (Noorani 2000, pp. 260-61).

Even in the Constituent Assembly, fears were expressed that the Article may be misused. Replying to the debate on 4 August 1949, Ambedkar, inter alia, said:

> I do not altogether deny that there is a possibility of these Articles being misused or employed for political purposes. But that objection applies to every part of the Constitution which gives power to the Centre to over-ride the provinces.... *The proper thing we ought to expect is that such Articles will never be called into operation and that they would remain a dead letter.*

The Sarkaria Commission on Centre-State Relations had recommended: 'Article 356 should be used very sparingly, in extreme cases, as a measure of last resort, when all available alternatives fail to prevent or rectify a breakdown of constitutional machinery in the state. All attempts should be made to resolve the crisis at the state level before taking recourse to the provisions of Article 356' (GOI 1988, p. 15).

The NCRWC (National Commission to Review the Working of the Constitution) had recommended:

> Normally, President's Rule in a state should be proclaimed on the basis of Governor's report under Article 356(1). The Governor's report should be a "speaking-document", containing a precise and clear statement of all material facts and grounds, on the basis of which the President may satisfy himself, as to the existence or otherwise of the situation contemplated in Article 356. (Pylee 2006, p. 771)

The following examples illustrate the gross misuse of the Article over the years, starting with the very first year after the adoption of the Constitution. Granville Austin, American historian and noted scholar of the Indian Constitution, has written:

> The first use of President's Rule was a far cry from the Constituent Assembly's intentions, growing (sic) as it did from an internal Congress dispute. The Government of Punjab in 1951 held a majority in the legislature, and the Governor's report to President Rajendra Prasad that the constitutional machinery had broken down was an *official fiction*. Additionally, the Centre, and not the Governor, had initiated the letter to the President. Leading the Congress Parliamentary Board, Prime Minister Nehru, against [President Rajendra] Prasad's remonstrance, ordered Chief Minister Gopichand Bhargava to resign despite his having a majority. Nehru claimed that the law and order situation was worsening, but his arguments to Prasad that Bhargava was not acting 'straight' and that it was inevitable for parties to give directions to their members told a different story.... The office of Governor for the first, but hardly the last, time had been mangled between the Congress Party and the Constitution to the detriment of even limited federalism and of representative democracy. *It was widely acknowledged that Nehru had set the country a bad example.* (Austin 1999, pp. 606-7)

The other instance of use of Article 356 in the Nehru era was when the duly elected Communist government in Kerala was dismissed by the Centre. D.R. SarDesai and Mohan have underlined that:

> It is indeed sad that the Congress Party, in keeping with its historically derived "catch-all" character, ended up sacrificing the federal rules of the game for the purpose of maintaining its hegemony in the political system. The net result of this was that *no non-congress chief*

minister lasted his full term in office in the Nehru era.... Nehru did use Presidential Rule, although for a limited number (six) of times and under pressure from within his own party. In fact, the party initiated the process of "politics of defection", thrived on it under the very watchful eyes of its "god-father" and legitimized the process by accommodating defectors with political prizes. (SarDesai and Mohan 1992, pp. 234-5)

These 'glorious' traditions were carried forward by subsequent Central governments, whether belonging to the Congress or other political parties, by dismissing the duly elected state governments on over 120 occasions. But not all these can be called arbitrary decisions. Of the 57 instances of President's Rule from 1951 to 1987 (excluding the mass dissolutions of state governments ordered by the Janata and Congress (Indira) governments in 1977 and 1980 respectively), the Sarkaria Commission thought 23 were inevitable, 15 had been without allowing other claimants to test their strength, and 13 had taken place when the ministry commanded a majority. (GOI 1988, pp. 186-9) *This means that about 50 per cent were due to the wishes of the Central government.*

The NCRWC, under the chairmanship of former CJI, M.N. Venkatachaliah, considered that Article 356 represented 'a giant instrument of constitutional control of one tier of the constitutional structure over the other [and] raises strong misapprehensions'. However, after considering all aspects, the Commission was not in favour of the deletion of Article (GOI 2002, pp. 168-9). The Sarkaria Commission on Centre-State Relations had come to the same conclusion. Having seen the working of the Centre-state relations closely, this author too holds the same view. Equally importantly, it was necessary to ensure that this Article would be used as a remedy of last resort, and not the first, as had been done over the years. And this was ensured by the *Bommai* judgment (1994) referred to hereafter.

The invocation of Article 356 had become particularly contentious on a few occasions such as the dismissal of the S.R. Bommai government in Karnataka in 1989, which led to the famous judgment of the Supreme Court restricting the use of the Article; dismissal of the Kalyan Singh Government in UP in 1997 but due to public protests, the order had to be taken back; and dismissal of the Rabri Devi Government in Bihar in 1999, but the resolution could not be passed in the Rajya Sabha and as a result the order imposing President's Rule had to be revoked.

However, on two occasions, when its use could not only have been fully justified but would have been widely welcomed, the Centre did not act under Article 356. The first was in Uttar Pradesh *before* the demolition of the Babri Masjid in December 1992, as detailed in my book, *The Babri Masjid-Ram Mandir Dilemma: An Acid Test for India's Constitution*, and the second in Gujarat *after* the Godhra pogrom in February 2002. On both occasions, the Centre did not act and played, instead, to their own political ends, i.e., of the ruling Congress and the BJP, respectively. For the 1984 anti-Sikh riots as also the communal riots in North East Delhi in February 2020, the Centre itself was responsible for the failure to maintain law and order in Delhi, but there is no provision in the Constitution to impose President's Rule at the Centre!

In recent years, imposition of President's rule in Uttarakhand and Arunachal Pradesh by engineering defections had become highly contentious and was challenged by the Congress Party in the Supreme Court.

Nehru must not have visualised that his short-sighted policy in this matter would, years later, set in motion forces which would undercut the very foundation of the federal structure in the country. The permanent distrust created between the Centre and the states, not just those belonging to the Opposition parties but also other political parties in the ruling coalitions, is evident from their opposition to enlarging the jurisdiction of the Central government in any field, whether it be the Central Bureau of Investigation (CBI), Railway Protection Force, National Counter-Terrorism Centre (NCTC), enactment of a law to deal with terrorism and communal violence, or the enactment of a Central law on Lokayuktas.

As Austin has stated, after Kerala was placed under President's Rule in 1959, B. Shiva Rao, the well-known constitutional expert, had suggested to the then Congress president, Indira Gandhi, that a 'board of advisors' be constituted to 'greatly strengthen the president's position so that there would not be any impression in the public mind that in matters such as this the president was guided by the Party Cabinet (sic) in power at the Centre' (Austin 1999, p. 607). As was to be expected, this advice fell on deaf ears. In any case, Indira Gandhi, who misused this provision blatantly in her long tenure as Prime Minister, would have been the last person to heed such sane advice.

Former CJI, K. Subba Rao, wrote: 'It is said that in issuing the said proclamations [for imposition of President's Rule] the Governors and the President acted as the agents of the central ministry...and the Congress Party manipulated the said proclamations in a bid to regain power in those states where it was defeated' (Austin 1999, p. 607).

Noorani has written that a broad consensus on the amendment of Article 356 emerged in the meetings of the standing committee of the Inter-State Council (ISC) on 10 May and 17 June 1997 on the following points: Parliament's approval should be obtained *before*, rather than after, the state government's dismissal; issuance of a show cause notice by the Union government to the delinquent government citing the grounds for the threatened action, and seeking a reply within a week; and ratification of the President's proclamation by a two-thirds vote by both Houses of Parliament. However, no consensus could be reached in the meeting of the ISC and the proposal was given up (Noorani 2000, p. 259).

V.R. Krishna Iyer, former judge of the Supreme Court, in his essay, 'Some Mutational Reflections on the Constitution', has made a strong plea that President's rule should be imposed on a state only after a resolution to that effect is passed by both Houses of Parliament by a majority of all members and two-thirds of those present. Ideally, he suggests that Articles 356 and 357 should be omitted. Dharma Vira, former Cabinet

Secretary and Governor of West Bengal and Karnataka, in his essay, 'Inadequacy and Impracticability of the Present Constitution', has argued that 'the power to impose President's rule needs to be reduced' (Kashyap 1992, pp. 43, 157).

Fortunately, the Supreme Court, in *S.R. Bommai v. Union of India* unanimously held that a presidential proclamation issued under Article 356 of the Constitution *is not completely beyond judicial review*. It was held that the President's satisfaction has to be based on objective material and further that the objective material available either from the Governor's report or from other information or both must indicate that the government of the state cannot be carried on in accordance with the provisions of the Constitution. Consequently, the validity of the proclamation issued by the President under Article 356 (1) is judicially reviewable to the extent of examining whether it was issued on the basis of any material at all or whether the material was relevant at all or whether the proclamation was issued in the mala fide exercise of power (Laxminath 2002, pp. 294-5).

In spite of this clear warning by the Supreme Court, the UPA government brazenly dissolved the Bihar Assembly in 2006. The decision was taken at a Cabinet meeting at midnight and sanction for the proposal was obtained by fax from the President who was then in Moscow. The Supreme Court made a scathing observation on the Governor, Buta Singh, for manufacturing a 'perverse' and 'mala fide' report, and said, 'the Council of Ministers should have verified the report before accepting it as gospel truth'. The Supreme Court made it clear that it would intervene to stop gubernatorial misdemeanours and violation of constitutional norms, and the decision to dissolve the Assembly was clearly taken to prevent Nitish Kumar from becoming the Chief Minister (*The Economic Times*, 25 January 2006). As a result, Governor Buta Singh had to resign in disgrace. Earlier, on 21 October 1997, President K.R. Narayanan—who used to be called a textbook President—had rejected the advice of the Council of Ministers to impose President's Rule in Uttar Pradesh. In contrast, R.

Venkataraman earned a well-deserved stricture from the Supreme Court in 1994 in the *Bommai case* in relation to the proclamation of 21 April 1989 imposing President's Rule in Karnataka. Two other proclamations which Venkataraman had signed were also struck down: one relating to Nagaland (1988) and the second relating to Meghalaya (1991).... *A clear majority of six judges on a nine-member bench ruled that the material submitted by the Government of India to the President could be called for and examined by the courts. Any claim to privilege would also be decided by the courts* (Noorani 2000, pp. 269, 271).

These pronouncements by the Supreme Court have put a decisive end to the misuse of Article 356. By its decision in the *Bommai case* the Court reasserted the original objectives underlying Article 356. As a result, there is no longer any need to consider the abolition or any amendment of this Article. This case underlines the importance of checks and balances in a democracy.

How far India has travelled over the years can be seen from the statement of Nehru in the Constituent Assembly that 'no court, no system of judiciary can function in the nature of a third House [of Parliament], as a kind of third House of correction. So it is important that with this limitation the judiciary should function' (Dhavan and Thomas 1992, pp. 69-70). However, in a series of cases, the judiciary effectively had to take over the role of Parliament. As a result, the Indian judiciary has emerged as the most powerful organ of the state enjoying the highest credibility in the country.

Institution of State Governor

Article 153 is an innocuous provision of the Constitution which states, 'There shall be a Governor for each state'. But it has become one of the most controversial provisions. P. Upendra, a former Minister in Andhra Pradesh and at the Centre, writes in an essay titled, 'The Ramlal Episode: A Breach of Democracy': '*One of the most blatantly misused instruments of our Constitution is the institution of Governors.... A time may also come* when the institution of Governor may be dispensed with.... Whatever the future may hold, it is necessary to avoid more Ramlals [Governor of AP] if Indian democracy is to survive' (*The Governor 1985*, pp. 106, 130).

The institution of Governor is clearly a vestige of India's colonial past. When the relevant provisions of the draft Constitution came up for discussion in the Constituent Assembly, there was considerable discussion on whether it should be an elected post and whether special powers ought to be given to the Governor, but no questions were raised about whether this institution was necessary at all. Nehru, who had called the privy purses given to the former rulers of princely states 'anachronistic', did not consider the continuance of the institution of Governor 'anachronistic' in the Indian Republic! Conducting all business of the state government 'by order and in the name of Governor', when he hardly ever was consulted on the relevant matters, did not make any sense. The provision in Article 164 that 'the Ministers shall hold office during the pleasure of the Governor' also appears odd in a democracy. These provisions showed the Constitution makers' fascination with the British Raj.

Jawaharlal Nehru treated governorships as sinecures for accommodating elderly politicians or loyal civil servants who were to be put to pasture and could not be usefully utilised elsewhere. Eminent journalist, G.K. Reddy, has invited attention to the fact that

> [Chief Minister] Pandit Pant had [Governor] Giri transferred abruptly from Uttar Pradesh when he found him to be unaccommodating and inconvenient. The then Maharashtra Chief Minister, Morarji Desai, prided himself on not forwarding any file of consequence to the Governor even for routine approval. [Governor] Pattabhi Sitaramayya complained bitterly that he generally read in newspapers of the orders and notifications issued in his name. (Bhagyalaxmi 1992, p. 9)

Former West Bengal Governor, Dharma Vira, believed that Governors 'generally' functioned 'objectively', but that they have been guided by the wishes of the powers that be at the Centre. However, he asked, can Governors act independently when they 'hold office at the pleasure of the Ministry in power at the Centre?' (Austin 1999, p. 607).

The Marxist Chief Minister of Kerala, E.M.S. Namboodiripad, in his picturesquely titled essay, 'A Spoke in the Federal Wheel', has written:

> The Kerala and West Bengal coalitions were rocked with dissensions among their constituents to such an extent that they were on the point of breaking down. Of these two, Kerala could be 'managed' (although after two years) by enticing a few of the constituents away from the coalition and engineering the fall of the government without resort to the intervention of the Governor. In West Bengal, however, the office of the Governor had to be utilised [by the Centre] and it was done earlier than the collapse engineered in Kerala. The way in which it was manipulated became a matter of constitutional history, drawing the attention of two Conferences—that of the State Assembly Speakers and of the Governors of states. Having discussed the question, the Conferences drew up guidelines on how the Governor should act in similar contingencies in the future.... During the second tenure of Indira Gandhi's Prime Ministership (particularly in 1984), these guidelines were grossly violated in three states—Sikkim, J&K and AP—the occupants of the gubernatorial office [in Sikkim and AP] were active Congressmen sent as Governors to create trouble for the elected Ministries, while in the third—J&K—the job was done by a civilian. (*The Governor* 1985, p. 97)

Nani Palkhivala, in his article, 'Ram Lal: The Shameless Governor', has stated:

> Nineteen eighty-four may go down in Indian history as the year of disintegration.... Federalism is in peril.... People's faith in democratic

institutions has been violently shaken and they have begun to wonder whether the office of Governor is *worse than an expensive superfluity*.... Let us never forget that it is not the Constitution which has failed the people; it is our chosen representatives who have failed the Constitution. (Palkhivala 1994, pp. 56, 59)

Palkhivala also lamented how Tamil Nadu Governor Prabhudas Patwari was dismissed (October 1980): 'It was constitutionally unauthorized, and the manner of the dismissal was not only uncivil but uncivilized.... Even a subordinate deserves to be treated with more courtesy' (Palkhivala 1994, p. 61).

B.K. Nehru, who had the distinction of serving as Governor in Assam, J&K and Gujarat, has, in his book *Nice Guys Finish Second*, shown how the office of Governor has been politicised and devalued and how he was transferred from J&K (April 1984), like a civil servant,[8] for failing to abide by the *diktat* of Indira Gandhi to sack Chief Minister Farooq Abdullah and install Gul Shah. B. K. Nehru has stated:

> The inducement for defecting had then to be substantial. The standard rate was two lakh rupees in cash and a ministership; this latter would, of course, provide the defector with a substantially larger cash return even though his career in office might be short. *The funds were provided by my friend Tirath Ram Amla, a staunch and tried Congress worker, and were supplied to him in cash from Congress Party money in Delhi, transported in the mail pouches of the Intelligence Bureau.* The use of official machinery for party purposes had by then become so commonplace that it did not call for any eyebrows to be even slightly raised. (Nehru 1997, pp. 620-1, 626-7)

---

8. When Principal Secretary to Prime Minister rang up B.K. Nehru to hurry up with his departure from Srinagar, Nehru had shouted back at him to say that his departure date had been fixed and he was not a bloody *chaprasi* [peon] to be turned out at a moment's notice. Dharma Vira, Governor of West Bengal, had used exactly the same words to the Cabinet Secretary of his time about his not being a 'bloody *chaprasi*'.

B.K. Nehru has emphasised,

> The concept of what a Governor was and what he was supposed to do has changed completely. The erosion of the original concept commenced fairly early after Independence. It started with Governors being "transferred" from State to State during their five-year tenure of office, a practice totally alien to the letter and spirit of the Constitution. The Governor's position now is very clearly *(sic)* that he is not an independent official, that he is under the orders of the central government and, more often than not, he is an agent or an active member of the party in power at the Centre.... Homi Talyarkhan, then Governor of Sikkim, proudly announced to me that he had taken action in Sikkim which would ensure that the Congress Party would always remain in power in that State. He hoped that I was doing the same in J&K. (Nehru 1997, p. 618)

During Vajpayee's NDA regime (1999-2004), several prominent loyal BJP workers were appointed as Governors. These included: K.R. Malkani (Pondicherry, as it was known at the time), S.S. Bhandari (Gujarat), Bhai Mahavir (Madhya Pradesh), Vishnukant Shastri (Uttar Pradesh), Suraj Bhan (Himachal Pradesh), and Kedarnath Sahni (Sikkim).

As seen earlier, the Congress had followed the practice of rewarding its party leaders in this manner right from Independence and this practice continued during the period Congress Party was in power. At least two Governors—Ram Naresh Yadav (MP) and Aziz Qureshi (Uttarakhand)—publicly declared their gratitude to Congress president Sonia Gandhi for their appointment. Ram Naresh Yadav called on Sonia Gandhi for advice (?) before writing to the chief minister to reconvene the Assembly session to discuss the no-confidence motion against the government (*The Indian Express*, 29 July 2013). Apart from the highly questionable propriety of such an action, it is its brazenness which is so striking. H.R. Bhardwaj, Governor of Karnataka, went to the extent of declaring that he was a Congressman first. The offices of Governors and ministers have become interchangeable (Sushilkumar Shinde, Jagmohan, S.M. Krishna). Governors are looked upon as representing the Central government and not the President of India. Most Governors are blatantly partisan in their dealings with the state governments and, as a result, are often perceived as instruments of the ruling party at the Centre. P. Venkatasubbaiah, Romesh Bhandari and Buta Singh, the then Governors of Karnataka, UP and Bihar, respectively, had to resign following strictures by the Supreme Court for doing New Delhi's bidding. Another Governor, Bhanu Pratap Singh, had to be dismissed. The C&AG (Comptroller and Auditor General) report had noted how Devanand Konwar, the then Governor of Bihar, had travelled by air on 53 occasions to various cities in 2011-12, with nothing on official records to show why. The then Education Minister of Bihar, P.K. Shahi, said he was ashamed to admit that Vice-Chancellors were being appointed on payment. Indeed, a joke that suggested that appointments to offices of Vice-Chancellors and college principals were available on equated monthly instalments (EMI) went viral in the state. The then Deputy Chief Minister, Sushil Kumar Modi, and many of his Cabinet colleagues, in an unprecedented move, demanded a CBI inquiry into the allegations against the Governor (*Outlook*, 25 March 2013). The Supreme Court had pronounced that the appointments made by Devanand Konwar as Chancellor were not only 'illegal' but also 'contemptuous'. The court noted that the decision of making these appointments, by way of three notifications, was taken without an effective consultation with the state government and in 'contemptuous disregard' of the orders passed by the Patna High Court.

The Bench noted: 'What is most shocking is that the Chancellor selected two Vice-Chancellors and one Pro-Vice-Chancellor despite the fact that they were facing prosecutions under the IPC [Indian Penal Code], SC/ST [Scheduled Caste/Scheduled Tribe] Act and the Prevention of Corruption Act...against some other persons, there were charges of wrongful withdrawal of TA [travelling allowance], DA [dearness allowance]' (*The*

Indian Express, 20 August 2013).

Konwar was merely transferred to another State as Governor and was not asked to resign. N.D. Tiwari, Governor of AP, had to resign after serious allegations surfaced about his sexual exploits. The long list of Governors who had to resign due to allegations included Prabhat Kumar, Romesh Bhandari, Sheila Kaul, Motilal Vohra, Bhanu Pratap Singh, Chenna Reddy, Jagmohan, Bali Ram Bhagat, Krishna Pal Singh, to name a few. At least two Governors were involved in the *Hawala* scandal (1991) and had to resign.

The partisan attitude of Governors is often evident in matters pertaining to the imposition of President's Rule under Article 356 of the Constitution. In such cases, inevitably, there is a demand for the recall or transfer of the Governor, hardly befitting the high constitutional office.

The lowest point was reached in 1990, when the V.P. Singh Government took the decision to ask for resignations of all Governors appointed by Rajiv Gandhi. Some Governors resisted this move, while others protested. B.G. Deshmukh, who was then Principal Secretary to the Prime Minister, has written:

> Romesh Bhandari, Lieutenant Governor of Delhi, declined to resign and 'dared the Prime Minister to sack him. I suggested the usual bureaucratic *via media* of giving Bhandari an inconvenient posting and he was thus appointed Lieutenant Governor of Andaman and Nicobar Islands. Since he had political ambitions and did not want to be away from Delhi, he resigned and we got him out of the Prime Minister's way' (Deshmukh 2004, p. 253).

Equating Governors with civil servants was thus complete!

The position in the Narendra Modi regime is no better. *India Today* (5 October 2020, pp. 48-51) has brought out how the role of state governors had come under a cloud in a number of states—namely, Uttarakhand, Arunachal Pradesh, Manipur, Goa, Karnataka, Maharashtra, Madhya

Pradesh and Rajasthan. As the *Indian Express* commented editorially, 'The BJP has long been an advocate of federalism and, as a party of (sic) the Opposition, it has spoken fervently of the independence of Governor's office. But its record in government has been scarcely different from that of the Congress. Since 2014, the Narendra Modi government has replaced 26 Governors and seven lieutenant governors with its own candidates' ('Governor's Rule', 24 January 2018, p. 10).

Almost all Governors, appointed by the Modi government, are from the BJP/RSS cadres. Some of them seem to forget that they are holders of constitutional office and are expected to sever their connections with their political party and its mentor, the RSS.

Some Governors seem to forget that they are not expected to interfere in state administration as seen in the case of Goa and Telangana. At the time of writing this book, the relations between Jagdeep Dhankhar, Governor of West Bengal, and Mamata Banerjee, Chief Minister, seem to be particularly strained. The standoff (*India Today*, 13 January 2020, p. 21) in Jadavpur University lowered the image of the Governor as also the state government. The Governor has denounced the incident as a 'total collapse of rule of law'. He has publicly stated that the Chief Minister has used foul language against him. There is an escalating war of words between the two. The Governor has alleged that the Raj Bhavan was under surveillance of the state police and documents from his office were either leaked or being 'procured'. As a result of the strained relations with the Chief Minister, the Prevention of Lynching Bill is reportedly pending for Governor's approval. He is called *rajnitipal* (adept at politicking) rather than *rajyapal* (head of the state) by some persons in the state. The Governor has publicly stated that getting 'yes-men' as VCs began soon after the TMC (Trinamool Congress Party) came to power in 2011 (*India Today*, 13 January 2020, p. 21). The TMC has demanded that the Governor should be booked for 'obstructing money laundering probe' (*The Indian Express*, 27 November 2020, p. 12). The TMC members of Parliament have written to the President of India for removal of the Governor 'for serious breach of oath of office' (*The Indian*

Express, 31 December 2020, p. 8).

In 2020, the rift between Goa Chief Minister Pramod Sawant and Governor Satya Pal Malik led to the Governor's transfer to Meghalaya. However, in spite of the much more unseemly and unending tussle between the West Bengal Chief Minister and Governor, referred to above, Dhankhar is continuing as the Governor. Is this because he is 'acting like a BJP mouthpiece', as Banerjee has publicly alleged? Obviously, the Centre found it convenient to retain Dhankhar in Kolkata in view of the elections in the state.

In 2015, the then Governor of Assam, P.B. Acharya, had been at loggerheads with the state Chief Minister Tarun Gogoi of the Congress. The Chief Minister had written to the President of India alleging that the Governor had converted the Raj Bhavan into an annexe of the BJP office and had requested the President to replace Acharya. The Chief Minister has also castigated the Governor for his comment, 'Hindustan is for Hindus' (*The Indian Express*, 29 November 2015, p. 4).

In January 2018, the ruling CPI-M in Kerala criticised the then Governor, P. Sathasivam, former CJI, for editing out a reference critical of the Centre and the BJP from the text of his address to the state Assembly.

His successor, Arif Mohammad Khan, has been criticised by Chief Minister Pinarayi Vijayan for his view that the state Assembly had no right to pass a resolution against the Citizenship Amendment Act (CAA) enacted by Parliament. The Governor publicly joining issues with the political parties in the state on an issue like the CAA can be seriously questioned. The Opposition Congress-led United Democratic Front in Kerala is pressing for adoption of a resolution in the state Assembly, demanding recall of the Governor (*The Sunday Guardian*, 2-8 February 2020, p. 6). The latest in the series is the letter written by Governor of Maharashtra Bhagat Singh Koshyari to Chief Minister Uddhav Thackeray on 13 October 2020 requesting for early opening of places of worship in the state, amidst the raging Covid-19 pandemic (*The Indian Express*, 14 October 2020, p. 1). It was an indiscreet act on the part of the Governor to release the letter to the media. More objectionable was the tone and contents of the letter which was hardly befitting the constitutional position he occupies. The letter mockingly asked the Chief Minister if he had turned 'secular', obviously referring to the strong Hindutva stand of the Shiv Sena, before forming a coalition government in the state with the two Congress parties. Koshyari calls himself *Lokrajyapal*, rather than *Rajyapal*, his official designation. In the appeals filed to the Governor of Maharashtra against the decisions of the ministers, the past practice was to forward such appeals to the Chief Minister for disposal. Instead, the Governor has started giving personal hearing to the appellants in the Raj Bhavan, effectively discharging executive functions, not in consonance with the position of a constitutional head of state (*Loksatta*, 4 March 2021, p. 1). Sharad Pawar, president of the Nationalist Congress Party, which is a partner in the coalition government in Maharashtra, has charged that Koshyari is the first Governor of Maharashtra who has flouted the constitutional norms of his office. Sanjay Raut, Shiv Sena MP, has said, 'It is not the case of a cold war, there is an open war between the Governor and the government' (*The Week*, 28 February 2021, p. 42).

Some of the non-BJP state governments were agitated about the three farm laws passed by Parliament in 2020 and were keen on calling a special session of the state legislature to pass resolutions denouncing the actions of the Central government. However, some Governors dragged their feet in agreeing to convene the legislature session. Kerala Governor Arif Mohammad Khan went to the extent of publicly justifying the actions of the Central government. The Governor of Maharashtra, B.S. Koshyari, has not taken a decision on the proposal sent by the state government for nomination of persons to the state legislative council, though several weeks have elapsed. The issue is likely to be taken to the high court. These developments have raised serious questions of propriety.

It can be seen that in some cases the Governors' actions, in their ex-officio capacity, as Chancellors of Universities, had become controversial. In these cases, the Governors had taken decisions by using their personal discretion under the relevant statute. There is divergence of judicial opinion on whether the Governor enjoys protection under Article 361 of the Constitution in such cases. 'The MP and AP High Courts have taken two different views.... The answer [to the question whether the Governor has protection] appears to be in the negative' (Democracy and Federalism 1995, p. 45).

Thus, over the years, the Governor's office has been politicised. It may be recalled that the Committee of Governors under the Chairmanship of Bhagwan Sahay (1971) had unambiguously stated that the Governor was an independent head of state drawing his authority from the Constitution. He was not concerned with and was above political parties and was not subordinate in any way to the Government of India. However, the Governors and the Central government have observed these precepts more in the breach.

L.P. Singh and Govind Narain, both former Union Home Secretaries and Governors, have quoted the decision of a five-member Constitution Bench of the Supreme Court (AIR 1979, SC 709) delivered on 4 May 1979 to underline that the Governor was not to function as an agent of the Central government:

It is no doubt true that the Governor is appointed by the President which means in effect and substance the Government of India, but that is only a mode of appointment and it does not make the Governor an employee or servant of the Government of India. *Every person appointed by the President is not necessarily an employee of the Government of India.* So also it is not material that the Governor holds office during the pleasure of the President. It is a constitutional provision for determination of the term of office of the Governor and it does not make the Government of India the employer of the Governor. His office is not subordinate or subservient to the Government of India. He is not amenable to the direction of the Government of India, nor is he accountable to them for the manner in which he carries out his functions and duties. His is an independent constitutional office which is not subject to the control of the Government of India. *He is constitutionally the head of the state in whom is vested the executive power of the state* and without whose assent there can be no legislation in exercise of the legislative power of the state. (*The Governor* 1985, pp. 44, 58)

No other ruling of the Supreme Court has been so far removed from reality! The constitutional precepts elucidated by the Supreme Court have remained just that. No government has taken notice of them all these years.

Dharma Vira raised a question:

How do we create an atmosphere in which the governor can operate independently and with objectivity?.... At present, the normal tenure of a Governor is five years, but he holds his office only at the pleasure of the President. The President, however, is guided in all matters by the advice of his Ministers. Thus, in actual fact, Governors hold office at the pleasure of the Ministry in power at the Centre. Such a situation leaves the Governor completely at the mercy of the Centre, and in most cases this tends to obstruct his independence and objectivity—particularly when quite a few Governors have been appointed as a consequence of political patronage. It is therefore necessary to evolve some system of selecting Governors with great care. The practice of consulting the state chief ministers prior to appointing Governors in their respective areas has more or less been reduced to nullity; the practice should immediately be revived. There should also be a greater security of tenure for Governors. The Constitution should ensure that a Governor cannot be removed except through processes which have to be observed in the case of judges of the Supreme Court. (*The Governor* 1985, p. 88)

All these have remained fond hopes. There has been no change in the treatment and functioning of Governors over all these years.

The salient guidelines suggested by the Sarkaria Commission on Centre-State Relations (1988), the NCRWC (2002), and the Punchhi Commission (2010) regarding the selection and appointment of Governors have been blatantly disregarded by successive governments at the Centre. The most comprehensive of these were the recommendations of the Sarkaria Commission which had suggested that a person to be appointed a Governor should satisfy the following criteria:

- He should be eminent in some walk of life.
- He should be a person from outside the state.
- He should be a detached figure and not too intimately connected with the local politics of the state, and
- He should be a person who has not taken too great a part in the politics generally, and particularly in the recent past.

The Commission had also suggested the following guidelines in respect of the office of Governor:

- It is desirable that a politician from the ruling party at the Union is not appointed as a Governor of a state which is being run by some other party or combination of other parties.
- In order to ensure effective consultation with the state chief minister in the selection of a person to be appointed as Governor, the procedure of consultation should be prescribed in the Constitution itself by suitably amending Article 155.
- The Governor's tenure of office of five years in a state should not be disturbed except very rarely and that too for some extremely compelling reasons.
- Save where the President is satisfied that, in the interest of the security of the state, it is not expedient to do so, the Governor

whose tenure is proposed to be terminated before the expiry of the normal term of five years, should be informally apprised of the grounds of the proposed action and affording *(sic)* reasonable opportunity for showing cause against it.

- As a matter of convention, the Governor should not, on demitting his office, be eligible for any other appointment or office of profit under the Union or a state government except for a second term as Governor or election as Vice President or President of India. Such a convention should also require that, after quitting or laying down his office, the Governor shall not return to active partisan politics (GOI Part I, 1988, p. 135).

The National Commission to Review the Working of the Constitution (NCRWC) has supported the above criteria for selection of a Governor and has added that the persons belonging to the minority groups should continue to be given a chance as hitherto (Pylee 2006, p. 770).

I have given this somewhat lengthy quotation to show that none of these salutary recommendations and guidelines have been observed by any of the Union governments, no matter to which political party they belonged.

Justice V.R. Krishna Iyer, in his essay (Kashyap 1992, pp. 43, 157), has called the Governors 'boneless wonders', and has suggested that Articles 200 and 110 providing for the Governor's and President's assent, respectively, to Bills are not necessary. The Speaker's certification of the Bill as passed should be enough. Dharma Vira is of the view that Governors should be appointed on merit and not on political considerations. Also, they should not be subject to removal at the will of the Centre (Kashyap 1992, pp. 43-44, 157). Vira has also lamented that the practice of consulting the state chief ministers prior to appointing Governors in their respective areas has more or less been reduced to a nullity (*The Governor* 1985, p. 88).

Discontent over reservation of bills by Governors for President's assent has been evident all these years. In 1952, Morarji Desai, then Chief Minister of Bombay, complained that the Governor sending the state's Essential Supplies Act to the President and then asking him to delay his assent 'was inappropriate...very extraordinary and would set a very awkward precedent...'. President Rajendra Prasad commented unfavourably that during the years 1953-56, as many as 1,114 of the 2,557 laws enacted by state legislatures had come to him for approval. From 1977 to November 1985, a similar number of bills was reserved for the President's assent, and all but 90 received assent (Austin 1999, p. 591).

Several state governments followed the example of Maharashtra which had passed the Maharashtra Control of Organised Crime Act (MCOCA) to deal more effectively with such crimes. The Act provided for enhanced punishment, constitution of special courts, authorisation for interception of wire, electronic or oral communications, special rules of evidence, protection of witnesses and admissibility of confessions made before police officers above a certain rank. Karnataka, AP and Delhi had enacted such laws with the prior approval of the President. But, the Gujarat Act was kept pending for the President's approval for an inordinately long time, the unstated reason being suspicion, after the 2002 Godhra riots, that the minorities may be persecuted by the state government under the provisions of the Act. Openly, of course, this reasoning was never divulged.

Parimal Dabhi has written:

> Irked that the UPA was not clearing the bill, Modi, then CM, wrote to then President Kalam seeking approval for the bill on the ground that similar bills were in operation in Maharashtra, Karnataka, AP and Delhi. In 2006, the Gujarat Assembly passed a resolution asking the Centre to clear the bill. In 2007, Modi wrote twice to the then Prime Minister Manmohan Singh to intervene and expedite the bill. In 2008, after the serial blasts in Jaipur, Modi wrote another letter to Singh on the bill. Later that year, the Gujarat Cabinet passed a resolution for immediate approval of the bill.... (*The Indian Express*, 1 February 2016, p. 9)

Why should it be necessary for the Centre to scrutinise the bills passed by state legislatures? This should appropriately be left for judicial review.

The Sarkaria Commission has recommended that in dealing with a bill presented to him under Article 200, the Governor should not act contrary to the advice of his Council of Ministers merely because, personally, he does not like the policy embodied in the bill (GOI, Part I, 1988: 157). The NCRWC has recommended that there should be a time limit—say a period of six months—within which the Governor should take a decision on whether to grant assent to or reserve a bill for consideration of the President (Pylee 2006, p. 770).

In the light of the experience of the working of the Governors over the last 73 years, it needs to be seriously considered whether there is any need at all for the institution of Governor. This office was copied from the GOI Act, 1935. The office was certainly important during the colonial period but I have serious reservations on its need in a democratic India.

I have carefully gone over the responsibilities of the Governor enumerated in the Constitution. *The fiction* created by Article 154 about the executive power of the state vesting in the Governor and his exercising it directly or indirectly through officers subordinate to him, etc. is just that and, being unnecessary, should be done away with.

The Supreme Court has laid down that all matters pertaining to the majority support enjoyed by a political party should be tested on the floor of the House. The Governor is not expected to count heads of legislators supporting any particular candidate or to verify and satisfy himself of such support on the basis of any documentary evidence, as used to be done earlier.

As for calling a session of the legislature, the chief minister can approach the Speaker of the Assembly and the Chairman of the Council. The intermediary of the Governor is not necessary to summon the House. Similarly, the assent of the Governor is not necessary to prorogue either of the Houses of the state legislature. It can be done by their presiding officers, on request by the chief minister. The Legislative Assembly can be dissolved by the Speaker on the advice of the chief minister.

The ceremonial address of the Governor to the first session of the legislature every year is also redundant. The chief minister, in his address, can indicate to the House what programme the government has in mind for the session.

Approval of the Governor is also not necessary for introduction of financial bills. After all, as leader of the House, it is the responsibility of the chief minister to be answerable for all actions.

Once a bill is passed by the House, certification thereof by the Speaker or the Chairman of the Council should be adequate. There is no need to have the assent of the Governor. There is also no need to reserve a bill/Act for prior approval of the Governor. If the bill exceeds the powers of the legislature or is in contravention of any Central law, the matter can be decided by the High Court/Supreme Court.

The power to grant pardon or to suspend, remit or commute sentences in certain cases is anachronistic, and a vestige of the colonial past and of the days of royalty. It is high time this practice is discontinued. Once the court has given the final ruling in a case, there should be no need for any review by any other authority. This should apply equally to the powers of the President for remission of sentences, grant of pardon, etc.

The only point on which the Governor has some role is in regard to selection of the person who is to be called to form the government after election. As stated earlier, the question of who should be called to form the government is no longer of unfettered discretion in view of the principle of floor test referred to above. But, the Election Commission of India could be given this responsibility. In view of the division of powers envisaged in the Constitution, I am not in favour of involving the Chief Justice of High Court in any matters pertaining to the role of the Governor except administering oath or affirmation to the chief minister and his ministerial team.

As for the special responsibilities cast on the Governors of Maharashtra and Gujarat in respect of development boards under Article 371 of the Constitution, serious thought needs to be given to the advisability of continuing this provision. Giving such powers to the Governors, overriding the wishes of a democratically elected government, was clearly against the grain of the Constitution. Therefore, the opening words of this Article are: 'notwithstanding anything in this Constitution...'. The experience of the working of the development boards in Maharashtra over the last several decades also shows that they have not served any purpose. It is high time this Article is abolished.

In the light of the above, I am of the view that the institution of Governor should be abolished. Looking to the importance of the subject, the proposal may be remitted to the Law Commission of India to elicit public opinion and for detailed examination thereafter.

The institution of Governor provides a spoils system as in the United States and enables the party in power to provide political patronage for its leaders at least for five years, if not longer. Major political parties, with prospects of coming to power, are not therefore likely to agree to abolish the institution of Governor. If abolition of the institution is not considered feasible or advisable, the following few steps should be taken to at least remove the major irritants in Centre-state relations. *First*, a committee may be constituted for selection of persons for appointment as Governor. The committee may consist of the Prime Minister, the Chief Justice of India, the Speaker of the Lok Sabha, the Union Home Minister, the Leaders of Opposition in both Houses, and two non-political, eminent persons of high reputation and integrity. The names of such persons may be decided by the government in consultation with the CJI. *Second*, the process of consultation with the chief minister should be laid down by formal orders on the subject. *Third*, a panel of three names may be sent to the chief minister from which he can indicate his preference. *Fourth*, bills should not be reserved for assent of the Governor. *Fifth*, the Governor should not object to any part of his address to the legislature, even if it is critical of the Central government or the party in power at the Centre. The Governor is head of the state. It is well understood that his speech is prepared by the state government and it is submitted to the Governor only after its approval by the Cabinet. As such, when the Governor delivers the address, it reflects the views of the state government and not of the Governor. It is high time these irritants are removed.

Transition Towards a True Federation?

The resistance of some Part B states to the control exercised by the Centre became evident when the state of Mysore conveyed to the GOI in 1951 that it was determined to resist constitutionally the interference of the Centre. Soon thereafter, the State of Travancore-Cochin too prevailed on the GOI to give it exemption from Central control (Alexandrowicz 1957, pp. 160-1).

Austin has noted that the gravest threats to secede came from Tamil Nadu [in 1950s], [and later] Punjab and the Nagas (Austin 1999, p. 562).

As discussed in Chapter 4, the creation of linguistic states in 1956, much against the wishes of the then ruling Congress Party stalwarts comprising Nehru and Patel, was proof of the assertiveness of the states in redrawing the map of India.

During the Nehru and Shastri period of hegemony of the Congress Party, any dispute between the Centre and the states was discussed and settled across the table at the party level and it never became a Centre-state problem. However, the Lok Sabha election in 1967 was a turning point with non-Congress governments coming to power in some states. The leftist governments in Kerala and West Bengal refused to give protection to the Central government offices in their states during the Central government employees' strike in 1968. The GOI had to write to the states inviting their attention to their obligations under Article 256 of the Constitution which, inter alia, laid down that 'the executive power of every state shall be so exercised as to ensure compliance with the laws made by Parliament and any existing laws which apply in that state'. When, even this had no effect, the Central Reserve Police Force (CRPF) was deployed for protection of the Central government offices and establishments. Later, this led to the Central government establishing the Central Industrial Security Force (CISF).

Speaking in the Lok Sabha on 6 August 1969, Y.B. Chavan, the then Union Home Minister, said:

> At this particular moment, I will have to take very careful note of the important aspects of the political reality in India today—that is the centre-state relationship. I do not want to say anything which will be construed as something which is intended to run down the government of a state. That is not my intention. The most important reality of today's politics is that there are different parties running different administrations, and there is a change in the emphasis of their politics.

Some members suggested that Chavan should act more firmly like a strong home minister. Chavan said: 'I do not want to be a Home Minister who makes brave speeches. I was told about the HM [Home Minister] of 1948-49. I must remind them [Hon'ble Members] that India of 1968-69 is not India of 1948-49' (Godbole 1996, pp. 68-9).

The Government of Tamil Nadu made a proposal in 1968 to have its own state flag. After stiff resistance by the Centre, this proposal was given up, though earlier, as a part of the Delhi Agreement between Nehru and Sheikh Abdullah in 1952, the GOI had agreed to J&K having its own state flag, as a special case. A proposal for a state flag has also been mooted by the Government of Karnataka in 2018 which is supported by both the Congress and the BJP. The implications of this are discussed in Chapter 4.

Durga Das has written:

> He had talks spread over six hours with him [Sheikh Abdullah] and his principal lieutenant, Mirza Afzal Beg, in May 1968 and these led me to the conclusion that he wants an honourable way of re-entry into India, if possible through special relations in which the Valley would

enjoy more autonomy than the other parts of India. The Sheikh is not alone in entertaining this desire. The late E.N. Annadurai, then DMK Chief Minister of Madras, and Namboodiripad, the Marxist Chief Minister of Kerala, expressed similar opinions. My talks with them in the last quarter of 1967 threw light on the issue of centre-state relations. Both wanted the centre to shed many of its powers and to confine itself to external affairs, defence, communications and international commerce. Annadurai wanted the Lok Sabha to be an indirectly elected Council of States in which each state would be equally represented. (Das 1969, pp. 411-2)

The Centre-state issues came to the fore with the appointment of the Rajamannar Committee by the Government of Tamil Nadu in September 1969. To give a flavour of the thinking of the committee, some of its important recommendations are given below:

- Unless the party that happens to be in power at the Centre develops conventions to shed its party affiliations in the matter of its relations with the states, the federal government cannot effectively function in our country.
- Articles 356 and 357 may be entirely repealed.
- Article 365 states that where any state has failed to comply with, or to give effect to, any directions given by the Union, it automatically attracts Article 356. Who is to decide whether or not a state has complied with and given effect to those directions? It is again the Union Cabinet and here too it is arguable whether the issue can be agitated in a court of law. It follows that Article 365 has to be deleted.
- The power to present an address to the President for the removal of a judge of the High Court from office should be vested in the state legislature.
- The power regarding the salaries and allowances, leave and

pension of High Court judges should be vested in the state legislatures.

- The Governor should be appointed always in consultation with the state Cabinet. The other alternative would be to make the appointment in consultation with a high power body especially constituted for the purpose.
- The Governor should be rendered ineligible for a second term of office as Governor or any other office under government.
- A specific provision should be made in the Constitution enabling the President to issue Instrument of Instructions to the Governors.
- The provision in the Constitution that the Ministry holds office during the pleasure of the Governor should be omitted.
- The provisions confining emergency to a state be omitted.
- Article 360 relating to financial emergency should be omitted.
- The expression 'internal disturbance' in Article 352 should be interpreted to mean that it must be comparable in gravity to the repelling of external aggression.
- Recruitment to All India Services should either be by transfer of members of the existing gazetted services under the control of the states or by direct recruitment or by a combination of both these methods, if need be *by holding an examination confined to each state.*
- Article 312 should be amended to omit the provision for the creation of new All India Services in future.
- Preferably English may be the medium of examination for the All India Services, although recruitment may be on a statewise basis.
- It should be expressly provided in the Constitution itself that *the territorial integrity of a state should not be interfered with in any manner,* except in accordance with any of the following three alternatives:
  - i. The consent of the state is obtained.
  - ii. The issue should be referred to, and decided by, a high-level judicial tribunal to be constituted for the purpose, and its

decision should be binding on all the parties.
iii. The opinion of the people of the area or areas concerned should be ascertained by holding a special poll (GOTN 1971, pp. 137,140, 221-224).

The creation of All India Services (AIS) was approved by the conference of Premiers of Provinces in October 1946 under the chairmanship of Vallabhbhai Patel. In his concluding remarks on 22 October 1946, Patel had stated, 'Except in the matter of control, we are agreed on all points.... There is very little difference and I think that difference will disappear' (GOI 1967, p. 138). However, the issue of control of AIS has continued to come up again and again. The two recent examples are of Tamil Nadu and West Bengal. Transfer of AIS officers serving in the states to the Centre by GOI, without approval of the state government, is being seen as infringing the federal spirit. It can be seen that the Rajamannar Committee had effectively asked for rewriting the Constitution. Importantly, the committee was presided over by Dr P.V. Rajamannar, Chief Justice of Madras High Court, from 1948 to 1961, and had two prominent members drawn from public life. And this was the view of only one of the states. One can imagine how diverse and contentious the demands will be if the issues are placed before all the states. The memoranda submitted by the states to the Sarkaria Commission (Part II of the report), in reply to the questionnaire circulated by the Commission, bring out the dissatisfaction of the non-Congress state governments on Centre-state relations. The Congress Party, with Indira Gandhi at the helm, was in power at the time at the Centre and in several states. I have quoted elsewhere the statement of Austin that, in informal discussions with him, even the chief ministers of the Congress-ruled state governments had expressed views on the Inter-State Council, which were contrary to the views expressed by the AICC (All India Congress Committee), but they did not dare to take a position opposed to their party line, formally. These winds of change must not be ignored.

The West Bengal Cabinet adopted a document pertaining to the Centre-state relations at its meeting on 1 December 1977 and released it for wide publicity. The demands therein were more or less the same as those made by the Rajamannar Committee. The main demands were: residuary powers should be with the states and not the Centre; Articles 200 [assent to bills by the Governor], 201 [bills reserved for consideration], 249 [power of Parliament to legislate on matters in the State List], 356 [provision in case of failure of constitutional machinery], and 312 [All India Services] should be deleted; elections to the Rajya Sabha should be direct as in the case of the Lok Sabha; all states must have equal representation in the Rajya Sabha, except those with a population of less than three million; both the Houses of Parliament must have equal powers; the Seventh Schedule should be revised so that the states are given exclusive powers in respect of certain categories of industries; and 75 per cent of the total revenue raised by the Centre from all sources should be allocated to the states (Pal 1985, pp. 319-21).

The conclave of non-Congress chief ministers held in Srinagar in 1983 was a major milestone in the long journey in search of full federalism, as opposed to the quasi-federalism prevailing in the country. The demands put forth by the conclave articulated several major grievances of the states such as misuse of the institution of Governor, misuse of Article 200 (assent to bills by the Governor), Article 257 (control of the Union over states in certain cases), and Article 356 (provision in case of failure of constitutional machinery in states), to name a few.

On 9 July 1998, West Bengal Chief Minister Jyoti Basu asked Prime Minister Atal Bihari Vajpayee to convene at the earliest a meeting of chief ministers to discuss the correct import of Article 355 [duty of the Union to protect States against external aggression and internal disturbance]. He said he had already written to him asking for a meeting of the Inter-State Council. Significantly, while each of the BJP's election manifestos in 1989, 1991 and 1996 pledged the establishment of the Council to settle all inter-state and Centre-state disputes, the pledge was omitted in the

1998 manifesto as well as in the so-called National Agenda (Noorani 2000, p. 275).

Over time, a number of legislative proposals had to be given up due to the resistance by the states. One of these was to have a Central legislation on custodial crimes, which has always been a matter of serious concern. As Union Home Secretary in 1991-93, I was anxious that such a Central legislation should be undertaken to make persons in charge of the custody solely responsible for persons in their custody, to cast the onus of proof of absence of human rights abuses on these officers, to make judicial inquiry mandatory in certain situations, to make publication of the report of the judicial inquiry compulsory in each case, and to provide for financial compensation to the victims of custodial crime. Even after my holding meetings with the Chief Secretaries and Directors General of Police of the states, and Union Home Minister S.B. Chavan holding a meeting of the Chief Ministers, the states could not be persuaded to agree to the enactment of a Central law on the subject and the proposal was given up (Godbole 1996, pp. 282-3).

The main question is whether we, as a nation, are committed to addressing the question of undocumented migration with any seriousness of purpose. It is futile to be under the misconception that the problem is confined only to Assam. It is shocking that states like West Bengal and Bihar have continued to deny the existence of the problem. As Union Home Secretary, I was concerned a great deal with massive illegal migration from Bangladesh. I convened a meeting of the Chief Secretaries of the concerned states on 24 March 1992 to discuss a package of measures to be adopted on an all-India basis. It came as a surprise to me that even at the official level, there was reluctance on the part of some states, and particularly West Bengal and Bihar, to deal with the problem firmly. This was obviously at the behest of the political direction of the state governments. I pursued the matter further and persuaded S.B. Chavan, Union Home Minister, to convene a meeting of the Chief Ministers. Accordingly, the meeting was held on 28 September 1992. In the background paper circulated for the conference, it was highlighted that Assam, West Bengal, Bihar, the North Eastern states and some other states in the country, including the Union Territory of Delhi, had been severely affected by the problem. The paper had underlined the fact that undocumented migrants seemed to be 'using West Bengal as a corridor to migrate to other parts of India. Parts of Bihar had been affected seriously. Large numbers have come to Delhi and have settled down in several other areas.'

A comprehensive package of nine measures was proposed to deal effectively with this huge problem. It was, however, shocking to see that the then Chief Minister of West Bengal, Jyoti Basu, and of Bihar, Lalu Prasad Yadav, were reluctant to approve the press note of the conference proceedings. Chavan had to exert a great deal of pressure to persuade them to do so. It is interesting to see that the stand of Jyoti Basu on the subject has not changed even though the Communists have been ousted and the Trinamool Congress has taken over (Godbole 2020, pp. 319-20).

The argument of federalism continues to be used by the states to oppose even other worthwhile proposals made by the Union government. Two recent examples bring this out. The railway police, belonging to the Ministry of Railways, are responsible only for the watch and ward duties and have no police powers. Debroy has stated:

> Contrary to what some people think, RPF doesn't stand for Railway Police Force – it is the Railway Protection Force. There is a railway police force too – it is the Government Railway Police (GRP). It is part of the state police. Law and order and policing on railways, including on trains, is the responsibility of the GRP. *The RPF was never meant to be a police force, not in the strict sense. A force doesn't become "police" unless it is "enrolled" under the Police Act (1861). The RPF isn't that, even if it is headed by someone from the Indian Police Service and even though it is an "armed force" of the Union.'*

It was proposed that the railway police be given police powers under the Police Act. Such a proposal made by the Ministry of Railways was strongly opposed by some states on the ground that it would dilute their police powers!

Another proposal pertained to enactment of a Central law on Lokayuktas who had been repeatedly urging in their annual conferences that a uniform all-India law should be enacted to increase their powers and make their institutions more effective. This proposal was opposed by some states on the ground that it would militate against the federal spirit of the Constitution. The alternate proposal for enactment of a model law on the subject by Parliament, which could be adopted by the states with such modifications as are considered necessary, was also objected to by some states.

One of the foremost concerns pertains to the working of the police in the country. The police are no longer looked upon by the common person as an upholder of the rule of law but have become an extended arm of exploitation by the political party in power. The image and credibility of the police has reached its nadir. No amount of exhortation by commissions of inquiry, statutory commissions such as the Human Rights Commission, or the higher judiciary has made any difference to the conduct and behaviour of the police. This is largely because of the support which the police receive from the political party in power. This nexus between the politicians and the police has become the bane of the system. This is evident from the fact that even the directions, given by the Supreme Court to the Centre and the states in the *Prakash Singh case* way back in 2006 regarding the restructuring of the police departments, have not been implemented by most states. Importantly, some of the directions were aimed at reducing the political interference in the functioning of the police, and ensuring fixity of tenure of field officers. The GOI has been unable to persuade the states to take necessary actions.

The very ill-considered decision by the Government of India not to have an all India Police Act to replace the old, archaic Police Act of 1861 due to the resistance of the states is indeed unfortunate. Even with the division of legislative powers in the Seventh Schedule of the Constitution, the Government of India could have taken the initiative to enact such a law as was done, for example, in the case of the Urban Land Ceiling Act. Article 249 of the Constitution gives power to Parliament to legislate with respect to a matter in the State List in the national interest. 'Police' and 'public order' are the basic responsibilities of the government. While the states could be free to make any changes in the Central law, in its application, to suit the local requirements, there are a number of precepts which should be considered sacrosanct and must form part of the national Police Act. Illustratively, these include the basic structure of police at different levels, their designations, hierarchy of police structure, composition of police, fixity of tenure, representation for minorities, reservation policy, personnel policies, empowered staff selection committees, grievance redressal committees, understanding of and focus on human rights, minimum use of force by police, sensitivity in dealing with weaker sections, women and children, promoting communal harmony, upholding the secular fabric of society, and maintaining the strictest standards of discipline. There can hardly be any difference of view on these basic prerequisites for a police force to meet the requirements of a new India. The National Police Commission, in its eighth and concluding report submitted as far back as 1981, had given a draft bill for the purpose (GOI 1981, pp. 51-60). Seventeen states have passed new Police Acts, but they are more with a view to circumventing the directions of the Supreme Court. The remaining states have passed executive orders which are against the letter and spirit of the Court's directions. The Centre is yet to pass the Model Police Act drafted by the Soli Sorabjee Committee, over a decade ago. Why are we shying away from enacting a Police Act at the national level?

The second generation economic reforms cannot be pushed beyond a point without the cooperation of the state governments. The Central government could push through the first generation reforms in the 1990s as they mostly pertained to subjects in the Union List. It is no longer so.

Several reforms have to be in respect of subjects in the State List. A case in point is that of the Central Land Acquisition Act. Ramesh and Khan's observations are significant:

> We knew that we did not have legislative competence to enact a new law on reporting [transactions in land]. So we took an existing law, passed before the Constitution came into force, and moved amendments to it: the Indian Registration Act, 1908 (which prescribes the procedure for the registration of documents by local authorities). The purpose of these amendments: mandate the computerization of land records and make them accessible to all at the lowest level, that is, at the block and district level.... We stepped up the Land Records Modernization Programme. Though unenforceable [by the Centre] it seeks to provide states with support to update and modernize their land records to boost transparency. Originally launched in 2008, it had languished until earlier this year [2014] with only four states actually following the programme guidelines.... And what we desperately need (but have not been able to figure out how, yet) is to enact a law making land titles 'conclusive' instead of 'presumptive'.... But the catch is that the Constitution of India classifies 'Land' as a state subject. This means that given India's quasi-federal structure, only states are free to make laws on the subject. So in effect, the Union cannot enforce what it commands. (Ramesh and Khan 2015, pp. 131-3)

This is indeed revealing. When a review of the Seventh Schedule is undertaken, a dogmatic view will have to be avoided in the larger national interest.

The position of some of the state governments on the Citizenship Amendment Act (CAA), the National Population Register, and the National Register of Citizens (NRC) has raised serious constitutional questions on the sustenance of the federal structure in the country. These subjects are squarely in the jurisdiction of the Central government but some states are not prepared to implement the GOI policies, including the laws passed by Parliament. Kerala became the first state to pass a resolution in the Legislative Assembly demanding abrogation of the CAA. Kerala Chief Minister Pinarayi Vijayan wrote to 11 non-BJP chief ministers urging them to consider taking similar step. Kerala also moved the Supreme Court against the Act. West Bengal Chief Minister Mamata Banerjee has issued public advertisements against the CAA and the National Register of Citizens (NRC) and has assured people that these will not be implemented in the state.

I had written in *The Wire* on 27 October 2018:

> A few weeks ago, West Bengal Chief Minister, Mamata Banerjee, roared, "They say they will start the exercise [National Register of Citizens] in Bengal. I want to see who dares to do that. *We are Bengal tigers*. It will not be so easy. Before you start anything here, remember that your days will be finished in 2019 [when the Lok Sabha elections were due]." We know that India is a country of stark contrasts. In Tripura and Jharkhand, politicians are anxious that the NRC be taken up in their states immediately. Tripura has approached the Supreme Court for the purpose, while the Chief Minister of Jharkhand, Raghubar Das, has requested the Union Home Minister for urgent action. Das has vowed to deport all foreigners residing illegally in the state. (Godbole 2020, p. 318)

In June 2018, four non-Congress Chief Ministers—AP, West Bengal, Kerala and Karnataka—rallied behind Arvind Kejriwal, Chief Minister of Delhi, in his fight against the Lt. Governor. They urged the Centre to 'rise above politics', solve the 'constitutional crisis' and not 'restrict the federal system' (*The Indian Express*, 17 June 2018, p. 1).

A Central law needs to be enacted for the Central Bureau of Investigation (CBI). *This subject has been under discussion for the last five decades.*

Such an enactment will require a Constitutional amendment for which concurrence of at least half the states will be required. The states have been resisting the proposal due to the misuse of the CBI by successive Central governments of different political parties over the years, by starting investigations against state leaders belonging to political parties opposed to the Central government, to settle political scores. To address these legitimate apprehensions, I have been suggesting for some time that a high level governing board should be created for the CBI consisting of, apart from the Prime Minister and the concerned Central ministers, a few chief ministers, by rotation. This proposal needs to be placed before the Inter-State Council for resolution in a spirit of give and take.

The Supreme Court had condemned the spate of lynchings in 2018 as 'horrendous acts of mobocracy', lamenting also the apathy of bystanders, mute spectators, police inertia and grandstanding on social media by the perpetrators of these crimes. The Supreme Court had suggested that the Central government should issue a directive to state governments under Article 256 of the Constitution. The Court also suggested that a separate law be enacted to create a deterrent against the tendency to take the law into one's hand. Let us deal first with the question of issuing a directive to state governments under Article 256. This Article which deals with the obligations of states and the Union lays down that 'the executive power of every state shall be so exercised as to ensure compliance with the laws made by Parliament and any existing laws which apply in that state, and the executive power of the Union shall extend to the giving of such directions to a state as may appear to the Government of India to be necessary for that purpose'. I seriously doubt whether the Central government is competent to give any directive under this Article to the states, on a subject which clearly falls in the 'State List' in the Constitution. The states will consider it as going against the principles of federalism, which is now a favourite hobbyhorse of all Opposition parties (*The Citizen*, 16 August 2018).

The Supreme Court also wanted Parliament to enact a law 'to control increasing incidents of mob lynchings and making it a cognizable, non-bailable and non-compoundable offence, in a time-bound manner'. However, in view of the insistence of the states on their rights under the Constitution, the Central government has left the subject to be dealt with by the states. It needs to be seriously considered why there cannot be a Central law on the subject instead of each state enacting its own law. To bring in turf issues does not appear to be justified.

The Communal Violence (Prevention, Control and Rehabilitation of Victims) Bill, 2005, was mooted by the UPA government. It provided for enhanced punishment, setting up of special courts, relief to and rehabilitation of victims and so on. It envisaged giving powers to the Central government to give directions to the state government and to issue notification declaring any area within a state as a communally disturbed area and to deploy Central armed forces, wherever necessary. It was envisaged that where it was decided to deploy armed forces, an authority known as Unified Command should be constituted by the Central government or the state government for the purpose of coordinating and monitoring such deployment (GOI 2007, pp. 242-4). The proposal was stoutly objected to by the state governments as an unnecessary interference in their jurisdiction. The Central government's own record in handling communal riots, as seen from the anti-Sikh riots in 1984 and the North East Delhi communal riots in February 2020, does not inspire much confidence in its capacity to handle such calamities.[9] But, in a democracy, there must be checks and counter-checks. What a government nearer home cannot do, a government at the national level may be able to do. Looking to the experience of handling of the major communal riots, as can be seen from my book, *The Babri Masjid-Ram Mandir Dilemma* (2019, pp. 142-171, 205-13), this subject needs to be addressed in the national perspective, keeping aside the rhetoric of federalism. I do not

---

9. The Delhi High Court expressing anguish over the communal violence had directed the Delhi police to register FIR against those responsible for hate speeches saying, 'this city has seen enough violence and let it not repeat 1984', when anti-Sikh riots claimed over 2,700 lives in Delhi alone (*The Indian Express,* 27 February 2020, p. 1).

agree with the recommendation of the Second Administrative Reforms Commission that such a legislation is not necessary and such situations can be handled under the existing laws such as the IPC (Indian Penal Code) and the CrPC (Criminal Procedure Code) by strengthening them by incorporating provisions for: enhanced punishments for communal offences; setting up of special courts; giving powers of remand to Executive Magistrates in cases of communal offences, etc. (GOI 2008, p. 212). I am firmly of the view that looking to the experience of dealing with major communal riots so far, such a new legislation needs to be enacted without delay.

The terms of reference of the Fifteenth Finance Commission pertaining to devolution of resources based on the 2011 population census data are raising North-South issues among the states. When the delimitation of parliamentary constituencies is taken up on the basis of latest population figures, it will open a Pandora's Box of inter-state issues of parity and regional balance. Varghese K. George has stated:

After the 2031 Census, India will switch to a pan-country delimitation of parliamentary constituencies, as opposed to the current practice of redrawing constituencies without affecting the number of seats in individual States. This will result in reduced parliamentary representation for States with higher success in checking population growth, typically through better social welfare and education strategies.... Constitutional amendments have mandated that the distribution of parliamentary representation among various States be based on the 1971 Census, until the first Census after 2026. The effort was to avoid disadvantaging states that stabilised their populations. But the result is, for example, that around 1.7 million people can elect a member of the Lok Sabha from Kerala, while in Rajasthan it takes 2.7 million people. It has long ceased to be "one person, one vote".... Political power in India will shift to northern States such as Uttar Pradesh, Rajasthan, Madhya Pradesh, Bihar, post-2031. Kerala could

> lose six of its current 20 Lok Sabha seats and Tamil Nadu could lose
> 11 of its 39. (*The Hindu*, 31 May 2018)

Writing in 1994, S.V. Kogekar, in his essay, 'Some Observations on the Constitution of India', had rightly underlined that 'the makers of the Constitution have conceived the relations between the Union and the states very much from the point of view of the present alignment of political forces. Any upsetting of the present balance must inevitably lead to a crisis in those relations' (Grover and Arora 1994, p. 103).

Reference must be made to the most disconcerting situation arising out of the actions of the Government of Punjab in regard to the Sutlej Yamuna Link Canal in total disregard of the inter-state agreements and the Supreme Court decisions. All political parties in the state are a party to this atrocious situation. Equally disconcerting is that the Centre has been unable to do anything in the matter. Serious questions on federalism raised by this case are discussed fully in Chapter 4.

Rising sub-nationalism, increasing intolerance in inter-state dealings of states, and excessive reliance on 'sons of the soil' policies are posing serious threat to federalism. Highly restrictive domiciliary policies are undercutting the fundamental rights of Indian citizens. These matters too are discussed at length in Chapter 4.

In the light of experience so far, there are serious doubts whether the Inter-State Council established by the V.P. Singh government in 1990, which has remained grossly underutilized and neglected, could be a useful forum for arriving at an amicable resolution of these politically complex problems. This is discussed at length in Chapter 5.

2

Integration of Jammu and Kashmir – The Critical Fault Line

Introduction

The Kashmir problem continues to be the most important fault line, even after the abrogation of Article 370 on 5 August 2019. The Kashmir problem in its entirety is dealt with comprehensively in Chapters 2 and 3. This chapter covers abrogation of Article 370 which was a complete break with the past starting with the accession of the princely state of J&K to India in October 1947, aggression by Pakistan, and India approaching the United Nations. The other major sections are: the genesis of Article 370; the 1972 Delhi agreement which was more responsible than even Article 370 for creating the impression of special status given to J&K; the Simla Agreement in which an opportunity was lost to settle the Kashmir issue;

and finally the 1975 agreement between Indira Gandhi and the National Conference leader Sheikh Abdullah in which yet another opportunity was lost to address the main issue of the future of Article 370.

Abrogation of Article 370

Union Home Minister Amit Shah's announcement in the Lok Sabha on 5 August 2019 about the abolition of Article 370 came like a bolt from the blue. It was received with a thunderous applause. This subject had been on the agenda of the ruling BJP right since the days of Shyama Prasad Mookerjee in the 1950s. In a bold political move, the BJP decided to implement it and played a masterstroke by abrogating the Article. I call this a masterstroke as, before doing so, the BJP withdrew its support to the coalition government of Mehbooba Mufti's PDP (Peoples Democratic Party) which led to the state being brought under the President's Rule under Article 356. As a result, all powers of the state legislature accrued to Parliament, and the Governor could exercise the powers of the state government of giving concurrence to the abrogation of Article 370. Simultaneously, the state was downgraded into two union territories— one comprising Jammu and the Kashmir valley, and the other Ladakh. The Jammu and Kashmir Reorganisation Bill 2019 was passed by both houses of Parliament with over two-thirds support, 351 Ayes, 072 Noes and 001 Abstention in the Lok Sabha. Importantly, there were dissensions in several Opposition parties, like the Congress, which opposed the move to abolish Article 370 with several young MPs in these parties supporting the bill. Even Mamata Banerjee's Trinamool Congress staged a walkout rather than be seen as opposing the Bill. The move has been challenged in the Supreme Court and is still pending though over a year has elapsed.

Equally important have been the pronouncements made by India that J&K in its entirety, as at the time of its accession to India, is an integral part of India. On 22 February 1994, Parliament had passed a resolution that the whole of J&K (including the PoK, northern areas and Aksai Chin) form an integral part of India and any attempt to separate it from the rest of the country would be resisted by all necessary means. Since then, India has been making statements that it will not rest till the areas occupied by Pakistan and China come back to India. Prime Minister Modi, for the first time, declared from the ramparts of the Red Fort on 15 August 2019 that the unfinished task of the Kashmir agenda was the liberation of the occupied areas. The liberation of Gilgit and Baltistan is thus also a part of this agenda. This is not going to be easy by any means but can be used as a bargaining chip to settle border issues with Pakistan and China.

External Affairs Minister S. Jaishankar declared on 17 September 2019 that India expected to have 'physical jurisdiction' over PoK (Pakistan-occupied Kashmir) 'one day'. This went beyond the Parliament resolution of 1994. Since this region also included Aksai Chin, China is reported to have been disturbed, leading to its adventurous moves along the border in Ladakh in June-July 2020. I have not been able to understand *why India was silent* in 1963 when Aksai Chin was transferred by Pakistan to China, or when PoK was made into a province of Pakistan in 1974. Meek diplomatic protests did not get us anywhere. The Gilgit-Baltistan Legislative Assembly has in March 2021 demanded provincial status from the Pakistan government.

Earlier, America was anxious to use Pakistan as a gateway for establishing relations with China, just as currently Pakistan is used as a gateway for handling Afghanistan. During the agitation in East Pakistan following the atrocities committed by the Pakistan Army, America did not want the breakup of Pakistan. More importantly, it did not want India to make any inroads into PoK. Declassified American government papers show that, on 10 December 1971,

[Under Secretary of State John] Irwin calls in Jha [L.K. Jha, Indian Ambassador in USA] and states that the US cannot countenance India's taking of any territory which would have a 'most profound and long-lasting effect on US-Indian relations.' *He then asks Jha to obtain assurances from his government that India has no intention of taking any territory, including any part of Azad Kashmir.* (Kalyani Shanker 2010, p. 349)

Against this background, the recent pronouncements by the GOI of taking over PoK, leave aside Aksai Chin that is in possession of China, are bound to be resisted not just by Pakistan and China respectively, but also by several other countries.

Former Chief Minister Mehbooba Mufti was despondent about the abolition of Article 370 and said, 'Today the people of J&K who reposed their faith in institutions of India like Parliament and the Supreme Court feel defeated and betrayed. By dismembering the state and fraudulently taking away what is rightly and legally ours, they have further complicated the Kashmir dispute' (*Legal Notes*, August 2019, p. 24).

After the release of the Kashmiri leaders from detention, People's Alliance for Gupkar Declaration has been formed in Srinagar to fight for the restoration of Article 370. Former Chief Minister and National Conference chairman Farooq Abdullah, in his interview with Karan Thapar, went so far as to say that *they* [people of Kashmir] *would rather be ruled by the Chinese.* A point he reiterated when he was asked if he really meant this (*The Wire*, 23 September 2020). In his further press statement, he hoped that China will help in the reinstatement of Article 370. One would have overlooked these ludicrous statements as those of an ageing, frustrated politician, but he has been the chief minister of J&K and also a Central minister.

Mehbooba Mufti has made a shocking statement that she would not raise the national flag in the state till J&K's flag is re-recognised. Looking to the catastrophic experience of dealing with Kashmir so far, these demands will not find any support at the national level.

It is gratifying to note that the seven mainstream Gupkar parties decided to fight the elections to the district development councils that were held in December 2020. It is for the first time that direct elections to these bodies were held and till the state Legislative Assembly comes into being, they will be the main fora for public debate and discussion. The newly-elected DDC members of all political parties are now clamouring for more powers and better status, the green shoots of nascent democracy at the ground level.

The amendments in the land laws in J&K effected in October 2020 are alleged to have given rise to fears of demographic changes, though agricultural land has been excluded therefrom. This led to a complete shutdown in Kashmir valley. Gupkar parties are trying to use this issue for rallying their supporters. As seen from the section below on Article 370, the fundamental rights in the Indian Constitution should have been made applicable to J&K right from the beginning, as was being insisted upon by the Constituent Assembly members and Vallabhbhai Patel.

Apprehensions were expressed by some North Eastern states that certain 'special' privileges enjoyed by them under Article 371 (A to I) would also be withdrawn after the abrogation of Article 370. However, there is an important distinction between Article 370 and these other Articles. While Article 370 was always a 'temporary' provision, the other provisions were consciously designated as 'special' provisions. As can be seen from the discussion in Chapter 3, there was persistent demand in J&K that Article 370 should be amended to delete the word 'temporary' and replace it with the word 'special'. The GOI has clarified that there is no proposal to change the special provisions pertaining to the other states.

According to the policy followed thus far in respect of amendments of the Constitution, Article 370 will now disappear altogether from the text of the Constitution. But, as former CJI M. Hidayatullah had observed in the *Golaknath case*, 'Constitution is not a sonnet written on water.... In America, prohibition was once introduced and then later withdrawn; but both the Articles are found in the Constitution. Our Parliament would have erased the earlier Article as if it was never enacted' (Hidayatullah 1979, p. viii). There is a great deal of merit in Hidayatullah's argument. I hope Article 370 would continue to be shown in the text of the Constitution with a note that it was abrogated in August 2019. Incidentally, Article 35A, which was introduced by a Presidential Order issued under Article 370, does not appear in the text of the Constitution at all, presumably as it was not enacted by Parliament by following the prescribed procedure. In a sense, this Article was truly a sonnet written on water! But it is not too late to correct these past omissions. Now the text of the Constitution should appropriately show Articles 370 and 35A as a part of the Constitution and their abrogation in August 2019.

The Kashmir Imbroglio

While matters pertaining to 554 princely states were handled by the States Ministry under Vallabhbhai Patel's leadership, Nehru had kept the Kashmir question exclusively with himself. So much so that he appointed a junior Minister, Gopalaswami Ayyangar, to handle it in the United Nations and Parliament, under his own personal supervision. The responsibility for all decisions pertaining to the handling of Kashmir question must, therefore, be placed squarely on Nehru himself.

It has to be accepted that at times Nehru's pronouncements on Kashmir created wrong impressions about the GOI's policies on the subject. Nehru often used the term 'autonomy' in the context of Hyderabad and J&K but it was in the sense in which the Governors' Provinces enjoyed autonomy in British India. He had no objection to the same kind of autonomy being given to Hyderabad and J&K. But, this was never made explicitly clear and therefore created an impression that the GOI was prepared to give 'autonomy' to J&K. He often used the word 'sovereignty' in the context of J&K. When asked on 27 January 1952 about his reaction to Prime Minister of Iran's suggestion to the Indian Ambassador that Kashmir should become independent and sovereign, Nehru said, 'It is for the people of J&K to decide'. This was largely because of his practice of thinking aloud and speaking extempore. And, this was not confined just to what he spoke. In the context of Sheikh Abdullah's visit to Paris in January 1952, Nehru had written to him, 'You should have an independent position and not be made a formal member of Indian delegation. You will be in a better position to help and advise and meet people in that independent capacity' (*JNMF-Jawaharlal Nehru Memorial Fund*, vol. 17, p. 438). Scores of such instances can be cited. Since Kashmir was a very live international issue at that time, such pronouncements often led to considerable misunderstanding.

The Kashmir problem became complicated due to Nehru's strained relations with Maharaja Hari Singh, the ruler of Kashmir. Nehru was arrested and detained in Kashmir, on the instructions of Hari Singh, only a few weeks before Nehru was to be anointed as India's prime minister! This was partly due to Nehru's proximity to Sheikh Abdullah who, at that time, was also under detention in the state.

Nehru's reply to Maharaja Hari Singh dated 5 July 1952 brings out his combative approach on the question of abolition of monarchy and shows how untenable it would have been in dealing with the complex issues pertaining to princely states whose resolution was so important for the unity and integrity of India during the formative years. Significantly, the letter brings out Nehru's unhappiness with the 'generous settlement' arrived at earlier by Patel with other rulers (*JNMF*, vol. 19, pp. 425-8).

It needs to be noted that it was not clear that the people in Jammu and Ladakh regions or for that matter the large remaining parts of the Kashmir state at the time, including Pakistan-occupied Kashmir, to which the Constitution-in-the-making of J&K was expected to apply, wanted the Maharaja to be removed. It is not even clear if all the people in the Kashmir valley wanted the Maharaja to go. But this was the prime demand of Sheikh Abdullah's National Conference. In fact, Sheikh Abdullah had made it a prestige issue to do away with hereditary monarchy and he was least interested in observing even common courtesies in executing the plan. As brought out in V.P. Menon's account, Sheikh Abdullah refused to pay Kashmir's share of the privy purse to be given to the Maharaja and, it was paid entirely by the government of India, till it was abolished.

In castigating the Maharaja, Nehru had, in his letter, charged that the Maharaja '[had] left Srinagar at the dead of night [in October 1947] for

Jammu. Many of your officers followed your example and the state was left without leadership or means of defence'. This too is not correct. Jammu was very much a part of Kashmir state and was, and continues to be, the winter capital of the state. Further, Nehru was fully aware that it was V.P. Menon, Secretary, Ministry of States, who was sent to Srinagar by the government of India to assess the situation on the ground, had advised the Maharaja to leave for Jammu to avoid his possible capture by the tribal raiders who were expected to reach Srinagar in less than 48 hours. This has been brought out by a number of authors, including Balraj Krishna (p. 371) and Narayani Basu (pp. 370-71).

As far as the accession of Kashmir to India is concerned, it is abundantly clear that under the provisions of the Indian Independence Act, what was prescribed was the ruler's request for accession duly accepted by the Viceroy. Nehru has tried to belittle the Maharaja's role by saying that 'Indeed, because your [Maharaja's] request had been powerfully supported by the National Conference, representing the people of Kashmir, that we decided to accept the accession'. This is factually incorrect. The government of India itself had made clear, including to the United Nations, that the accession was constitutionally and legally complete as soon as the Maharaja's request was accepted by the Viceroy. The question of wishes of the people was totally extraneous to the legal procedure laid down for accession of the state to India.

In his letter dated 30 November 1947 to Nehru, Mehr Chand Mahajan, Prime Minister of J&K, wrote almost despondently:

> Gilgit is in enemy hands. Muzaffarabad district is in their possession. The Poonch area, excepting the town of Poonch, is also in their occupation and the district of Mirpur and part of Jammu district have been taken by them.... It is only by a direction from you that these positions can be regained. It is felt that with this vast area of the state in enemy hands, even negotiations on our side with Pakistan will not be very successful. It appears that unless we have a whip

hand these negotiations may not be satisfactory.... If the plebiscite goes against us, there is no other alternative but abdicate.... There is pessimism about the results of the plebiscite here. Even if the plebiscite goes against Pakistan, it is felt that the trouble will still not end and the fighting will go on. (Durga Das 1971, p. 100)

This feeling of uncertainty about the results of the plebiscite was also raised in Nehru's letter to Patel dated 17 April 1949 in which he referred to:

a growing Hindu agitation in Jammu province for what is called a zonal plebiscite. The idea is based on the belief that a plebiscite for the whole of Kashmir is bound to be lost and therefore let us save Jammu at least. You will perhaps remember that some proposal of this kind was put forward by the Maharaja some time back. It seems to me that this kind of propaganda is very harmful for us. Whatever may happen in the future, I do not think Jammu province is running away from us. If we want Jammu province by itself and are prepared to make a present of the rest of the state to Pakistan, I have no doubt we could clinch the issue in a few days. *The prize we are fighting for is the valley of Kashmir.* This propaganda for a zonal plebiscite is going on in Jammu, in Delhi and elsewhere. It is carried on by what is known as the Jammu Praja Parishad. (Shankar 1977, pp. 346-7)

Doubts continued to persist regarding the feasibility of a plebiscite. Patel wrote to Nehru on 3 July 1950 to say:

Both the National Conference and Sheikh Sahib are losing their hold on the people in the Valley and are becoming somewhat unpopular.... I agree with you that a plebiscite is unreal. Not only that, it would be positively dangerous because my own feeling is that once talk [for plebiscite] starts, the non-Muslims in Jammu and Kashmir would start feeling uneasy and we might be faced with an exodus to India.

> This would be an additional point to emphasise in respect of our stand that the conditions preliminary to plebiscite should be fully and effectively fulfilled before we can talk of it. (Durga Das 1971, p. 317)

Instead of taking action to get back the Pakistan-occupied territories, Nehru conveyed to the Maharaja by his letter dated 23 December 1947 the decision of the Government of India to approach the UN to get the aggression vacated (Durga Das 1971, p. 126).

One of the main criticisms against Nehru's handling of the Kashmir question is that he stopped the advance of Indian troops resulting in the declaration of ceasefire when the Indian Army had an upper hand and could have got the whole of Kashmir valley vacated of the invading tribals and Pakistani aggressors. Dharma Vira, who was joint secretary to the Cabinet, has stated that this decision was taken by Nehru at the behest of Mountbatten who ostensibly did not want two Commonwealth countries to go to war with each other. Vallabhbhai Patel had opposed this move and was of the opinion that the Army should be given a free hand to oust the invaders from the valley. Nehru went along with the advice of Mountbatten. This led to a part of the valley, named Azad Kashmir by Pakistan, remaining permanently in the possession of Pakistan. Shockingly, this also led, over a period of time, to a large part of the strategically located portion of Ladakh, Aksai Chin, being ceded by Pakistan to China.

The other very ill-advised decision taken by Nehru was to refer the Kashmir question to the UN which internationalised the dispute. This calamitous decision was taken by Nehru also at the instance of Mountbatten, overriding the opposition of Vallabhbhai Patel and others.

It is interesting to note that Shyama Prasad Mookerjee, the then tallest Jan Sangh leader and a member of the first Nehru Cabinet, had admitted in Parliament in August 1952 that:

> he was a party when the decision was taken to refer the Kashmir issue

to the U.N.O. That is an obvious fact. I have no right and do not wish to disclose the extraordinary circumstances under which that decision was taken and the great expectations which the Government of India had on that occasion but it is a matter of common knowledge that we have not got fair treatment from the United Nations which we had expected. We did not go the U.N.O. with regard to the question of accession, because accession was an established fact. We went there for the purpose of getting quick decision from the U.N.O. regarding the raids which were then taking place by persons behind whom there was the Pakistan Government...we should withdraw ourselves, so far as consideration of the Kashmir case is concerned, from the U.N.O. (Mukherjee 2007, pp. 245-6)

The involvement of the UN put serious restrictions on India in handling the Kashmir question.

Questions were raised in the Constituent Assembly on whether the accession of J&K, being conditional on plebiscite being held, was complete. Maulana Hasrat Mohani doubted whether the Prime Minister's description of the accession being complete was altogether correct. Prof K.T. Shah also seemed to imply what the Maulana contended. Gopalaswami Ayyangar however defended the government's stand (Noorani 2011, p. 55).

Deliberate and motivated allegations were made that India had sent its army into Kashmir even before the Instrument of Accession was signed. Doubts were also raised about the Instrument having been signed on 26 October 1947. Owen Bennett Jones, who was a BBC correspondent in Pakistan from 1998 to 2001, has, in his book, *Pakistan: Eye of the Storm*, also raised doubts in this regard. Pakistan issued a statement on 30 October 1947 in which they characterized the Kashmir accession as being 'based on fraud and violence and as such cannot be recognised'. Interestingly, Sir Patrick Dean, representing the British government before the Security Council, said, 'We consider it unrealistic to consider the status of Kashmir purely in terms of the legal effect of the Maharaja's Instrument of Accession' (Srivastava 1996, p. 173). The UN Security Council had raised questions on the J&K Constituent Assembly passing a resolution approving accession of the state to India.

Former Chief Justice of India, Justice Anand, has in his article 'Kashmir's Accession to India' stated that:

> the Instrument of Accession was *unconditional, voluntary* and *absolute*. It was not subject to any exceptions; it bound the state of J&K together legally and constitutionally. However, after the Instrument of Accession had been accepted by the Governor-General of India, Lord Mountbatten wrote a semi-official letter to Maharaja of Kashmir. Among other things written in the letter it was provided that, "It is my government's *wish* that, as soon as law and order have been restored in Kashmir and its soil is cleared of the invader, the question of Kashmir's accession should be settled with reference to the people." This statement has figured as the most controversial feature of Kashmir's accession to India. Critics of the accession have steadfastly maintained that this stipulation renders the accession conditional. The present writer is of the opinion that this statement does not and cannot affect the legality of the accession which was sealed by India's official acceptance. This statement is not part of the Instrument of Accession.... The Indian Independence Act did not envisage conditional accession.... The only documents relevant to the Accession were the Instrument of Accession and the Indian Independence Act.... Mountbatten...was probably expressing a pious hope, a declaration without legal effect. (Italics in original) (Anand 1964, pp. 81-82)

As for the dispatch of the armed forces to J&K, V.P. Menon has quoted from the note prepared by the three British Commanders—the Chiefs of the Army, Air Force and Navy—to show that it was only 'on the afternoon of 26th October we finalised our plans for the dispatch by air of troops to Kashmir. At the first light on the morning of 27th October, with the Instrument of Accession signed, the movement by air of Indian forces to Kashmir began' (Menon 2014, p. 361).

Article 370 – A Temporary Provision

This temporary provision of the Constitution, interpreted by a section of Kashmiris as giving special status to J&K in its relationship to the Indian Union, has been solely responsible for creating the feeling of separateness and alienation, and generating the demands for autonomy. Article 370 had to be incorporated in the Constitution only to safeguard the position of J&K state in the Indian Union which had acceded to India on 26 October 1947, just a few weeks after India's independence, but its most unfortunate by-product was a separate constitution for J&K. In view of the importance of the subject, the full background thereof has been brought out in Appendix 2. It can be seen therefrom that *ordinarily the Government of India would have preferred to treat J&K State like other States in the category of Part III States. The main difficulty in adopting this procedure was that the Premier of this State, Sheikh Abdullah, had definitely expressed his inability to extend the content of the accession of the State beyond the three subjects till the Constituent Assembly of the State had taken a decision in the matter. The Sheikh was most anxious that the accession of the State should continue in respect of the three subjects of Defence, Foreign Affairs and Communications only.* During the course of the discussion in the Drafting Committee meeting, it was pointed out that the scheme embodied in the Draft Constitution visualized that all states in Part III would accept List I (Union List) and List III (Concurrent List) and in addition accept all provisions relating to fundamental rights and the provisions relating to the High Courts and Supreme Court. *It was further pointed out that if the quantum of accession of Kashmir State was not extended, difficulties would arise in respect of the citizenship of the subjects* of Kashmir state as also in connection with the operation of the provisions regarding fundamental rights and Supreme Court in respect of this state. The Government of India had therefore considered the matter in its various aspects and were of the opinion that in view of the peculiar situation in respect of Jammu and Kashmir state *it is desirable that the accession should be continued on the existing basis till the state could be brought to the level of other states. A special provision had therefore to be made in respect of this state on the basis suggested above as a transitional arrangement.* It may be added that 'naturalization' was already covered by the existing Instrument of Accession signed by the Ruler of the state and this could meet the requirements in respect of citizenship of the subjects of this state. While Parliament had unfettered powers to legislate for any subjects in the Union and Concurrent Lists, in so far as J&K is concerned, except in respect of Defence, Foreign Affairs and Communications, it could do so only with the concurrence of the state legislature. Over a period of time, of the total 395 Articles in the Indian Constitution, 260 Articles were extended to J&K. Of the 97 entries in the Union List, 94 were applied to the state. Similarly of the 47 entries in the Concurrent List, 26 were applied. These include, among others, Article 356 regarding imposition of President's Rule, jurisdiction of the Supreme Court, the Election Commission of India and the Comptroller and Auditor General of India. Out of the 12 Schedules in the Indian Constitution, seven were applied to J&K (Noorani 2014, pp. 435-6).

It is important to note again that *Article 370 was only a transitional arrangement till the state acceded to India fully.* Part XXI of the Constitution of India describes this provision as 'temporary', as opposed to 'special' provisions pertaining to some other states. But, due to the intransigence of the state leaders, this had become almost a permanent feature of the Constitution. They argued that the Article was meant to give a special status only to J&K state, as opposed to all other states in the Indian Union.

Sheikh Abdullah in his book, *Flames of the Chinar*, has stated:

When we started a dialogue with the Central leadership regarding

Article 370 we realised that it was not easy to persuade them to accept our point of view. N. Gopalaswami Ayyangar, while moving a resolution regarding Article 370, could not hide the true sentiments of the Indian leaders.... "We all hope that in future the State of Jammu and Kashmir will get over the hurdles and completely merge with the Union, like the rest of the States...". Not hopeful about the resolution of the Kashmir problem by the United Nations, we started preparing ground to convene the Constituent Assembly. *Our move was opposed in Delhi. Even Jawaharlal was hesitant. But the National Conference was firm,* [and] *in 1950 we adopted the following resolution:* ..."National Conference is not prepared to allow this uncertainty to continue. We believe that the time has come when the people should take the initiative. We appeal to the people to convene a Constituent Assembly." *Eventually, the circles in Delhi agreed to convening of the Constituent Assembly.* (Abdullah 1993, pp.113-5)

Sheikh Abdullah's objectives were thus clear right from the beginning. The genesis of Nehru agreeing to Abdullah's proposal of having a separate Constitution for J&K lay in Article 370. Even the President of India, Rajendra Prasad, was taken aback. Nehru and his colleagues remained in their own imagined world hoping to persuade Abdullah to agree to the full integration of J&K with India.

Shyama Prasad Mookerjee had rightly asked in his much-quoted speech in Parliament:

May I ask—was not Sheikh Abdullah a party to this Constitution? He was a member of the Constituent Assembly; but he is asking for special treatment. Did he not agree to accept this Constitution in relation to the rest of India, including 498 states? If it is good enough for all of them, why should it not be good enough for him in Kashmir? (Mukherjee 2007, pp. 247, 250)

The first draft of Article 370 (then numbered 306A) presented by the state government, headed by Sheikh Abdullah, can be seen in Appendix 3. It shows that Abdullah had envisaged that Kashmir's accession to India would be *kept confined in perpetuity* only to the three subjects mentioned in the Instrument of Accession. He did not visualise extending the provisions of the Indian Constitution to Kashmir year after year by issue of Presidential Orders. Since it was not possible to agree to this draft, Nehru entrusted the drafting of the Article to K.M. Munshi, Gopalaswami Ayyangar and Abdullah. According to Munshi, 'Abdullah was unhappy with the Article as we drafted, and though he was scheduled to support the Article before the Constituent Assembly', Munshi feared he might absent himself from the proceedings. But instead Abdullah chose to lodge his protest by staging a walkout, though not formally.

The war-like conditions in J&K, part of the state being under Pakistani occupation, reference to UN, etc. were cited as reasons for making the temporary provision of Article 370. But the reality was quite different as can be seen from Appendix 2. The real reason was the opposition of Sheikh Abdullah to the full integration of the state by going beyond the Instrument of Accession, coupled with his insistence on having a separate Constitution for J&K. Surprisingly, Nehru supported the latter enthusiastically. But if these real reasons had been divulged, the members of the Constituent Assembly would have been incensed and opposition to Abdullah would have increased further. Hence, the window dressing of special conditions by Gopalaswami Ayyangar which forced the government to make this temporary provision. Nehru also keeps up this pretence in his note dated 3 July 1952 on Kashmir's integration:

Kashmir, like other states, acceded to India on three subjects in October 1947 under rather peculiar circumstances. Later, other [princely] states became more integrated in regard to additional subjects and they accepted the Constitution of India in its entirety. This development did not take place in regard to Kashmir because of those special reasons—war with Pakistan, reference to UNO, etc., and therefore Kashmir's accession was continued to be limited to those three subjects. (*JNMF*, vol. 18, p. 423)

It is high time this pretence is given up.

Outwardly, it looked as if Article 370 had a smooth passage in the Constituent Assembly since it was passed without any discussion. But this is far from the truth. The first draft of the Article was finalised by Gopalaswami Ayyangar in consultation with Sheikh Abdullah and the approval of Nehru was taken before he left for abroad. V. Shankar, ICS, Private Secretary to Patel, has written:

Sardar [Patel] had not been consulted. *The Congress Party in the Constituent Assembly was strongly, even violently, opposed to the draft Article which gave special position to the state.* On *(sic)* principle, opinion in the party was that Kashmir should accept the Constitution on the same terms as other states; and in particular the provision that basic Articles, e.g. fundamental rights as enshrined in the Constitution would not apply to the state, was greatly resented. (V. Shankar 1977, pp. 220-1)

Vishnu Sahay, Secretary for Kashmir Affairs in the GOI, had in his letter to Shankar dated 14 October 1949 written:

Sheikh Abdullah has sent an alternative draft which merely says that the provisions of the Constitution shall apply to Kashmir only in regard to the acceded subjects and that the Dominion Parliament shall be entitled to legislate only in respect of the acceded subjects. A further proviso is made that the Government of Kashmir shall mean His Highness the Maharaja acting on the advice of the Council of Ministers as at present constituted and not on his personal judgment or discretion. (Shankar 1977, pp. 363-4)

This clearly brings out what Sheikh Abdullah wanted—accession of J&K to be confined only to the three subjects mentioned in the Instrument of Accession, for ever. No provision was to be made to extend the other provisions of the Constitution of India to J&K or its further integration with India, in any manner.

Abdullah with his often 'imagined grievances in regard to the policy that the Government of India was following in relation to Kashmir' was adamant on several points. When Gopalaswami sent the revised draft, prepared to accommodate the points raised by Sheikh Abdullah, to Patel, he [Patel] replied by his letter dated 15 October 1949 to say:

I find there are some substantial changes over the original draft, particularly in regard to the applicability of fundamental rights and directive principles of state policy. *You can yourself realise the anomaly of the state becoming part of India and at the same time not recognising any of these provisions. I do not at all like any change after our party has approved of the whole arrangement in the presence of Sheikh Sahib himself.* Whenever Sheikh Sahib wishes to back out, he always confronts us with his duty to the people. Of course, he owes no duty to India or to the Indian government, or even on a personal basis, to you and the Prime Minister who have gone all out to accommodate him. *In these circumstances, any question of my approval does not arise. If you feel it is the right thing to do, you can go ahead with it.* (Noorani 2011, pp. 61-2)

There was also stiff opposition to the Article in the Congress Parliamentary Party meeting. Gopalaswami Ayyangar could not convince the agitated members and it seemed that the Bill would be defeated in the House. As Nehru was away on a long foreign visit, Ayyangar approached Patel to intervene and use his influence on the members to accept the draft Article. Though Patel had serious reservations as above, he graciously agreed to intervene, purely because of his loyalty to Nehru and to avoid any embarrassment to Nehru by defeat of the proposal in the Constituent Assembly. *Such was Patel's hold over the Party that after his intervention, the Article was passed without much discussion.*

The language of Article 370 makes it clear that it was not intended to be permanent. Ayyangar, in his speech in the Constituent Assembly while moving the Bill for its adoption, had stated:

> We have said Article 211 A will not apply to J&K state. But that cannot be a permanent feature of the Constitution, and [I] hope it will not be. So the provision is made that when the Constituent Assembly of the state has met and taken its decision both on the Constitution for the state and on the range of federal jurisdiction over the state, the President may on the recommendation of that Constituent Assembly issue an order that this Article 306A [later renumbered as 370] shall either cease to be operative, or shall be operative only subject to such exceptions and modifications as may be specified by him. (Noorani 2011, p. 71)

Thus, logically, the Article was expected to be inoperative at the end of the term of the Constituent Assembly of the state. Instead, it continued till 5 August 2019.

The Article was not in keeping with Abdullah's wishes. Another bone of contention was about the Explanation to Clause 1 (b) (ii) which states: 'For the purpose of this Article, the Government of the State means the person for the time being recognised by the President as the Maharaja of Jammu and Kashmir and acting on the advice of the Council of Ministers for the time being in office under the Maharaja's Proclamation dated the fifth day of March 1948.' Abdullah wanted words 'as at present constituted and not acting in his discretion or in his individual judgment', instead of the words 'for the time being in office'. When the amendment proposed by Sheikh Abdullah was not accepted by the government, in his letter to Gopalaswami Ayyangar dated 17 October 1949, Abdullah threatened that if the position is not rectified, 'no course is left open for us but to tender our resignation from the Constituent Assembly'. In his reply dated 18 October, Gopalaswami had clarified that 'the words in the Explanation as agreed to between us are "Council of Ministers appointed under the Maharaja's Proclamation dated 5 March 1948". The words appearing in the Article as passed yesterday are "the Council of Ministers for the time being in office under the Maharaja's Proclamation dated 5 March 1948"' (Durga Das 1971, pp. 306-8).

Abdullah later held a grievance that had the formulation proposed by him been retained, the Sadar-e-Riyasat would not have been competent to dismiss him as Prime Minister in 1953.

Vallabhbhai Patel in his letter dated 3 November 1949 had conveyed to Nehru the difficulties which had arisen in getting this Article passed:

> Sheikh Sahib went back on the agreement which he had reached with you in regard to the provision relating to Kashmir. He insisted on certain changes of a fundamental character which would exclude in their application to Kashmir the provisions relating to citizenship and fundamental rights and make it necessary in all these matters, as well as others not covered by the accession to three subjects, to seek the concurrence of the state government which is sought to define as the Maharaja acting on the advice of the Council of Ministers appointed under the Proclamation of 5 March 1948. After a great deal of discussion, I could persuade the party to accept all the changes except the last one, *which was modified so as to cover not merely the first Ministry so appointed but any subsequent Ministries which may be appointed under that proclamation.* Sheikh Sahib has not reconciled himself to this change, but we could not accommodate him in this matter and the provision was passed through the House as we had modified. After this he wrote to Gopalaswami Ayyangar threatening to resign from the membership of the Constituent Assembly. Gopalaswami has replied asking him to defer his decision

until you returned. (Durga Das 1971, p. 310)

When the bill was passed, Abdullah walked out in protest with the threat that he was going back to Kashmir. Patel sent Mahavir Tyagi (senior MP) to the railway station to deliver a stern message: 'Sheikh Sahib, the Sardar says you could leave the House, but you cannot leave Delhi.' A speechless Abdullah got down from the train, cancelling his departure (Krishna 2005, p. 394).

Referring to Article 370, Abdullah had said in July 1953:

When Article 370 was devised, we felt reassured by the statement of Sardar Patel that the Instrument of Accession would be the final basis of the Indo-Kashmir relationship. Subsequently, when the Delhi Agreement came up before the Council of States [Rajya Sabha] on August 5, 1952, Shri Gopalaswami Ayyangar stated that Article 370 was not a permanent feature of the Constitution and "when the time came" this provision could be wiped off from the Constitution. This clearly shows that...such assurances come with a good deal of mental reservation. The ground has been shifting from time to time ever since the Instrument of Accession was signed and it has been made abundantly clear to us that ultimately the special position accorded to our state in the Constitution would be taken away. You can well imagine the reaction of such a threat to the local rights and privileges of the majority community [Muslims], particularly at a time when they are subjected to much psychological pressure from many quarters which threaten to undermine the ideals that made them turn towards India. (Bhattacharjea 2008, p. 179)

This once again shows that Abdullah had not reconciled himself to Article 370. His insistence was that Kashmir's relationship to India should be based only on the Instrument of Accession and that Article 370 should be a permanent feature of the Constitution. This made no sense since he was a party to the drafting of the Article, except for the last change which was made at the insistence of members of the Constituent Assembly. And there was nothing objectionable in the change.

However, Abdullah continued to maintain that Article 370 was not temporary. In his statement in the state Constituent Assembly on Delhi Agreement, he reiterated:

> The fact that Article 370 has been mentioned as a temporary provision in the Constitution does not mean that it is capable of being abrogated, modified or replaced unilaterally. In actual effect, the temporary nature of this Article arises from the fact that the power to finalise the constitutional relationship between the state and the Union of India has been specifically vested in J&K Constituent Assembly. It follows that whatever modifications, amendments or exceptions that may become necessary either to Article 370 or any other Article in the Constitution of India in their application to the J&K state are subject to the decisions of this sovereign body. (Noorani 2014, pp. 163-4)

The White Paper on Indian States, published by the GOI in 1950, had clearly stated:

> Steps will be taken for the purpose of convening a Constituent Assembly [of J&K] which will go into these matters [of extending the Indian Constitution to J&K] in detail and when it comes to a decision on them, it will make a recommendation to the President who will either abrogate Article 370 or direct that it shall apply with such modifications and exceptions as he may specify. Thus, the state's Constituent Assembly's decision was to mark a finality to the exercise of the President's powers under Article 370. (Noorani 2014, p. 427)

The President of India persisted with his objections [for an elected

Head of state] till as late as November 7, 1952 *insisting that the Constituent Assembly should come to a decision on all matters relating to the state's Constitution....* The Prime Minister of India was in a bind. He had agreed with the President's views on the legality but termination of the royalty was also part of the Delhi Agreement. He was under pressure from Sheikh Saheb and his colleagues (Noorani 2014, p. 428).

The use of Article 370 to gradually extend the provisions of the Indian Constitution to J&K has come in for repeated comments. On 21 August 1962, Nehru in reply to the letter from Pandit Prem Nath Bazaz, a progressive Kashmiri Pandit, had written:

As a matter of fact, much has been done in spite of the Article [370] in the Constitution which is supposed to give special status to Kashmir *and gradually what little remains will also go.* The question is more a sentimental one than anything else. Sentiment is sometimes important but we have to weigh both the sides and *I think no change should be made in the matter for the present.* (Jagmohan 1991, p. 251)

M.C. Chagla, former Chief Justice of the Bombay High Court and the then Union Education Minister, said on the floor of the Rajya Sabha on 24 February 1964, 'The Prime Minister (Jawaharlal Nehru) the other day spoke of the general erosion of Article 370. I only hope the erosion is accelerated and *I also hope that very soon the Article will disappear from the Constitution of India. After all, it is transitional and temporary. I think the transitional period has been long enough'* (Sharma 2011, p. 31).

Chagla also wanted the separate Constitution of J&K to be scrapped.

Gulzarilal Nanda, the then Union Home Minister, on 4 December 1964 said in the Lok Sabha that *Article 370 was the 'tunnel through which a good deal of traffic had already passed; more will pass now'.*

The Sarkaria Commission on Centre-state relations had observed:

There is no limitation on the exercise of this power in relation to one or more of the provisions of the Constitution of India. It is important to note that the process of extending the various provisions of the Constitution to the state has been gradual and founded on consensus and experience to the mutual advantage of the Union and the state. (Sharma 2011, pp. 31-2)

It is pertinent to note that all through the years, the Congress Party, which was in power, was convinced about the need to abolish Article 370 but, to put it mildly, was waiting for an opportune time, and to put it bluntly, *did not have the political courage to abolish it.*

Through a series of constitutional and statutory steps taken over the years, J&K was being fully integrated with India like any other former princely state, except for a few vestiges of the past. The most important among these was Article 370 which continued as an emotional link with the past. A.S. Dulat, former RAW chief, had stated: 'Article 370 is by now merely symbolic. *It is a fig leaf for Kashmir*—so why would anyone want to take that away from them? Perhaps if Sheikh Abdullah had not been arrested in 1953, we would not have (sic) be having this debate in 2014' (Dulat 2015, p. 314). But, as seen later, it was by no means a mere fig leaf. It was primarily responsible for perpetuating the myth of special status of J&K. Its implications within J&K were significant.

Jagmohan, in his book, *My Frozen Turbulence in Kashmir*, has brought out an important facet of Article 370. He has written:

The people of Jammu region nurse a long-standing grievance that, under cover of Article 370 and the state Constitution, the decisions over the years have been so manipulated by the Valley leaders that the power structure in the state has permanently tilted in favour of the Kashmir region. For the Lok Sabha, Jammu returns one member for every 1.4 million people, while Kashmir sends one representative for every one million. Jammu's total area is 70 per cent larger than Kashmir's and has 45 per cent of the state's population. But Jammu has only 32 seats, out of 76 in the state Assembly, and Kashmir has 42. While Jammu returns one member for every 90,000 [for state legislative assembly], Kashmir returns one for every 73,000. While three new districts were suddenly created in the Valley in 1979, none of the three districts recommended by the Wazir Commission (1981-83) has been created in Jammu region. The distribution of Plan funds is also unfair. (Jagmohan 1991, p. 244)

Jagmohan has further stated that Ladakh too received a raw deal for years together:

The Ladakhis too are highly resentful that the leverage of Article 370 has been placed in the hands of Kashmiri leadership. They have been complaining that instead of being made "free sons of free India", they have been thrown "at the mercy of the Kashmiris". They are often heard saying, "If India is going to keep us under Kashmiri domination, then it is as bad as being under the Chinese." As early as 1949, in an impassioned plea to Prime Minister Nehru for taking Ladakh directly under the care of the Union Government, the Ladakhi Buddhist Association said, "Tibet is the cultural daughter of India, and we of the 'lesser Tibet' seek the bosom of the gracious mother to receive more nourishment for growth to full stature...." ...The violent agitation of Ladakhi Buddhists in July-September 1989 was an expression of their strong resentment against what they called the Kashmiri domination and exploitation. (Jagmohan 1991, p. 245)

Over the years, there has been persistent demand to make Ladakh a Union Territory. When I visited Ladakh in 1991 as Union Home Secretary this demand was unanimously pressed. Even the legitimate demand of Ladakh for some regional autonomy was not met till August 1995 when the elections to the first Leh Autonomous Hill Development Council were held.

The constitutionality of Article 370 came to be challenged at least thrice in the context of tenancy laws, preventive detention law, etc. In *Prem Nath Kaul v. State of Jammu and Kashmir* (AIR 1959 SC 749), the Supreme Court reviewed several Constitutional orders issued by the President of India under Article 370 and upheld them as valid. The court observed:

> The Constitution-makers were obviously anxious that the said relationship [between the state and India] should be finally determined by the Constituent Assembly of the state itself; that is the main basis for, and purport of, the temporary provisions made by the present Article.... Until the Constituent Assembly [of the state] reached its decision in that behalf, the constitutional relationship between the state and India continued to be governed basically by the Instrument of Accession. (p. 761)

In *Sampat Prakash* (*Sampat Prakash v. The State of J&K* (AIR 1970 SC 1118), the Supreme Court held that Article 370 had never ceased to apply to J&K and therefore the President could validly pass Constitution (Application to J&K) orders in 1959 and 1964 extending the time for giving protection to any law. It was argued by the petitioner that the will of the people expressed through the instrument of a Constituent Assembly would determine the Constitution of the state as well as the sphere of Union jurisdiction over the state. Article 370 could only have been intended to remain effective until the Constitution of the state was formed...and thereafter the Article must be held to have become ineffective. The court did not uphold these arguments and declared:

> The purpose of introducing this Article was to empower the President to exercise his discretion in applying the Indian Constitution while that situation remained unchanged.... There are, however, much stronger reasons for holding that the provisions of this Article continued in force even after the Constituent Assembly of the state

had passed the Constitution of the state.... This [Clause (2)] clearly envisages that the Article will continue to be operative and can cease to be operative only if, on the recommendation of the Constituent Assembly of the state, the President makes a direction to that effect.... *The Constituent Assembly of the state did not desire that this Article should cease to be operative and, in fact, expressed its agreement to the continued operation of this Article by making a recommendation that it should be operative with the modification only.*... It seems to us that when the Constitution used the word "modification" in Article 370 (1), the intention was that the President would have the power to amend the provisions of the Constitution if he so thought fit in their application to the state of J&K.... We must give the widest effect to the meaning of the word "modification" used in Article 370 (1) and in that sense it includes an amendment.' (pp. 1122-25)

In *Mohd. Maqbool Damnoo v. The State of J&K* (AIR 1972 SC 963), the Supreme Court asserted that the Second Amendment made by the 1965 Presidential Order 'was not by "back door"...it is quite clear that the Governor is competent to give the concurrence stipulated in Article 370 and perform other functions laid down by the Jammu and Kashmir Constitution.... *What the state government is at a particular time has to be determined in the context of the Constitution of J&K*' (pp. 963, 968-9).

It was surprising to see Nehru strongly defending the relevant provision in the Delhi Agreement on which Article 35A, which gave preferential treatment in the services and acquisition of property rights to the 'citizens' of J&K, was based. The Article had become highly controversial since it was against the letter and spirit of the Constitution of India which provided for only one (Indian) citizenship and not a dual citizenship. It also militated against the fundamental rights. There were two extreme views on the subject. According to Haseeb Drabu, former Finance Minister of the state, the Article was enacted through a constitutional process and its repeal would be a blow to federal India (*The Indian Express*, 30 March

2019, p. 8). Arun Jaitley, former Union Finance Minister, argued that it was constitutionally vulnerable (*The Indian Express*, 29 March 2019, p. 4), while Mahesh Jethmalani, senior advocate of the Supreme Court, is of the view that it is manifestly unconstitutional and it is time to get rid of it (*The Indian Express*, April 2019, p. 9). While the points pertaining to the right to acquire and hold property and discrimination made between the residents and citizens of J&K remain, the context has changed with respect to the services with several other state governments stipulating similar preferential treatment in the services for persons domiciled in their states, not just in the government sector but also the private sector. This is discussed at length in Chapter 4. There will be no authoritative pronouncement on Article 35A as the pending writ petitions in the Supreme Court will now be treated as withdrawn since the Article has become inoperative.

The Delhi Agreement, 1952 – A Bigger Mistake

Nehru could have solved the tangle of Article 370 in the early years but he failed to address the problem firmly and decisively. Instead, in a series of discussions with Sheikh Abdullah and his colleagues, *Nehru and his Cabinet sub-committee members* agreed as under:

i)   While the residuary powers of legislature are vested in the Centre in respect of all states other than J&K, in respect of the latter, they should be vested in the state itself.

ii)   In accordance with Article 5 of the Constitution of India, persons who have their domicile in J&K shall be regarded as citizens of India. However, the J&K legislature was given powers to make laws for conferring special rights and privileges on the 'state subjects' in view of State Subjects Notifications of 1927 and 1932; the state legislature was also empowered to make laws for the 'state subjects' who had gone to Pakistan on account of communal disturbances of 1947, in the event of their return to Kashmir.[1]

iii) As the President of India commands the same respect in the state as he does in other units of India, Articles 52 to 62 of the Constitution relating to him should be applicable to the state. It was further agreed that the power to grant reprieves, pardons and remissions of sentences, etc. would also vest in the President of India.

iv) The Union government agreed that the state should have its own flag in addition to the Union flag, but it was agreed by the state government that the state flag would not be rival to the Union flag; it was also recognised that the Union flag should have the same status and position in J&K as in the rest of India, but for historical reasons connected with the freedom struggle in the state, the need for continuance of the state flag was recognised.

v) There was complete agreement with regard to the position of the Sadar-i-Riyasat; though the Sadar-i-Riyasat was to be elected by the state legislature, he had to be recognised by the President of India before his installation as such.... With regard to the powers and functions of the Sadar-i-Riyasat, the following was mutually agreed upon:

   (a) The Head of the state shall be a person recognised by the President of the Union on the recommendation of the legislature of the state;

   (b) He shall hold office during the pleasure of the President;

   (c) He may, by writing under his hand addressed to the President, resign his office;

   (d) Subject to the foregoing provisions, the Head of the state shall hold office for a term of five years from the date he enters upon his office;

---

1. It is in pursuance of this agreement Kent that –Article 35A was introduced in the Indian Constitution in 1954. It empowers the J&K legislature to frame a law without attracting a challenge on the grounds of violation of right to equality of the people from other states or any other right under the Constitution.

(e) Provided that he shall, notwithstanding the expiration of his term, continue to hold the office until his successor enters upon his office.

vi) With regard to the fundamental rights, some basic principles agreed between the parties were enunciated; it was accepted that the people of the state were to have fundamental rights. *But in view of the peculiar position in which the state was placed*, the whole chapter relating to 'Fundamental Rights' of the Indian Constitution could not be made applicable to the state, the question which remained to be determined was whether the chapter on fundamental rights should form part of the state Constitution or the Constitution of India as applicable to the state.

vii) With respect to the jurisdiction of the Supreme Court of India, it was accepted that for the time being, owing to the existence of the Board of Judicial Advisers in the state, which was the highest judicial authority in the state, the Supreme Court should have only appellate jurisdiction.

viii) There was a great deal of discussion with regard to the 'Emergency Powers'; the GOI insisted on the application of Article 352, empowering the President to proclaim a general emergency in the state. The state government argued that with the existence of its powers over defence (item 1 of the Union List), in the event of war or external aggression, the GOI would have full authority to take steps and proclaim emergency but the state delegation was averse to the President exercising the power to proclaim a general emergency on account of internal disturbance. In order to meet the viewpoint of the state's delegation, the GOI agreed to the modification of Article 352 in its application to Kashmir by the addition of the following words at the end of clause (1) of the Article: "but in regard to internal disturbance at the request or with the concurrence of the government of the state".

ix) Both the parties agreed that the application of Article 356, dealing with the suspension of the state Constitution and Article 360 dealing with financial emergency was not necessary (GOJ&K 1998, pp. 77-79).

The agreement was approved by Parliament on 7 August 1952 and by the Constituent Assembly of J&K on 21 August 1952.

The language of the agreement gives the impression that it was an agreement between two sovereign powers rather than being one between the Union government and the state government. It is shocking how one-sided it was with the GOI agreeing to several very unreasonable proposals of the state government such as a state citizenship, separate flag, elected Head of the state, non-application of fundamental rights in the Indian Constitution, curtailed emergency powers, curtailed jurisdiction of the Supreme Court and so on. More than Article 370, this agreement gave the impression that the special status of J&K was recognised by the GOI.

On signing the agreement, Abdullah was jubilant and said, 'the main consideration before our government was to secure a position for this state which would be *consistent with the requirements of maximum autonomy* for the local organs of the state power which are the ultimate source of authority in the state while discharging obligations as a unit of the federation' (GOJ&K 1998, pp. 79-80).

Sheikh Abdullah has recalled: 'Communal elements did not like the Delhi Agreement. The Indian media was also critical. Some newspapers went to the extent of writing that *instead of Kashmir acceding to India, in fact, India had acceded to Kashmir*' (Sheikh Abdullah 1993, p. 118).

Although India had conceded a number of Abdullah's demands such as the state flag, state citizenship, division of powers, etc. he was still not satisfied. Y.D. Gundevia has stated in his book, *The Testament of Sheikh Abdullah* (1974), Nehru had told Sheikh Abdullah, 'Oh, we will bind you in chains of gold, don't worry'. But even this did not help.

While moving a resolution on the state's flag in the J&K Constituent

Assembly on 7 June 1952, Abdullah had used the words, 'National Flag of Jammu and Kashmir'. He tried to defend it by saying, 'Because this flag was first prepared by the National Conference, it runs by the name of national flag.' Mir Qasim opposed it and moved an amendment that the word 'National' be deleted (Noorani 2011, p. 114). This amendment was accepted but it showed the real intentions of Abdullah in calling the state flag a 'national' flag.

Several major princely states which merged with India also had their own flags. For example, Bikaner had a flag of its own. The Maharaja of Bikaner had, on the occasion of flag hoisting ceremony on 15 August 1947, stated:

> To the Bikaner flag the loyalty and allegiance of all patriotic citizens of the state are legitimately due. *There is no question of the Indian national flag superseding the flag of Bikaner any more than the new Dominion of India superseding the sovereignty of this state.* Bikaner continues to be a sovereign state even though it has acceded to the Dominion of India and as such *our flag not only maintains its separate character* but shall proudly reign supreme in Bikaner, rising as before during the five centuries of its existence. (Munshi 2013, p. 423)

But, after their full merger with India, the state flags lost their status. Against this background, it was surprising that J&K's separate flag was agreed to by Nehru.

Abdullah was keen on bringing about very early change in the Headship of the state. Here too, Nehru supported him enthusiastically, perhaps because what he could not do in India to abolish the privy purses and privileges of erstwhile rulers of princely states, Abdullah was doing so swiftly. In his letter to Abdullah dated 5 June 1952, Nehru wrote: 'By removing Hari Singh and laying down the elective rule for the Head of the state, you not only carry out your declared policy but *create a good impression on large numbers of people in Kashmir as well as on people in*

"Azad Kashmir" and to some extent, even in Pakistan.'

Nehru had, however, to bring to Abdullah's notice, its likely implications for 'Kashmir's accession to India'. Nehru had also to bring to the notice of Abdullah by his letter dated 7 August 1952 that the draft notification sent by the state government was not in keeping with the agreed upon formulation. Nehru wrote:

> This wording has been changed, and the change will immediately be noticed by those who have carefully argued this point in Parliament here.... In the First Schedule, among the qualifications for the state President is that he should be a State subject of Class I. Thereby you are perpetuating in your Constitution the various divisions of state subjects and classes which were made many years ago, and which you said were out of date and were going to be revised. (Noorani 2011, pp. 125-6, 149)

But, this classification of citizens continued without any change.

In spite of the generosity shown by the GOI, the implementation of the agreement was not forthcoming. In the Working Committee of the ruling National Conference there was sharp criticism of the government's policy. There was a serious rift in the Cabinet itself. The differences of opinion reached a peak when Sheikh Abdullah, instead of implementing the agreement, started advocating secession, which would make Kashmir an 'independent state' (GOJ&K 1998, p. 80).

Ajit Bhattacharjea, a veteran journalist and former editor of *Hindustan Times* and *The Indian Express*, has brought out these developments in detail. On 10 February 1953, Nehru appealed to Abdullah to give full effect to the Delhi Agreement: 'It would help us greatly if some indication came from your government about the early implementation.... That would partly disable any big agitation.' However, the spread of the Jammu agitation was pushing Abdullah in a different direction, as conveyed in a confidential note for Nehru sent by him to Bamzai, Kashmiri scholar and historian.

The note quotes Abdullah as writing:

> Even the Delhi Agreement is not going to satisfy certain elements in India.... I cannot continue to keep people in the valley on tenterhooks. So far the people in the valley have been silent because they knew that I will not barter away their interests. Moreover, *how can we have peace in the state if the solution which India and Kashmir adopt is not acceptable to Pakistan....* If today Jammu has rebelled, it is not far off when we lose all sympathy in the valley. *In the circumstances, independence is best because Pakistan would never agree to a unilateral arrangement and our borders will always be attacked by them. Tell Panditji to have a solution which will be honourable to all—Pakistan, India, Kashmir and to him.*

According to the confidential note, Abdullah made district-wise suggestions for separating an independent Kashmir from Jammu and Ladakh that would remain with India. Kashmir would consist of Uri, Titwal, Gurais, Zojila, Trangbal, and the Jammu side of Ramban (Doda district). This presumably represented Abdullah's first preference. He also suggested a variety of solutions in a separate note entitled 'Possible Alternatives for an Honourable Settlement between India and Pakistan on the Kashmir Issue'. These included proposals floated earlier: for the entire state to be independent, guaranteed by India, Pakistan and the UN; the entire state to be under UN trusteeship for 10 years, after which the people could opt for either India or Pakistan; the entire state to be a condominium of India and Pakistan.

Nehru could see no way out. On 1 March 1953, he despairingly wrote to Maulana Azad:

> I fear that Sheikh Sahib's mind is so utterly confused that he does not know what to do. All kinds of pressures are being brought to bear on him and he is getting more and more into a tangle. There is nobody

with him who can really help him very much because he does not trust anyone fully, and yet everyone influences him.... My fear is that Sheikh Sahib, in his present state of mind, is likely to do something or take some steps, which might make things worse. (Bhattacharjea 2008, pp. 173-4)

More shocking than Sheikh Abdullah's thinking is Nehru's almost paternalistic reaction as though Abdullah's thinking was nothing much to be worried about. Nehru continued to believe that without Abdullah's support, the Kashmir valley would be lost. He was therefore prepared to turn a blind eye to Abdullah's machinations. Looking to this situation, it was appropriate of B.N. Mullick, Deputy Director of Intelligence Bureau, to brief Nehru about the doings of Abdullah which were going to cost India dearly.

As Bhattacharjea has rightly stated, 'The Delhi Agreement and Jammu agitation had let loose forces demanding the state's complete merger with the India Union. Abdullah found that "Jawaharlal Nehru and Maulana Azad were interested in the [merger] proposition, but did not agree with the strategy"' (Ajit Bhattacharjea 2008, p. 183).

Against this background, it was not surprising that on 8 August 1953, the Sadar-i-Riyasat Dr Karan Singh (son of erstwhile Maharaja Hari Singh) dismissed Sheikh Abdullah from the post of Prime Minister and dissolved the Cabinet. When questioned in the Lok Sabha, Nehru said, 'This was an internal matter and we did not wish to interfere' (GOJ&K 1998, p. 82). I find it impossible to believe that Nehru had nothing to do with it. Kashmir was a very sensitive issue, both domestically and internationally, and such an important matter could not have been left by him to the Sadar-i-Riyasat, who was just 22 years old and a total novice in politics.

In his first policy statement on taking over as the Prime Minister, Bakshi Ghulam Mohammad bitterly deplored the idea of an 'independent Kashmir' under the patronage of the United States of America, which he said 'would be a threat to the freedom and independence of Indian and Pakistani people. He praised India with which Kashmir had entered into indissoluble links'. The constitutional relations between Kashmir and India had entered a new phase (GOJ&K 1998, p. 82).

Noorani has stated that after the Delhi Agreement, both Nehru and Abdullah found their popularity dwindling in their respective constituencies. Till then Abdullah was strongly opposed to a plebiscite despite the fact that he had a most unpleasant experience of breach of faith by Vallabhbhai Patel, Abul Kalam Azad and N. Gopalaswami Ayyangar just before Article 370 was adopted by the Constituent Assembly on 7 October 1949. Had the agreed draft not been altered unilaterally, Abdullah's dismissal on August 8, 1953 would have been constitutionally barred, beyond the slightest doubt. When Nehru pressed him to conclude the Delhi Agreement and thereafter to implement it while at the same time foreclosing all possibilities of a settlement with Pakistan.... Abdullah's mind turned to other options. It is a matter of opinion whether it was a bargaining ploy to set aside the Delhi Agreement or indeed to settle the future of the state once and for all. Nehru panicked and Abdullah was put in jail (Noorani *EPW*, 1999, p. 272).

The Simla Accord[2]

It is rightly said that while the armed forces of India acquitted themselves well in each of the conflicts/wars with Pakistan, it is the political executive which failed the country and often gave away what was won by the armed forces at great sacrifice. The 1972 Simla Accord was no exception. The manner in which the final Accord was arrived at during the last couple of hours, by Indira Gandhi and Zulfiqar Ali Bhutto discussing the matter by themselves, without any aides present, remains a mystery. 'I hear a voice from the darkness,' Indira Gandhi had told a reporter (Akbar 1991, p. 174), just before the final conclave began.

---

2. Partly based on my book, *Indira Gandhi: An Era of Constitutional Dictatorship* (2018).

Under the accord of 2 July 1972, India agreed to return 5,000 square miles of the territory it had captured in West Pakistan, and to persuade Bangladesh to agree to the return of over 90,000 Pakistani prisoners of war who had surrendered to the joint Indo-Bangladesh command. India retained 400 square miles of *its own territory* in PoK, which it had recovered from Pakistan control during the war. A new line of control (LOC) in Jammu and Kashmir (in place of the old ceasefire line of 1949) was set up by the two sides who agreed not to upset it by the use or threat of force. *Both sides also agreed to discuss a final, peaceful settlement of the Kashmir question bilaterally* (Kaul 2000, p. 94).

Indira Gandhi's and Bhutto's interpersonal relationship was by no means very cordial, before the Simla encounter. Katherine Frank, in her book, *Indira: The Life of Indira Nehru Gandhi*, has brought out the relationship between Bhutto and Indira Gandhi:

> The *froideur* [coldness] that accompanied their first meeting in person was hardly surprising. Three months earlier, in an interview with the Italian journalist Oriana Fallaci, Indira had described President Bhutto as "unbalanced". Bhutto was so enraged by this that he summoned Fallaci to Karachi in April and denigrated those involved in the fourteen-day Indo-Pak war. Bhutto branded Mujib Rahman 'a congenital liar' with 'a sick mind'. As for Indira Gandhi, she was 'a mediocre woman with mediocre intelligence. There is nothing great about her.... It's that throne that makes her seem tall.... And also the name she bears.' Indira and Bhutto found one another repellent. (Frank 2001, p. 344)

Though Kashmir was to be the substantive issue in the Simla discussion, as M.J. Akbar has written in his book, *Kashmir – Behind the Vale*, Karan Singh, who was Sadar-i-Riyasat of J&K for 18 years and was a member of Indira Gandhi's Cabinet at the time, was not included in the delegation, even though several other Central ministers formed part of it. Since the

Accord was never placed before the Cabinet for approval, at no stage did Karan Singh have any opportunity to take a look at it. 'Karan Singh never hid his resentment, and still believes that it was the "gang" of Kashmiri Pandits who finessed him. Dogra suspicion of the Pandit runs deep. [Maharaja] Hari Singh's advice to his son used to be to trust anyone before a Pandit (Akbar 1991, p. 179).

Much has been written about Bhutto's strategy to have his way in the talks. According to Akbar's version, Bhutto mixed emotion with extremely subtle deference and switched his pitch from give and take of politics to a higher morality: Only a person as strong and popular as Mrs Gandhi could take a generous extra step for peace; he could not return to Pakistan with the stigma of surrender, he would be destroyed politically. And so on and so forth. Bhutto told her that Pakistan was now convinced that it could never win a war with India, that Kashmir was lost. But he could not commit that on paper. '*Bharosa Keejiye*', Bhutto pleaded; trust me. 'He played this card beautifully'. Indira Gandhi trusted him (Akbar 1991, p. 179).

This was totally in keeping with P.N. Haksar's logic. According to Sharada Prasad, 'Haksar was one of the principal shapers of Indira Gandhi's Bangladesh policy.... In Simla, a few months later, with D.P. Dhar taking ill, the task of making assessments and advising the prime minister fell largely on Haksar' (Sarkar 1989, p. 189). Haksar had advised the prime minister not to put Bhutto in the predicament of going back empty-handed or having given away too much. In this light, the outcome was a foregone conclusion and it is not surprising that Bhutto got what he wanted.

T.N. Kaul's (the then Foreign Secretary) observations in this regard are significant:

Indira Gandhi has been criticised for not getting 'a final settlement' of the Kashmir question at Simla in 1972, when India was the victor. She tried hard but Bhutto said if he agreed to a final settlement at

Simla he would be overthrown and the military would take over power and increase tension with India. *When I suggested it at the conference table, Bhutto, addressing Mrs. Gandhi, said, "Madam, I assure you that within two weeks of my return to Pakistan, I shall prepare the ground for it (a final settlement of the Kashmir question)".*

After the agreement, P.N. Dhar, her secretary, who was outside [the room] has said that there was a verbal understanding between Mrs Gandhi and Mr Bhutto that a final settlement of the Kashmir question along the Line of Control (LOC) would be made.

There is no record of this and when I asked Mrs. Gandhi the next day, she said, "I do not trust Bhutto, but I wanted to make a gesture to the people of Pakistan with whom we have ultimately to settle this question and live peacefully together. I did not want to keep the 5,000 sq. miles of West Pakistan territory. I would have antagonised the people of Pakistan and [it would have] been a millstone around our neck. Besides, we have always preached against keeping territory occupied in war." I believe, she was afraid of rousing criticism in her own party, and certainly in the BJP and the Opposition, if she settled on the LOC at that time, as we had been claiming the whole of J&K as Indian territory. But she could have stood firm on a final settlement along the LOC and Bhutto would have had to give in since he could not go back empty-handed to Pakistan (as his intelligence boss told an Indian friend in Simla). (Kaul 2000, pp. 116-117)

The apprehension about the likely opposition from the BJP and other Opposition parties does not seem to be justified. In a seminar organised by *Kirloskar* magazine—the oldest and widely circulated Marathi monthly—in 1990 (mimeo) L.K. Advani and Balraj Madhok had expressed disappointment that the opportunity to settle the Kashmir problem finally by converting the LOC into the international border was lost during the Simla discussions. As for likely opposition from within the Congress, Indira Gandhi's position at the time was so supreme that even senior leaders like Y.B. Chavan and Jagjivan Ram did not have the courage to speak out their mind during the discussion.

This whole thing, thus, gets curiouser and curiouser. If there was one time when this question could have been settled permanently, it was at the Simla meeting. But, Indira Gandhi's own position was far from clear, as can be seen from what she told Kaul. Personally, I believe that she was unduly influenced by Haksar's thinking and the outcome was as per Haksar's advice. Apparently, no strategy had been worked out in advance, and the position to be taken at the talks, the fallback position to be taken, the strong and weak points, etc. had not been discussed inter-ministerially or in the cabinet sub-committee before talks with Bhutto, except for whatever briefing Indira Gandhi had from Haksar and the two Dhars (D.P. and P.N.) This was in keeping with her style of working.

Akbar has stated that an impression was sought to be created by the Government of India that the Kashmir issue had been solved. 'But within weeks the External Affairs Ministry realized—although it was not yet telling—that India had been sold a pup, and a nasty little mongrel at that.' However, he himself has quoted what Farooq Abdullah had told him about his visit to Pakistan after the Simla Accord.

> The most significant meeting during that tour...was with Bhutto. In an interview to the author, Farooq revealed: "When I went to Rawalpindi in 1974 from England, the entire bureaucracy of Pakistan and Bhutto's secretary himself told me that a final solution has been arrived at: there can be nothing more. What we (the Pakistanis) have got (in Kashmir) we are keeping. What they have got they are keeping, and that is how it is. Bhutto confirmed this." Farooq flew to Delhi, where he briefed Mrs. Gandhi in the presence of P.N. Dhar— by now the principal secretary. (Akbar 1991, pp. 180, 186)

Benazir Bhutto, in her book, *Daughter of the East – An Autobiography*, has described how tense and unsure the Pakistan delegation and her father were during the negotiations and about the final outcome:

I was sitting on the floor of my bedroom when my father suddenly appeared in the doorway. "Don't tell anybody," he said with a new gleam in his eyes, "but I'm going to use this protocol visit to try one last time with Mrs. Gandhi. I have an idea. But don't be disappointed if there are no results." And he was gone.... "If there is an agreement, we'll say a boy has been born. If there is no agreement, we'll say a girl has been born." "How chauvinistic", I commented, but no one was listening.... I was upstairs in my bedroom when "Larka hai! Larka hai! A boy has been born! A boy has been born!" rang out through the house at 12.40 am. "How did you do it, Papa?" I asked him as the sombre silence in the house lifted to be replaced by the humming sound of one delegate passing on the news to another. "I saw that she was very tense during our visit," my father told me. "After all, failure was not only a set-back *(sic)* for us, but for her, too. Both our political opponents would use it against us. She kept fiddling with her handbag and gave the impression that her tongue did not relish the taste of the hot tea in her cup. So I took a deep breath and talked non-stop for half an hour.".... "Did she agree?" I asked my father with mounting excitement. "She didn't disagree," he said, lighting a cigar. "She said she would consult her personal advisers and let us know at the dinner tonight."

"Mrs Gandhi agreed to return either the prisoners of war or the territory," my father said to me when he came upstairs later. "Why do you think I chose the territory?" "I really don't know, Papa," I said, quite shocked. "The people in Pakistan would have been much happier if the prisoners had been freed." "And they will be freed," he assured me. "Prisoners are a human problem. The magnitude is increased when there are 93,000 of them. It would be inhuman for

India to keep them indefinitely. And it will also be a problem to keep on feeding and housing them. Territory, on the other hand, is not a human problem. Territory can be assimilated. Prisoners cannot. The Arabs have still not succeeded in regaining the territory lost in the 1967 war. But the capturing of land doesn't cry out for international attention same way as prisoners do. (Benazir Bhutto 1988, pp. 64-66)

Here was a real hard-headed politician and statesman speaking. This was in sharp contrast to the idealistic advice given by Haksar to Indira Gandhi, based on an academic understanding of consequences of the Treaty of Versailles! There is no reference in Benazir Bhutto's account of any informal understanding on the Kashmir problem arrived at between her father and Indira Gandhi. Even if there was such an understanding, Bhutto was not going to share it even with his own daughter! On 4 July 1972, the Simla agreement won the unanimous approval of the National Assembly of Pakistan; even the Opposition joined in the tributes.

It may be recalled that the word Pakistan (literally meaning land of the pure) was, according to Rehmat Ali who coined it in 1933, an acronym of Punjab, Afghania (North West Frontier Province), Kashmir, Sindh and Balochistan. It was not therefore surprising that Z.A. Bhutto, in his book, *The Myth of Independence*, published *well before the Simla agreement*, had made his views on Kashmir and its importance for Pakistan clear. Bhutto had written: '*If a Muslim majority [region] can remain a part of India, then the raison d'être of Pakistan collapses.... Pakistan is incomplete without Jammu and Kashmir both territorially and ideologically*' (Devasher 2016, pp. 14, 285).

Against this background, no credence should have been placed on any oral commitments made or assurances given by Bhutto.

One of Bhutto's aides, who was also very close to the Americans, fully briefed P. Sterba (*The New York Times* correspondent) on the understanding that his leader had reached with Mrs Gandhi. In his news analysis, which appeared within hours of the signing, Sterba, after referring to the inflexible positions of the two governments on the Kashmir problem, wrote: 'These positions have been drummed into the minds of the peoples of each side to the point where any compromise would be viewed largely as a "sell-out" in both countries. And for years, such a sell-out would have probably toppled the rulers who agreed to it.' Sterba added:

> President Bhutto, Pakistan's first civilian leader in fourteen years, came to Simla ready to compromise. According to sources close to him, he was willing to forsake the Indian held two-thirds of Kashmir that contains four-fifths of the population and the prized valley called the "Vale", and agree that a ceasefire line to be negotiated would gradually become the border between the two countries. The key word is 'gradually'.... President Bhutto wants a softening of the ceasefire line with trade and travel across it and a secret agreement with Mrs Gandhi that a formally recognised border would emerge after a few years, during which he would condition his people to it without riots and an overthrow of his government. (Dhar 2000, pp. 196-197)

Dhar has stated that this was the understanding between the leaders of the two countries and this was the Simla Solution to the Kashmir problem. The agreement that was signed at Simla in the first hours of 3 July 1972 was the launching pad for an implementation of the Simla Solution. Dhar has written:

> It was in the context of an utter disregard for the Simla commitments by Pakistan that I decided to make public the substance of the Simla understanding. I did this through a two-part article which was published in *The Times of India* in April 1995. Pakistani response to this came in an avalanche of statements and comments from the government, political leaders, columnists, and editorial writers

questioning the veracity of what I had said. About the only person in authority who did not react was Pakistan's prime minister, Benazir Bhutto.... Humayun Gauhar [Pakistani columnist] called it Bhutto's diplomatic artistry. Writing on this subject in the *Political and Business Weekly* of 15 May 1995, Gauhar wrote: "If it took a private talk between Mr Bhutto and Mrs Gandhi in which he made certain commitments to her but he was clever enough not to have written [them] down in the Simla Agreement or on a separate piece of paper, then it was diplomatic artistry of the highest order. He would have known better than anyone else that such private secret agreement, which is only verbal, was worthless. Face it Mr Dhar, even if we accept what you say, Mr. Bhutto fooled your prime minister."

Dhar has stated that the reaction in India too was not different from what Humayun Gauhar had stated—namely, that India had lost on the negotiating table what its armed forces had gained in the battlefield (Dhar 2000, pp. 198-200).

As for the Indian strategy for the Simla meeting, Dhar has confirmed that Haksar gave his soft approach a strong intellectual justification by references to comparable episodes in European history.... Haksar repeatedly referred to the baneful consequences of the harsh terms the Treaty of Versailles had imposed on the vanquished.... Haksar's intellectualism did not convince all his colleagues and some were sceptical of his approach to Bhutto.... Though Indira Gandhi had some reservations about Haksar's arguments, she went along with him. *Y.B. Chavan and Jagjivan Ram were unhappy about the return of POWs and territories to Pakistan without adequate quid pro quo, but did not, as was their wont, articulate their misgivings clearly enough* (Dhar 2000, p. 206). Dhar's assessment seems reasonable. Indira Gandhi's style of working was so authoritarian that the cabinet form of government was mere window dressing on paper. All decisions were made by the prime minister with the advice of her coterie. It was not therefore surprising that the two senior-most ministers, Chavan and Jagjivan Ram, did not have the courage or inclination to express their views on such a critical matter openly and clearly.

The Pakistan delegation's assessment was that though all the bargaining chips were stacked in India's favour, India's excessive anxiety about avoiding the failure of the talks at any cost became its major handicap. Inevitably, the wording of the accord did not reflect the Indian position on Kashmir. Bhutto is reported to have absolutely insisted on retaining as the opening commitment of the pact, 'That the principles and purposes of the Charter of the United Nations shall govern the relations between the two countries'. So where was the question of the Kashmir issue being withdrawn from the United Nations agenda, asked Pakistan.

Pakistan also began to draw attention to the sentence in the agreement which reads: '...the representatives of the two sides will meet to discuss further the modalities and arrangements for the establishment of durable peace and normalization of relations...(including) *a final settlement of Jammu & Kashmir.'*

This is shocking, to say the least. I wonder if anyone on the Indian side had even cared to read the draft agreement before it was signed. An excessively high-level and high-powered delegation, which must have kept the MEA (Ministry of External Affairs) out of negotiations and drafting, must have led to this kind of most awkward situation.[3] And yet, the Government of India was euphoric about the success of the negotiations and how the Kashmir problem had been solved by making it only a bilateral dispute. In fact, this is the line still being taken by India. However, since bilateral discussions have not gone anywhere during the last four decades, and, in recent years, India has refused to talk about

---

3. Akbar has written: 'The summit began on a note of tragedy, when D.P. Dhar had to be hospitalized with heart trouble. On a more tragicomic note, [foreign secretary] T.N. Kaul stomped off, possibly because of an imagined slight; he would return' (Akbar 1991: 176-179). This conjecture was not true. Kaul has stated, 'I left Simla on the evening of 2 July 1972, for Chandigarh to see off the Pak delegation next morning, because I did not think a settlement with Bhutto was likely' (Kaul 2000: 117).

Kashmir till the question of cross-border terrorism is addressed, a number of countries including the United States, China, Iran, and Turkey have started showing interest in mediating to find a solution to the Kashmir problem. As if this was not enough, some Kashmir leaders like Farooq Abdullah and his son Omar, Hurriyat Conference leaders and others have also suggested that, if necessary, help from friendly countries may be taken in the matter. This shows that the Simla Accord for which Indira Gandhi has been given credit was a non-starter. *To put it bluntly, in fact, Bhutto managed to fool India (India is Indira?)*.

In 1974, Z.A. Bhutto made Pakistan-occupied Kashmir (PoK) constitutionally a province of Pakistan *without much protest from India* (Dhar 2000, p. 196). Was it because this was in keeping with India's thinking of converting the LOC into an international border?

Reference must also be made to paragraph 5 of the Agreement which stated: 'This Agreement will be subject to the ratification by both countries in accordance with their respective constitutional procedures....' (Kaul 2000, p. 222). In India international agreements do not have to be approved by Parliament but this is not so in Pakistan. It was clear that the final settlement of the Kashmir question in the Simla Agreement would not have been approved by the Pakistan Parliament.

The Simla Agreement was discussed in Parliament and the impression one gets is that all political parties except the Jan Sangh, precursor of the BJP, supported it. Indira Gandhi replied to the debate in the Lok Sabha on 31 July 1972 and in the Rajya Sabha on 2 August 1972. Her reply in both the Houses was rambling, in the style of her father Jawaharlal Nehru. Her whole emphasis was on peace having been established as a result of the agreement. She made no mention of any understanding arrived at with Bhutto on Kashmir, or why the territory won in the war was given back, without getting anything in return. The Pakistani prisoners of war were released later in consultation with Bangladesh (GOI 1975, No. 66, p. 652-667).

C.S. Pandit, noted author and political commentator, has written:

On the international plane, Indira's main worry was the complete standstill obtaining on the implementation of the Simla agreement. Ever since India had withdrawn its troops from the occupied Pakistani territory, Pakistan seemed to have lost all interest in any further implementation of the accord. Bhutto was only using the POWs hold (sic) in India as a big stick to beat India with in international forums.... Despite all this, Indira herself wrote to Bhutto on 24 January offering further steps towards normalization of relations under the Simla agreement. He rejected the offer in his reply sent late in February, saying that any steps towards restoring normal relations between India and Pakistan must wait until the POWs returned home. (Pandit 1977, p. 130)

Attention may be invited to how efforts made during the Janata regime (1977-1980) to bring out the truth on the so-called secret understanding reached during the Simla discussions proved futile due to the inexplicable ruling given by the Lok Sabha Speaker that there was no urgency to discuss the matter. The Leader of the Opposition had given a notice of an adjournment motion to discuss:

the conduct of the minister for external affairs [Atal Behari Vajpayee] in violating the oath of secrecy by his announcement at two public meetings alleging a secret understanding between Mr. Bhutto and the former prime minister and claiming in his speech in the House on April 18 that this information was from official documents he came into contact with (sic) in his capacity as the minister.

Giving his ruling, the Speaker declared that the oath of secrecy was not a blanket one. The oath of secrecy provided in the Constitution forbade a minister from disclosing information made available to him or which became known to him, except as might be required for due discharge of his duties as such minister.... The question of whether a particular disclosure made by a minister was required for the discharge of his duties as such minister, was a very difficult question to decide. On this matter there could always be differences of opinion. More importantly, the Speaker observed that though the question raised was no doubt a matter of public importance, *he was unable to hold that it was a matter of such urgent public importance as to warrant disrupting the listed business of the House* (Kashyap 1997, pp. 396-398). An excellent opportunity was thus lost to reveal the full details of the matter once and for all. After this ruling, the Janata Party could have asked one of its MPs to ask for a discussion on the subject in Parliament. In fact, I have not been able to understand why Indira Gandhi and later governments should have kept this information secret, once it was clear that Bhutto had gone back on his assurances.

The 1975 Agreement with Sheikh Abdullah

The totally indefensible act of the high-handed detention of Sheikh Abdullah for nearly 11 years was brought to a close with his unconditional release on 5 June 1972. According to Dulat, who headed R&AW for a number of years, after Pakistan's defeat in the 1971 war and the creation of Bangladesh, Sheikh Abdullah realized that 'Pakistan was no match for India. For Kashmiris, the 1971 war had a huge impact' (Dulat 2015, p. 312).

Perhaps, the only gain from the Kashmir Accord signed in 1975 was the successful negotiations held by the GOI with Sheikh Abdullah in which agreement was reached on the following points:

- Article 370 would continue;
- Residuary powers would remain with J&K Assembly. Delhi would retain control of any legislation dealing with the sovereignty of India;
- Kashmir could alter or modify any provisions, but only with the consent of the President of India;
- The state could review legislation [made] after 1953 on [entries in] the Concurrent List, and President's assent 'would be

sympathetically considered';
- Article 356 and the powers of the Election Commission would remain as they were.

'No agreement was possible', however, on the question of the nomenclature of the Governor and the chief minister; Abdullah wanted a return to Sadar-i-Riyasat and Wazir-i-Azam, respectively.

Importantly, after this accord, the Plebiscite Front [which was Sheikh Abdullah's creation], which was in existence for 25 years, was wound up.

Frank's assessment is quite interesting. She has stated:

> Bhutto called the Kashmir Accord a 'sell-out' and maintained that it violated the 1972 Simla Accord. From Indira's point of view, the agreement with Abdullah had laid to rest the idea of plebiscite; it confirmed the irrevocable accession of the state to India and thereby put halt to the movement for Kashmiri self-determination. In his autobiography, Sheikh Abdullah explained that he had only agreed to cooperate in order to regain power, "but soon had to regret my decision". (Frank 2001, pp. 366-367)

It is important to note that the retention of Article 370 was reconfirmed. Particular attention may be invited to the assertion by Sheikh Abdullah in his letter to the prime minister dated 11 February 1975 that '*the accession of the state of Jammu and Kashmir to India is not in issue. It has been my firm belief that the future of Jammu and Kashmir lies with India* because of the common ideals that we share' (Noorani 2011, p. 413).

But later, this itself was disputed by some political parties in J&K, with the active support from Pakistan. This was not just a step back to square one, but minus one!

3

Kashmir – Never-Ending Search for Answers

Introduction

This chapter deals with the evolution of the Kashmir problem starting with the inscrutable role played by Sheikh Abdullah who continues to be an enigma to this day; persistent demands in the Kashmir valley for special status, *azadi* and autonomy; strenuous efforts made by India to resolve the issues; the nefarious role played by Pakistan; litany of blunders over the years in dealing with this crucial issue; and, finally, what lies ahead.

Sheikh Abdullah – An Enigma

Sheikh Abdullah was a person of many faces and colours. His statements often lacked consistency. No two persons agree on what his real game plan was.

To begin with, Abdullah was a strong supporter of Kashmir's accession to India. In his hard-hitting speech at the UN Security Council in February 1948, Abdullah had highlighted that aggression by Pakistan, and not Kashmir's accession to India, was the real issue which had to be addressed by the UN. Abdullah had declared, '*We do not believe in the two-nation theory.... We believe that religion has no place in politics*' (GOJ&K 1998, pp. 91, 94).

Whatever may have been his motivations later, Abdullah was most unequivocal in his support for Kashmir's accession to India in his opening address to the Constituent Assembly of J&K on 5 November 1951. His speech often read like that of the head of a newly independent country, rather than of a state of the Indian Union. Abdullah invariably used the word 'country' while referring to J&K. Quoting from the memorandum submitted to the Cabinet Mission, Abdullah stated, 'The fate of the Kashmiri Nation is in balance'. Abdullah dealt extensively with the merits and demerits of the state's accession to India. Talking about the points in favour of acceding to Pakistan, he said that it was a Muslim State but 'Pakistan is a feudal state in which a clique is trying by these methods to maintain itself in power...*religious affinities alone do not and should not normally determine the political alliances of the State....* These days economic interests and a community of political ideas more appropriately influence the policies of States.' As an alternative, he also placed before the House the idea of making Kashmir an 'Eastern Switzerland' and explained why this was not a feasible option. And finally he urged that it was in the best interest of Kashmir to go with India (GOJK 1998, pp. 44-69). But this was only one side of the story. Different facets of Abdullah's personality came to light over time.

Sheikh Abdullah, who was a member of the Indian delegation to the UN, while talking to the American audience on 28 January 1948, raised a third alternative—independence of Kashmir. 'It would be much better if Kashmir were independent and could seek American and British aid for development.' Abdullah raised the same proposition with US Ambassador Henry F. Grady in Delhi on 21 February 1948, except that this time he whittled down his demands to 'internal independence with defence and foreign affairs *controlled by India and Pakistan*'. Josef Korbel, a member of the United Nations Commission for India and Pakistan (UNCIP), has confirmed that when the commission visited Srinagar in July 1948, *Abdullah suggested the 'division of the country'*. According to Korbel, the Kashmir leader asserted that 'if this is not achieved the fighting will continue...and our people's suffering will go on'. The UNCIP was perplexed as to whether he was speaking on his own or reflecting the latest Indian view (Sarila 2005, p. 377).

Patel's assessment of Sheikh Abdullah was quite different from that of Nehru. B.N. Mullick, who was then the deputy director of the Intelligence Bureau, was asked by Nehru to give his independent assessment of the situation on Kashmir. He has written:

> Sardar Vallabhbhai Patel was unhappy [about my assessment]. This report of mine apparently went against the views which he had held about Kashmir in general and Sheikh Abdullah in particular. *He suspected that the Sheikh was not genuine and was misleading Pandit Nehru* and was not happy that the report should have been given such wide circulation.... I got a summons to see the Sardar the next day.... He asked me why I had sent a copy of the report to Jawaharlal without consulting him. I replied that I had submitted the report to the Director.... Sardar then said that he did not agree with my assessment of the situation in Kashmir in general and of Sheikh Abdullah in particular.... The Sardar then gave me his own views about Sheikh Abdullah. *He apprehended that Sheikh Abdullah would ultimately let down India and Jawaharlal Nehru and would come out in his real colours*; his antipathy to the Maharaja was not an antipathy to a ruler as such, but to the Dogras in general and with the Dogras he identified the rest of the majority community in India. In his slow voice, *he firmly told me that my assessment of Sheikh Abdullah was wrong*, though my assessment of the public opinion in Kashmir valley

about accession was probably correct.... Events, as they turned out subsequently, proved that *the Sardar was right and I was not.* Within three years we found ourselves fighting against Sheikh Abdullah. Sardar Patel was dead by then. Yet, I feel that possibly events might have turned out differently and the subsequent pain, turmoil, and embarrassment could have been avoided.... *Probably, things would not have come to this pass at all if the Sardar was still living, because Sheikh Abdullah had a very wholesome respect and fear for* [sic] *him.* And, if Rajagopalachari had continued as the Home Minister, his genius would have found a solution which, whilst satisfying the Sheikh, would yet have kept Kashmir firmly within India (Mullick 1971, pp.15-17).

V. Shankar has written, 'Even in 1949, Abdullah had started his dreams of an independent Kashmir, not aligned either to India or to Pakistan. We find in this correspondence [*Sardar Patel: Selected Correspondence 1945-1950*, vol. I] both Sardar and Gopalaswami Ayyangar "ticking him off"....' (Shankar 1977, p. 221).

Vallabhbhai Patel had become so dissatisfied with Abdullah's style of functioning that in his letter dated 17 February 1949, Patel sarcastically wrote to Gopalaswami Ayyangar: 'Jammu and Kashmir seems to be an independent state and the Government of India appear to have abdicated their functions in advance of the abdication of the Maharaja!' (Durga Das 1971, p. 259).

Gopalaswami replied to Patel saying, 'I am sending a message to Sheikh Abdullah that I condemn his action and that I feel that what he has told Michael Davidson [correspondent of *The Scotsman*] and what the latter has published will have the most serious and mischievous consequences both in India and abroad' (Shankar 1977, pp. 351-2).

In his further letter to Gopalaswami dated 1 May, Patel wrote: 'He wants [lands of] absentee landlords, most of whom have gone to Pakistan, to be expropriated. At the same time, he has got (*sic*)...large tracts of valuable irrigated lands vacant lest non-Muslims should settle down on them, and this is at a time when elsewhere we are asking for every inch of land to be cultivated' (Durga Das 1971, p. 266).

Balraj Krishna's assessment that Abdullah had agreed to Kashmir's accession apparently not so much on secular considerations as to ensure, first and foremost, his freedom from Jinnah, whose hatred for him is evident from the cynical remark, 'Oh, that tall man who sings Koran and exploits the people'. Liaquat Ali had contemptuously called Abdullah: 'This quisling—an agent of the Congress for many years…' (Krishna 2005, p. 371).

In his interview to Michael Davidson of *The Scotsman*, published on 14 April 1949, Abdullah had said:

> Accession to either side cannot bring peace. We want to live in friendship with both Dominions. Perhaps a middle path between them, with economic cooperation with each, will be the only way of doing it. But an independent Kashmir must be guaranteed not only by India and Pakistan but also by Britain, the United States and other members of the UN…. Yes, independence guaranteed by the UN may be the only solution. But why do you talk of partition? (Durga Das 1971, p. 266)

Nehru had expressed his shock at this interview and felt that it 'will have most serious and mischievous consequences both in India and abroad'. Patel was so angry that in his letter dated 1 May 1949 to Gopalaswami, he wrote: 'A vehement exponent of accession to India seems to have been converted to an "independent Kashmir"….' (Durga Das 1971, pp. 266-7).

Ajit Bhattacharjea, a veteran journalist and former editor of the *Hindustan Times* and the *Indian Express,* has written:

> In May 1949, a report in London's *Sunday Observer* attracted notice in New Delhi. It reported Abdullah as saying, "Accession to either

side cannot bring peace. We want to live in friendship with both Dominions. Perhaps a middle path between them with economic cooperation with each other will be the only way to do it. However, an independent Kashmir must be guaranteed not only by India and Pakistan, but also by Great Britain, the US and the UN".... Most of these suggestions, as well as others emanating from the UN discussions, focussed on the Valley, leaving the rest of the state to India and Pakistan. [Later] Abdullah's vision expanded from the Valley to the entire state. (Bhattacharjea 2008, p. 150)

The *Press Trust of India (PTI)* reported Abdullah as having said in a public meeting at Ranbir Singh Pora (Jammu district), on 10 April 1952 that:

Kashmir's accession to India would have to be of a restricted nature as the communal spirit still existed in India. While the Indian Government, unlike the authorities in Pakistan, were trying to curb communalism, they had not succeeded fully, and "so far as Kashmir was concerned it wanted to preach the mission of secular democracy both to India and Pakistan". He also said that many Kashmiris feared about their fate in the event of something happening to Nehru. Sheikh Abdullah added that the Indian press and some correspondents in the state were "indulging in misconceived criticism of Kashmir's desire for a special status" and warned that if they persisted in their attitude, they might "finally destroy the union of Kashmir with India". (*JNMF*, vol. 18, 1996, p. 383, footnote 2)

Abdullah accused the *PTI* of 'viciously' distorting his speech at Ranbir Singh Pora. Replying to Nehru's letter of 25 April, Abdullah said that he had been gravely wronged as even the authorised version of the speech had failed to change Nehru's impression created by the *PTI* report (*JNMF*, vol. 18, 1996, p. 384, footnote 2 and p. 389, footnote 2).

In April 1952, when Gopalaswami Ayyangar wanted to bring about a measure of financial integration between India and Kashmir by extending the jurisdiction of C&AG to the state, Sheikh Abdullah made a highly provocative speech at Ranbir Singh Pora saying *'Kashmir's accession to India will have to be of a restricted nature'* and described arguments in favour of the full application of the Indian Constitution to Kashmir as *'unrealistic, childish and savouring of lunacy'*. In another speech two weeks later, he said, 'It would be better to die than submit to the taunt that India was our bread giver. Kashmir is not eager for India's aid.' Mullick has stated that when these speeches were reported to Nehru, *he 'mildly rebuked the Sheikh'* for this. Sheikh Abdullah, of course, promptly denied the more objectionable portions, but there is no doubt that he was trying to assert his independence. According to Mullick, Nehru believed that 'we were in Kashmir because of the Sheikh, and if the latter resiled, India's position would be difficult' (Mullick 1971, pp. 25-6). No wonder Patel did not share this view.

Mullick was of the view that 'Once having tasted power, Sheikh Abdullah wanted to be a dictator under the facade of democracy and started toying with the idea of an independent Kashmir.... Sheikh Abdullah has proved to be completely unreliable—unreliable to the people of India and of Jammu and Kashmir.... In actual fact, he led Kashmir step by step further away from India' (Mullick 1971, pp. 194-7).

Noorani has stated that, from 1947 till 1953, Nehru was profuse in proclaiming his commitment to hold a plebiscite while Sheikh Abdullah opposed it from 1947 to 1952. *The roles were reversed in 1953.* In his note to Sheikh Abdullah dated 25 August 1952, Nehru stated: '[In our discussions in Srinagar] you told me that there were only two courses open for Kashmir—either full integration or full autonomy, whatever that autonomy might mean' (Noorani in *EPW* 1999, pp. 268, 271). Looking back, one can see how true it was. There could not be a halfway house. Full integration is what has been brought about by the abrogation of Article 370.

Against this background, the stand taken by Sheikh Abdullah in the Constituent Assembly of India which led to the incorporation of Article 370 is not surprising. What is surprising is that Nehru continued to support Sheikh Abdullah for so long thereafter.

V.P. Menon has brought out an interesting but important facet of the Kashmir problem:

> Fears regarding the likely attitude of popular ministries [towards the erstwhile rulers] were not entirely groundless. Take the case of Kashmir: *No sooner had Sheikh Abdullah secured complete power he insisted that the Maharajah should stay out of the state.* It was on Sardar's persuasion that the Maharajah agreed to do so, though reluctantly. The government of India negotiated a settlement in regard to his privy purse and other matters. *Sheikh Abdullah refused to honour the agreement and the government of India are still [till abolition in 1971] paying the privy purse from their own coffers.* (Menon 1956, p. 486)

Nehru wrote in his letter to the chief ministers on 12 January 1958 that Sheikh Abdullah, who was released from his internment, had 'given expression to violent sentiments in regard to the J&K Prime Minister Bakshi Ghulam Mohammad, the Sadar-i-Riyasat Karan Singh, and India. He had attacked the Constituent Assembly of the state and the Constitution it produced. He appears to be on the warpath.... He appears to be appealing to communal passions.' In a further letter to the chief ministers dated 18 May 1958, Nehru lamented that Sheikh Abdullah had to be rearrested and detained. Nehru said:

> But the fact remains that Sheikh Abdullah by his activities made it difficult for any government to remain quiet. It has been a matter of deep grief to me that an old colleague who has in the past played such a brave part in our national movement and in the liberation of

Kashmir, should have drifted away so far and should have sought to rouse communal passions. He has been connected also with other undesirable activities. (Parthasarathi 1989, pp. 3-4, 48-49)

Looking back at the events of the period, I think it was an error in political judgment to detain Sheikh Abdullah in this manner and to make him a martyr. Instead, he could have been sidelined. This is particularly so since, as Nehru himself had mentioned in his letter to chief ministers: 'Apart from some *hartals* [closures] on the day of his arrest, there has been hardly even a demonstration.... Only four persons have been arrested including Sheikh Abdullah. Indeed life flows on in Kashmir calmly and without a ripple on its placid surface' (Parthasarathi 1989, p. 49).

C. Bilqees Taseer has quoted several speeches of Sheikh Abdullah in 1964 which are disturbing. He vigorously advocated the strengthening of the Plebiscite Front as [the] most suitable instrument for realizing Kashmiris' wishes. In another speech he said, 'the eyes of the world are seeing that Kashmiri people reject the Indian claim that Kashmir's accession to India is final'. He added that the people of Kashmir would not rest content until they were given an opportunity to decide their future freely (Taseer 2005, pp. 328-9).

In a speech in Srinagar on 28 March 1969, Sheikh Abdullah said that if a Congress candidate had the right to say that India was good, another person who felt that Kashmir's future would be good in Pakistan should have the freedom to say so. The Central government considered the statement to be not only totally misconceived but also improper and deplorable (Rajya Sabha Debates, 30 April 1969).

In the resolution adopted at the meeting of the Working Committee of the Plebiscite Front [which was Sheikh Abdullah's creation] held in Srinagar on 14 December 1969, the Front said it considered Article 370 of the Constitution as the only basis for a relationship of Kashmir with India on a temporary basis, subject to a plebiscite, and as and when the Article is abrogated India shall cease to have any *locus standi* in Kashmir.

The government considered the resolution as wholly misconceived and a total distortion and misinterpretation of the facts and history of the Constitution (Godbole 1996, p. 79).

During the course of negotiations on the 1975 Agreement, Abdullah, in his letter dated 29 December 1974 to Prime Minister Indira Gandhi, wrote in anguish:

> I have no doubt in my mind that the manner in which the Government of India systematically eroded both the letter and spirit of the special provision of the Union Constitution jeopardised the very foundation of the relationship so laboriously built over the years of tireless effort and dedication. I recall with pain and anguish that once a former Home Minister of India publicly characterised Article 370 as a 'Tunnel' obviously implying that through it the internal autonomy of Kashmir will be eroded and that exactly was assiduously accomplished behind our back after 9th August 1953 [after his arrest].... Myself and the Plebiscite Front leaders were purposely kept behind the bars or externed from the state at the time of every general election to the state legislature or the Parliament in the years 1957, 1962, 1967 and 1972. As if this was not enough, large scale rigging in elections was taken recourse to. (Noorani 2011, pp. 410-11)

While under detention in Delhi, in his interview with Gundevia (*The Testament of Sheikh Abdullah*, 1974), Abdullah said that there was a gradual victory of right-wingers, reactionaries and petty men around Nehru, and Nehru was fighting the battle almost single-handedly. He had the support of only Rafi Ahmed Kidwai, Amrut Kaur and perhaps B.R. Ambedkar. Even Rajendra Prasad was opposed. Abdullah said, 'Sardar Patel and several others had no faith in me. Nehru first resisted the campaign of vilification against me but ultimately he succumbed.'

As stated earlier, the challenge posed by Sheikh Abdullah should have been met politically rather than taking recourse to the drastic measure of detaining him. Such actions sullied the image of India at home and abroad. Writing about the conspiracy case, Abdullah has stated: 'It took five years and cost two and half crore rupees.... The case became a joke. The global mood was reflected in the following headline which appeared in the *Observer* (published from London) dated 16 December 1963 – "Sheikh Abdullah on Trial But India in the Dock"' (Sheikh Abdullah 1993, p. 144).

Nehru's Kashmir policy lacked direction. This drift continued for years as a part of Nehru's legacy, till August 2019 when Article 370 was abrogated, and the state was divided into two Union Territories.

Even for an ardent admirer of Nehru like me, his policies on China and Kashmir continue to be highly questionable. This is more so in respect of Kashmir, which he insisted on handling himself, rather than permitting Sardar Patel, who was instrumental in bringing about the peaceful integration of 552 princely states, to deal with it.

Some features of the Kashmir story need to be understood and appreciated without any political baggage. **First**, Sheikh Abdullah was not the accepted leader of the entire J&K state. He was the leader of the Kashmir valley. His leadership was challenged even in Jammu and Ladakh, leave aside the part of Kashmir which is under Pakistan occupation. **Second**, while Kashmir's accession to India was complete on 26 October 1947, the Constitution of India was finalised two years later on 26 November 1949. This long intervening period was enough to finalise Kashmir's Constitutional relationship with India, as in the case of other states by bringing about its full integration. The reasons for not doing so cited in Nehru's note dated 3 July 1952—namely, 'war with Pakistan, reference to UNO, etc.' do not hold water. 'Chiefly because of the reference to the UN, we did not take this matter up and allowed things to continue in the transitional and rather vague state,' Nehru had stated (*JNMF*, vol. 18, 1996, p. 423). The Government of India had taken this stand in its discussions with the UN from time to time. This was merely a gloss. The reference to the UN was about Pakistan's aggression and not Kashmir's accession to and integration with India. *The real reason for leaving the position of India's relationship with Kashmir vague was the opposition of Sheikh Abdullah to Kashmir's full integration with India beyond the three subjects*—defence, external affairs and communications—mentioned in the Instrument of Accession, and his insistence on having a separate Constitution for Kashmir. If Sheikh Abdullah had been permitted to have his say, Article 370 would have been a permanent part of India's Constitution! Nehru was anxious not to state these real reasons as this would have led to sharp reactions in India and much stronger opposition to Sheikh Abdullah than there already was, from his own Congress Party.

Third, Nehru, in keeping with his Socialist ideology, was taken in by Sheikh Abdullah's insistence on the abolition of *zamindari* in Kashmir without paying any compensation to landholders. It is for this reason that Abdullah did not want the fundamental rights in the Indian Constitution to be extended to Kashmir. Patel was strongly opposed to this stand by Abdullah but Nehru was sympathetic to it. By the first amendment in 1951, the Constitution of India was amended to introduce the 'device' of the Ninth Schedule to keep the 12 agrarian enactments pertaining to land reforms out of the purview of the Supreme Court. Later, of course, this became a monstrosity with nearly 285 diverse enactments getting excluded from the Apex Court's scrutiny. This ugly chapter in India's judicial history was finally put an end to by the decision of the Supreme Court in 2006.

Fourth, Nehru was also taken in by Abdullah's insistence on doing away with the monarchy in J&K. Nehru considered the continuance of the arrangements of privy purses arrived at by Vallabhbhai Patel with India's princely rulers 'anachronistic' but could not do anything about them, due to Patel's pre-eminent position in the Congress Party.

Fifth, the most important question was about Nehru's thinking. Unbelievably, Nehru was questioning, 'Must all constituent units of the Republic of India have exactly the same relation to the Union, as embodied in the Constitution and various Lists of subjects [Seventh Schedule of the Constitution], or can there be a variation?' (*JNMF* vol. 19, 1996, pp. 423-8). Abdullah was also aware of what Nehru had written to him: 'My own view about the Constitution has all along been that it is always better to have a brief and flexible Constitution. We have made a mistake, I think, in having too long and complicated a Constitution of India and we are regretting it...it comes in the way all the time' (Noorani in *EPW* 1999, p. 270). It is difficult to believe that Nehru, who was one of the prime architects of India's Constitution, was prepared to jettison the Constitution itself in order to keep Kashmir in India! Sadly, Vallabhbhai Patel was no longer alive, for he alone could have averted such a catastrophe. Attempting to make such basic changes in the Constitution would have opened the Pandora's box.

Finally, the question remains—what did Abdullah want? Did Abdullah want to merge Kashmir with Pakistan? Or, did he want Kashmir to remain independent? Abdullah was well aware that Kashmir would not be given any autonomy by Pakistan. He was also pragmatic enough to realise that Pakistan would not permit Kashmir to remain independent. Independence of Kashmir was therefore not a feasible option, howsoever close it might have been to his heart.[1] His best bet was to remain in India but with the very limited ties as in the original Instrument of Accession signed by the Maharaja. This way Kashmir would be a protectorate of India and he would be the Sultan-e-Kashmir. Durga Das has written: 'The secret talks between Abdullah and some intermediaries from the US had broken down because he wanted to be a "hereditary sultan" while the negotiators maintained that they could sell to the US Congress only

---

1. B. K. Nehru, who was Governor of J &K from 1980-84, has written: 'His [Sheikh's] objective was not the gradual integration of the state of Jammu and Kashmir into the Indian Union. What he wanted instead was the eventual creation of a separate independent state consisting of at least the Valley together with such Muslim areas of Jammu division as could be tagged to it' (B. K. Nehru 1997: p. 593). The same was the assessment of Durga Das who wrote: 'Sheikh Abdullah has been hoping that somehow New Delhi will be constrained to make Kashmir independent' (Das 1969: p. 410).

presidency, not a sultanate!' (Das 1969, pp. 410-1).

Incidentally, at one stage, the Drafting Committee of the Constitution was thinking of providing for a separate category of states classified as Part E[2] and making a special provision therein for the 'protected' states to be governed on the basis of agreements ensuring their *virtual accession* in respect of the three subjects of defence, foreign affairs and communications. Sikkim was being considered as a state in this category (Munshi 2013, pp. 475-6). J&K could have qualified for inclusion in this category, if Sheikh Abdullah had pressed for it. It is anybody's guess what the reaction of Nehru, Patel and the Constituent Assembly would have been, but this would have changed the course of history.

Demands for Special Status, *Azadi* and Autonomy

It is necessary to note that when one talks of the Kashmir problem, it is the problem of the Kashmir Valley. The other two parts of the erstwhile J&K—namely, Jammu and Ladakh, were never a part of the problem.[3] A sizeable section in the Kashmir valley had never reconciled itself to Kashmir's accession to India. It is often said that the insurgency in Kashmir began in the 1980s. But this is far from true. As Sati Sahni has shown in his book, *Kashmir Underground*, 'use of violence and force to change the order of things in J&K certainly took birth the same day as Pakistan' (Sahni 1999, p. 18). Sahni has traced in detail the part played by secessionists and sympathisers of Pakistan right since the accession of the state to India. Since the separatist movement began in the 1980s,

---

2. At that time, the First Schedule of the revised draft Constitution had divided the states and UTs into four parts: A,B, C and D.

3. Before the Partition, Jammu province had a Muslim majority. According to the 1941 census, 70 per cent of the population were Muslims, and over 90 per cent in Kashmir *(sic)*. After the ceasefire, however, Hindus were in majority in the areas of Jammu under Indian authority.... Many Muslims had moved from Hindu-dominated areas in the wake of the Partition.... One of Abdullah's first efforts in his newly assumed office of head of the state administration was to restore communal peace in Jammu city and assuage the hurt of terrorized Muslims (Bhattacharjea 2008, p.159).

at least 1,000 Pandits have been killed, roughly 16,000 homes have been burnt and 350,000 have been displaced in one of the most sordid acts of ethnic cleansing.

The Constitution of J&K clearly states that the Constitution has been framed 'in pursuance of the accession of this state to India....., to further define the *existing relationship of the state with the Union of India as an integral part thereof ....' Article 3 states, 'The state of Jammu and Kashmir is and shall be an integral part of the Union of India'*. Article 4 states, 'The territory of the state shall comprise all the territories which *on the fifteenth day of August 1947*, were under the sovereignty or suzerainty of the Ruler of the state' (Chitaley and Rao 1959, pp. 4180-2). But this did not matter to the secessionists, who continued to press their demands for *azadi* (freedom).

Memorandum by the National Conference: The clamour for special status, autonomy, or self-rule had continued unabated. The memorandum submitted by the National Conference to the Prime Minister on 4 November 1995 stated that there was nothing irreversible in Article 370 which began the entire process of dilution of the state's autonomy. An election just for the sake of an election would be a farcical exercise which would fail to carry conviction with the people. It would be another short-sighted step in pursuit of the Centre's obduracy in refusing to deal with the political problem in keeping with the principles of secularism, democracy, federalism and solemn obligations under the Delhi Agreement (Noorani 2014, p. 420).

State Autonomy Committee: The Farooq Abdullah Government set up a 10-member committee on 29 November 1996 under the chairmanship of Dr Karan Singh to examine the restoration of autonomy of the state. Karan Singh, however, resigned on 31 July 1997. Thereafter, the committee functioned under the chairmanship of Ghulam Mohiuddin Shah. The committee submitted its report in April 1999.

The terms of reference of the committee were:

(i) To examine and recommend *measures for the restoration of autonomy to the state of J&K consistent with the Instrument of Accession, the Constitution Application Order, 1950, and the Delhi Agreement of 1952.*

(ii) To examine and recommend safeguards that may be regarded necessary for incorporation in the Union/state Constitution to ensure that the Constitutional arrangement that is finally evolved in pursuance of the recommendation of the committee is inviolable.

(iii) To also examine and recommend measures to ensure a harmonious relationship for the future between the state and the Union.

Specific attention may be invited to the following important recommendations:

1. Temporary, Transitional and Special Provisions (Part XXI)
    (i) *The word 'Temporary' be deleted* from the title of Part XXI of the Constitution of India and the word 'temporary' occurring in the heading of Article 370 be substituted by the word 'special'.

2. Legislative Relations (Part XI)
    (i) Matters in the Union List *not connected with* the three subjects of Defence, External Affairs and Communications and/or ancillary thereto but made applicable should be excluded from their application to the state.

    (ii) All modifications made in Article 246 [subject matter of laws made by Parliament and by the legislatures of states] in its application to the state subsequent to the 1950 order should be rescinded.

    (iii) Articles 248 [residuary powers of legislation], 249 [power of Parliament to legislate with respect to a matter in the State List in the national interest], 250 [power of Parliament to legislate with respect to any matter in the State List if a proclamation of Emergency is in operation] and 251 [inconsistency between laws made by Parliament under Articles 249 and 250 and laws made by the legislatures of states] whether applied in original or substituted/modified form should be omitted from their application to the state.

In keeping with the tenor as above, the committee recommended doing away with changes made in respect of elections, application of fundamental rights, finance, property, contracts and suits, etc., All India Services and so on. *In short, the clock was to be reset to what obtained in 1950 on adoption of the Constitution of India. All that mattered was the Instrument of Accession and the Delhi Agreement of 1952, and the Presidential Orders issued to implement them. Everything else would be erased.* The committee had also underlined that:

Article 370 had acquired a dangerously ambiguous aspect. *Designed to protect the state's autonomy* [?], it has been used systematically to destroy it. A compact is necessary between the Union and the state which makes ample redress and finalizes their relationship by declaring a 'Constitutional understanding' that Article 370 can no longer be used to apply to the state of J&K any other provisions of the Constitution of India beyond the ones extended under the 1950 Order and the Delhi Agreement, 1952. This could be embodied in a new Article that specified the agreement as part of the unamendable basic structure of the Indian Constitution.

The state Cabinet endorsed the recommendations of the committee and formed a four-member ministerial committee. The GOI was requested to set up a ministerial committee to initiate a dialogue on the report. The report was discussed in the Legislative Assembly for seven days in April and June 2000. The motion to endorse the report and approve action as above was approved by the House. The BJP, Congress, Panthers Party,

Janata Dal and Awami League, however, opposed it and staged a walkout (Noorani 2014, pp. 420-2, 434-458).

Justice Saghir Ahmad's Report, 2009*:* The Working Group V, set up in pursuance of the decisions concerning the establishment of five working groups by Prime Minister Manmohan Singh, had the following mandate: Strengthening relations between the state and the Centre and to deliberate on:

(1) Matters relating to the special status of J&K within the Indian Union;

(2) Methods of strengthening democracy, secularism and the rule of law in the state;

(3) Effective devolution of powers among different regions to meet regional, sub-regional and ethnic aspirations.

As regards (1) above, the National Conference (NC) made a demand for autonomy of the state, while the PDP pressed for 'self-rule'. Muzaffar Hussain Baig (PDP founder member, quit the party in November 2020) elaborated on the concept of 'self-rule':

There is a difference between the autonomy demand of NC and the 'self-rule' demand of PDP. While autonomy essentially relates to centre-state relations, 'self-rule' has several other connotations: external dimension of relationship between India and Pakistan; centre-state relations; *application of the self-rule not only to J&K but also POK and areas occupied by China*; border between India and Pakistan; regional issues, and so on.

The PDP demanded that Articles 356 and 357 pertaining to emergency powers of the GOI were not necessary in respect of J&K. The head of the state should be called Sadar-i-Riyasat. All India Services are not necessary in J&K. Article 370 should be a permanent feature of the Constitution. There is enough scope for economic and trade relations with POK. The local police should play a stronger role, replacing the role of the Central forces including military operations.

The demand of the NC was for restoration of the autonomy of the state which had been eroded over a period of time. It was contended that erosion of autonomy was the primary cause of discontent in the state and this fact was accepted at different times. For example, Prime Minister P.V. Narasimha Rao had observed, 'Sky is the limit and short of independence, the demands can be accepted'. However, the NC boycotted the 1996 parliamentary elections. Thereafter, Prime Minister Deve Gowda promised 'maximum autonomy to be discussed with peoples' representatives'. The NC therefore contested the 1996 Assembly elections and obtained a two-third majority as it had stressed in its election manifesto that autonomy was the prime consideration for the state. The committee for restoration of autonomy set up by the state government examined the issues and the report of the committee was approved by the state legislature but was summarily rejected by the GOI even without any discussion or detailed examination.

The continuance or strengthening of Article 370 was widely debated by the Saghir Ahmad Working Group. The report of the P.B. Gajendragadkar Commission of Inquiry indicates that even in November 1968, that is to say, almost 18 years after the coming into force of the Indian Constitution, there was no recommendation that Article 370 should be abolished. 'The position remained the same and there had been no material alteration in the circumstances as [only a] few voices were raised and are still raised for abrogation of Article 370, while there are other voices which strongly plead for the continuance of this Article'. The Gajendragadkar formula that it is for the people of the state of J&K to decide how long to continue Article 370 in its present form and when to make it permanent or abrogate [it], is still relevant.... This position has continued since 1950.... *The Working Group recommends that the question of Article 370 should be settled once and for all and the state of uncertainty in respect of this Article should be given a final shape* (Noorani 2014: pp. 459-472).

Report of the Group of Interlocutors: Following the All Party Parliamentary Delegation's visit to J&K in September 2010, the Manmohan Singh government appointed on 13 October 2010 a group of interlocutors. The Group comprised Dileep Padgaonkar, veteran journalist and former editor of *The Times of India*, as chairman, and Radha Kumar and M.M. Ansari as members. The mandate given to the Group was to hold wide-ranging discussions with all sections of opinion in J&K in order to identify the political contours of a solution and the roadmap towards it. In order to fulfil this mandate, the Group was tasked with spending about a week each month in the state. The Group, after extensive interactions with more than 700 delegations in all the 22 districts in the state and three round table conferences, made some significant recommendations which reflected the main demands voiced before it. Some of the important recommendations are given below:

- *Delete the word 'temporary'* from the heading of Article 370 and from the title of Part XXI of the Constitution, and replace it by the word 'Special' as it has been used for other states.
- Governor: The state government, after consultation with Opposition parties, shall submit a list of three names to the President. The President can ask for more suggestions if required. The governor will be appointed by the President and hold office at the pleasure of the President.
- Article 356: The action of the Governor is now justiciable in the Supreme Court. The present arrangement should continue with the proviso that the Governor will keep the state legislature under suspended animation and hold fresh elections within three months.
- Article 312: The proportion of officers from the AIS should be gradually reduced in favour of officers from the state civil service without curbing administrative efficiency.
- The nomenclature in English of the Governor and the Chief

Minister should continue as at present. Equivalent nomenclatures in Urdu may be used while referring to the two officers in Urdu.

- Parliament will make no law applicable to the state unless it relates to the country's internal and external security and its vital economic interest, especially in the area of energy and access to water resources.
- These changes should be harmonised in all parts of the former princely state. All opportunities for cross-LOC cooperation should be promoted. This will require substantial Constitutional changes in POK.
- All appropriate measures be taken to regard J&K as a bridge between South and Central Asia.
- The list of subjects out of List II [State List] in the Seventh Schedule that could be transferred to the regional councils is listed in detail in the report.

The Group also made some recommendations to take the political dialogue forward:

(a) Resume the GOI-Hurriyat dialogue at the earliest opportunity.
(b) Agreement between India and Pakistan should be entered into to promote civil society interactions for J&K on both sides of the LOC.

The above discussion shows that through all the years, the preponderance of public opinion in J&K was in favour of giving larger autonomy to the state and making Article 370 a permanent feature of the Constitution. There was also a demand to reduce the Centre's hold over the state by reducing the role of All India Services and taking other steps. As none of these demands were in keeping with the thinking of the political parties which formed the GOI, from time to time, no action was taken on any of these recommendations and they fell into a bottomless pit. As the late

Padgaonkar told me in one of my talks with him, Union Home Minister Sushil Kumar Shinde took no trouble to read the report of the Group and had evinced no interest even in discussing the matter. Clearly, successive governments were in a bind. None of them had the political courage to address these issues, least of all the future of Article 370, till the NDA government announced the decision in August 2019 to abrogate the Article and to untie the Gordian knot.

A Series of Efforts to Resolve Issues

The state of J&K is a vast and mountainous territory and comprises areas acquired or conquered by the Dogra dynasty over the years. The implications of holding a statewide plebiscite were examined by UN experts minutely. Owen Dixon, in his report to the Security Council, said, 'The state of Jammu and Kashmir is not really a unit geographically, demographically, or economically. It is an agglomeration of territories brought under the political power of one Maharaja. That is the unity it possesses' (Gupta 1996, p. 476). Neither India nor Pakistan was sure of the outcome of the plebiscite in this region of great religious, linguistic, cultural and ethnic diversity. Talk of plebiscite was therefore just academic. As stated elsewhere, Sheikh Abdullah's hold was also largely confined to the Kashmir valley. The Kashmiri Muslim with his commitment to *Kashmiriyat* is different from the Punjabi Muslim. Therefore, the idea of partitioning J&K was considered by India right from the beginning.

Dr Ambedkar, in the written statement on his resignation from the Nehru Cabinet, tabled in the Lok Sabha on 10 October 1951, had, inter alia, expressed the view:

> The real issue to my mind is not who is in the right but what is right. Taking that to be the main question, my view has always been that the right solution is to partition Kashmir. Give the Hindu and Buddhist part to India and the Muslim part to Pakistan as we did in the case of India. We are really not concerned with the Muslim part of Kashmir.

> It is a matter between the Muslims of Kashmir and Pakistan. They
> may decide the issue as they like. (LSS 1951, p. 1322)

Mountbatten was anxious to settle the Kashmir dispute before he relinquished the Governor-Generalship in June 1948. At his behest, V.P. Menon and Gopalaswami Ayyangar drew up a plan for the partition of the state, complete with maps (which left Gilgit to Pakistan). It is difficult to believe that the Indian government remained ignorant of this exercise. Nothing came of it but the proposal was not kept confidential. V.P. Menon, on 23 July 1948, told the chargé d'affaires of the US Embassy in Delhi that *the Government of India will accept settlement based on accession of Mirpur, Poonch, Muzaffarabad and Gilgit to Pakistan.* Such a statement cut the ground from under the US stand that to leave the occupied areas in Pakistan control 'would be highly unacceptable to GOI'. A few days later in July 1948, *Nehru is reported to have told Josef Korbel, member of the UNCIP (United Nations Commission for India and Pakistan), that 'He would not be opposed to the idea of dividing the country between India and Pakistan.'* This meant leaving Gilgit to Pakistan.

In his letter to Patel from Paris dated 27 October 1948, Nehru had given a gist of his discussions. Nehru, inter alia, wrote:

> [As for the plebiscite] People cannot get rid of the idea that Kashmir
> is predominantly Muslim and therefore likely to side with Muslim
> Pakistan.... The position I have taken up about Kashmir is either a
> full acceptance of the UN Commission's resolution on ceasefire, or a
> partition on the lines we have previously talked about, i.e., Western
> Poonch, etc., Gilgit, Chitral, most of Baltistan, etc. to go to Pakistan.
> Neither of these is acceptable to Liaquat Ali. (Durga Das 1971, p.
> 249)

On 20 February 1948, Nehru wrote to Krishna Menon, the Indian High Commissioner in the UK: *'Even Mountbatten has "hinted at partition of*

Kashmir''', Jammu for India and the rest including lovely Vale of Kashmir to Pakistan. This is totally unacceptable to us.... *Although if the worst comes to the worst I am prepared to accept Poonch and Gilgit being partitioned off.*

Y.D. Gundevia, former Foreign Secretary, in his book, *Outside The Archives* (1984) (Kindle edition 2013), has written about how Nehru was keen on settling the Kashmir issue during his lifetime 'by even making territorial concessions and territorial adjustments'. Nehru had realised that it would be impossible to make Pakistan vacate the territory acquired by it by aggression. *Nehru was anxious not to leave the Kashmir problem as his legacy* and was therefore even prepared to modify the ceasefire line somewhat in favour of Pakistan. Towards this end, six rounds of talks were held during 1962-63 with Pakistan Foreign Minister, Z.A. Bhutto, in Rawalpindi, New Delhi, Karachi, Calcutta, again in Karachi, and finally again in Delhi, in May 1963. At one stage, Ayub Khan, President of Pakistan, was inclined to settle but finally there could be no agreement. The Indian team comprised Swaran Singh (Minister for Steel and Mines), Krishna Menon, Y.D. Gundevia (Foreign Secretary), G. Parthasarathy (journalist, educationist and diplomat) and Shankar Prasad.

Sheikh Abdullah had also made efforts, during his visit to Pakistan in 1964, to find an amicable solution of the Kashmir problem. He proposed a confederation of India, Pakistan and J&K! Interestingly, India's Cabinet Committee on External Affairs had approved the proposal but Ayub Khan was totally opposed to it.

As stated in Chapter 2, efforts were made during the discussions on the Simla Accord in 1972 to bring about the division of J&K along the LOC,[4] but Prime Minister Z.A. Bhutto, on returning to Pakistan, went back on the informal understanding reached with Prime Minister Indira Gandhi. Pakistan was not prepared to accept any compromise unless the Kashmir Valley was given to it.

After Sheikh Abdullah's death, Kashmir politics was unstable, most of

---

4. Of the total area of J&K at the time of accession, 48 per cent is with India, 35 per cent with Pakistan and 17 per cent with China.

the time. Bakshi Ghulam Mohammad (J&K Prime Minister from 1953 to 1964) had a very dubious reputation but with his strong hold over the National Conference party it was not easy to dislodge him. This task was performed by the diminutive Lal Bahadur Shastri, then Union Home Minister. D.R. Mankekar writes:

> Releasing Bakshi's grip on the affairs of Kashmir was a consummation long devoutly wished for by many in New Delhi. But even Nehru did not find (sic) the gumption to set about it. And thus Bakshi ruled in Srinagar like an absolute despot, his right none to dispute and his misrule none to question. Now this little man from New Delhi had done the trick with ease of a David felling a Goliath. (Srivastava 1996, p. 75)

In spite of the serious efforts made by successive governments at the Centre, the mistrust has continued. Rigged elections, unfair election practices, misuse of Article 356 of the Constitution, partisan role played by Governors at times, have all been partly responsible for this situation. But, these were not unique to J&K and for the same reasons had alienated a number of other states. One of the other main factors responsible for the alienation was the repeated arrests and detention of Sheikh Abdullah for nearly 11 years. He was first arrested on 9 August 1953 and was released in January 1958. He was again arrested on 29 April 1958 and released on 8 April 1963. He was yet again arrested on 7 May 1965 and released on 2 January 1968. He was rearrested and was finally released on 5 June 1972. Involving him in a conspiracy case, which had to be dropped, also contributed to damaging the image of the Central government. Finally, Abdullah was reinstated as the chief minister with the support of the Congress Party!

Vajpayee's term as prime minister has gone down in history for the concerted efforts made by him to build bridges not just with Kashmir but also with Pakistan. Dulat in his book, *Kashmir: The Vajpayee Years,* has detailed extensively the efforts made by Prime Minister Vajpayee to commence a dialogue with the Hurriyat Conference, which was anathema till then. Vajpayee also visited Pakistan twice—first on 20 February 1999 on the bus trip between Delhi and Lahore. It was the first visit by an Indian Prime Minister to Pakistan after Rajiv Gandhi's visit in 1989 when the Lahore Declaration was signed. Vajpayee wrote in the visitor's book at Minar-e-Pakistan, the monument to Muslim League resolution of 23 March 1940 calling for the creation of a country for Muslims in the Indian subcontinent: 'A stable, secure and prosperous Pakistan is in India's interest. Let no one in Pakistan be in any doubt. India sincerely wishes Pakistan well.' Vajpayee had told Pakistan Prime Minister Nawaz Sharif, 'One can choose one's friends, but neighbours are permanent.' His hosts were overwhelmed (Dulat 2015, pp.17-18).

It was a travesty that when Vajpayee's Lahore visit was on, Pervez Musharraf, the then Army Chief, was planning the takeover of Kargil, ostensibly with the approval of Nawaz Sharif, which eventually led to the Kargil War! As if this was not enough, the terrorist attack on the J&K Assembly in Srinagar on 1 October 2001, and the attack on the Indian Parliament on 13 December 2001, with active help from Pakistan, brought home the point that it was futile to make any efforts to improve relations with Pakistan.

Dulat has further written: '[After the passing away of Vajpayee] Abdul Ghani Bhatt said, "if Vajpayee had [been given] time, India and Pakistan would be moving together today." My friend, co-author and former ISI Director-General, Gen. Asad Durrani, once remarked, "How Pakistan could do with Vajpayee as PM". Can we still doubt that Atalji's is the only way forward in Kashmir?' (*India Today*, 3 September 2018, p. 55).

Shakti Sinha, Vajpayee's private secretary, has recalled, 'Vajpayee seized upon Prime Minister Nawaz Sharif's interview, in which he said he would be happy to host Vajpayee in Lahore. Contrary to the MEA advice, which suggested a reaction only after a formal invitation was received, he said he would be happy to go to Lahore (*India Today*, 3 September 2018, p.

57). Rakesh Sood, a former diplomat, who was involved in arranging Vajpayee's Bus *Yatra* (ride) to Lahore, has written:

> Vajpayee spoke without a text at the civic reception and when he concluded by reciting the lines from his poem '*Jung na hone denge*' (we will not permit a war to take place), there was not a single dry eye in the audience. Sharif wisely refrained from a long response, merely telling him that Vajpayee could now well win an election in Pakistan too. (Ibid, p. 49)

Unfortunately this unforgettable attempt remained just that, and had no lasting impact on future India-Pakistan relations.

In an interview with *APN* editor-in-chief Rajshri Rai in Dubai in 2014, Musharraf had revealed that at the Agra Summit (2001),

> We had agreed to the LAC being the official border during our talks. But then entered Lal Krishna Advani and ruined the whole thing. I was very upset and wanted to return without meeting Atal *ji*. But my diplomatic team advised me to meet him before leaving. I asked him: "Is there anyone more important than you in India and Pakistan? But had I known this, I would have done my homework on that person." Atal *ji* remained silent, and then patting me, said that someday a solution would be found.... The best time for dialogue was when I was in talks with Vajpayee *ji*. I want both the countries to have strong and popular governments, so that their citizens accept their decisions. (*India Legal*, 10 September 2018, p. 23)

Speaking in Parliament on 4 November 1995, Prime Minister P.V. Narasimha Rao went as far as to say, 'Short of *Azadi* (independence), Constitution of India contains scope to permit autonomy to any limit.' Rao underlined that:

Kashmir was an integral part of India, Article 370 would not be abrogated, and autonomy of the state would be strengthened within the parameters of our Constitution, keeping in view the aspirations of the people, and with reference to all the regions of the state. The state was reassured that in case the state government came up with any proposal to change the central laws made after 1953 on matters in the Concurrent List, the grant of assent to the Bill would be sympathetically considered. Regarding nomenclature of the chief minister, if the state legislature amended the state Constitution to provide for the title "Wazir-e-Azam", we would have no objection; similarly as regards "Sadar-e-Riyasat", the state legislature might initiate action amending the state Constitution.[5] (Kashyap 2000, p. 261)

Thus, the GOI was prepared to go even beyond the 1975 Agreement between Indira Gandhi and Sheikh Abdullah, when such a change in the nomenclatures was not agreed to.

Narasimha Rao also took over the work of Kashmir affairs from the Ministry of Home Affairs and placed it in the Prime Minister's Office. In reality, it made no difference. Nothing significant was achieved.

As Dulat has written:

Linked to the Kashmir paralysis was the missed window of opportunity with Pakistan, when Musharraf was at the height of his power from 2004 to 2007. This is something Dr [Manmohan] Singh himself admitted at his last press conference on 3 June 2014: that there was a golden opportunity for a deal with Pakistan, particularly during the 2006-07 winter, that was missed. It all centred on what Musharraf himself in 2006 called his 'four-point formula' for Kashmir.... The formula was: making borders irrelevant by allowing free movement

---

5. These nomenclatures were changed to chief minister and Governor respectively in 1966 by amendment of the J&K Constitution.

of Kashmiris across the LOC; self-governance which meant autonomy but not independence; demilitarisation; and a mechanism for joint management. It had big implications for Pakistan's stand on Kashmir: it meant that the LOC was being accepted; that the long held demand for plebiscite would be set aside; that self-governance would replace the demand for self-determination; that Kashmiris would talk to Delhi; and that Kashmir was no longer the unfinished business of Partition.... After Musharraf no Pakistani picked up his four-point formula in fear that they would lose out in Kashmir.... The solution to the India-Pakistan-Kashmir Gordian knot was given to Dr Manmohan Singh on a platter in 2004. When he left office in 2014, he had not accomplished what was within his grasp. No wonder Kashmiris call his tenure their "lost decade".   (Dulat 2015, pp. 278, 285)

Manmohan Singh's 10 years in office as Prime Minister was a lost decade in another sense as well. He had taken a number of initiatives to look at some of the basic issues such as the welfare of minorities, and socio-economic factors holding back the development in J&K. As for the first, the Sachar Committee (2006) and Justice Ranganath Misra Commission (2007) had made very significant recommendations. Their implementation would have changed the social landscape of India but no action was taken on them. In fact, the reports were not even discussed in Parliament! The same was true in respect of J&K. As seen earlier, the report of the Group of Interlocutors was shelved without any action. The fate of a number of other reports was the same.

The Group of Interlocutors has stated that realizing the gravity of the prolonged turmoil in the state which led to misgovernance, economic frustration, and alienation among people, particularly the youth, the Central government undertook several diagnostic and prescriptive studies. On the basis of research findings, these studies tried to design policies and suggest implementation of strategies to redress the grievances of the people and to lay a strong foundation of infrastructure for faster economic growth. These studies were as follows:

- Report of the task force on development of J&K under the chairmanship of Dr C. Rangarajan, November 2006.
- Report of the working group on economic Development under the chairmanship of Dr C. Rangarajan, March 2007.
- Report of the working group on ensuring good governance under the chairmanship of N.C. Saxena, 2007.
- Report of the special task force on developmental needs of Ladakh region under the chairmanship of Dr Narendra Jadhav, January 2011.
- Report of the special task force to examine the developmental needs of Jammu region under the chairmanship of Dr Abhijit Sen, February 2011.
- Report of the state finance commission under the chairmanship of Dr Mehmood-ur-Rehman, November 2010.
- Report of the expert group on employment under the chairmanship of Dr C. Rangarajan.

Thus, in the five years from 2006 to 2011, at least seven comprehensive research and policy-oriented studies have been accomplished.... The recommendations were reported to be at various stages of implementation. But reliable evidence on the extent of implementation is lacking (Group of Interlocutors 2010, pp. 64-5).

Ahead of the first anniversary of abrogation of Article 370, Lieutenant Governor of the Union Territory of Jammu and Kashmir G. C. Murmu announced that nearly five years since the announcement of the Prime Minister's Development Package, only 49 per cent of the funds allocated towards 54 projects (excluding Ladakh) have been utilised. The package was announced by Prime Minister Narendra Modi at a rally in Srinagar on 7 November 2015. In the last about five years, only nine projects were completed and eight substantially completed (*The Indian Express*, 21 July 2020, p. 1). Thus, on both the fronts of political dialogue and economic development, matters continued to be in a drift.

Reference must also be made to the efforts made by Prime Minister Narendra Modi to improve relations with Pakistan. Modi invited the prime ministers of neighbouring countries for his oath-taking ceremony as prime minister in 2014 and held talks with Pakistan Prime Minister Nawaz Sharif in Delhi on 27 May 2014. He was also the first prime minister to pay a personal, informal visit to Pakistan to participate in Prime Minister Nawaz Sharif's family function on 25 December 2015. But these gestures too did not yield anything in terms of taking India-Pakistan relations to any higher level.

To reduce the feeling of alienation in J&K, Prime Minister V.P. Singh went out of his way to appoint Mufti Mohammad Sayeed as India's first Muslim Home Minister (1989). Earlier, he was tourism minister in the Rajiv Gandhi government (1986). Ghulam Nabi Azad, Farooq Abdullah and his son Omar Abdullah, Saifuddin Soz and several other Kashmiri leaders also worked as ministers at the Centre.

Over the years, persistent efforts were made by the GOI to hold elections not just for Parliament and state legislature but also for the local bodies in J&K. However, the turnout in these elections in the Kashmir valley has been most disappointing. In the municipal body elections held in October 2018, the turnout in the first phase was just 1.1 per cent in Anantnag, which is in the constituency of the former chief minister Mehbooba Mufti. For the valley as a whole, it was just 3.3 per cent, while there was nearly 80 per cent voting in Jammu. In the third phase, Srinagar recorded a turnout of 1.8 per cent, while 81 per cent voting was recorded in Jammu. Local polls ended with just 4.2 per cent turnout in the valley in the final phase. There was no candidate or there was no vote cast in many wards. Of the 149 wards in which polls were held in one of the four phases in the valley, no votes were cast in 92 wards and there were no candidates in 23 (*The Indian Express*, 9 October 2018, p. 1). Both the NC and the

PDP had given calls for boycott of polls of local bodies. The position in parliamentary polls was no different. Farooq Abdullah had been elected from Srinagar with just about 10 per cent of votes. The blame for this lies entirely on the political parties and other organisations like the Hurriyat for giving calls from time to time to boycott elections. As the adage goes, 'You can take a horse to water but you cannot make him drink'!

Pakistan – The Constant Instigator

The history of the Kashmir problem is replete with references to the devious role played by Pakistan. Below are some instances of its repeated references over the years.

After the war with Pakistan in 1965, the Tashkent Declaration was signed by India and Pakistan in which the following points were agreed to by both the nations: renunciation of force for settlement of disputes; non-interference in each other's affairs, and observance of ceasefire terms on the ceasefire line in J&K. During the negotiations, Prime Minister Lal Bahadur Shastri had emphasised the importance of renunciation of force and maintenance of good neighbourly relations so that both the countries might attend to their economic problems in peace. During the discussion in the Lok Sabha on 16 February 1966, members of several parties expressed reservations on whether Pakistan would abide by the terms of the agreement. Frank Anthony, for example, said Pakistan could not be expected to treat the Kashmir issue as India's internal affair. It would be unrealistic to believe that there was going to be any let-up, internal and external, on the part of Pakistan with regard to Kashmir (Kashyap 1996, pp. 26-29).

During the discussion in the Lok Sabha on the international situation on 22 December 1967, Indira Gandhi stoutly denied that she was being pressurised internationally on Kashmir. The government would not tolerate anyone dictating to her on Kashmir, she declared. Inder J. Malhotra 'flayed Pakistan for violating the terms of the Tashkent Declaration, and had demanded that relations with Pakistan should not be improved at the cost of the interest of the people of Jammu and Kashmir'. Intervening in the debate, Minister for Defence Swaran Singh had admitted, 'We cannot live in peace unilaterally.' Attitude of China and Pakistan was of continued hostility (Kashyap 1996, pp. 313-14, 318).

Making a statement in the Lok Sabha on 2 May 1990, External Affairs Minister I.K. Gujral reiterated India's stand that Pakistan's continued intervention in J&K and its support and encouragement to terrorism there, were not conducive to the maintenance of peace in the region and that such an approach would be detrimental to India-Pakistan relations. He stressed that adventurist brinkmanship on the part of Pakistan in relation to J&K could generate unpredictable events which might become uncontrollable. According to Gujral, Pakistan's Foreign Minister had denied that his country was encouraging subversion and terrorism in India (Kashyap 2000, p. 70).

On 20 August 1990, Saifuddin Soz demanded withdrawal of the Disturbed Areas Act. Chitta Basu (All India Forward Bloc leader) felt that the government should have a very firm Kashmir policy in the interest of the nation's security, unity and integrity. Replying to the discussion on 21 August 1990 in which 20 other members had participated, Home Minister Mufti Mohammad Sayeed said that Pakistan was planning to create insurgencies in Kashmir and making it difficult for the Indian forces to control the situation. The government had taken several steps to check infiltration and had taken action against those responsible (Kashyap 2000, p. 34).

Making a statement in the Lok Sabha on Foreign Secretary-level talks on 19 August 1992, Minister of State for External Affairs R.L. Bhatia stated that the Prime Ministers of India and Pakistan, during their meeting in Rio de Janeiro in June, had agreed that it was necessary to reduce tensions and set the bilateral dialogue back on track. During the course of the meeting, India had reiterated that Pakistan's continued support to terrorism and subversion and interference in India's internal affairs must be stopped (Kashyap 2000, p. 257).

The burning down of the highly revered Charar-e-Sharief mosque by terrorists led to angry reactions in the Lok Sabha. The matter was raised by way of an adjournment motion on 15 May 1995. Minister of State for External Affairs Salman Khursheed said that the situation in J&K could not be blamed entirely on any single event, person or decision. Prime Minister Narasimha Rao said the whole country was feeling the anguish of the disaster. Terrorists from Pakistan—trained, armed, funded and dispatched by Pakistan—were responsible for this tragedy (Kashyap 2000, pp. 258-9).

Prime Minister Narasimha Rao had, in his statement in the Lok Sabha on 4 November 1995, expressed the concern of the nation for the people of J&K and the aim and determination [of the government] to restore peace and democracy to that state which had been ravaged by terrorism, sponsored from across the border, for six years. The Prime Minister had appealed to all sections of the people of the state that they should firmly stand up to the terrorists and help in the process of bringing about peace and their own representative government.... On the question of financial package, it was stated that already 70 per cent of the funding of the entire expenditure of the state, both developmental and non-developmental came from the Centre...and the government would formulate [a package of] further financial and development benefits for the state in due course (Kashyap 2000, pp. 261-2).

Union Home Minister S.B. Chavan made a statement on J&K in the Lok Sabha on 28 November 1995 and said that the state had to be brought under President's Rule on 18 July 1990 *in the wake of large-scale violence and terrorism unleashed from across the border, which had led to a breakdown of the normal constitutional and administrative machinery in the state....* Pakistan was increasingly resorting to infiltration of its own and other foreign nationals into the state to try and take direct control of the so-called 'insurgency', since the local militancy was clearly on the wane.... The government had also decided to go in for elections of the state legislature in December 1995 (Kashyap 2000, pp. 259-61).

In his 1997 Independence Day address in Srinagar, Chief Minister Farooq Abdullah had stated that Pakistan had embarked upon a proxy war when it failed to achieve its designs by aggressions. 'Our youth were indoctrinated, misled, trained in terrorist activities and ultimately put on the path of destruction....' Blaming Pakistan for the troubles in the last eight years, he said that the 'Pakistan-sponsored militancy soaked the state in blood, with our hearts wounded and eyes full of tears'. Hardly any section of the population remained unaffected. Our intellectuals, academicians, religious leaders, scholars, professionals, literary personalities, media persons, public men and public servants, women and even children were not spared (*The Tribune*, 15 August 1997, p. 5).

The anti-India activities of the All Party Hurriyat Conference (APHC) were overlooked by India for years together, mainly with a view not to antagonise public opinion in Kashmir. These activities included receipt of funds from Pakistan and its funding of the agitations in the state. The latest in the series of such activities was the Pakistan medical colleges racket by which seats in these colleges were arranged by the Hurriyat Conference for Kashmiri students on payment of hefty capitation fees.

It is a travesty that Pakistan has been waging an undeclared 'thousand cuts' proxy war against India all these years. The last few years have seen increasing support for terrorist activities from Pakistan. As stated earlier, this was evident from the attack on the J&K Assembly in Srinagar on 1 October 2001 and on Parliament on 13 December 2001. This was followed by the attack on the Air Force base at Pathankot on 4 January 2016 by terrorists from across the border. Pakistan, as usual, denied their involvement in the attack. India took the very unusual step of inviting Pakistan security agencies to visit the site of the attack and see the evidence first hand. This gesture too did not serve any purpose.

After another terror attack on a CRPF convoy in Pulwama on 14 February 2019, in which 40 *jawans* [constables] died, India launched its first major surgical strike on Balakot to destroy a training camp for terrorists in Pakistan. The chargesheet filed by the NIA (National

Investigation Agency) in the Pulwama case in August 2020 has pinpointed how the Pulwama attack was a well-planned criminal conspiracy hatched by the Pakistan-based leadership of the terrorist organisation Jaish-e-Mohammed (JeM). It has listed key evidence including the 'forensically matched' voice of JeM chief Masood Azhar's brother Rauf Asghar discussing the attack, and the Pakistan government identity card issued to Azhar's nephew Mohammed Umar Farooq, the key conspirator (*The Indian Express*, 26 August 2020, p. 1). Pakistan had stoutly denied its involvement in the attack but its Science & Technology Minister Fawad Chaudhry said in the National Assembly during a debate on 29 October 2020: '*Humne Hindustan ko ghus ke maara* (We hit India in their home). Our success in Pulwama is a success of this nation under the leadership of Imran Khan. You and us are all part of that success.' Attempts were made by Pakistan to disrupt the elections to the District Development Councils which were to be held in November-December 2020. This was evident from the encounter of JeM terrorists by the Indian Army in Nagrota in Jammu on 19 November 2020. A large cache of weapons and explosives was recovered from them. Prime Minister Modi said this was a nefarious plot by Pakistan to target grassroots democracy in J&K.

Cross-border violations and firings by Pakistan have continued unabated. The ceasefire violations by Pakistan went up from 605 in 2019 to 930 in 2020. With Chinese aggressive postures in Ladakh, the spectre of fighting wars on two frontiers simultaneously is a worrying prospect for India.

India, in its generosity, had granted the Most Favoured Nation (MFN) status, providing for non-discriminatory access to its domestic markets, to Pakistan in 1996. Under the WTO norms, member countries are mandated to give this status to each other on a reciprocal basis but Pakistan had never extended the MFN status to India. After the Pulwama attack, this concession was withdrawn by India in 2019.

No stone has, thus, been left unturned by India to make Pakistan see reason. But, with the active support of China, Pakistan has got away without any international chastisement. With Pakistan's Afghanistan leverage, the United States too has not been a restraining force. In spite of India's persistent efforts, Pakistan has still not been blacklisted by the Paris-based global watchdog, Financial Action Task Force (FATF), and continues to be on its terror grey list since 2018, mainly due to the strong support of China and the soft-peddling by the United States. The games played by foreign powers have continued to this day.

A Litany of Blunders

The above discussion brings out the series of blunders made by the Government of India in dealing with the Kashmir problem.[6] Satya Pal Malik, the erstwhile Governor of J&K, had admitted as such when he said, 'India's mistakes alienated J&K, my job is to make space for talks.... India is being presented as an occupation force. But Kashmir is not an occupied territory. It came to us of its own free will' (*The Indian Express*, 4 October 2016, p. 1). However, no talks ensued during Malik's term.

India is clearly in a cul-de-sac. *First*, Kashmir should have been left to be dealt with by the States Ministry under Vallabhbhai Patel who had brought about the integration of 553 princely states in the shortest possible time. V. Shankar, ICS, Private Secretary of Vallabhbhai Patel, has written, 'Kashmir was an emotional issue with the Prime Minister. Gopalaswami had a Kashmir past of his own; only Sardar could bring to bear on the problem an outside view, to some extent, however, conditioned by his own views on Muslim politics (V. Shankar 1997, p. 222). It is not clear how Patel would have solved the Kashmir problem but, looking to the immense role played by Patel in safeguarding Kashmir's future in the initial years, as brought out by Balraj Krishna, it would be safe to say that Patel would not have given in where Kashmir's integration with India

---

6. B. K. Nehru, who was the Governor of J&K from 1981 to 1984, has written in his autobiography: 'From 1953 to 1975, the chief ministers…had been nominees of Delhi. Their appointment to that post was legitimised by the holding of farcical and totally rigged elections in which the Congress Party led by Delhi's nominee was elected by huge majorities' (Nehru 1997, p. 614).

was concerned. Of course, there was no escape from Nehru handling the subject after Patel's demise in December 1950.

Second, there are reasons to believe that it was at the instance of Sheikh Abdullah that Nehru decided to divest Patel of the charge of Kashmir. It was quite clear that Patel did not trust Sheikh Abdullah and would not have given him a free hand, as Nehru did.[7]

Third, as seen in the section 'The Kashmir Imbroglio' (in Chapter 2), the acceptance of Maharaja Hari Singh's request for accession to India was made unnecessarily controversial by linking it with the GOI's intention of holding a plebiscite. This gave an opportunity to Pakistan (and some other countries sympathetic to it) to raise questions about the validity of accession. But later, the idea of plebiscite being unworkable was given up and concerted efforts were made by India for the partition of J&K. These too did not succeed.

Fourth, when it was intended to hold a plebiscite to ascertain the wishes of the people on accession of the state to India, there was no need to agree to a separate Constitution for J&K.[8] This was not agreed to by the GOI in the case of any other state, even bigger than J&K. But, step by step, Sheikh Abdullah led India towards his goal of confining J&K's integration only to the three subjects listed in the Instrument of Accession. And, knowingly or unknowingly, India walked into the trap.

Fifth, Nehru's excessive reliance on Mountbatten led to a number of wrong decisions such as stopping the Indian Army from taking over all areas of J&K in possession of Pakistan, giving up the idea of authorising strikes against the raiders' camps in Pakistan, and, most importantly, referring the question of Pakistan's aggression on Kashmir to the UN.

---

7. Rajmohan Gandhi has written, 'Viewing Abdullah as the key to Kashmir's future and believing that Patel would mishandle him, Jawaharlal decided to manage Kashmir himself' (Gandhi 1990, p. 446). According to Balraj Krishna, Nehru was acting under Abdullah's influence (Krishna 2005, p. 388).

8. Even in the case of Hyderabad, the GOI had agreed that its accession would be provisional and subject to the ratification by the people of Hyderabad (Munshi 2013, p. 475). But it was given up later.

Sixth, it was a mistake not to clearly name Pakistan as an aggressor in the complaint to the United Nations. In his press conference, Nehru had stated, 'We have deliberately not asked that Pakistan should be declared an aggressor or sanctions should be imposed because that is not in our opinion the way to seek a settlement' (*JNMF*, vol. 16, 1994, p. 363), though in its complaint to the Security Council, India had said: 'The GOI request the Security Council to call upon Pakistan to put an end immediately to the giving of such assistance which was an act of aggression against India.' The complaint had also stated: That the invaders were allowed transit across Pakistan territory; that they were allowed to use Pakistan territory as a base of operations; that they included Pakistan nationals; that they drew much of their military equipment, transportation and supplies (including petrol) from Pakistan; and that Pakistan officers were training, guiding and otherwise actively helping them. In spite of this enunciation, in the hearings before the UN, India was often made to look like the guilty party, guilty of taking the law into its hand. As Srivastava has said, 'In the Security Council, the petitioner became virtually the accused' (Srivastava 1996, p. 151).

Sheikh Abdullah has shed a new light on the Pakistan tribals' invasion in his book, *Flames of the Chinar*:

> Pakistan had made several manoeuvres to occupy Kashmir. Their prime reason was the fear that Afghanistan may incite the tribals to attack Pakistan and, therefore, their attention had to be diverted. Abdul Qayyum Khan, the Chief Minister of the NWFP at the time, was the mastermind behind all this. He was a lawyer of Kashmiri stock, who had earlier joined the Khudai Khidmatgars of Khan Ghaffer Khan, and had risen to become Deputy Leader of the Congress Parliamentary Party in the Central Legislative Assembly. *At first M.A. Jinnah was not in favour of the tribal raids* but Abdul Qayyum Khan managed to persuade him. After destroying Kashmir, when they reached Rawalpindi, the raiders started repeating their

antics. When the public raised hell they were hurriedly shoved back into their mountain homes. *In May 1964, when I visited Pakistan, I discussed the events of 1947 with President Ayub Khan, who sadly confessed that Abdul Qayyum Khan had dreamt of becoming the king of Kashmir and, it was his overwhelming desire which caused this madness.* (Sheikh Abdullah 1993, pp. 103-4)

The veracity of this version needs to be ascertained from independent sources, as it could have been floated to discredit Khan Abdul Ghaffar Khan and his Khudai Khidmatgar.

Seventh, relying excessively on Sheikh Abdullah to the extent of stating in the UN that India had agreed to the accession of J&K mainly because of the support extended by Sheikh Abdullah. Strictly, under the provisions of the Indian Independence Act, 1947, all that was required for accession to be accomplished was a request by the state's ruler to accede and the acceptance of the request by the Governor General. In the process, the position of the GOI became untenable when Sheikh Abdullah started speaking about Kashmir's limited accession and even independence, and the authority of the state to set its own policies on all matters not falling in the purview of the Instrument of Accession.

Eighth, the Delhi Agreement was the prime culprit in creating the Kashmir problem. Almost everything in it became contentious. It was unbelievable but Nehru agreed to practically everything Sheikh Abdullah pressed for. It was all the more surprising that it was *ostensibly* the decision of the Cabinet committee, and not of Nehru alone! Looking to the sensitivity of the issues and the likely controversy, Nehru had taken the very unusual step of associating the Cabinet committee in the negotiations with Sheikh Abdullah and his team. However, with Nehru's towering personality, the other members of the Cabinet committee must have been overly influenced.

Ninth, the repeated arrests of Sheikh Abdullah and his detention for nearly 11 years raised serious questions about India's credibility.

Tenth, several pronouncements and statements by the GOI in Parliament regarding Article 370 created the wrong impression that the Article was being grossly misused. One such statement was by Union Home Minister Gulzarilal Nanda that this Article was a tunnel through which the Indian Constitution was being extended to J&K! In fact, as declared by the Supreme Court, Article 370 was a deliberate device created in the Constitution for extending the provisions of the Indian Constitution to J&K. There was nothing surreptitious about it.

Eleventh, a valuable opportunity was lost in 1972 for solving the Kashmir problem, once and for all, during the negotiations on the Simla Agreement by converting the LOC into an international border.

Twelfth, the second opportunity was when the 1975 agreement between Indira Gandhi and Sheikh Abdullah was signed. The abolition of Article 370 could have been pressed for acceptance at that time. Instead, it was specifically agreed that Article 370 would continue. This was clearly opposed to the provisions of the Constitution which had termed it as a temporary provision. It would have been logical to get its abolition agreed to by Sheikh Abdullah, who was responsible for its inclusion.

Thirteenth, the third opportunity was when President Musharraf suggested his four-point programme in 2006. This too was lost by India's ineptitude.

Fourteenth, treating the insurgency with kid gloves for too long was one of the main reasons for the continued violence in J&K. Farooq Abdullah, the erstwhile Chief Minister, and Rajesh Pilot, the then Minister of State for Internal Security in the Ministry of Home Affairs, were fond of describing the terrorists as 'misguided youth', though they were being properly trained, financed and guided from across the border by Pakistan. Farooq Abdullah had also said that 'the militancy was on the wane' (*The Tribune*, 15 August 1997, p. 5). Foreign funding which was largely responsible for the insurgency, stone-throwing episodes and agitations was, till recently, not put down with a firm hand. A private member's bill on making Sharia law applicable in the state was passed in the J&K legislature, despite points raised about its larger consequences (*The Indian Express*, 10 February 2007, p. 2).

Fifteenth, deployment of the army for years together in the Kashmir valley has given the impression that it is an occupation army. I have been advocating for quite some time that the army should be withdrawn from civilian areas and moved to the outer peripheries and the border, and the role of looking after civilian areas should be entrusted to the Central paramilitary forces, supplemented by the state's armed police, and the armed police of other states, if necessary.

Sixteenth, the Armed Forces (J&K) Special Powers Act, 1990 (AFSPA), giving special powers and protection to the armed forces, has become highly controversial. Understandably, it has not been possible for the Central government to repeal or amend the Act. If the above suggestion to withdraw the army from civilian areas is implemented, this major irritant will go away.

Seventeenth, Pakistan's role in instigating, funding and supporting the insurgency in J&K must be addressed with a new sense of urgency. The issue needs to be resolved by discussion with Pakistan. The GOI's stand that there can be no dialogue with Pakistan till it gives up its role in terror attacks is proving counterproductive. Efforts must also be continued to bring international pressure on Pakistan, for whatever it is worth. *India must also use other leverages available to it to make a headway in finding a permanent solution.*

What Does The Future Hold?

At long last, with the abrogation of Article 370, the last hurdle in the integration of J&K has been removed. The division of J&K into two Union Territories became effective on 31 October 2019.

Dr Aman Hingorani, eminent lawyer and author of *Unravelling the Kashmir Knot*, has in an extensive interview to *The Indian Express* (1 September 2019, p. 11) argued, 'It is New Delhi which has defined the constitutional relationship between India and the state, and not the state defining its constitutional relationship with India.' But, as seen from the above discussion, this was the contentious issue all along. In any case, it will be far from the truth to say that, even after making Article 370 inoperative, there is an emotional integration or bonding between the Kashmir valley and India. This was never a problem with Jammu and Ladakh regions.

Public reaction to the abrogation of Article 370 has been muted in the valley mainly due to the complete political vacuum created by the GOI by keeping leaders of non-BJP parties under preventive detention for months together. Invocation of the provisions of the Public Safety Act against top leaders and political workers, including the three former Chief Ministers—Farooq Abdullah, his son Omar Abdullah, and Mehbooba Mufti—and keeping them under detention for months together was totally indefensible. Mufti was the last to be released, after 14 months, on 13 October 2020. It is shocking that Mehbooba Mufti has been denied passport on the ground that her travel abroad would be 'detrimental to the security of India'. The Supreme Court had held in *Maneka Gandhi v. Union of India* (AIR 1978 SC 597) that a citizen's passport cannot be impounded for an indefinite period of time. To get over this difficulty, the reason of security of India seems to have been put forward. It is difficult to believe that a former chief minister of a state can be a threat to national security. This shows the insecurity of the ruling establishment in Delhi. Such short-sighted actions of the GOI are self-defeating.

Severe restrictions on social media and the press are still continuing. The new media policy framed by the J&K administration in June 2020 is harsh. Arbitrary denial of internet facilities is difficult to justify. This oppressive atmosphere must be done away with at the earliest. Prime Minister Modi's new *mantra* for Kashmir, '*Vikas* and *Vishwas*' (development and trust), needs to be translated into reality. Otherwise, it will remain just a political rhetoric.

Unfounded fears were being entertained that with the abrogation of Article 35A non-Kashmiris will make inroads and take away the land and employment opportunities from the locals. The recent data show that of the 3.7 lakh persons who have been given domicile certificates, 78 per cent are from the Jammu region (*The Indian Express*, 1 August 2020, p. 1).

The PDP-BJP coalition government which was in power from February 2015 to July 2019 was a major step forward in 'bringing North Pole and South Pole together' (*The Indian Express*, 28 February 2015, p. 1), However, Mehbooba Mufti, on taking oath as Chief Minister, said, 'It was like drinking a cup of poison' (*The Indian Express*, 29 July 2018, p. 5). A similar effort made some years earlier with the Congress and the NC joining hands demolished the credibility of the NC. To some extent, this was repeated in the recent coalition of the PDP and the BJP.

The Kashmir chapter in India's history can never be complete without discussion of the massive extermination and exodus of Pandit families from the Valley starting from the late 1980s, brought out by Ashok Bhan, senior advocate, Supreme Court and a displaced Kashmiri Pandit (*The Sunday Guardian*, 20-26 September 2020, p. 13).

Sheikh Abdullah has devoted a chapter in his book to 'The Role of Kashmiri Pandits'. He has stated:

Although they constitute a microscopic minority, their influence is widespread. In fact, during different periods of history, they were used as instruments of tyranny.... The Mughal rulers of India won over the loyalty of the Kashmiri Pandits and *used them as informers and spies against the Muslim nobility*.... They bitterly opposed the 'Quit Kashmir' movement against the Maharaja.... With their superb capabilities, the Pandits can serve as a bridge between Kashmir and the rest of the country.' (Sheikh Abdullah 1993, pp. 170-2)

As seen in the section on the Simla Accord in Chapter 2, Karan Singh too had expressed his apprehensions about the role of Pandits.

In the Muslim majority areas in the valley, Pandits were the minority Hindus. Nearly 60,000 Kashmiri Pandit families are registered as migrants after the onset of militancy in the valley. For the last 30 years they are leading the lives of refugees in their own country. Farooq Abdullah, who was the chief minister of J&K thrice, has demanded a probe by a retired judge of the Supreme Court into the exodus of Kashmiri Pandits. 'It will clear many minds around the globe that it was not Kashmiri Muslims who threw them out' (*The Indian Express*, 3 August 2020, p. 2). Several questions arise from this statement. Why is Farooq Abdullah talking about such an inquiry now? He could have easily appointed such a committee during his long tenure as chief minister. If local Muslims were not responsible for their exodus, who was responsible? He holds former Governor of J&K Jagmohan Malhotra responsible for exodus—'He took them away' on the false promise of ensuring their return within three months. Justice Sachar, in his book *In Pursuit of Justice: An Autobiography*, has stated, 'I personally think that Jagmohan's strategy was a mistake. It made it all too easy to communalize the situation and created all sorts of problems' (p. 216). Why did Abdullah not have this enquired into when he was the Chief Minister? Why could he not help create a congenial atmosphere for their return and rehabilitation? Silence on these questions is deafening! It is some consolation that the GOI has now decided to resettle all displaced Kashmiri Pandits in the valley by 2022 (*The Sunday Guardian*, 14-20 February 2021, p. 1). Let us hope this gets translated into reality.

As stated earlier, the grievances of J&K are no different than those of other states in the country. They include electoral malpractices, the often partisan role played by the Governor, and misuse of powers by the Central government, including the provisions of Article 356 of the Constitution. Answers to these have to be found urgently on an all-India basis. But this cannot be a ground for asking for special treatment for J&K, as a section of Kashmiri leaders have been doing. The keenness to maintain separate identity is not of J&K alone. It is so in every state, as can be seen from discussion in the following Chapter 4. If harnessed properly, this can be India's strength.

The financial distress of the state was articulated at length by the

Committee on Economic Reforms for J&K (1998), of which I was the Chairman. The committee, in its 350-page report, had asked the state government to set its house in order and had also suggested some relief to be given by the Central government. The state government declined to take any remedial steps and instead took the stand that the Centre alone could save it ('Blaming each other', *The Indian Express*, 28 October 1998, p. 9). This was nothing new. With large assistance from the Centre, J&K has consistently taken a soft line on economic reforms.

Denying internet access to Kashmir valley for months together had come in for considerable criticism both in India and abroad. In view of the improved security situation, 4G mobile internet services were restored in the whole UT after a lapse of 18 months on 4 February 2020. The security concerns in regard to misuse of social media, not only in J&K but also in other parts of the country, need to be addressed without loss of time. Repeated stone-throwing episodes in J&K were ascribed to misuse of social media. The communal riots in North East Delhi in February 2020 were also partly due to large-scale misuse of social media. Cases of lynching in several parts of the country were due to the deliberate spread of false stories through social media. In this context, the suggestion made by Pavan Duggal, Supreme Court lawyer and President of Cyberlaw Asia, deserves serious consideration: 'We need new India-specific laws that will tackle challenges thrown by social media and over-the-top (OTT) applications like WhatsApp. Existing cyber laws predate social media and cannot deal with these challenges' (*India Today*, 23 July 2018, 50-1). The GOI has announced a new policy on the subject which has been challenged in at least two high courts. The Supreme Court has also expressed reservations on the adequacy of the policy to deal with the situation effectively.

Looked at in the larger perspective, the Kashmir question opened up a debate on the basic issues of Centre-state relations. Reference may be made in this context to how Nehru too was debating these issues with himself when the Delhi Agreement was under discussion. In a note recorded on

3 July 1952, Nehru wrote: 'Must all constituent units of the Republic of India have exactly the same relation to the Union, as embodied in our Constitution and various Lists of subjects, or can there be a variation?.... This is not a practical proposition and, even from the larger point of view, it is desirable to have a certain flexibility in our Constitution (*JNMF* vol. 18, 1996, pp. 423-5).

Interestingly, these musings of Nehru were within just about two years of the adoption of the Constitution of which he was one of the prime architects. The implications of what Nehru was advocating are huge. Most importantly, it would imply a loose federation (and not a union of states), with arrangement between each state and the Union being worked out on a case-by-case basis. It would also detract from the proposition of having a strong Centre on which the Constitution is based. It would give leverage to the states to bargain for the best terms for their association with the Union. The Delhi Agreement is an apt example of what such a policy would imply. One can imagine such agreements being entered into with various states. I have serious reservations on adoption of such a policy. It is bound to lead to disintegration of the Indian Union. Therefore, any discussion with states for greater powers and autonomy must be held within the boundaries of the Constitution. There has been an agreement among all major political parties in this regard as seen from the way they have dealt with the Kashmir problem when in power in the GOI. The abrogation of Article 370 is a reflection of the same policy. B.K. Nehru had written: 'The long-term aim of India should be the full integration of the people of J&K with the people of India' (B.K. Nehru 1997, p. 592). This has at last been achieved.

Serious thought now needs to be given to normalising the situation in Kashmir valley. After the abrogation of Article 370, constitutionally, Kashmir's integration is now complete. But, emotionally, has the valley bonded with India? The answer will have to be categorical 'No'. The spate of killings of BJP functionaries since July 2020 is a deliberate attempt by secessionists and Pakistan to delay the process of normalisation. I would suggest the following 12-point programme towards this end.

1. Jammu and the Kashmir valley must be given full statehood. This will restore the dignity and status it had enjoyed till August 2019 when it was converted into a Union Territory, and will mend the hurt public feelings. But this is unlikely till the delimitation of Assembly constituencies is given effect to. This process needs to be expedited. Unfortunately, some political parties seem to be abstaining from the deliberations of the Delimitation Commission on the plea that their petitions against the abrogation of Article 370 are still pending in the Supreme Court. The LG of J&K has said, 'Those demanding early Assembly elections must cooperate with the Delimitation Commission for completion of the exercise at the earliest (*The Indian Express*, 23 February 2021, p. 7).

2. Ladakh should continue as a Union Territory, particularly in view of its strategic location and China's recent aggressive postures. As brought out earlier, Ladakh was always unhappy as a part of J&K state and felt that it was being neglected and its development needs were being overlooked.

3. A time-bound plan must be prepared for the withdrawal of the army from the civilian areas of J&K, in consultation with all political parties. The army is also generally reluctant to take up the task of tackling counter-insurgency operations in civilian areas, except as a short-term measure. As GOC of Indian Army's Srinagar-based 15 Corps Lt Gen. Anil Kumar Bhatt has said, 'We will go back to barracks once things stabilise.... Even in Punjab, we pulled out as soon as the situation stabilised. We have reduced our footprints in Mizoram and Tripura and we'll do so.... as the situation improves' (*Outlook*, 27 August 2018, p. 20). The responsibility of stabilising the situation is entirely in the hands of the government, political parties and the civil society. It is only through political dialogue and enunciation of appropriate policy

measures that this can be brought about. But for this to become possible, a dialogue is necessary between the government on the one side, and political parties and civil society on the other.

Fortunately, the situation was better on all parameters in 2020. While there were 584 law and order incidents in 2019, the figure came down to 143 in 2020. Militancy-related incidents also came down to 243 in 2020 from 255 of 2019. While 157 militants were killed in 2019, the figure rose to 222 in 2020. However, militant recruitment went up from 143 in 2019 to 174 during the year. Also, during the year 2020, more than 12 political activists, most of them belonging to the BJP, were killed by militants (*The Week*, 6 December 2020, p. 27).

4. An open offer could be made by the government that withdrawal of the military from the civilian areas would be done, on an experimental basis, if maintenance of peace is ensured by the people at large. During this period, the law and order duties may be entrusted to the state police, supplemented by the Central paramilitary forces. If necessary, armed police of other states may be requisitioned for deployment in J&K.

5. A country can choose its friends but it cannot choose its neighbours. All efforts made in the past to partition J&K have failed. Pakistan is hell-bent on getting the Kashmir valley. In a sense, it's an existential fight for the Pakistan Army which is spearheading the insurgency in Kashmir. Once the Kashmir problem is settled, the hold of the Pakistan Army on the country's policies will be greatly reduced. However, significantly, Pakistan Army Chief General Qamar Javed Bajwa has made a plea to bury the past and to move forward (*The Indian Express*, 19 March 2021, p. 1). The leaders of BJP and its affiliate organisations must also stop issuing statements about their dream of *Akhand Bharat* (united India) comprising India, Pakistan, Bangladesh, and Afghanistan which have created legitimate fears and insecurities

about India's intentions. No sane person should ask for India's unification with these countries. The problem has become more complex with China's entry in the J&K conundrum. A national consensus needs to be evolved on how to deal with Pakistan. Among an array of other measures, dialogue needs to be resumed with Pakistan, supplemented by international pressure to prevail on Pakistan to stop its support to insurgency and terrorist activities from within its borders.

6. A time-bound programme must be worked out for using other leverages such as the earliest use of the waters allotted to India under the Indus Water Treaty.

7. Leaders of political parties and organisations still under detention should be released immediately. Cases against other persons jailed for their involvement in agitations, stone-throwing incidents, etc. should be reviewed with a view to effecting their release. Only those involved in acts of terror, violence or support to insurgency should be continued in detention.

8. Fortunately, the elections to the District Development Councils (DDCs) were conducted smoothly at the end of 2020. J&K had deliberately delayed the ushering in of democratic decentralisation, though the Constitution of J&K contained a specific provision for empowerment of village panchayats. The committee on economic reforms for J&K (1998) under my chairmanship had made a series of recommendations in this regard, which remained unimplemented. On paper, there were enactments in place, which included the J&K Panchayat Raj Act, 1989, and the J&K State Finance Commission Act, 2011. The committee on devolution of powers to the panchayats (2011) had also made some pertinent recommendations. But due to lack of implementation, there was no impact on ground. Village panchayat elections were first held in 1971. Thereafter they were held for some panchayats only in 2011. For the remaining

panchayats, they were held in 2018, but were boycotted by the National Conference and the Peoples Democratic Party (PDP). The 73rd amendment of the Constitution became applicable in J&K after a lapse of 28 years and elections were held to the newly created DDCs, *Halqa* (area) panchayats, and block development councils in December 2020. Against this background, it was surprising to see Haseeb A Drabu, former finance minister of J&K, in his article 'Junior MLA, senior Panch' in *The Indian Express* (24 December 2020, p. 8) totally misrepresenting the facts and calling it 'a framework of disempowerment'. The DDC elections were a welcome development. Grassroots democracy has to be established and nurtured, if the superstructure of democratic governance at the state and national levels is to be sustained. The issues of autonomy of state, preserving the identity of the state, and special status for the state are certainly important but they do not fall in the jurisdiction of the local bodies at the district and lower levels. It is immaterial how many DDCs are controlled by the Gupkar Alliance and how many by the BJP. What matters is that after a long time, elections in J&K were held without calls for boycott and without any violence. There cannot be a greater encouraging indicator of normalisation of the situation in the state.

9. This process of normalisation can be facilitated only if a number of restrictions currently in operation in the state are lifted at the earliest, as a conscious policy. The media must not only be permitted but also be encouraged to operate freely. An important element of this has to be the policy on government advertisements. This is particularly relevant in the post-Covid-19 period of economic slowdown and other hardships. It is necessary that the advertisement policy is transparent. Locking up the premises of the *Kashmir Times*, which was somewhat critical of the government, has sent a very wrong message.

10. Emotional, cultural and social bonds need to be built between the people of J&K and the rest of the country. Conscious efforts need to be made for the purpose at non-government level.

11. Kashmir's problems and development needs have been examined closely by a number of high-level expert committees. Their recommendations have, however, largely remained on paper. A dialogue should be started with all stakeholders to give a fillip to the time-bound implementation of these recommendations. Improving investment climate in the state has to be an important element of any new strategy.

12. Basically, the task of bringing the Kashmir valley into the mainstream of the country has remained incomplete. This should not be left to the government alone. The role of the private sector will be important in these endeavours. It is a challenge which must be accepted nationally by the civil society at large and political parties of all hues.

This war for integration, peace and normalcy is more difficult than even the proxy war which India has been fighting in Kashmir for several decades. It implies building bridges of trust. This is going to be a long haul. There are no easy, ready-made solutions. This onerous task can be achieved only if India speaks with one voice and rises unitedly.

4

Other Major Fault Lines

Introduction

In this chapter, we shall discuss five major fault lines—namely, intermixing of religion and politics; linguistic states; growth of sub-nationalism; the Frankenstein of domiciliary requirements; and the official language. Their potential capacity for damage is substantial but sadly, there is very little awareness, leave aside understanding, of the gravity and the imminent dangers these fault lines pose for India's federalism. Finding remedies for these fault lines is a challenge which will call for ingenuity, far-sightedness and statesmanship of the highest order.

Intermixing Religion and Politics

While the Constitution was in the making, at a press conference in Delhi on 12 October 1947, Nehru had said: 'We cannot think of any state which might be called communal or religious state. We can only think of a secular, non-communal, democratic state in which every individual to whatever religion he may belong, has equal rights and opportunities' (Dhavan and Paul 1992, p. 164).

With the Partition of the country and the holocaust accompanying it, communalism was the foremost concern of the Constituent Assembly. In the Constituent Assembly (Legislative), a resolution was moved on 3 April 1948 by M. Ananthasayanam Ayyangar (who was later the first Speaker of the Lok Sabha) to ban communal parties. Ayyangar proposed that it was time to separate religion from politics. There was an almost unanimous acceptance of the resolution barring the single dissenting note of Ishaq Seth.

Nehru welcomed the resolution and said that:

> The government would do everything in their power to achieve the objective behind the resolution.... There might have been in the past various reasons which came in the way of such policy being given effect to, although I think even *in the past those of us who accepted any measure of communalism erred and acted unwisely, and we have suffered greatly for our unwisdom.* The combination of politics and religion in the narrowest sense of the word resulting in communal politics was a *most dangerous combination and must be put an end to....* This Resolution mentions administrative and legislative measures to be taken to give effect to it.... The right course for the government will be to consider this matter and to see what administrative and—more specially—what legislative measures are necessary to gain this end; and then later when this House meets again for another session, to consider any recommendations in that respect as far as legislative measures are concerned.... Meanwhile, no doubt our new Constitution will have taken shape also and it will help us then to consider those legislative measures in terms of that new Constitution. *But we need not wait till then.* (GOI 1949, pp. 47-9)

H.V. Kamath asserted that he would yield to none in his 'desire to see the early liquidation of those communal organisations which have become a cancer eating into the vitals of our body politic, which have rent our motherland in twain and which led to the martyrdom of Mahatma Gandhi. These calamities have overtaken us because these communal organisations have functioned on a political plane'.

Shyama Prasad Mookerjee emphasised that it was

> no use passing a pious resolution; if we are really anxious to uproot communalism from the political sphere in India altogether, we will have to see that there is no place for communalism of any kind whatsoever in the Constitution of our country. You cannot justify reservation on ground of religion or caste and in the same breath say that you want to banish communalism from the political life of India. (Kashyap 1994: pp. 321-2)

It was significant that Mookerjee, the only member representing the Hindu Mahasabha, did not oppose the resolution but his reference to reservation based on castes was confounding since the resolution was meant to address inter-religious communal strife and not caste-based differences.

Finally, the following resolution was passed:

> Whereas it is essential for the proper functioning of democracy and the growth of national unity and solidarity that communalism should be eliminated from Indian life, this assembly is of opinion that no communal organisation which by its constitution or by the exercise of discretionary power vested in any of its officers and organs, admits to or excludes from its membership persons on grounds of religion, race and caste, or any of them should be permitted to engage in any activities other than those essential for the bonafide religious, cultural, social and educational needs of the community, and that all steps, legislative and administrative, necessary to prevent such activities should be taken.

Since the Constituent Assembly was deliberating on the Constitution at the time, a suitable provision could have been made at least in the Directive Principles of State Policy, to begin with, leaving it to the government to take appropriate constitutional and legislative steps later, after wider consultations. This would have given the concept a constitutional status. It appears from Nehru's speech that he was serious about it and wanted to take further action without loss of time. But, inexplicably, no follow-up action was taken during his 17-year tenure as prime minister and the Constitution is also silent on the subject.

Any such constitutional amendment now would have to be passed by a two-thirds majority in both Houses of Parliament. Thereafter, the bill will also have to be ratified by half the state legislatures. This would have been possible only when Jawaharlal Nehru, Indira Gandhi or Rajiv Gandhi were prime ministers. In spite of the massive mandate they enjoyed, the Congress Party's proclaimed commitment to secularism, and Nehru's strong support to Ayyangar's resolution, no steps were taken by any of them to separate religion from politics. This speaks volumes. Inevitably the question arises, 'What was the politics of it all?' The only conclusion one can draw is that these three strong prime ministers, with huge national popularity and parliamentary majorities, were not sure whether the proposal would be acceptable to their own party!

Rajiv Gandhi's tenure was noteworthy in this regard. In the 1984 election held after the tragic assassination of Indira Gandhi, Rajiv Gandhi had won an unprecedented three-fourths majority (401 seats), creating history by surpassing the record of 371 seats won by the undivided Congress Party under Nehru in 1957. Unfortunately, he used this mandate to pander to the demands of fundamentalists in both the Muslims and the Hindus by enacting the Muslim Women's (Protection of Right on Divorce) Act and opening of locks of the Ram temple in the Babri Masjid in Ayodhya, thereby showing how religion could be used to further the cause of politics.

The situation has degenerated over the years due to the menace of religious fundamentalism increasing enormously in all religions. The issues pertaining to secularism came to the fore prominently after the demolition of the Babri Masjid on 6 December 1992 and the country-wide communal riots which followed. As I have discussed in detail in my book, *The Babri Masjid-Ram Mandir Dilemma—An Acid Test for India's Constitution,* (2019), the GOI failed to protect the Masjid, in spite of information available to it that the government of Uttar Pradesh was not inclined to take any steps to do so. Along with the Masjid, the secular credentials of the Narasimha Rao Government too were shattered.

To rehabilitate its image, the Rao government on 29 July 1993 introduced two bills in Parliament for delinking religion from politics. The first related to the amendment of the Constitution to provide that the State shall have respect for all religions, and to confer power on Parliament to ban any association or body of individuals if it promotes or attempts to promote disharmony or feeling of enmity, hatred or ill-will between different classes of citizens on grounds of religion, race, place of birth, residence, language, caste or community. The bill further provided that making use of religion, including religious symbols, for the purpose of getting elected to Parliament or state legislature or promoting or attempting to promote feeling of enmity, hatred or ill-will would be a ground for disqualification.

The second bill was to amend the Representation of the People Act (RPA) so as to provide that no association or body shall be registered by the Election Commission of India as a political party if the association or body bears a religious name, since such a religious name could be said to contain an appeal to vote for the political party on grounds of religion which would be detrimental to the cause of secular democracy. A provision was also proposed under which a complaint could be made to the high court within whose jurisdiction the main office of the political party is situated, for cancelling the registration of the political party where such political party bears a religious name or the memorandum or the rules and regulations of the political party no longer conform to the proposed provisions. A time limit of 90 days was laid down within which political parties with religious names would be required to change such names and conform to the new law.

These bills were, however, introduced in Parliament without any effort to build a consensus on the relevant issues among political parties. Clearly, the government did not want to share the credit for the proposed amendments with the political parties. As was to be expected, both the bills met with stiff resistance, not just from political parties in the Opposition but also the media, intellectuals and a large cross-section of society. As a result, the move was shelved by withdrawing the bills (Kashyap 1993, pp. 51-63).

The importance of this subject is borne out by the following judgment of the Supreme Court. In *Ebrahim Sulaiman Sait v. M.C. Mohammed and Anr (AIR 1980 SC 354)*, the court had observed,

Reading the speech as a whole it cannot be denied that its tone is communal, *but in this country communal parties are allowed to function in politics.* That being so, how an appeal to the voters, such as the one made in the speech in question should be viewed in the context of corrupt practices mentioned in the Act, has been explained by Gajendragadkar, C.J., speaking for the court in *Kultar Singh v. Mukhtiar Singh*: "It is well known that there are several [political] parties in this country which subscribe to different political and economic ideologies, but their membership is confined to, or predominantly held by, members of particular communities or religions. *So long as law does not prohibit the formation of such parties and in fact recognises them for the purpose of election and parliamentary life, it would be necessary to remember that an appeal made by such candidates of such parties for votes may, if successful, lead to their election and in an indirect way, may conceivably be influenced by considerations of religion, race, caste, community or language. This infirmity cannot perhaps be avoided so long as parties are allowed*

> *to function and are recognised, though their composition may be predominantly based on membership of particular communities or religion".*

This helplessness of the highest court of the land is telling.

Another important judgment of the Supreme Court was in *S.R. Bommai v. Union of India* (AIR 1994 SC 2092). While dealing, inter alia, with the case of the dismissal of the three state governments of Madhya Pradesh, Himachal Pradesh and Rajasthan by the Centre in 1992, Justice P.B. Sawant and Justice Kuldip Singh, who wrote the judgment, stated:

> Secularism is one of the basic features of the Constitution. While freedom of religion is guaranteed to all persons in India, from the point of view of the state, religion, faith or belief of a person is immaterial. To the state, all are equal and are entitled to be treated equally. In matters of state, religion has no place. *No political party can simultaneously be a religious party. Politics and religion cannot be mixed. Any state government which pursues unsecular policies or unsecular course of action acts contrary to the Constitutional mandate and renders itself amenable to action under Article 356.*

There is no dissent or qualification or reservation by any of the other judges on this part of the judgment. Soli Sorabjee has rightly stated that 'the propositions are over-broadly stated' (*Journal* Section (1994) 3 SCC, p. 30).

In the comprehensive article on the judgment, Justice H.R. Khanna, former Judge of the Supreme Court, has written:

> The decision of the court in respect of the three states in question would have serious repercussions on the survival or coming into power of BJP in any state.... It would also warrant the dismissal of all BJP governments if and when they come into power in any state....

Yet ever since the commencement of the Constitution we have had political parties like Muslim League, Akali Dal and Hindu Mahasabha. Some of these parties like Akali Dal have formed state governments, yet no one has so far thought of dismissing such government because of the label of the party or its allegiance or affinity to some religion… No judgment of the Supreme Court, in the opinion of the writer, can and should ignore the ground realities of political life in the country. Life of law, it is said, is not logic, but experience, and one may add, taking due cognisance of the political and social realities. Constitutional law cannot operate in vacuum or choose to reside in some higher region cut off from the world of existing political and social realities.'(Khanna, AIR 1994 Journal Section, p. 156)

Reference may also be invited to the thoughtful and thought-provoking report of the Concerned Citizens Tribunal on Gujarat Riots in 2002 in which it has been suggested that the government should suitably amend electoral laws so as to disallow parties that espouse a particular religion, and which act or behave by word of mouth, print or any other manner with a view to secure power through a religious policy, to contest elections to parliament, to the assembly, to the municipal corporations [or] to panchayats. Justice Krishna Iyer was the Chairman and Justice P.B. Sawant and Justice Hosbet Suresh, among others, were the members of the Tribunal.

In spite of these overwhelming concerns, it is a harsh reality that no steps are likely to be taken in the foreseeable future to separate religion from politics. In the recent times, considering the massive mandate which the BJP enjoyed, such a proposal could have been moved during Narendra Modi's term as prime minister. But the BJP, with its ideology of ushering in *Hindu Rashtra* (Hindu nation), cannot be expected to take any such suicidal step! Looking to the fragmented and highly polarised polity and lack of a credible Opposition party at the national level, it is unlikely in the near future for a ruling political party at the Centre to have two-thirds majority in both the Houses of Parliament and its own party governments in half the states in the country. It is also unlikely to create a national consensus on this issue, howsoever important it is for the future of the country. It is, thus, an inevitable reality that this fault line will remain as it is for the foreseeable future and its consequences will have to be borne by the country, whatever the cost.

One way to address the menace of vote-bank politics, which has been primarily responsible for intermixing religion and politics, is to lay down by law that a candidate must win at least 50 per cent plus one vote for being declared elected. The National Commission to Review the Working of the Constitution (NCRWC) supported this idea in its report submitted in 2002. After some initial hesitation, the Election Commission of India has also declared that it would have no difficulty in giving effect to it. The present first-past-the-post system results in a majority of legislators getting elected on a minority vote. The proposed change will make democracy more representative and force candidates to seek the support of all cross-sections of the constituency and not appeal to voters only on the basis of caste, community, creed or religion. I hope political consensus can be developed at least on this point. Enacting such a legislation will be a small step forward.

The NCRWC has referred to the tensions generated between communities by inciting feelings of hatred on the basis of caste, community, religion, race or language during election campaigns and has regretted about ineffective implementation of laws. The Commission has recommended that *these offences should be made punishable with mandatory imprisonment for three years* instead of discretionary, as currently provided under Section 125 of the Representation of the People Act, 1951. (GOI 2002, p. 496) Though nearly two decades have elapsed since the submission of the report, no action has been taken on this recommendation. This would have considerably helped the cause of communal harmony.

The NCRWC has also referred to a number of judicially deduced fundamental rights, which include freedom of press, freedom of information, right to travel abroad, right to privacy, remedy for violation of Article 21 and so on (GOI 2002, p. 10). Looking to the Supreme Court judgments referred to above, the Court could have declared the separation of religion and politics as fundamental to safeguarding secularism in the country and directed that suitable legislative and administrative action should be taken by the government but this has not happened so far.

The importance of this subject for India's future must not be underestimated. There was jubilation in the country among large cross-sections after the demolition of the Babri Masjid and the commencement of the construction of a grand Ram temple in September 2020. Demands are now being made to amend the Places of Worship (Special Provisions) Act, 1991, which prohibits conversion of any place of worship and to provide for the maintenance of the religious character of any place of worship as it existed on the 15th day of August, 1947 so as to 'liberate' the Kashi Vishwanath temple from the Gyanvapi Mosque (Varanasi), and the Krishna Janmabhoomi temple in Mathura. The constitutional validity of the Act has been challenged in the Supreme Court. In March 2021, the district court in Varanasi has directed the Archaeological Survey of India to conduct a study of the Gyanvapi Mosque regarding traces of any temple before construction of the mosque. This decision is challenged in the high court.

One does not know whether the demands will stop here. The Uttarakhand government has announced its decision to take over the management of Badrinath and Kedarnath temples. Is this the secular India ordained by the Constitution?

Linguistic Reorganisation of States

K.M. Munshi, a jurist and a member of the Constituent Assembly, has written passionately about the dangers of linguism:

> Linguism...denotes the belief that language is the product of a mystic

folk-unity and its speakers have an inalienable right to govern the region which they occupy. It identifies language with culture and equates culture with political frontiers.... *It has all the characteristics of a sub-nationalism.* All other language groups within the particular language area are to be treated as aliens.... Linguism, even when it is related only to a region of a nation, soon becomes a positive, intolerant, expansionist sentiment. As Wheare puts it: "*The danger is that the region may inspire a loyalty greater than that of the Union and that in time of conflict the Union will fall apart.*" In India, this is no longer a distant danger; it has become an ever-present menace.... The political ambition of a linguistic group can only be satisfied by the exclusion and discrimination of other linguistic groups in the area...the rule of the majority, exercised most often under the title of democracy is a true tyranny.... It has been the common experience the world over that linguistic claims have led to interminable boundary disputes leading to unending bitterness, ceaseless insistence on revision of boundaries and eventual disruption.... *Linguism is the most vulnerable aspect of the nation ideology and the most indefensible when applied* to regions in a nation-state like India. (Munshi 2012, pp. 222-5)

Munshi has strongly argued that modern linguism has no historical basis since India was not a federation of pre-existing sovereign states. The seeds of linguism were sown in India by the Indian National Congress in 1908 and the principle was approved in the Scheme of Provincial Autonomy set forth in the GOI's dispatch of 25 August 1911 and the consequent separation of Bihar from Bengal. The seed struck roots in 1917 when the Congress recognised the demand of the Telugu-speaking people to have a separate province.

Ever since 1921, the Indian National Congress had given expression to its opinion in favour of the creation in British India of administrative units based on linguistic homogeneity; and as early as 1928 the All Parties

Committee (Nehru Report) emphasised the desirability of creating linguistic provinces. This principle was subsequently officially adopted by the Congress and included in its election manifesto in December 1947. Earlier, on 27 November 1947, Nehru had accepted in the Constituent Assembly the principle underlying the demand for linguistic provinces, subject to the requirements of security and stability of India. In reply to a question by N.G. Ranga, Nehru emphasised, 'The first essential therefore is for India as a whole to be strong and firmly established, confident in her capacity to meet all possible dangers and face and solve all problems. If India lives, all parts of India also will live and prosper' (Gopal and Iyengar 2003, p. 45). Subsequently, the Government of India made a statement that Andhra could be mentioned as a separate unit in the new Constitution, as was done in the case of Sind and Orissa by the Government of India Act, 1935. However, the Drafting Committee suggested that a commission should be appointed to enquire into and work out all relevant matters not only as regards Andhra but also other linguistic regions.

Accordingly, the President of the Constituent Assembly appointed a commission consisting of Justice S.K. Das, retired judge of the Allahabad High Court; Panna Lal, a retired member of the Indian Civil Service (ICS); and Jagat Narain Lal, a member of the Constituent Assembly. K.M. Munshi was appointed as Associate Member insofar as the question of Bombay was concerned. The commission submitted its report on 10 December 1948.

Even in 1948, *this was a highly controversial inquiry leading to bitter differences and extreme positions on the subject. The commission received about 1,000 written memoranda. Oral evidence of over 700 witnesses was recorded.* The provincial governments preferred to remain neutral and did not offer their cooperation to the commission.

In his memorandum submitted to the Das Commission, Dr Ambedkar had bluntly stated: 'In discussing the question of creating such linguistic provinces, it would be very short-sighted to omit from one's consideration the future structure of GOI...one must therefore consider the effects which linguistic provinces would have on the working of the Central government (Munshi 2012, p. 228).

After hearing the arguments on both sides, the commission had ably summarised the arguments against the formation of linguistic provinces: the intolerance which they breed against the minority speaking a different language in the same province, the inter-provincial isolation and antagonism which they bring into existence, the parochial patriotism which they emphasize as against the growth of the nascent national feeling and lastly the bitterness which is likely to be generated as a result of marking off the boundaries of these provinces between rival claimants, and the allotment of the capital cities of Madras and Bombay. The actual experience has shown how true the commission's reservations were.

The future of Bombay and Madras cities troubled the commission a great deal. The commission noted:

> *The future of Bombay, therefore, seems to us by itself a very strong argument against the formation of linguistic provinces.* And if these provinces are ultimately decided upon, *we suggest that Bombay and possibly Madras should be kept wholly outside the vortex of linguistic politics* and disposed of in the best way possible in their own interest and in the interests of the country as a whole and not on linguistic considerations alone.

The commission recommended:

- *The formation of provinces on exclusively or even mainly linguistic considerations is not in the larger interests of the Indian nation and should not be taken in hand.*
- The existing provinces of Madras, Bombay, Central Provinces and Berar present serious administrative problems for which an administrative solution is urgently necessary and it is for the Centre to find a satisfactory solution to these problems.

- The aforesaid problems do not call for an immediate reformation of provinces. As soon as Indian [princely] States have been integrated and the country has stabilized itself and other conditions are favourable they may be reformed and *convenient administrative provinces set up.*

- *In the formation of new provinces, whenever such a work is taken in hand, oneness of language may be one of the factors to be taken into consideration along with others; but it should not be the decisive or even the main factor. Generally speaking, bilingual districts in border areas, which have developed an economic and organic life of their own, should not be broken up* and should be disposed of on considerations of their own special needs.

- Similarly, *the cities of Bombay and Madras should receive special treatment and be disposed of in the best interest of India as a whole and in their own interest.* Subject to the above and other relevant and paramount considerations, if some new provinces come into being and produce more or less linguistic homogeneity they need not be objected to.

- If any powers are necessary for the Centre for a proper solution of the administrative problems in the provinces, the Constitution should provide for them.

- We find that no new provinces out of those referred to us [Andhra, Kerala, Karnataka and Maharashtra] should be formed for the present (B. Shiva Rao 1968, pp. 439, 443, 456, 482-3).

It can thus be seen that irrespective of the position adopted by the Congress Party on linguistic states before Independence, the very first commission on the subject appointed after Independence had expressed strong reservations on the formation of linguistic states.

In 1948, a committee consisting of Nehru, Patel and Pattabhi Sitaramayya, former president of the Congress Party, examined the subject afresh in the light of conditions of free India. They reported in a very different tone from anything that the Congress had advocated previously. They said: 'When Congress had given the seal of its approval to the general principle of linguistic provinces, *it was not faced with the practical application of the principle and hence it had not considered all the implications and consequences that arose from this practical application*' (Tyson 1966, p. 147).

Both these reports could have been useful to the Centre in resisting the demands for linguistic states. But Nehru was disinclined to oppose the popular demand, in spite of his own serious reservations on the subject, brought out below.

D.V. Tahmankar has stated that Patel was firmly opposed to making language the sole basis of creation of a state. But, the Congress Working Committee yielded to the clamour of the Telugu-speaking 'hotheads' and issued a directive for creating the Andhra state. As Union Home Minister, the responsibility for implementing the directive was Patel's, but he declined to pursue this as the directive was not a Cabinet decision. Instead, Patel expressed himself strongly against the linguistic reorganisation of states. Speaking in Trivandrum on May 14, 1950, he said: 'Some people say they want provinces on a linguistic basis like Andhra, Tamil and Kerala. What will be its effect in the north or in the west, nobody cares to consider. We should cease thinking in terms of different states or provinces. *Instead we should think that we are Indians and should develop a sense of unity.*'

Speaking to students of Allahabad University, Patel condemned people who pursued narrower objectives at the cost of wider national interests, saying, 'the need of the hour is to safeguard the unity, integrity and security of the newborn state from disruptive forces' (Tahmankar 1970, pp. 273-4).

Tahmankar has emphasised that the disintegration of provinces such as Madras and Bombay under the guise of linguistic redistribution came about only after Patel's death.

However, in the election manifesto of the Congress Party, prepared by Nehru and adopted at the AICC session in Bangalore on 14 July 1951, it was stated: 'The Congress expressed itself in favour of linguistic provinces many years ago. A decision on this question ultimately depends on the wishes of the people concerned.... Where such a demand represents the agreed views of the people concerned, the necessary steps prescribed by the Constitution, including the appointment of a boundary commission, should be taken (*JNMF* 1994, p. 12).

It can thus be seen that in spite of the Das Commission and the Nehru, Patel and Sitaramayya Committee expressing their reservations on the subject, Nehru was reluctant to take a stand on the subject and preferred to follow the populist course of action. The Congress Party manifesto prepared by him reflected this.

The decision of formation of Andhra Pradesh was announced by Nehru in Parliament on 19 December 1952. But Nehru's misgivings were clear. Nehru wrote to chief ministers on 22 December 1952:

> The decision in fact had been taken long ago, and it was only a lack of agreement among the parties concerned that delayed its implementation.... I have little doubt that this decision will open out other demands for linguistic provinces and we shall have to face them realistically. *And yet, I must confess to a feeling of regret that we are going along these lines.* How far they will take us, I do not know. (Parthasarathi 1987, p. 206)

Some Andhra leaders such as T. Prakasam, T. Vishwanatham and others started protesting stoutly against the decision to keep Madras city out of the new Andhra State. Nehru wrote:

> It is perfectly true that the Andhras have had an important share in building up that city and much of their cultural life has centred around it. But it is equally true that Madras city is the intellectual, cultural nerve-centre of Tamil Nadu. If the Madras state could have continued jointly as now, everyone could have had their own share in it. But,

unhappily, this was not to be and the people of Andhra *Desha* felt strongly that they should have their own special province.... *What is still more likely to add to our burdens is the demand for other so-called linguistic states. A blank 'no' cannot be said where feeling is strong.* I hope, however, that whatever other steps we might have to take will be after careful consideration. (Parthasarathi 1987, pp. 215-6)

The agitation for linguistic states had started building up in several states. For example, Shankargonda, president, Hubli Taluka Congress, undertook an indefinite fast from 28 March 1953 to press the demand for the formation of Karnataka state by 2 October 1954. Nehru had severely criticised such agitations as '*narrow and bigoted mentality* which, if it succeeded, could only bring ruin to India'. In his letter to chief ministers dated 10 April 1953, Nehru wrote:

I feel that after the establishment of Andhra state, we should consider this whole problem of reorganisation of state boundaries in a realistic and dispassionate way.... *The purely linguistic approach is obviously not good enough.* It is hoped, therefore, to appoint towards the end of the year, some kind of a high-powered commission to go into this matter fully without fuss. (Parthasarathi 1987, pp. 298-99)

Accordingly, the States Reorganisation Commission (SRC) was set up on 29 December 1953. The commission attracted more public attention than any comparable inquiry of its kind. *It received 1,52,252 communications of one kind or another from the general public, including about 2,000 'well-considered memoranda'. The commission examined 9,000 witnesses, travelled 38,000 miles and visited 104 places. The inquiry also revealed dangerous underlying fissiparous tendencies.* In one of the closing passages of their report, the commission said:

It has been *most distressing to us to witness, during the course of our inquiry, a kind of border warfare in certain areas in which old comrades-in-arms in the battle for freedom have pitted against one another in acrimonious controversy,* showing little appreciation of the fact that the states are but the limbs of the same body politic and that territorial readjustments between them should not assume the form of disputes between powers. *Deliberate attempts to whip up popular frenzy by an appeal to parochial and communal sentiments; threats of large-scale migration; assertion such as that if a certain language group is not allowed to have an administrative unit of its own, its moral, material and even physical extinction would follow as an inevitable consequence; and finally incidents such as those in Goalpara, Parlakimedi, Ludhiana and Amritsar; all point to an acute lack of perspective and balance.*

The commission recognised the dangers of the situation when they observed:

One view which is strongly held by certain sections of public opinion is that only a unitary form of government and division of the country into purely administrative units can provide the corrective to the separatist tendencies. We feel however that in existing circumstances this approach would be somewhat unrealistic. *Other methods have therefore to be found to keep centrifugal forces under check.* (Tyson 1966, pp. 148-9)

We have seen a replay of these sad happenings in the Telangana agitation in recent years.

The commission, inter alia, recommended that '*it is neither possible nor desirable to reorganize states on the basis of a single test of either language or culture*; a balanced approach, which takes all relevant factors into account, is necessary. Financial viability has an important bearing on reorganisation proposals, but it has to be considered along with other relevant factors.'

The commission had also urged that 'it would be desirable to avoid, as far as possible, wide disparities in resources between the various states. The wishes of the people should be regarded as an important factor bearing on reorganisation but they have to be considered along with other relevant factors' (GOI 1955, pp. 308-11).

These and other principles enunciated by the commission clearly show that this was, in a large measure, an exercise in the use of discretionary powers. There were no rational outcomes. One prominent example of this was the fact that the well-argued note of dissent (or just a 'note' as the commission preferred to call it) by one of the members of the commission, K.M. Panikkar, proposing that UP state be divided into three was rejected. The recommendation made by Panikkar was eminently reasonable and, in fact, satisfied a number of criteria laid down by the commission itself. Similarly, the inclusion of the Marathi-dominated areas such as Belgaum, Karwar and Nipani in Karnataka, by overlooking the representations made by the people of the area, was questionable. The agitations in these areas are still continuing though over six decades have elapsed since the reorganisation of states. Such agitations have seen stern action by the Government of Karnataka. For instance, in the agitation on 1 November 2018, proclaiming it as Black Day since on this day Belgaum was allotted to Karnataka, the Marathi-speaking demonstrators were lathicharged (*Loksatta*, 2 November 2018, p. 10). A controversy erupted over the alleged removal of the statue of Shivaji in Belgaum's Manguti village, leading to large-scale agitations and demonstrations at several places in Maharashtra and Karnataka (*The Indian Express*, 9 August 2020, p. 2). This high-handedness has been happening each year. Ministers in the Maharashtra government wore black bands on 1 November 2020 to express their support for Marathi-speaking people living in Maharashtra-Karnataka border areas. Agitations were also held in several towns and villages in these areas to protest against their inclusion in Karnataka. The clashes in the border areas led to suspension of road traffic between the two states in February 2021.

The issue of injustice done to the Marathi-speaking areas is now pending in the Supreme Court since 2004! One of the arguments put forth by the Government of Karnataka is that the Supreme Court should not intervene on such a 'political question'. However, K. Subba Rao, former CJI, in his book, *Some Constitutional Problems*, has asserted:

> The argument that political questions must be kept out of the Court's jurisdiction is not sound. When a matter comes before the court, its jurisdiction does not depend upon the nature of the question raised, but on the question whether the said matter is expressly or by necessary implication excluded from its jurisdiction.... It is often said that the court is not competent to deal with political questions. This argument involves ignorance of the court's functions. Questions of wide-ranging variety—social, economic, political, scientific or technological—directly or indirectly, arise for consideration before courts. Assisted by experts on the subject, learned counsel argue complicated questions before the court and it is never suggested that the courts cannot decide such questions. (Subba Rao 1970, pp. 197-8)

The SRC report was discussed at length in the two Houses of Parliament. *The debate lasted 55.5 hours in the Lok Sabha and 41 hours in the Rajya Sabha. As many as 244 members representing various shades of opinion participated freely.* Intervening in the debate on 21 December 1955, Nehru said:

> While members here represent their constituencies, they do something more. They are not only members of this or that particular area of India, but each Member of Parliament is a member *for India and represents India,* and at no time can we afford to forget this basic fact that India is more than the little corner of India that we represent. We know, all of us, that *we have to face certain forces which may be called separatist, that is to say—I am not using the word in*

any bad sense—it nevertheless means that people's attention is being diverted more to local problems of India. There should be really no conflict between the two but it is a question of the method in our thinking (sic), in our minds, in considering our problems. (Kashyap 1995, pp. 129, 131)

It is unbelievable to see the extent to which Nehru was on the defensive in putting across his point of view, in the face of the tidal wave of sentiments in favour of linguistic states.

C.D. Deshmukh, the then Finance Minister, was in favour of the minority recommendation of K.M. Panikkar that UP be divided. Deshmukh has written: '[It] had no backers, and Govind Ballabh Pant rejected energetically even the relatively minor adjustment of transferring Lalitpur tahsil, hanging like a thin pendant into Madhya Pradesh, to the latter state; "only over my dead body" he is reported to have said apropos of this' (Deshmukh 1974, p. 224).

In his letter to the chief ministers on 26 October 1955, Nehru stated:

Constituted as I am, I fail to understand why this question [of reorganisation of states] should rouse so much passion and excited debate, not to mention threats of some action or other. *I feel unhappy and distressed at the picture of India that I see before me today.... If people go about saying that they will not accept a decision unless it is according to their own views, then that is the negation of democracy.... Something of the fierceness of the approach of a bigoted religion comes into consideration of linguistic provinces. Each person thinks that his doxy is orthodoxy.* (Parthasarathi 1988, p. 287)

Nehru could not have expressed his anguish more strongly but it fell on deaf ears and Nehru, as a democrat, did not want to go against the public feelings on the subject, howsoever unreasonable they were.

Reorganisation of the then Bombay state had become a major worry for the government. Nehru is often blamed for his indecisiveness as seen in this case. The GOI decisions swung from one extreme to another. The future of Bombay city was the crux of the problem. In his broadcast on 16 January 1956, Nehru announced the government's decision that Bombay city should be centrally administered, Vidarbha merged into Maharashtra state, and Saurashtra and Kutch incorporated in Gujarat state. C.D. Deshmukh, the then Union Finance Minister, resigned since he did not wish to share the responsibility of separating Bombay city from Maharashtra.[1] He was critical of Nehru making the announcement without taking the Cabinet into confidence and bypassing the Lok Sabha. Nehru contested this by stating that the draft bill was placed before the Cabinet on two occasions and passed, when Deshmukh was present.

Later, on 6 August 1956, this decision was changed with the formation of a bigger bilingual Bombay state, comprising Maharashtra, Gujarat and Bombay city, after 220 MPs in Lok Sabha submitted a memorandum suggesting this course of action. The bigger bilingual experiment met with stiff resistance both in Maharashtra and Gujarat. Nehru lamented the *'growth of the spirit of violence, almost bordering on anarchy, which has been evident in India during the past year or so.... What happened in Gujarat was politically painful, because it was least expected'* (Parthasarathi 1987, p. 435). This decision weakened the Congress in Maharashtra so much that in the 1957 Lok Sabha elections all Congress Party candidates lost, except Y.B. Chavan from Satara and Balasaheb Bharde from Ahmednagar. And finally, after all this 'Ramayana', Maharashtra state was created with Bombay remaining its capital. Gujarat state was formed with Saurashtra and Kutch.

An interesting sidelight of his resignation was brought out by C.D. Deshmukh:

---

1. C.D. Deshmukh has written how [prominent Congress Party leaders] Deogirikar, Pataskar and Altekar, who had suggested to Deshmukh they should all resign together, backed out the next day saying 'the Congress Working Committee would not allow us to resign'! (Deshmukh 1974, p. 225).

> Although the matter was of no interest to me, people have wondered why, after my point of view had been conceded, the Prime Minister had not asked me to come back into the Cabinet. *My belief is that he was influenced in this matter by G.B. Pant who had, in his turn, been influenced by industrial magnates not to give me any further opportunity of perpetuating socialistic measures.* In any case, T.T. Krishnamachari was always at hand, cheerfully prepared to carry the burden of the Finance Ministership. (Deshmukh 1974, p. 227)

Thus, crony capitalism and industrialists influencing the appointment and removal of ministers was in operation even during the Jawaharlal Nehru era! India witnessed this again in Vajpayee's NDA regime (removal of Jagmohan from the Ministry of Communications) and Manmohan Singh's UPA I and II regimes (appointment of A. Raja as Telecommunication Minister, and removal of Mani Shankar Aiyar and Jaipal Reddy from the Ministry of Petroleum).

To counter the demand for creation of a separate state of Vidarbha in Maharashtra, and Kutch and Saurashtra in Gujarat, Article 371 of the Constitution was enacted immediately after the reorganisation of states in 1956. The most significant words were: 'notwithstanding anything in this Constitution'. Special responsibility was cast on the Governor for establishment of separate development boards for Vidarbha, Marathwada and the rest of Maharashtra or, as the case may be, Saurashtra, Kutch and the rest of Gujarat. The Governor was given the responsibility for equitable allocation of funds for developmental expenditure and an equitable arrangement providing adequate facilities for technical education and vocational training, and adequate opportunities for employment in services, etc.

Giving such overriding powers to the Governor was a negation of democracy. Curtailing the powers of the elected government was against the basic framework of the Constitution. In Maharashtra, these development boards have been in operation for over three decades but have served no purpose at all. The term of these boards is now over but with the somewhat strained relations between the Governor, who is a BJP appointee, and the coalition government of Shiv Sena and the two Congress parties, and fearing the assertiveness of the Governor, the term of the development boards has not been extended so far. The BJP has, however, threatened to launch an agitation over the issue. In the meanwhile, the demand for a separate state of Vidarbha is being raised time and again, but has not gathered enough strength yet.

In the speech in the Lok Sabha on 21 December 1955, Nehru spoke about the place of language in the reorganisation of states. It shows how far Nehru was removed from the narrow state prejudices and was a true statesman far removed from the common prejudices and failings, someone who belonged to the whole of India. Nehru had said:

I am not greatly interested where a particular state boundary is situated, and find it very difficult to get passionate or excited about it.... Infinitely more important is what happens on either side of the boundary, what happens within the state—more especially in the great multilingual or bilingual areas—and what happens to people inside a particular state who may, linguistically or in any other sense, form a minority.... Each member [of Parliament] is not only a member for this or that area of India, but a member for India as a whole. He represents India.... I am constantly compelled to think in larger terms, not only in national terms but in international terms.... *I repeat that I attach the greatest importance to language but I refuse to associate it necessarily with a state.... Every culture and every manifestation of culture should be encouraged. There is no exclusiveness about culture. The more inclusive you are, the more cultured you are.* The more barriers you put up, the more uncultured you are.... I personally welcome the idea of bilingual or multilingual areas. For my part, I would much rather live and have my children brought up in bilingual or trilingual areas than in a unilingual area.... The

Bombay Municipal Corporation has schools in fourteen languages, because Bombay is a great city with many language groups.... *It is the primary responsibility of the majority to satisfy the minority in every matter....* Talking about religion in the broad sense of the word, the votaries of the Hindu religion in our country greatly outnumber the others. Nobody is going to push them from that position; they are strong enough. Therefore, it is their special responsibility to see that people following other religions in India feel satisfied that they have full freedom and opportunity. If this principle is applied, most of these troubles and grievances will disappear. (Gopal 1980, pp. 520-3)

This is one of Nehru's most thoughtful and thought-provoking speeches and fully brings out his deep understanding of India and its problems. But, the profound message was overlooked by his own party, leave aside the others.

Alexandrowicz considers linguistic reorganisation of states such an important event as to change the very character of India's quasi-federalism. Redrawing the federal map of India hardly justifies the classification [any longer] of India as a quasi-federation (Alexandraowicz 1957, p.170).

Creation of Telangana: – Adding a New, Cultural Dimension

The States Reorganisation Commission (SRC) had recommended that the Telugu-speaking areas of Hyderabad state, which historically had constituted the Telugu region, be made into a separate state, called Hyderabad. The commission appreciated the strong sentiments that existed in favour of such a separate state but it also recognised the substantial benefits that would materialise if it were combined with the Andhra state to create '*Visalandhra*' [larger Andhra], an idea that had been mooted by the Andhra Mahasabha in October 1942. Perhaps not being able to make up its mind, the commission said that the new state of Hyderabad should come into being immediately, and after five years, if two-thirds of its legislature so wished, it should be merged with Andhra (Ramesh 2016, p. 22-3). The Congress leadership, however, decided to bring about the integration of the two parts immediately. Those were the days when the ruling Congress Party was enamoured of bigger states (as opposed to BJP's ideology of smaller states), whether it was a bigger bilingual state of Maharashtra and Gujarat, or even combining West Bengal and Bihar.

As Nehru said, '...so that barriers are fewer and progress is faster.... The new proposal was that a greater Andhra should be created with its two regions having their own separate identity and say in their development. It also envisaged safeguards for the people of Telangana regarding their land, admissions to schools and colleges, language, jobs, etc.' (Ramesh 2016, p. 25).

Andhra was the first linguistic state, created in 1953, against the wishes of the central Congress Party leaders, only to put an end to the sustained political agitation culminating in the death of Potti Sriramulu, who had given an ultimatum of 'fast unto death'.

The agitation for a separate state of Telangana has been going on for decades. Way back on 22 August 1969, in reply to a debate in the Lok Sabha, the then Union Home Minister, Y.B. Chavan, had urged, 'The problem of regional development has to be tackled as a problem of development. It cannot be made a problem of reorganisation of a state' (Godbole 1996, p. 68). This was the policy adopted by the GOI for years together and as a result, even the Constitution was amended in 1974 to incorporate Article 371D to make special provisions with respect to AP to provide 'for equitable opportunities and facilities for the people belonging to different parts of the state in the matter of public employment and in matters of education'. None of these ideas made any headway and it took 58 years to correct the mistake and give the Telanganaites their due.

In the meanwhile, when the Telangana agitation was at its peak again in 2010, the UPA 2 government did not know what to do, and it took the usual course of appointing, on 3 February 2010, a committee to hold consultations with all stakeholders. The Srikrishna Committee for Consultations on the Situation in Andhra Pradesh 'did not find any real evidence of any major neglect by the state government in matters of overall economic development. However, there are some continuing concerns regarding public employment, education, and water and irrigation' (GOI 2010, p. 441).

The committee was faced with the situation of dealing with the demand for reorganisation of AP on the basis of cultural differences. It was like two brothers fighting for separation of their ancestral property. *The Indian Express* had pithily brought this out in a full page article, 'CM *vs.* CM: what one has, the other wants' (*The Indian Express*, 26 August 2015, p. 10).

The supporters of Telangana urged the Srikrishna Committee to concede the demand for a separate state on the basis of:

A strong regional identity based on a distinctive culture[2]. Distinctiveness is asserted on the basis of a cultural self formed through 1) historical experience common to the people of the region—especially during the Nizam period which binds them together while distinguishing them from coastal Andhra and Rayalseema people, 2) a distinctive dialect born out of the synthesis of several languages—primarily Telugu and Urdu but further enriched by languages such as Marathi and Gondi, and presently being called Telangana Telugu, 3) other distinct cultural forms which are moulded by a specific regional topography, climate and other factors, resulting in a separate cuisine or diet, region-specific festivals, etc., 4) the social composition of the region comprising higher percentages

---

2. C. Rajagopalachari (Rajaji) was requested by *Hindustan Times* for an article for its Andhra Supplement on Tyagaraja, the great composer of Carnatic music who lived in the nineteenth century. Rajaji had conveyed that Tyagaraja was a good Tamilian of Tanjore district and that only Tamilians knew how to sing his compositions properly and that he was unable to contribute any article that will hand over Tyagaraja to the Andhras (Ramesh 2016, p. 156).

of what may be called disadvantaged or non-upper caste groups—SCs, OBCs, STs, Muslims, leading to 5) a Telangana 'self' which sees itself as being more diverse and cosmopolitan than Andhra-Seema Telugus. (GOI 2010, p. 391)

Srikrishna Committee has said:

Although India has broadly followed the policy of linguistic states, creation of new territorial divisions on the basis of cultural differences is inconceivable, given the range of diversity. However, if the cultural hegemony of one region over another translates into deliberate and systematic discrimination in employment or participation in cultural or political life, then it becomes a matter of serious concern and has to be addressed by the state.... To address cultural grievances, the state can make a more concerted effort that cultures of various groups—not just of regions—are given space to grow. (GOI 2010, p. 416)

Jairam Ramesh, in his book *Old History New Geography: Bifurcating Andhra Pradesh*, has written about how the proposal met with stiff resistance from Andhra Pradesh, how the chief minister of AP had 'hyper-aggressively opposed the bifurcation, defying his party leadership' and resigned, the opposition which the bill faced in both Houses of Parliament and so on. Earlier, the Andhra Pradesh legislative assembly and council had rejected the Andhra Pradesh Reorganisation Bill, 2013.[3] After wavering for several years, the GOI was determined to bifurcate the state irrespective of opposition. With Hyderabad going to Telangana, the residual AP would be a financially weak state. As an inducement, it was declared that the Polavaram multipurpose project would be a national project and will be implemented by the GOI, and AP will be given special

---

3. In 1955, the Fifth Amendment of the Constitution was passed by which a bill for reorganisation of a state can be introduced in either House of Parliament on the recommendation of the President. The consent of the state concerned is not required.

category status.[4]

Accordingly, apart from Prime Minister Manmohan Singh making an announcement to this effect in Parliament, a provision was also made in the AP Reorganisation Act. It was shocking that the Modi government went back on it on the specious plea that the 14th Finance Commission had abolished such categorisation. Looking to the facts of the case, an exception could have easily been made but, for reasons best known to it, the Modi government did not do so. The Government of India has also been remiss in fulfilling its commitment regarding the Polavaram project which has led to considerable delay in the completion of the project.

Bifurcation of AP was clearly a political decision by the UPA 2 government in the hope that TRS (Telangana Rashtra Samithi) would merge with the Congress Party and it would be able to remain in power in the new Telangana state. However, K. Chandrashekar Rao, president of TRS, preferred to retain his party's separate identity. Finally, Telangana state came into being on 4 March 2014.

The creation of Telangana state on the basis of purely cultural differences may now set the stage for the next round of reorganisation of states. The rising expectations of major castes like Reddys and Kammas in AP, the Lingayats and Vokkaligas in Karnataka, and Marathas in Maharashtra will have to be watched with some apprehensions. The reservation granted to Marathas has raised the fears of a backlash from other backward communities in Maharashtra. The constitutional validity of reservation for Marathas, which has taken the total reservations in the state to over 68 per cent, is now pending in the Supreme Court, which has stayed the reservation decision of the state government.

---

4. 'Special category status' had been extended over the years to eleven states for the purpose of normal Central assistance that was provided to all states annually. Thirty per cent of the total resources available for such assistance was earmarked for these eleven states which repaid only 10 per cent of the amount, the balance 90 per cent being a grant. The non-special category states got assistance on the basis of 70 per cent loan and 30 per cent grant. These special category states also got special advantage in externally-aided projects.

Rise of Sub-nationalism

Signs of increasing provincialism had worried the Centre even in the early years of Independence. Shyama Prasad Mookerjee, who was then a Minister in the Nehru Cabinet, had written to Vallabhbhai Patel with a request to raise this issue in the conference of Prime Ministers of Provinces. In reply, Patel had said that he too had similar anxieties on the subject. These trends have got further accentuated with the linguistic reorganisation of states.

K.M. Munshi has asserted that he had raised his voice against the dangers of linguism as a distinct menace to national solidarity. He had also raised an important question about the difficulties which would be created for the Supreme Court:

> The Supreme Court will have to close down. For, if it is to function, every judge of the Supreme Court – I am omitting for the moment the lawyers practicing therein – must know the language of every Province, which is impossible to provide for.... It may lead to a break-up of India. Instead of remaining united, India may end in becoming like Europe – faced with the prospect of chaos and disorder.

Munshi had stated: '*Sardar [Patel] characterised the impatient champions of re-distribution of provinces on linguistic basis as "assassins of nationalism"*' (Munshi 2012, pp. 227-230). As stated earlier, Jawaharlal Nehru had often expressed himself against linguistic states.

Speaking in the Lok Sabha on language riots during 1960, Nehru said:

> We are discussing here, whatever we may say about Assam or Bengal, is really ourselves...how superficial is the covering of what we like to call 'nationalism' which bursts open at the slightest irritation. It is amazing how all higher considerations are swept away when communal passions are roused. It is not only the Assamese or Bengalis who are guilty in this regard. Each one of us is a guilty party.

When we talk about our nationalism, each person's idea of nationalism is his own brand of nationalism.... It is very grave tragedy for people in one state to be driven out either by force or through sheer panic. Panic is so infectious that it is difficult to deal with it. (Kashyap 1995, pp. 235-6)

Clearly, Nehru implied sub-nationalism or provincialism when he used the word 'nationalism' in this speech.

Nirmal Mukarji, former Cabinet Secretary and Governor of Punjab, in his essay, 'A More Federal India', writes:

Reorganisation of states on linguistic or tribal grounds marked the beginning of a new era, for it sowed the seeds of sub-nationalism. There are two contrasting views about Indian sub-nationalism. Centralists regard it as subversive of the unity and integrity of the country and disparagingly refer to it as regionalism. Those of a federal persuasion look at it positively arguing that only strong building blocks at the state level can lend strength to the large and diverse entity that is India.... Sub-national states transformed the country's policies but failed to bring about a corresponding change in the Constitution. (Baxi et al. 1999, p. 130)

The Sarkaria Commission on Centre-state relations had, in its report submitted in 1988, stated:

One state government has observed, 'With the reorganisation of states on a linguistic basis, these are no longer mere administrative sub-divisions of the country with their boundaries for the most part a historical legacy. *These are now deliberately reorganised homelands of different linguistic groups. These groups are, in fact, growing into distinct nationalities'....* The very idea of 'homeland' within a country implies a pernicious discrimination between the so-called original inhabitants or 'sons of the soil' and so-called 'immigrants' or 'outsiders' from other states. Practice and promotion of such unhealthy ideas eventually lead to creation of two or more classes of citizens all over the country. (GOI 1988, p. 16)

The Commission to Review the Working of the Constitution had surveyed India's achievements and failures over the 50 years since Independence. The Commission had come to the sad conclusion that 'Fraternity', the noble ideal of brotherhood of man enshrined in the Preamble of the Constitution, has remained unrealised. The people of India are more divided amongst themselves than at the time of country's Independence (GOI 2002, p. 47). This is fully brought out by the narration below.

With state assembly elections due in April 2021, West Bengal has become a major battleground, with the BJP making a big push to capture the state. Mamata Banerjee, Chief Minister, has been projecting the BJP as an 'outsider', out to vanquish 'Ma' or the motherland, and calling it as an assault on Bangla pride. It is for the first time that a national political party ruling at the Centre is being dubbed as an 'outsider', and raises serious concerns about the growing sub-nationalism in the country. In the process, national icons like Subhas Chandra Bose and Rabindranath Tagore have been converted into regional leaders. The TMC has made a poll promise that Bengal will be run by Bengalis, not 'outsiders', insulating the state from Hindi heartland culture, aggressive Hindutva (*India Today*, 15 March 2021, p. 57) .

A new facet of linguistic pride has come to light with the observation of Professor Imankalyan Lahiri of Jadavpur University: 'The attempt to arouse linguistic pride is Mamata's conscious move to weaken the Hindu consolidation [of votes]' (*India Today*, 19 October 2020, p. 35).

The anti-Hindi agitations led to the growth of the Dravidian Movement with its political face being the Dravida Munnetra Kazagam (DMK). The intense love for one's mother tongue is evident in the Tamil saying that even if you hurl abuse at God in Tamil, he will forgive you.

Chinmay Tumbe, in his book *India Moving: A History of Migration*, has highlighted how 'the much-hallowed Indian diversity is routinely tested by claims on ethnicity, region and language, pitting the insiders or 'sons of the soil' (and presumably daughters) versus the proverbial *mlecchas* or outsiders' (Tumbe 2018, pp. 218-9). One of the earliest instances of this was under the Nizam's rule of Hyderabad state in the late 19th century. The state was founded by Asaf Jah in 1724 after the collapse of Mughal power. His subjects were known as *mulkis* (the word '*mulk*' meaning country). Salar Jung tried to recruit non-*mulki* or immigrant Muslims to improve the administration. Later due to the agitation by Muslim *mulkis*, a policy was instituted in 1868 to recruit only *mulkis* into government administration. After the linguistic reorganisation and creation of Maharashtra in 1960, the Shiv Sena started an anti-Tamilian (the *Lungiwalas*) agitation in 1966. *Lungi*, the typical attire of Tamilians, was caricatured to represent those Tamilians who stole jobs from Marathi-speaking locals. Later, the ire shifted against the *bhaiyyas* from UP and Bihar who were engaged in low-paying jobs. In the late 1960s, a similar anti-migrant movement was started by the Kannada Chaluvaligars in Bangalore against the other south Indian migrants in the city. Today, a similar mantle is donned by the Karnataka Rakshana Vadike. A few other states witnessed agitations at different levels and intensities, and they were also characterized by demands for the protection of jobs for locals, changes in language signboards and occasional violence (Tumbe 2018, pp. 220-1).

Agitations in Karnataka and Gujarat against migrants had led to their reverse migration, creating an adverse climate and fear among migrants all over the country. There have also been cases of violence against students from the North East and J&K in various states, further intensifying the alienation of these areas.

Assam is an extreme example where the complex and hazy maze of sub-nationalism runs deep. Another subset of identity which is emerging in that state is of Assamese-speaking community who identifies itself as the indigenous (or *khilonjiya* in Assamese) Muslims. Currently a census is underway to identify 'Assamese Muslims' – Goriya, Moriya, Julha and Deshi Muslims estimated to be 16 lakh in Assam's total population of 3.3 crore (*Outlook*, 24 February 2020, p. 22). The government has decided to set up a Development Corporation for Indigenous Muslims. In addition are the tribal overtones which had led to horrific riots in Nellie. The CAA (Citizenship Amendment Act) has raised fears among the Assamese that their language will be subsumed by the naturalisation of Bengali immigrants.

In his thoughtful article 'Anatomy of an anxiety', M.P. Bezbaruah (a retired IAS officer who served in Assam, and was later Member, North East Council), has written:

> Assamese society's pride was a tradition of tolerance and pluralism, flowing from Sankaradeva and embellished by persons like Ajan Fakir. Did Partition and its legacy create permanent fissures in the composite Assamese identity? Assam Accord (1985) accepted the need for a constitutional safeguard for the Assamese people. As old fears come to haunt Assam again, it is necessary to tread the path with great care and sensitivity. (*The Indian Express*, 22 May 2018, p. 9)

The report of the 14-member committee appointed by the Government of Assam, as a follow-up of the Assam Accord, is likely to open a Pandora's Box on the very question of the definition of Assamese people. The All Assam Students Union (AASU) members on the committee are learnt to have recommended 100 per cent reservation for the Assamese people and other indigenous communities in the elected bodies, while some other members had suggested 67 per cent reservation. The committee is also reported to have recommended the reintroduction of the Inner Line Permit in Assam (*Frontline,* 27 March 2020, p. 103).

One striking example of intensified sub-nationalism is raising of slogans by MLAs and MPs about the greatness of their state, language or historical state icons, after taking the solemn oath in legislature or Parliament. The rulings by presiding officers to desist from doing so, are openly resisted and opposed.

Recently, there has been a raging controversy over whether the 'Rasagolla', the delicious sweet dish or dessert, had its origin in Odisha or West Bengal. When the decision went in favour of Odisha, there was a spell of gloom in West Bengal!

Though movies are certified by the Central Film Censor Board of the GOI, it is not uncommon to see the states applying their own rules and if any part of a movie is perceived to offend local sensitivities of caste, creed, language or historical figures, movies are banned in the state. The same happens with books. It is becoming increasingly difficult to undertake any creative venture without fear of offending the regional, linguistic and cultural sensibilities. I have been advocating for some time that the Constitution should be amended to forbid state governments from taking such actions.

Manuraj Shunmugasundaram (media spokesperson for DMK) in his article 'Towards a southern brotherhood' has written that the rising discontent in South India could revive the idea of 'Dravidian Cooperation' once articulated by the DMK founder Annadurai. The conclave of finance ministers of southern states held in Thiruvananthapuram in April 2018 may have laid the foundation of Dravidian Cooperation based on natural sense of sub-nationalism and distinct national identity. The political aspects of the dialogue may include challenging the Centre's actions on imposition of Hindi or on beef, and the economic agenda could call for a review of the terms of reference of the 15th Finance Commission and its implications for devolution of resources (*The Indian Express,* 12 April 2018, p. 11).

Reference may be made to the discussions held in Kolkata in March 2018 between Mamata Banerjee, Chief Minister of West Bengal, and K.

Chandrasekhar Rao, Chief Minister of Telangana, regarding the formation of a federal front.

Garga Chatterjee (Kolkata-based political commentator) has perceptively written:

> If one looks at the map of non-BJP states in the Indian Union, it is the south and the east that form a continuous belt that prevents the spilling over of the [Sangh Parivar] Hindi-Hindu-Hindustan ideology into the holy waters of the Bay of Bengal and the Indian Ocean. This continuity is not incidental. *This is the zone of politics of federalism.* This is the zone whose absence would have created a Hindu *Rashtra* called Hindustan with Hindi as its national language in 1947. This is the zone whose presence created the flawed but still nominally federal democratic entity called the Indian Union as it exists. (*India Legal*, 21 May 2018, p. 21)

These are early warning signs of what lies ahead.

The political clout and leverage of southern states was brought home in the case pertaining to the removal of Justice V. Ramaswamy from the Supreme Court on the grounds of proved misbehaviour under Article 124 (4) of the Constitution. The charges of misbehaviour against the judge were found to have been proved by a committee comprising a judge of the Supreme Court, chief justice of a high court and an eminent jurist. However, when the motion for the removal of the judge was placed before Parliament, it was opposed by MPs from the southern states on the grounds of injustice to their brethren and the then Prime Minister P.V. Narasimha Rao succumbed to political pressure to save his minority government, and issued a whip to the Congress Party members to abstain from voting! As a result, the motion for removal of the judge failed.[5] The founding fathers of the Constitution could never have visualised such

---

5. The motion was rejected by 196 votes for it, none against and 205 abstentions. It needed 273 votes in its support for its adoption.

blatant disregard of constitutional provisions (Godbole 2011, p. 11).

Sub-nationalism is becoming increasingly intolerant everywhere. During the Cauvery waters agitations, even after the decision of the Supreme Court, regional flare-ups were seen in Karnataka and Tamil Nadu. Even showing of Tamil films was halted in Karnataka during this period.

Towns and cities are being renamed with a vengeance. To impress the significance of Tamil phonetics, the AIADMK government has issued orders amending the English spelling of 1,018 cities and places or giving them a totally new official name. For instance, the spelling of Coimbatore has been changed to 'Koyampuththoor' (*The Indian Express*, 12 June 2020, p. 1). Madras and Bombay, both metropolitan cities, have already become Chennai and Mumbai, respectively. One of the latest in the series is Allahabad being renamed as 'Prayagraj'. The same thing is happening in almost all states.

As a part of the Delhi Agreement in 1952, Nehru agreeing to a separate flag for J&K had become a major controversy. The Bharatiya Jan Sangh, BJP's predecessor, was at the forefront in this agitation. At least two other states—Tamil Nadu and Karnataka—have made a similar demand. Tamil Nadu did not persist with it, after strong objection by the GOI in 1968. However, in Karnataka this demand is being sponsored by both the BJP and the Congress Party. The design of the new flag has also been unveiled. The reasons adduced are 'Kannada *Swabhimana*' (Kannada pride), imposition of Hindi by the Centre, displeasure about bank recruitment policies which disregard Kannada, etc. In 2012, when the BJP was in power in the state, the then Chief Minister D.V. Sadananda Gowda decreed that the Kannada flag would be compulsorily hoisted on the state formation day (November 1) every year in government offices, schools and colleges. But since the rights to the flag were held by Kannada Paksha, a political party, the matter went to court and the move was stalled. Now the design of the new flag has been formally approved by the state government (*Outlook*, 26 March 2018, pp. 28-9).

It was after some 80 rounds of 'talks' with the National Socialist Council of Nagaland (IM) spread over 16 years that, in August 2015, the Central government signed what it called a 'Framework Agreement'. The NSCN (IM), however, called it an 'accord'. R.H. Raising, 'Home Minister' of NSCN (IM), claimed that New Delhi had agreed to allow the Nagas a separate flag and passport (*Outlook*, 11 July 2016, p. 26). The government has denied this, though the details of the Framework Agreement are yet to be made public. Thuingaleng Muivah, the chief of the NSCN-IM, said the Centre recognised the sovereignty of the Nagas when it signed the 2015 Framework Agreement. Muivah said they were not asking the GOI for a Naga national flag and a separate constitution, as 'recognise them or not, we have our own flag and constitution'. He said that 'the Nagas will co-exist with India sharing sovereign powers as agreed in the Framework Agreement and defined in the competencies.... But they will not merge with India.' Earlier, the NSCN-IM had for the first time released the details of the 2015 Framework Agreement, stating that the Centre had agreed to 'share the sovereign power' and to provide for an 'enduring inclusive new relationship of peaceful co-existence of the two entities' (*The Hindu*, 14 August 2020). In his interview to *The Indian Express*, Muivah said that the 2015 agreement was signed on the principle of 'co-existence and shared sovereignty'. The GOI through the Framework Agreement recognises the sovereignty of the Nagas. He said the Naga flag and constitution were non-negotiable and that the agreement included the idea of unification of all Naga-inhabited areas across Assam, Arunachal Pradesh and Manipur (*The Indian Express*, 15 August 2020, p. 16). He reiterated this in an interview with Karan Thapar for *The Wire* on 16 October 2020. 'Nagas will never join Indian Union, nor accept India's Constitution', he added.

Nandita Haksar, in her article 'Why the Indo-Naga Peace Process is dead?', has invited attention to the fact that Pakistan, China, the USA and Britain all played a role to keep alive the idea that the North East region was not a part of India. There was even a plan to make it a kind of Hongkong.... The Manipur government was worried that the Naga ceasefire plan was a part of the Naga homeland [project].... The NSCN vision of a future Naga society is a nation based on religion and their slogan Nagaland for Christ would make their nation a theocracy.... *The Naga national movement has become an identity movement* without any vision for a future that envisages a programme for the development of the Naga people (*The Radical Humanist*, October 2020, pp. 4-9). The Parliamentary panel report has observed that 'any final agreement will have some implications' for Manipur, Arunachal Pradesh and Assam and recommended that 'any agreement that may be finally arrived at must allay the fears of the stakeholders in these states and the state governments must be kept abreast with the emerging dynamics of the talks' (*Frontline*, 9 October 2020, p. 70).

'Odia pride rising, Odisha to get own anthem soon' was a banner headline in a newspaper recently. The demand to accord the historic Odia song *Bande Utkala Janani* (Hail Mother Odisha) the status of anthem is getting louder. A consistent rise in Odia pride—a strong sense of belongingness or feeling proud of being an Odia, among the general populace—in the recent years has no doubt given a strong impetus to this demand. Naveen Patnaik, who has been the Chief Minister of Odisha for 21 years now, cannot speak Odia but, ironically, Odia pride has risen phenomenally during his rule (*The Sunday Guardian*, 15-21 July 2018, p. 6). With the increasing assertiveness of the BJP, which has replaced the Congress as the main Opposition party, the Biju Janata Dal is reviving the plank of regionalism. The same phenomenon is seen in some other states such as West Bengal.

Bihar too adopted a song titled 'Bihar, the Garland of India' as the state song five years ago. The aim was to invoke Bihar identity. Odisha and Bihar have also made demands for their own state flags (*The Sunday Guardian*, 15-21 July 2018, p. 6).

The emergence of identity politics saw pitting of the *moolvasis* (original inhabitants) against outsiders in the area now known as Jharkhand. For well over a decade prior to the creation of Jharkhand, there was intense pressure for the protection of indigenous culture, tradition and language. The demand was for creation of a separate entity where the tribals would have complete control over their *jal* [water], *jungle* [forest] and *zameen* [land] (*The Indian Express*, 13 April 2016, p. 9). The domicile policy announced by the Jharkhand government has laid down that anybody who has lived in Jharkhand for 30 or more years for business, employment or any other reason and has immovable property is to be considered a resident of the state. The Jharkhand Mukti Morcha (JMM) is demanding that a 1932 survey be made the cut-off mark for the eligibility of being a resident. More than 9,000 people had been detained in the ensuing agitation (*The Indian Express*, 15 May 2016, p. 1).

Meghalaya has seen several instances of ethnic clashes—with Bengalis in 1979, Nepalese in 1987, and Biharis in 1992. As a part of the anti-Citizenship Amendment Act (CAA) agitation, the Confederation of Meghalaya Social Organisations and others have been leading a sustained campaign demanding introduction of the Inner Line Permit regime to regulate the entry of 'outsiders' into the state. A new law that will potentially require outsiders to register before entering the state is also being pressed for (*Outlook,* 16 March 2020, p. 26). There is a large population of Sikhs, belonging to backward classes, who have resided in Shillong for nearly five decades. They are being seen as migrants and are facing increasing antagonism, resulting in violence and lawlessness.

Andhra Pradesh has passed a new law making it mandatory for industrial and service sector units to limit the migrant workforce at 25 per cent, and employ three out of four employees from within the state. The government has given three years' time to implement this law. The first to be affected will be workers from Chhattisgarh, Jharkhand, Bihar and Odisha who work mainly in power plants. The Sri City Special Economic Zone (SEZ) will also be affected (*The Indian Express*, 9 August 2019, p. 4).

The Sutlej Yamuna Link (SYL) Canal is a blatant example of how Punjab even flouted the inter-state agreements and decisions of the Supreme Court by not only stopping the construction of the canal but even excavating the previously constructed part of the canal. The land acquisition for the SYL Canal had commenced way back in 1978. In 1981, an agreement was executed by Punjab and Haryana for sharing of waters of the Ravi and Beas rivers. The groundbreaking ceremony was performed by Indira Gandhi in 1982. The project was approved in the Rajiv Gandhi-Longowal Accord in 1985. In 1990, the Punjab terrorists did not want the construction of the canal to proceed and killed the chief engineer and 35 labourers working on the project. When Amarinder Singh's government came to power (2017), it got the Punjab Termination of Agreements Act passed by the Punjab legislature. The Shiromani Akali Dal (SAD) and the Congress Party were vying to take credit for the excavation of the canal. To settle his political scores with the Chief Minister of Haryana, Arvind Kejriwal, Chief Minister of Delhi, supported the Punjab government stand of denying any water to Haryana. In turn, Haryana has threatened to turn off Delhi's water supply. Even more distressing was that the Central government looked the other way. No action was taken during the UPA regime, when both the Central government and the state government were run by the Congress Party. Thereafter, the NDA government too has not been inclined to do anything in the matter. In the meeting of the chief ministers of Punjab and Haryana, held in August 2020 at the behest of the Supreme Court, the chief minister of Punjab has reiterated his stand on the subject and has warned that Punjab will go up in flames if the SYL Canal question is reopened. He has made the same point again in his interview at 'Idea Exchange' in the *Indian Express* on 7 September 2020. If Punjab has a case, it must endeavour to place it before the Supreme Court. It cannot be permitted to take the law in its own hand.

Manohar Singh Gill, former Agriculture Secretary to Government of India and Chief Election Commissioner, in his article 'When hope runs dry' has tried to justify the actions of Punjab on the ground that it has a small share of its own rivers, a farming crisis, and few off-farm jobs. He has pleaded that the solution doesn't lie in court (*The Indian Express*, 16 March 2016, p. 10). In view of the farmers' agitation against the three

Central farm laws, Haryana Chief Minister Manohar Lal Khattar has sought the Central government's intervention in the SYL issue so that the state could get its legitimate share of river water (*The Sunday Guardian*, 21-27 February 2021, p. 3).

Disregarding inter-state agreements and the Supreme Court rulings is not the way to settle such an important, complex dispute. Such actions would be a death knell for India's federalism. This case brings out the limitations of the Central government in taking any corrective action in such politically sensitive cases. Building up a national consensus on these sensitive issues is the only way to deal with them. Unfortunately, major political alliances (UPA and NDA) have shied away from taking any initiative in these matters.

Shiv Sena's Marathi plank comes alive time and again. In September 2015, Diwakar Raote, the then Transport Minister of Maharashtra, announced that one lakh three-wheeler auto-rickshaw permits would be given only to those who showed evidence of having stayed in Maharashtra for over 15 years and speak Marathi (*Loksatta*, 16 September 2015, p. 4). Counterpart of Shiv Sena, the Maharashtra Navnirman Sena's (MNS) firebrand chief Raj Thackeray asked his party workers to burn auto-rickshaws operated by non-Marathis. This led to a repartee by Bihar Deputy Chief Minister Tejashwi Prasad Yadav that Maharashtra was 'not the fiefdom of anybody's father' (*The Indian Express*, 11 March 2016, p. 5). Raj Thackeray halted the agitation only after drawing a flak from across the country. But he reiterated that almost 70-72 per cent of those issued permits were people hailing from outside the state (*The Indian Express*, 12 March 2016, p. 5).

The present coalition government in Maharashtra, comprising the Shiv Sena and two Congress parties, announced this year its intentions to bring forth a bill for reservation of 80 per cent of vacancies for the locals at the next session of the legislature.

The Jharkhand government has also approved a new policy of reserving 75 per cent of jobs up to a salary of Rs 30,000 per month in the private sector for local people (*The Indian Express*, 13 March 2021, p. 1).

The opposition to migrants is seen in several parts of the country. The north-eastern states seem to have an allergy to Hindi-speaking migrants. The year 2008 saw rampant attacks on migrants from UP and Bihar in Maharashtra. In Gujarat, an agitation flared up and mob attacks were launched against migrant workers from MP, Rajasthan, Chhattisgarh and UP in September-October 2018, and just within a week more than 50,000 migrants had to leave various towns and cities in Gujarat. The reason was the alleged rape of a 14-month-old toddler by a Bihari migrant.

Gujarat has decided to reserve 80 per cent of factory jobs in the state only for Gujaratis. This is in spite of a large migrant workforce contributing to Gujarat's rise as a manufacturing hub. According to the Economic Survey 2016-17, net migration among the 20 to 29-year-old group to Gujarat stood at nearly 3.5 lakh, which was one of the highest among Indian states.

Kamal Nath, the then Chief Minister of Madhya Pradesh, stated that youths in the state were losing jobs to migrant workers and announced that 75 per cent of vacancies in both the public and private sectors would be reserved for the locals. The present Madhya Pradesh Chief Minister, Shivraj Singh Chouhan, has announced that government jobs in the state would now be reserved for people from the state only. Describing it as an 'important decision', Chouhan said in a video message, 'We are making the required legal provisions for it. Resources of Madhya Pradesh are for the children of Madhya Pradesh' (*The Hindu*, 18 August 2020). Former Chief Minister Kamal Nath said Chouhan had, in fact, acted in accordance with decisions of the previous Congress government. 'Anyway, you woke up from sleep after 15 years today, regarding the employment of youth.'

UP has gone a step further by promising that 90 per cent of the jobs in every industrial unit in the state will be reserved for local youth.

The Haryana Assembly has passed the Haryana State Employment of Local Candidates Bill to reserve 75 per cent of jobs in the private sector for locals. It will cover all companies, societies, trusts, limited liability partnership firms and partnership firms located in the state (*The Indian Express*, 6 November 2020, p. 1). This was in spite of the fact that a similar bill which was reserved for President's approval earlier had been objected to by the Government of India. The state BJP election manifesto had emphasised that industries which give 90 per cent of their jobs to Haryana residents will receive special incentives.

Manipur passed a bill proposing that anyone who settled in the state after 1951 be barred from being recognised as a permanent resident. He will either have to leave or seek special entry and work permit. The bill has put the Central government in a quandary, as it fixes the cut-off year 20 years before Assam's disqualification year of 1971. In fact, Manipur became a state only in 1972. The state has apparently buckled under pressure from the dominant Meitei community (*The Indian Express*, 2 September 2018, p. 10).

In 2015, the imposition of a ban on the sale of meat for four days during the eight-day Jain festival of *Paryushana* led to an unsavoury controversy between Jains and Gujaratis on one side and the Thackeray brothers, on the other. An editorial in the Shiv Sena mouthpiece, *Saamana*, asked Jains to rein in their 'fanaticism'. The editorial warned that the Jain community's financial empire could be turned to ashes in a matter of minutes, and that unlike Muslims they did not have another country to turn to. Muslims at least have Pakistan for them (*The Indian Express*, 11 September 2015, p. 1).

The National Capital Region (NCR) comprises Delhi, Gurugram and Faridabad in Haryana, and Noida and Ghaziabad in Uttar Pradesh. But in the Covid pandemic, borders between these states were closed. Medical facilities in Delhi government-run hospitals and private ones were restricted only to the residents of Delhi. This was a negation of the concept of NCR.

State pride has, at times, led to unimaginable actions. During the 'Blue Star' Army Operation launched in the Golden Temple in 1984 to flush out Bhindranwale and other terrorists, some Sikh soldiers had deserted in protest. Later, they were proceeded against by the Army. The Government of Punjab decided to double the monthly allowance to the deserters and their dependents, and announced grant for fee of their wards in schools and medical colleges (*The Indian Express*, 11 September 2015, p. 1).

The boundary dispute between Assam and Mizoram and between Tripura and Mizoram led to the suspension of traffic between the states, digging of trenches along the border and even destroying a primary school building on the state border. It is not uncommon to see disputes regarding administrative control over a few border villages between states such as Andhra and Odisha, Maharashtra and Andhra, and between the states in the North East. This has vitiated the atmosphere in the concerned states. Is this the one India we have been talking about? These shocking developments showed the ugly face of provincialism.

The importance of these issues needs to be appreciated in the context of an emerging India in which internal migration is a major driving force speeding up economic development. Ambedkar had rightly said, 'An ideal society should be mobile, should be full of channels for conveying a change taking place in one part to another.'

Arvind Subramanian, the then Chief Economic Advisor to the GOI, must be complimented for bringing out the extent of migration in India in *The Economic Survey 2016-17*. The evidence showed that the annual inter-state migration flow was close to 9 million in 2011. Significant findings of the Survey may be noted: First, India is increasingly on the move—and so are Indians. Annually, the inter-state labour mobility averaged 5-6 million people between 2001 and 2011, yielding an inter-state migrant population of about 60 million and inter-district migration as high as 80 million. Second, migration is accelerating. In the period 2001-2011, according to census estimates, the annual rate of growth of labour migrants nearly doubled relative to the previous decade, rising to 4.5 per cent per annum in 2001-2011 from 2.4 per cent in 1991-2001. Third, a potentially exciting finding, for which there is tentative though not conclusive evidence, is that while internal political borders impede the flow of people, language does not seem to be a demonstrable barrier to the flow of people. Another interesting finding of this study is that the acceleration of migration was particularly pronounced for females and increased at nearly twice the rate of male migration in the 2000s (GOI 2017, pp. 265, 277).

The estimates of migrant labour displaced by the national lockdowns in March-April 2020 vary a great deal, but even the lower estimates are staggering. The Chief Labour Commissioner put the figure at 26 lakh. Chinmoy Tumbe puts it at 30 million or 3 crore or 15-20 per cent of the urban workforce. Amitabh Kundu, et al. estimate it at 22 million while Maajid estimates it at 5 million, in the first wave (*The Indian Express*, 8 June 2020, p. 7).

The Census 2011 counted 14.2 crore migrants in the decade preceding it, intra-district to inter-state. Top migrant destinations were Maharashtra, Delhi, Gujarat, Haryana, Karnataka and Punjab, in the descending order. The top migrant sources were UP, Bihar, Rajasthan, West Bengal, Odisha and Madhya Pradesh, in the descending order (*The Indian Express*, 28 July 2019, p. 12).

Looking to the experience of the last few years cited above, I believe that the rate of growth of migration and the rise in employment and productivity would have been much higher had there been a more congenial atmosphere in the states.

The outflow of labour has been mainly from UP, Bihar, MP, Jharkhand, Uttarakhand and West Bengal. The staggering size of inter-state migration and the human problem of their displacement shocked India's conscience during the long nationwide lockdown due to Covid 19 pandemic. Day after day images of thousands of migrants heading for their home states with their meagre belongings, men, women and children—walking, bicycling, sitting precariously on top of buses, crowding in bullock carts, trucks and railway bogies—brought home the enormity of the suffering of migrant labour in the country. After the partial lifting of the lockdown in most states, shortage of labour emerged as a gigantic problem hampering the normalisation of economic and commercial activity in the country.

The rise of sub-nationalism, domiciliary restrictions and agitations against migrant labour can be a catastrophe and pose serious problems, particularly in labour-intensive sectors such as infrastructure, real estate, small and medium enterprises and so on. The seriousness of the rapidly growing menace of sub-nationalism must be addressed with utmost urgency in the national perspective.

Creation of Smaller States – A Troubling Development

In his letter to chief ministers dated 16 January 1956, Nehru wrote:

> In considering these difficult questions of reorganisation, I have felt more and more that *we should have fewer and fewer and larger states.... I think it will be a worthwhile development later on for two or sometimes more states to join together to form a larger state.* A suggestion was made that West Bengal and Bihar should form one larger state. From any economic or planning point of view this is obviously desirable.... This suggestion, I was happy to find, met with a favourable response though obviously nothing could be done about it at this stage and it requires careful consideration. So also, at a later stage, we might have the joining together of some of the states in South India. (Parthasarathi 1988, p. 335)

The ball has now swung to the other extreme. During the last few years, the trend is towards the creation of smaller states such as in the North East, Goa, Chhattisgarh, Jharkhand and Uttarakhand. There are also demands for the creation of Gorkhaland in West Bengal, Bodoland in Assam, Vidarbha in Maharashtra, and Bundelkhand, Poorvanchal and Harit Pradesh in Uttar Pradesh. There is a demand for division of Karnataka and creation of a residual Mysore state. Voices are also being raised intermittently for separating Saurashtra and Kutch from Gujarat. A National Federation of Small States was formally established in August

2010, with headquarters in Lucknow, with a view to energise the creation of smaller states. These demands are based on various considerations which are not necessarily linguistic.

As seen from the experience of North Eastern states, there is no convincing evidence to show that small states perform better. These states were created either on an ethnic basis or to counter secessionist movements. The Srikrishna Committee studied the advantages of small states and came to the conclusion that the performance of the three small states—Uttarakhand, Chhattisgarh and Jharkhand created in 2000—through their decade-long existence, had been somewhat of a 'study in contrast'. In terms of governance, political stability and economic performance, Uttarakhand has done reasonably well. The state received 'special category status' as a hill state which facilitated a more generous funding pattern from the Plan funds which contributed to its rapid economic growth. Chhattisgarh, although it has seen political stability and decent economic growth, has continued to face serious internal security problems particularly from the Maoists. The state has not been able to control or even contain successfully the violence and extortions perpetrated by the Naxalites thereby causing a huge demand and burden on the resources of both the state and the Central exchequer. Jharkhand, unfortunately, despite initial signs of better economic performance, has failed to impress in most areas of governance. In 10 years, the state has had eight chief ministers, besides being under President's Rule twice. Its economic performance has been dipping steadily and internal security problems created by the Maoists/Naxals continue to exist. Unemployment in the state presently is among the highest in the country...*looking at their performance, it would be difficult to say whether mere creation of small states is a panacea for all ills and would ensure all round development of the region and its people. The other view is that the goals of development can best be served by providing good governance irrespective of the size of the state* (GOI 2010, pp. 439-40).

More serious are the implications of creating multiple sub-nationalities based on narrow considerations such as even diet, cuisine, apparel and culture, as was argued before the Srikrishna Committee in support of the demand for the creation of Telangana. Carried to its logical conclusion, in a country of such diversities, this will lead to a complete balkanisation of India.

India is a Union of states based on the concept of a strong Centre. The creation of small states will further weaken the bargaining power and leverages of states vis-à-vis the Centre. The polity will get more fragmented. Too many regional parties based on narrow focus and interests will further weaken the national perspective.[6]

In spite of all the disadvantages, linguistic states at least have the advantage of bringing the government closer to the people. Conducting government business in the language of the people has its merits which need not be overemphasized. But, further dividing unilingual states, purely for reasons of political expediency, must be avoided. An exception could be Uttar Pradesh, with its huge population (the strength of 80 Members in the Lok Sabha comprising 543 members, and 31 members in the Rajya Sabha out of the total of 242 members) and very large geographical area which pose humongous administrative problems. But such has been the politics of reorganisation of states that, in spite of the dissenting note given by K.M. Panikkar, member of SRC, suggesting splitting up of UP, this state has remained untouched, except for the carving out of a small hill state of Uttarakhand from it in the year 2000. This is reflected in the adage, 'UP i.e., India i.e., Bharat'!

If and when parliamentary constituencies are redrawn on the basis of the 2031 census, the representation of states in the Lok Sabha will be so lopsided as to pose a real challenge to India's federalism. Currently, the top five states with the highest number of Lok Sabha seats are UP, Maharashtra, West Bengal, Bihar and Tamil Nadu. They account for 249

---

6. It was for the first time in 1984 that as many as 57 per cent of the non-Congress or Opposition MPs elected were from regional parties. The percentage of votes cast in favour of regional parties also rose from 6.3 in 1962 to 20.8 in 1984 (Kashyap 1998, p. 244).

of the total 553 seats. The strength of AP, Bihar and Madhya Pradesh has been reduced after the creation of Telangana, Jharkhand and Chhattisgarh respectively. Due to the considerably lower rate of growth of population in the southern states during the last several decades, their representation is likely to go down, while that of the northern states will go up considerably. This iniquitous position is unlikely to be acceptable to the southern states and the entire basis for representation in the Lok Sabha and the Rajya Sabha will have to be examined afresh. The terms of reference of the Fifteenth Finance Commission had laid down that the Commission should use population data of 2011 and not 1971 when making recommendations on the allocation of tax revenues among states. This was to replace the compromise formula in place since 1976 which sought to give incentives to states to control their population growth. Southern states—Andhra Pradesh, Kerala, Karnataka and Tamil Nadu (and Telangana after the bifurcation of AP)—are up in arms. Creation of smaller states will further complicate this situation.

The Frankenstein of Domiciliary Requirements

Article 35A of the Constitution by which special protection was given to J&K citizens in respect of public employment and acquisition and holding of property in the state had become highly contentious. This protection was given to protect the rights which had accrued to the state citizens under the enactment made by the Maharaja of Kashmir in 1927. The writ petitions challenging the Article are still pending in the Supreme Court. With the abrogation of Article 370, this protection has also become inoperative as the concerned Article was incorporated in the Constitution by a Presidential Order issued in pursuance of Article 370. But, in view of domiciliary restrictions imposed by several states, the entire subject calls for a close review.

Now, the Permanent Residence Certificate (PRC) in J&K has a new name, Domicile Certificate. The Lt. Governor of J&K has clarified that all PRC holders can automatically get a domicile certificate. But those who have been staying in the state for years together, such as the Valmikis who were brought from Punjab, and displaced persons [after the Partition of the country] settled in J&K since 1947, who were earlier ineligible to get a PRC, will now be able to get a domicile certificate (*The Indian Express*, 21 July 2020, p. 2).

As stated earlier, the 'sons of the soil' concept has a long history. The Nizam of Hyderabad had issued orders in 1919 to protect the residents of the Telangana area and give them preference in government employment in their own region. These '*mulki* rules' had, however, become inoperative from 21 March 1959 when a law passed by Parliament—The Public Employment (Requirement as to Residence) Act, 1957—came into effect. Nevertheless, the law had provided that government employment in the Telangana area would be open only to those who had been residing there for not less than 15 years and could provide written evidence to this effect.... By its order dated 28 March 1969, the Supreme Court held the entire domicile rule to be unconstitutional (Ramesh 2016, pp. 29-30).

India's Constitution recognises only a single citizenship, that of India. Article 19 guarantees to every citizen the fundamental right to move freely throughout the territory of India, and to settle, acquire, hold and dispose of property in any part of that territory. As the Supreme Court observed in the *A.K. Gopalan's case,* these provisions are meant to remove provincial barriers and to establish that the citizens of India are citizens of one country, free to move, work, live and settle in any part of the country. The equality provisions of Article 15 forbid discrimination against citizens on the grounds of religion, race, caste, sex and place of birth. Significantly, language is not included in this list, but, according to eminent jurist H.M. Seervai, discrimination on the grounds of language is opposed to the basic concept of the unity of India to which a common citizenship and a common country testify (Seervai 1996, pp. 2585-6). Looking to the rise of provincialism brought out earlier, it is imperative to amend Article 15 of the Constitution to specifically bar discrimination based on language.

The next question which arises is that of state domicile. The domiciliary requirements laid down by state governments make a mockery of rights given by Articles 15 and 19 cited above, and Article 16 [equality of opportunity in matters of public employment]. As seen earlier, the division of states on linguistic basis and also reorganisation of states generally has introduced divisive and increasingly parochial tendencies which run counter to the whole spirit, and the numerous provisions of the Constitution, designed to promote unity of the country.

One of the main instruments used by the states to protect the interests of their residents, and to keep persons of other states from getting any benefits of working in the state, is to tighten the provisions of domiciliary requirements. Though there is a single citizenship for India, the courts have recognised the concept of state domicile. In *Radhabai v. Bombay*, the Bombay High Court had held: 'The persons residing in any state, such as the state of Bombay, and having an intention to continue residence in that state for an unlimited time or to make their permanent home in that state can therefore be said to have the domicile of that state.' However, in *State v. Narayandas Mangilal Dayame* (1957) Bom. 880, (58) A.B. 68, 59 Bom. L.R. 901, a *Full Bench of the Supreme Court had overruled Radhabai's case,* (1955) Bom. 1039, ('55) A. B. 439, 442, 57 Bom. L. R. 827, holding, among other things, '*...in India, we have one citizenship, the citizenship of India. We have one domicile—the domicile in India.*' Seervai has summarised the main points in the judgment for countering them. The Supreme Court had held:

> Now it is clear on a reading of the Constitution that it recognises only one domicile, namely, domicile in India. Article 5...is clear and explicit on this point and it refers only to one domicile, namely, "domicile in the territory of India". Moreover, it must be remembered that India is not a federal state in the traditional sense of the term. It is not a compact of sovereign states which have come together to form a federation by ceding a part of their sovereignty to the federal state. It has undoubtedly certain federal features but it is not a federal state

and it has only one citizenship, namely, the citizenship of India. It has also one single unified legal system which extends throughout the country. It is not possible to say that a distinct and separate system of laws prevails in each state forming part of the Union of India. The legal system which prevails throughout the territory of India is one single indivisible system with a single unified justicing system having the Supreme Court of India at the apex of the hierarchy, which lays down the law for the entire country. It is true that with respect to the subjects set out in List II [State List] of the 7th Schedule to the Constitution, the states have the power to make laws and are subject to the overriding power of Parliament, the states can also make laws with respect to subjects enumerated in List III [Concurrent List] of the 7th Schedule of the Constitution. But the legal system under the rubric of which such laws are made by the states is a single legal system which may truly be described as the Indian legal system. It would be absurd to suggest that the legal system varies from state to state or that the legal system of a state is different from the legal system of the Union of India, merely because with respect, the states have power to make laws. *The concept of 'domicile' has no relevance to the applicability of municipal laws, whether made by the Union or the states. It would not, therefore, in our opinion be right to say that a citizen of India is domiciled in one state or another forming part of the Union of India. The domicile which he has is only one domicile, namely, domicile in the territory of India.* When a person who is permanently resident in one state goes to another state with intention to reside there permanently or indefinitely, his domicile does not undergo any change; he does not acquire a new domicile of (sic) choice. His domicile remains the same, namely, Indian domicile. *We think it is highly detrimental to the concept of unity and integrity of India to think in terms of state domicile.* (Seervai 1991, p. 322)

I have deliberately given this extensive quotation as it is highly relevant for further consideration of the issues on hand. I fully agree with the arguments adduced therein. Seervai has argued that a common citizenship must not be confused with a common Indian domicile and that this judgment was not good law as it was a judgment *per incuriam* being contrary to the law laid down by the Supreme Court in *D.P. Joshi v. the State of Madhya Bharat* ([1955] 1 SCR 1215; AIR 1955 SC 334), in which it was held that in law there can be a state domicile under our Constitution and the requirement of domicile did not violate Article 15 (1) which allowed discrimination, inter alia, on the ground of 'residence' (Seervai 1991, pp. 316-7). Seervai has also argued that since certain laws, particularly personal laws, are applicable state-wise, the concept of state domicile is relevant and must be accepted. I do not want to enter into a debate on this point but from the point of view of the concerns discussed in this book and looking to the ways in which the concept of state domicile has undercut the rights given in Articles 15 (the state shall not discriminate against any citizen on grounds of religion, race, caste, sex, place of birth or any of them), 16 (equality of opportunity in matters of public employment) and 19 (right to reside and settle in any part of the territory of India) of the Constitution, fresh thought needs to be given to the subject and to carry out, if necessary, suitable amendments to the Constitution.

M.P. Jain, in his article 'Federalism in India', has stated that the very first seminar held by the Indian Law Institute, as far back as 1957, was on 'Inter-State Barriers to Movement of Commodities and Persons'. It had suggested a few topics for research, which included, among others, state discrimination against non-resident individuals including especially: (i) undue insistence on proficiency in a regional language as a prerequisite to recruitment into public service; (ii) state measures setting an unduly long period of time as prerequisite to the attainment of 'residence' by an Individual; (iii) discrimination against non-resident citizens on the right to acquire immovable property in particular localities; and (iv) restrictions on the admission of non-residents in the state institutions of higher learning (JILI-1964, 370).

Unfortunately, these issues are languishing all these years and have now become matters of serious concern. Even in the National Eligibility-cum-Entrance Test (NEET), merit is being relegated to the sidelines, while domicile criterion has become the overriding touchstone. State quotas are defeating the very purpose of the all-India medical entrance examination. Thus 85 per cent of seats in government colleges are reserved for 'domicile' students and only 15 per cent of seats are available to applicants from other states. Seats in the private colleges are also reserved on this basis (*Outlook*, 15 July 2019, pp. 28-29).

The SRC, while making its recommendations for linguistic reorganisation of states, had recognised the inherent dangers involved therein and had suggested enactment of a law by Parliament under Article 16(3)[7] to safeguard the freedom given by the Constitution under the said Article. Though five decades have elapsed, no thought has been given to it by successive governments of various hues, colours, and ideologies. Obviously, this is due to the fear of the likely political backlash. No political party being prepared to address such an important national issue is an eloquent commentary on India's democracy.

A Way Out

The SRC had strongly repudiated the 'home land' concept, which, according to it, negated one of the fundamental principles of the Indian Constitution—namely, 'equal opportunities and equal rights of all citizens throughout the length and breadth of the Union'. It had warned against exclusivity on the basis of any primordial identity—whether of birth, language, caste, region or religion. *The SRC had pointedly advised that the Indian nation and Indian states must provide space for the flowering*

---

7. Article 16(3) states: Nothing in this Article shall prevent Parliament from making any law prescribing in regard to a class or classes of employment or appointment to an office under the Government of, or any local authority within, a state or union territory, any requirement as to residence within that state or union territory prior to such employment or appointment.

of all cultures in their richness and variety. A 'sons of the soil' policy cannot really work in a socially diverse society in which the histories of migration are also multi-layered. Perhaps by sheer omission, 'culture' was not mentioned as a factor for claiming a separate identity and this is precisely what was latched on to by Telanganaites while pressing their demand for a separate state.

The SRC in its anxiety to safeguard national unity had made the following recommendations:

- The domicile tests in force in certain states operate to the disadvantage of minority groups. The GOI should, therefore, undertake a legislation under Article 16 (3) of the Constitution in order to simplify and liberalise the requirements as to residence.
- As far as possible, Public Service Commissions should be constituted to serve more than one state.
- Appointments to Public Service Commissions serving even single states should be made by President [of India] as in the case of appointments to joint Public Service Commissions.
- The services of the Governors should be utilised for enforcing the safeguards for linguistic minorities (GOI 1955, pp. 260-1).

Of these four recommendations, I find only the one pertaining to enacting a legislation under Article 16(3) of the Constitution valuable but it has been totally sidetracked by the GOI, and this has led to an alarming situation on the subject. The other three recommendations are neither workable nor are they likely to serve any purpose.

For bringing about greater coordination between states, Nehru created five zonal councils—Northern, Central, Eastern, Western and Southern— to 'deal with matters of common concern, promote inter-state concord *and arrest the growth of acute state consciousness'.* The experience so far has shown that the zonal councils have become mere appendages and have served no purpose whatsoever. In fact, it is high time they are abolished.

Nehru wanted states to take special steps to safeguard the interests of linguistic minorities. Experience has shown that the states are hardly interested in taking any steps in the matter. For example, the decision of the Karnataka government in November 2020 to set up a welfare board for the Maratha community met with stiff resistance from the Kannada activists who had given a threat of a strike if the decision was not reversed (*Outlook*, 7 December 2020, p. 7). Nehru had also contemplated the appointment of common Governors, establishment of common High Courts, and Common Public Service Commissions in certain regions (Parthasarathi 1988, pp. 335-337). None of these are workable. None of these initiatives materialised because of resistance by states. Thus, so far as linguistic states are concerned, none of Nehru's initiatives materialised. And with the enormous rise of parochialism, it is unlikely that any such proposals would even be entertained by the states, any longer.

When linguistic riots rocked Assam and Bengal, fearing that the unity of the nation was crumbling, Munshi wrote to Nehru on 29 May 1961 about his apprehensions. He suggested, inter alia, the following programme to avoid the 'linguistic balkanisation' of the country:

- The implementation of an all-India policy of preventing the states from enforcing unilinguality by law, executive action or patronage, but to accept multi-linguality in all the states.
- Establishment of all-India universities with English and Hindi as compulsory media. This can be done in the following manner: (1) by constitutional amendments taking power to establish Central universities, (2) by enlarging the affiliative scope of existing Central universities, and (3) by channelling the bulk of the grants of the University Grants Commission (UGC) to only such universities which, by accepting these media, acquire a national status.

Munshi followed it up by discussing the matter at length with Nehru.

Later, Nehru took steps to convene a conference [of chief ministers, educationists and others] in Delhi from 28 September to 1 October 1961.... Then came the Chinese invasion and the spectacle of India rising to [*sic*] one man to resist the aggressor. Unfortunately, this led to the wrong conclusion that the task was fulfilled and so no special effort was needed (Munshi 2012, pp. 235-40).

Munshi has rightly observed, 'The situation today is, if anything, much worse than what it was in 1961.' Unfortunately, no action was taken on any of the above points. Let us hope the same will not happen again in 2020, when the country has come together again in the face of Chinese aggression in Ladakh. If not addressed with a sense of urgency, these issues are so fundamental as to sap India's roots of nationhood.

The *Economic Survey 2016-17* has predicted an increasing rate of growth of migrants over the years. The Survey has noted:

> The acceleration in migration has taken place against the backdrop of discouraging incentives such as domicile provisions for working in different states, [and] lack of portability of benefits, legal and other entitlements upon relocation. To sustain this churn, these policy hurdles have to be overcome. Portability of food security benefits, healthcare, and a basic social security framework for the migrants are crucial—potentially through an inter-state self-registration process. While there do currently exist multiple schemes that address migrant welfare, they are implemented at the state level, and hence require inter-state coordination of fiscal costs of migration. The domestic remittances market, estimated to exceed Rs 1.5 lakh crore, can also be leveraged to enhance financial inclusion for migrant workers and their families in the source region. Such measures would vastly enhance the welfare gains of migration and encourage even greater integration of labour market in India. (GOI 2017, pp. 277-78)

The 'One Nation, One Ration Card' initiative of the Modi government is receiving good response and the number of states and UTs on the portability platform has increased to 24. This development was significant as the government had announced a national portability roll-out of ration cards across all states and UTs by 31 March 2021 (*The Indian Express*, 2 August 2020, p. 3).

Meghnad Desai in his column 'Out of My Mind' titled 'A grave danger' has invited attention to an important decision of the Supreme Court:

> Someone from outside a state is not eligible to claim reservation granted by the state. When a state grants reservations they are only for 'citizens' of the state and not outsiders. This strikes a crippling blow at the idea of a single citizenship for all Indians. No matter whether 'insiders' or 'outsiders', Indians should be free to live and work and enjoy reservations they qualify for, all across India.... In other words, state reservations are not open to all Indians.... The court's decision means that only the upper castes who are not entitled to reservations (and the non-Hindus) are able to enjoy the rights of mobility across India without paying a cost. (*The Indian Express*, 9 September 2018, p. 12)

However, as seen above, the right to mobility of all persons is also being circumscribed by the increasingly restrictive policies adopted by states, which completely undercut their fundamental rights.

Maharashtra had gone one step further by laying down region-wise quota for admissions to medical colleges. In September 2020, the state government scrapped the 70:30 region-wise formula for admissions in medical courses. 'Instead of the 70:30 quota, it would be "one Maharashtra, one merit", said Medical Education Minister Amit Deshmukh. Students and parents had since long been demanding the scrapping of the contentious 70:30 formula under which 70 per cent seats in medical colleges were reserved for students in their districts.

As stated in the previous section on domiciliary restrictions, Article

15 of the Constitution needs to be amended to prohibit discrimination based on language, and to make sure that domiciliary requirements are not permitted to undercut equal rights available to all citizens in matters of public employment, under Article 16.

Following the Supreme Court decision laying down a limit of 50 per cent on reservations in employment, a similar limit of 50 per cent could be laid down for recruitment of locals, leaving the balance 50 per cent for persons from other states. The question of non-availability of reservation benefits to migrants brought out in the above comment of Meghnad Desai also needs to be addressed for remedial action.

The Public Employment (Requirement as to Residence) Act, 1957, had a limited application and applied only to AP, HP, Manipur and Tripura. The 'Objects' of the Act had clarified that:

Clause (2) of Article 16 of the Constitution provides, inter alia, that no citizen shall, on grounds only of residence be ineligible for, or discriminated against in respect of, any employment or office under the State. *Parliament is, however, competent under clause (3) of the said Article to regulate the extent to which it would he (sic) permissible for a State to depart from the above principle.*

In considering this aspect of the question, the State Reorganisation Commission recommended that if any departure from the principle of non-discrimination on the ground of residence is to be authorised at all, it should be such as to cause minimum hardship and that necessary legislation in this regard should be undertaken.

On the basis of these recommendations, provision was made in this behalf in paragraphs 14, 15 and 16 of the memorandum on safeguards for linguistic minorities which was laid before Parliament in September, 1956. *It was stated in the memorandum that the Government of India did not consider it necessary or desirable to impose restrictions for any public employment and that it was proposed to repeal all the laws in force prescribing any requirement as to residence for any public employment.* It was further stated that in certain cases exceptions might have to be made for a transitional period to the general rule of non-discrimination in the Telangana area of the former Hyderabad State and in certain backward areas. In pursuance of this decision, it is now proposed to repeal all the laws in force prescribing any requirement as to residence within a State or Union Territory for any public employment in that State or Union territory. Exception, however, is being made in the case of Himachal Pradesh, Manipur and Tripura and the area transferred from the State of Hyderabad to Andhra Pradesh. *In respect of these areas, it is proposed to prescribe residential qualifications for a limited period not exceeding five years* in regard to non-gazetted services including the service of tehsildars. It is proposed to empower the Central Government to make rules for the purpose.

The action taken by the GOI was clearly inadequate. The question was not of just protecting the interests of linguistic minorities, and did not pertain to only a few states. This was convenient misinterpretation of the recommendation of the SRC! *If a legislation had been passed by Parliament debarring restrictions on public employment at that time itself, the problem could have been nipped in the bud.* This could also have been accepted as a *quid pro quo* for linguistic reorganisation of states, for which there was so much clamour.

Now the question has become important with restrictions being imposed on public employment by almost all states. The right to equality is often described as a 'meta' right, a right above all rights. But, *the issues involved have become politically sensitive and a national consensus must be evolved, if they are to be addressed without political wrangling and one-upmanship.* The ramifications of the issues may first be got examined by the Law Commission of India. Thereafter, a comprehensive paper could be prepared for discussion in the National Integration Council. The subject may also be discussed in the Inter-State Council. If necessary, advisory opinion of the Supreme Court may be sought under Article 143 of the Constitution. I am suggesting this overly judicious and cautious approach in view of the political sensitivities of the issues and their national importance.

Official Language

Language turned out to be the most divisive issue in the deliberations of the Constituent Assembly. So much so that at one stage, it looked as if the unanimous adoption of the Constitution itself could come into difficulties. Credit must be given to the sensitivity and the statesmanship of not just the top leadership of the Congress Party but also the strong advocates of Hindi and English for their willingness to accept a reasonable compromise.

The problem was truly immense. George Grierson (Irish linguist in British India) in his monumental work *Linguistic Survey of India* mentioned the existence of 179 languages and 544 dialects in undivided India. According to the 1951 Census of India, there were a total of 845 languages or dialects spoken in India. The 1961 Census mentioned 1,652 mother tongues of which 103 were foreign mother tongues. Eighty-seven per cent of the total population has, however, been classified as speaking the 14 major languages specified in the original Eighth Schedule to the Constitution, and English. Out of the 439 million people of India in 1961, only 30 million can be said to be bilingual. Thus, less than seven per cent know an Indian language other than their mother tongue. Hindi speakers were calculated at 30.37 per cent of the total population which are mostly in North India and English speakers at 0.05 per cent (Agrawala 1977, pp. 43-44).

Nehru genuinely believed that despite the vast size of the country, India has singularly few languages and these are intimately allied to each other. 'However numerous the difficult problems India has to solve, language clearly is not one of them,' he observed in 1937 (Agrawala 1977, p. 46). Similarly, in 1936, Nehru said that the day on which India achieves freedom, communal differences and jealousies will get solved automatically. His other statements like 'the communal problem was a wasteful diversion from the main campaign against the British', 'communal parties were giants with feet of clay, who would fade into nothingness in the light of the reason once the British were pushed out', showed how far removed he was from realities (Godbole 2014, p. 91).

O.P. Minocha in his article, 'The Impact of Gandhian Ideology on the Indian Constitution', has brought out an interesting sidelight that a small group, led by Nehru, did not want an official language to be prescribed by the Constitution (Grover 1987, p. 171).

K.M. Munshi was closely associated with the deliberations on evolving a language formula. He has narrated how in the early stages of the Constituent Assembly, the Sub-Committee on Fundamental Rights, following Gandhiji's lead, adopted the following formula:

> Hindustani, written either in Devanagari or the Persian script at the option of the citizen, shall, as the national language, be the first official language of the Union. English shall be the second official language for such period as the Union may by law determine. All official records of the Union shall be kept in Hindustani in both the scripts and also in English until the Union by law otherwise provides.

This formula was adopted in the hope that if the Muslim League came into the Constituent Assembly, it would prove sufficiently acceptable to both sides. In a dissenting note of 19 April 1947, Ambedkar had suggested that Hindustani should be made the language not only of the Union, but also of all the units, as otherwise 'linguistic diversity will make Indian administration impossible'. He had further stated: 'There is a great danger of the Hindustani language becoming Sanskritized by Hindi writers and Arabicized by Muslim writers. If this happens, Hindustani will cease to be a national language and will become a sectional language. Without a National Academy, the Hindustani language will not be able to overcome this danger.' But this suggestion was not found to be workable.

Munshi has written:

Shyama Prasad Mookerjee, Gopalaswami Ayyangar and myself, three representatives of non-Hindi-speaking Provinces, were anxious to produce a formula which would set the country in the direction of developing a national medium.... The Congress Party passed a resolution, moved by me, accepting Hindi and Devanagari as the national language and script respectively. There was a storm in the meeting. Nehru was very unhappy. Matters then stood adjourned to the last stage of the Constituent Assembly. In July 1949, a few of us met informally and drafted Articles making Hindi the official language and Devanagari the official script of the country, with English as the additional official language for a period of ten years. It was supported by about 80 members of the Constituent Assembly— the largest group in the Congress Party. A battle royal raged in the National Language Committee, at party meetings and in informal conferences. Ultimately three schools of thought emerged:

- Those Hindi enthusiasts who thought that Hindi should and could be introduced not only as the official language of the Union, but even in the high courts *straightway*;
- Those who wanted to retain English as it was before 1947, leaving Hindi to be studied as a second language, promoted in easy stages into an official language; and
- Those who thought English should be replaced by Hindi as the official language of the Union *progressively*, as and when Hindi was ready to perform in some measure the functions then performed by English.

The proposal of some south Indian representatives that Arabic numerals should be used in the Devanagari script immediately raised a fierce controversy. The South had, for several generations, adopted the Arabic numerals in Tamil, Telugu, Malayalam and Kannada, and they were used even in Sanskrit books. However, when it was discovered that the Arabic numerals were Indian, both in origin and by adoption in the south, the opposition to Arabic numerals lost its edge. (Munshi 2012, pp. 215-18)

In the wide-ranging discussion, a number of suggestions were made by members to resolve the language controversy. The All India University Teachers Convention had passed a resolution that there should be a common Devanagari script for all Indian languages. Speaking in the Constituent Assembly on 18 December 1948, O.V. Alagesan said:

> When it is recognised that the various provincial languages of India are more ancient, more developed and richer in content and expression than the common language, Hindi, it will be realised that this step will cause great dissatisfaction and heart-burning. It is said that there is no organic unity between the script and the language. I do not know. It is for eminent educationists to offer their opinion on the matter. All I can say is that there are certain special sounds in every language which can be expressed only by the ancient script with which the language has been associated. It is not possible otherwise. (LSS, vol. VII, 2009, p. 912)

It was through such a maze that a common ground had to be found.

It is out of these conflicts that the formula, which came to be known in the press as the 'Munshi-Ayyangar Formula', was drawn up as representing the most realistic approach to the problem, attracting the largest support. Nehru made an impassioned plea for the adoption of the Munshi-Ayyangar proposal, not because he thought it to be perfect but because this integrated solution was the result of continuous efforts, endeavour, thought and consultation.

In his letter to Munshi dated 19 August 1949, Vallabhbhai Patel had written:

> Language is a vital question in which it is necessary for us to take

both a long-range, and practical view of the problem. I know the feelings and strength behind the many currents and cross-currents in the party on this question. Happily, however, the range of controversy has been narrowed.... There seems to be a consensus of opinion as to the place of Hindi in Devanagari script. It will, and must, be the national or official language of India. (V. Shankar 1977, p. 497)

Ultimately, with several changes, it became part of Articles 343 [official language of the Union] and 344 [commission and committee of Parliament on official language] of the Constitution.

Speaking in the Constituent Assembly on the final draft of the Constitution on 18 November 1949, M. Ananthasayanam Ayyangar, member of the Drafting Committee, said:

Then there was the question of language, over which we thought there will be much controversy at one stage. Three or four times we met outside this House and also inside and ultimately we have resolved the question harmoniously. Hindi has been accepted as the *lingua franca* or the official language of India. These are all matters [including division of powers between the units and the Centre, having a common Constitution for the units and the Centre] each one of which for its resolution would have taken many months, if not years. We have resolved them all in the short period of time at our disposal. (LSS, Vols. X-XII, 2009, p. 662)

Most importantly, the compromise formula has worked and held good all these years.

Two new Articles were added (350A and 350B) by the Constitution (Seventh Amendment) Act, 1956. Article 350A contains a directive to every state and local authority to provide adequate facilities for instruction in the mother tongue at the primary level to children belonging to linguistic minority groups; Article 350B provided for the appointment of a special officer for linguistic minorities to ensure the observance of the safeguards provided for them.

The issue of official language continued to be sensitive and at one point it looked as if it would threaten the unity of the country itself. In a letter to Vijayalakshmi Pandit, Indian High Commissioner in London, on 9 February 1958, Nehru wrote:

> I wonder if you know how an agitation is spreading in Madras against the North on the plea that the North dominates over the South and does not look after its interests. *Indeed there is a party there which actually claims for separation from India. All this is rather mad. But then we have plenty of mad people in India. Rajaji also appears to have lost his head completely.* He is carrying on an aggressive agitation against Hindi and in favour of English.... Rajaji actually wants a whole part of the Constitution dealing with languages to be deleted and further wants English to be declared the official language of India.... *Rajaji has gone so far as even to hint support of the move for separating Madras state from India if his proposals are not wholly accepted.* (*JNMF* 2010, p. 346)

This was a saga of reversing the steps from the very precipice. Article 343 provided that the official language of the Union shall be Hindi in Devanagari script. The form of numerals to be used for the official purposes of the Union shall be the international form of Indian numerals. Equally importantly, it provided that for a period of 15 years from the commencement of the Constitution, the English language shall continue to be used for all the official purposes of the Union for which it was being used immediately before such commencement. The President could order the use of Hindi language in addition to the English language and of the Devanagari form of numerals in addition to the international form of Indian numerals for any of the official purpose of the Union. *Most importantly, it also provided for the use of English beyond the period of fifteen years by a Parliamentary legislation.* This period has since been repeatedly extended and, as it appears, this will continue in the foreseeable future.

As the constitutionally stipulated year 1965 for the switch-over from English to Hindi neared, the language issue again assumed such explosive proportions that at one stage it threatened to split the Congress Party. The Official Language Commission, set up on 7 June 1955 to suggest ways and means for impending switchover to Hindi, completed its task in a year and finalized its report but the prevailing situation at that time warranted a delay in its publication. When the report finally appeared in 1957, there were widespread protests in some non-Hindi-speaking areas—particularly some sections in the south. The majority report, while not prescribing any time limit for changeover to Hindi, had suggested that steps should be taken with all possible speed to replace English by Hindi in as many fields as possible, and to universalise Hindi by compelling every child to learn Hindi for four years by the time it completed its compulsory elementary education of eight years. They also exalted Hindi over the regional languages, as far as possible. The minority report, however, suggested that the regional languages should be permitted to come into their own in the first instance, and Hindi should be accommodated only when the Provinces had voluntarily accepted it and recommended its wider use. *The minority report had also recommended that constitutional recognition should be given to English as one of the Indian languages. One of the members in the majority group, R.P. Tripathi, had supported this recommendation* (Grover and Arora 1994, p. 189).

The proponents of Hindi and English were not prepared for any kind of compromise and the language controversy had become increasingly acute, especially in south Indian states. In a joint statement on 1 January 1958, the chief ministers of Madras, Andhra and Mysore described the Language Commission's recommendation to discontinue English after 1965 as impractical. During the debate on the language resolution at the AICC Session in Guwahati held from 16 to 19 January 1958 under the presidentship of U.N. Dhebar, K. Hanumanthaiya, S. Nijalingappa, C. Subramaniam and R. Venkataraman made a forceful plea for the continuance of English, and succeeded in making the Congress resolve that the changeover should be 'flexible and gradual'. While Hindi should be developed and made acceptable as a national language, it should not be 'imposed'. The resolution passed in the session declared that the official language for all-India purposes will have to be Hindi but the transition to Hindi would necessarily be gradual, and the continuation of English even after 1965 may be in the manner provided in Article 343 (3) of the Constitution which envisaged that English may continue after 1965 for such purposes as may be specified in law (Parthasarathi 1989, p. 11).

The issue was resolved, but only for the time being, with the proponents of English reconciling themselves to the formal introduction of Hindi after 1965 and the pro-Hindi people agreeing that the switch-over would be gradual with the continuation of English as an additional language for official purposes even though in effect it meant continuance of the status quo, i.e., the use of English as the only official language for all practical purposes. But, at least, it avoided major polarisation on the situation.

When the matter came up in Parliament, some sections wanted English to be included in the Eighth Schedule of the Constitution as one of the national languages. Replying to the debate in the Lok Sabha on 7 August 1959, Nehru contended:

While it [English] opened out windows of knowledge, it sat on top of our own languages and our own cultural traditions. To some extent that memory lingers though we should try to get rid of it and consider the matter more objectively and impartially.... I suggest two things. First, there must be no imposition. Secondly, *for an indefinite period, I would have English as an associate, additional language which can be used for official purposes.* I would have it so because I do not wish the people of non-Hindi areas to feel that certain advantages are denied to them. I would have English as an alternative language as long as the people require it and *I would leave the decision not to the Hindi-knowing people but to the non-Hindi knowing people.*... At the same time we have progressively to function in our own languages. We should have a foreign language to serve as a window to the modern age. (Kashyap 1995, p. 233)

Speaking in the Lok Sabha on 24 April 1963, Nehru said: 'Our progress should be in the direction of developing Hindi, not only as a regional language, but as a link language and maintaining English to serve that purpose so that there may be no gap' (GOI 1964, p. 67). This unexceptional declaration set the controversy to rest, at least for some time.

As for language of instruction, Nehru stressed that 'it should be fundamental policy of the state to encourage primary education in the mother tongue of the child, whatever it might be, provided of course there are sufficient children to take advantage of this. This has little to do with what the state language or what the provincial languages are' (Parthasarathi 1985, p. 245).

The Hindi Commission report, referred to earlier, had argued that only a small number of Indians spoke English. In a population of over 356 million [at that time], English was spoken by only 1.72 lakhs and understood by 38 lakhs. The population and percentage of English-speaking people has increased in multiples now. For example, in the Seventh Lok Sabha [1980-84], the language-wise break-up of the number of members who made and subscribed the oath/affirmation showed that, of the total 522 members, while 231 members used Hindi, as many as 168 used English (Kashyap 1998, p. 18).

When the Official Languages Bill was introduced in August 1963 [for extension of period for the use of English], there were some unseemly scenes on the floor of the House. In particular, the behaviour of one Hon'ble member was found to be not very happy or desirable. Nehru strongly deplored the tendency:

Yesterday, one Hon'ble Member.... behaved in a rather extraordinary manner in the precincts of this House. I do not know if that gentleman has the least conception of what Parliament is, what democracy is, and how one is supposed to behave or ought to behave...but I am not prepared to see this behaviour in the name of language which spoils democracy. (Kashyap 1996, pp. 131-2)

Kodanda Rao of the Servants of India Society, in his essay, 'The Hindi Commission Report', has highlighted,

The French language is current in Canada, Belgium and Switzerland. It is considered one of the official languages in these countries and not a "foreign" one because it originated in France. America does not consider the English language as "foreign" because it originated in England. C. Rajagopalachari went so far as to claim that the English language was the gift of Goddess Saraswati to India.... Belgium, Switzerland and Canada did not insist on the universality of a single language to preserve national unity or emotional integration. (Grover and Arora 1994, pp. 191-2)

The majority report of the Hindi Commission had rightly concluded (p. 269) that language was:

the loom, not the fabric; only a vehicle of thought, not the thought itself.... It is not language but education that is aimed at in the schools; it is not language but good government that is aimed at in the field of public administration; it is not language but justice that is sought in the law courts. That which lends itself to the most convenience is the correct solution of the language problem in the various fields. (Grover and Arora 1994, p. 193)

Ramchandra Guha has written:

On 26th January 1965, disregarding the warnings of southern states as well as leading Congressmen from south India, [Prime Minister Lal Bahadur] Shastri had English removed from governmental use, leaving Hindi as the country's sole "official" language. *Massive protests broke out in Tamil Nadu that were so fierce and intense that the Prime Minister was forced to acknowledge that the imposition of Hindi had been an error.* He did so in the most graceful manner possible, through a speech on All India Radio on 11th February 1965. Notably, he spoke in English. The Prime Minister began by conveying his "deep sense of distress and shock" at the "tragic events". To remove any "misapprehension" and "misunderstanding", *he said he would fully honour Jawaharlal Nehru's assurance that English would be used as long as the people of South India wanted.* Then he made four assurances of his own:

> First, every state will have complete and unfettered freedom to continue to transact its own business in the language of its own choice, which may be the regional language or English.
>
> Secondly, communications from one state to another will either be in English or will be accompanied by an authentic English translation.
>
> Thirdly, the non-Hindi States will be free to correspond with the Central government in English and no change will be made in this arrangement without the consent of the non-Hindi states.
>
> Fourthly, in the transaction of business at the Central level English will continue to be used. (Ramchandra Guha, *NDTV*, Opinion, 2 October 2020)

On 31 August 1967, M.C. Chagla, the then External Affairs Minister of India, who had been the Minister of Education earlier, tendered his resignation on a Cabinet decision with regard to the educational policy involving the proposed changeover from English to Hindi, which he regarded as a complete reversal of the policy which he had pursued as

Minister of Education and which had been accepted by the Cabinet. Seervai has written, 'As far as I have been able to ascertain, the policy in opposition to which Mr Chagla resigned has made little or no progress.' (Seervai 1996, p. 2584)

Now, there is greater acceptance of English in the country. After the process of globalisation began in the early 1990s, the context has changed completely and there has been increasing demand for English medium schools, even in rural and semi-urban areas in the Hindi belt. The Delhi government announced in May 2018 the launch of spoken English courses for students of government schools. The Chief Minister tweeted: 'Government school students mostly come from economically poor backgrounds.... This was their biggest demand.' In government schools in Odisha, English begins in Class II. In Gujarat, it was taught from Class V until 2013-14, when it was advanced to Class III, but without textbooks in the first two classes. In West Bengal, the Left Front government had stopped teaching of English before Class VI; it began the teaching of English from Class I in 2004. In places like Lucknow and even smaller cities and towns, a plethora of institutions offer spoken English classes. The latest in such developments is the Karnataka government's proposal to have an English medium section in 1,000 government schools as a pilot project to wean away parents from private schools. This has provoked protests from Kannada writers and intellectuals who fear that English will wipe out the native language. Across the country, with student numbers in government schools dropping and English seen as the only way forward, states have been introducing English medium. The medium of instruction in all government schools in J&K since 2003 is English. Punjab has started English medium sections in government schools from 2018. When the Ahmedabad Municipal Corporation started English medium schools, 21,000 students were reported to have shifted to it in the previous five years. In UP, 5,000 government primary schools have become English medium from April 2018. Every block in every district would have a minimum five and maximum seven such schools (*The*

Indian Express, 30 July 2018, p. 1).

Article 348 contains special provisions for the language of the Supreme Court and the High Courts in order to ensure that uniform administration of law is not rendered impossible by the use of regional languages. Subba Rao, former CJI, has forcefully underlined:

> Under our Constitution, the judiciary and the laws are the most important unifying and integrating forces. Though it provides for a federation, the judiciary is a unitary element. There is one hierarchy of judicial structure and the Supreme Court is its apex. All the courts decide questions arising both under the central laws and state laws. If English is replaced by different languages in different states, the said structure will crumble down. Under the Advocates Act, the Bar of India has been unified. There is one All India Bar. That has become possible only as English is the language in all High Courts and the Supreme Court and as English is the language of all laws, whether Central or state. Replacing English by different languages will destroy the unity of the legal profession. (Subba Rao 1970, pp. 235-6)

The Ministry of Education devised a three-language formula for the knowledge of the mother tongue, as well as Hindi and English. For those whose mother tongue is Hindi, the formula involves the learning of another Indian language, preferably a South Indian language. It also contained a regional language policy for the Union Public Service Commission examinations. Successful implementation of this formula should go a long way in finding a solution to the complex language controversy.

Sowmya Dechamma (assistant professor, department of comparative literature at the University of Hyderabad) in her article 'The Hindi Scare' has argued that the idea of one country, one language was bequeathed to us by colonialists. 'The Harappan civilisation precedes the Sanskritic/ Vedic culture. This means *Sanskrit was never the language of Harappan civilisation.* There are pointers towards the undeciphered language of the

Harappan civilisation as being proto-Dravidian. Do we then declare the Dravidian language as the national language?' (*The Indian Express*, 20 September 2019, p. 10)

After Narendra Modi's tenure as prime minister began in 2014, there is an increasing emphasis on the primacy of Hindi. Amit Shah, Union Home Minister, tweeted on Hindi *Diwas* (Day) in September 2019: 'Today, if one language can do the work of uniting the country, then it is the most spoken language, Hindi. There is so much influence of English on us that we cannot talk in Hindi without its help.' Shah further said that people should realise that if languages are lost to foreign influence, 'we will be severed from our culture'. Prime Minister's national broadcasts such as those dealing with the Covid-19 pandemic are no longer in both Hindi and English. They are only in Hindi. Considering that a large number of people in several states, particularly in the South, do not understand Hindi, this is clearly counterproductive and goes to alienate large sections of society.

The draft of the new education policy (NEP) put out for public comments in January 2020 had proposed making Hindi mandatory till Class VIII. This was objected to by a number of persons. Following protests, the reference to the three-language formula has been dropped from the final document. 'The three languages learned by children will be the choices of states, regions, and of the students, so long as at least two of the three languages are native to India,' it states (*The Indian Express*, 30 July 2020, p. 1-2). However, Tamil Nadu is still not happy. *The Hindu* has editorially commented:

> By rejecting the three-language formula advocated in the National Education Policy (NEP 2020), Tamil Nadu Chief Minister Edappadi K. Palaniswami has only reiterated the state's unwavering position on an emotive and political issue. Its two-language policy, implemented decades ago after a historic agitation against the imposition of Hindi, remains non-negotiable for almost the entire political class.

Opposition from the state had last year forced the Centre to amend the draft NEP and withdraw a proposal to teach Hindi as a third language in schools in non-Hindi speaking states. Yet in the NEP, approved by the Union Cabinet last week, it chose to push for the three-language formula, packaging it as a means to promote multilingualism and "national unity". Though the policy said that no language will be imposed on any State, it has expectedly cut no ice with parties in Tamil Nadu, which have risen in near unison to oppose the proposal. In fact, Palaniswami, citing "collective sentiments" of the people, noted that the proposal was "saddening and painful" and appealed to the Prime Minister to allow states to follow their own language policy. In a state that resisted multiple attempts to impose Hindi since 1937, political parties are understandably wary of any mandate to impart an additional language in schools. They fear this would eventually pave the way for Hindi to enter the state through the back door. Since 1985, the state has even refused to allow Jawahar Navodaya Vidyalayas to be set up as they teach Hindi. (*The Hindu*, 5 August 2020)

This shows that the stand of Tamil Nadu has not changed over all these years. This does not bode well for any hopes of a compromise. It is time the younger generation is left free to decide whether to learn Hindi than to bar its teaching in the schools altogether.

DMK president M.K. Stalin has written to Prime Minister Narendra Modi and Union Education Minister Ramesh Pokhriyal, urging them to halt the implementation of the NEP 2020, until the situation is conducive to follow the due process enshrined in the Constitution. His concerns seemed to be primarily two-fold: erosion of federalism, and the return of the three-language formula (*The Hindu*, 8 August 2020).

Politics over language found a new flashpoint after Kanimozhi, MP, said an airport security officer asked her if she was 'an Indian' because she said she didn't know Hindi. 'The issue is not about knowing Hindi or not. It is shameful (to say) I can be Indian only if I know Hindi,' Ms Kanimozhi is reported to have said (*The Hindu*, 14 August 2020). Instead of taking a casual interface in its stride, much is made of it to get maximum political mileage.

The Andhra Pradesh government had approached the Supreme Court challenging its State High Court's decision to strike down a government order of November 2019 that had made English medium education compulsory from classes I to VI in primary, upper primary, and high schools under all managements from 2020-21. It was to be gradually extended to each further class from the next consequent academic years (*The Hindu*, 3 September 2020).

Eminent jurist H. M. Seervai has stated: 'It would be strange indeed if after rejecting a two-nation theory, the language provisions and their implementation lead to the acceptance of a ten or twelve-nation theory based on language' (Seervai 1996, p. 2586). It is interesting to note that J&K has now five official languages—Urdu, Hindi, Kashmiri, Dogri and English. This has ended Urdu's 131-year reign as the only official language of the ethnically diverse J&K region. There are also demands for declaring Punjabi and Gujri as official languages (*Outlook*, 12 October 2020, pp. 16-18). Day will not be far off when the example of J&K will be followed by other states. This will give the concept of official language a whole new perspective, insofar as the states are concerned.

This brings us back to where we started this discussion. It is clearly not feasible to think of Hindi as a replacement for English as an official language, if the unity of the country is to be preserved. The replacement of English will be impossible due to the opposition from the southern states. In the light of the above, it makes no sense to consider English a foreign language. It must be given the recognition of an Indian language by including it in the Eighth Schedule of the Constitution.

Language continues to be a divisive issue though its intensity has reduced considerably. However, its potential capacity to strike at the roots of the country's unity must not be overlooked.

5

Towards A Cooperative Federalism

Introduction

In this concluding chapter we shall deal with some of the unfinished tasks whose completion would strengthen India's federalism. These include taking a fresh look at the future of union territories, setting up of a constitutional court, establishing a trade and commerce authority of India, pursuit of the remaining goals under the GST, exploring alternate mechanisms to resolve the Centre-state and inter-state issues in view of the disappointing performance of the Inter-State Council so far, and the way forward in the light of discussion in the book.

Future of Union Territories

Shiva Rao (member of the Constituent Assembly) has stated that at the time of India's Independence, scattered over India, were six small areas administered directly by the Central government—Delhi, Ajmer-Merwara, Coorg, British Baluchistan, the Andaman and Nicobar Islands, and Panth-Piploda (in the present-day Ratlam district of Madhya Pradesh). Because of their small size, they could not—except in the case of Coorg which had a Legislative Council of some kind—share in the system of representative government provided for in the Governors' Provinces and *for reasons historical and political they could not be merged in the neighbouring areas* (Shiva Rao 1968, p. 558). Constitutional Adviser B.N. Rau did not suggest any change in their status as Centrally-administered areas. The Provincial Constitution Committee met on 9 June 1947. By that time, it was clear that British Baluchistan would be a part of Pakistan. The Committee decided to refer the question of the other Chief Commissioners' Provinces to the Union Constitution Committee. The latter commended that *as an interim measure these areas should continue to be administered by the Centre and any change in this system could be considered subsequently.*

In the joint meeting of the Union and Provincial committees held on 18 July 1947, the question of responsible governments for only Delhi and Coorg was considered. It was later decided that Coorg, Ajmer-Merwara and Delhi should be designated as Lieutenant Governors' Provinces. N. Gopalaswami Ayyangar called them 'minor Provinces'. Later, as a part of the integration of princely states, Centrally-administered states such as Bhopal, Bilaspur, Cooch-Behar, Himachal Pradesh, Kutch, Manipur, Rampur and Tripura also became Centrally-administered territories for some time. At the revision stage of the Constitution, the schedule enumerating these states was altered as Part C states.

Currently there are eight union territories. The question of whether UTs need to be continued as such was never examined closely at any time. This was also true in respect of the Second Administrative Reforms Commission, though it made recommendations pertaining to the administration of various UTs.

Union Territory of Delhi

There has been persistent demand to grant statehood to Delhi but, being the seat of the national capital, it has rightly been retained as a union territory. I am of the view that it should remain so in the future. The Second Administrative Reforms Commission, in its report on 'State and District Administration' submitted in 2009, has suggested: 'The Union government may retain control over the broader aspects of security and law and order whereas traffic, local policing and enforcement of special laws could be handed over to the Delhi Government. In the long run, some of these functions could be transferred to the Municipal Corporation' (GOI 2009, p. 294). The movements of VIPs in Delhi which need careful coordination and handling is just one example why it will be best not to fine-tune the division of powers and leave the position as it is.

The Supreme Court judgment ([2018] 8 Supreme Court Cases 501) regarding the powers of the Lieutenant Governor has dealt comprehensively with the constitutional provisions and has underlined that except for the three reserved subjects—namely, public order, police and land, the powers of the elected government must be supreme and the decisions of the elected government thereon do not require concurrence of the Lt Governor. The court declared that the Lt Governor and the Council of Ministers must serve the constitutional norms, values and precepts. The judgment was silent on 'services'. I should note that the separate judgment of Justice D.Y. Chandrachud reads like a post-doctoral thesis. One is amazed at the depth of his research.

The National Capital Territory of Delhi (Amendment) Act, 2021, passed by Parliament in March 2021, has, however, made it clear that 'government' in the National Capital Territory of Delhi means the Lt Governor of Delhi. The Act gives discretionary powers to the Lt Governor even in matters where the Legislative Assembly of Delhi is empowered to make laws. The proposed legislation also seeks to ensure that the Lt Governor is 'necessarily granted an opportunity' to give his opinion before any decision taken by the Council of Ministers is implemented. This has been seriously objected to by the Delhi government and is expected to be challenged in the Supreme Court. The controversy brings out the inherent contradictions in the structure of a union territory with an elected legislature, particularly in the national capital. It also brings out the understandable reluctance of the

Centre to give powers of a full state to the government of NCR. Though a number of Opposition parties have criticised the move, the position is not likely to be any different with a Central government formed by any other political party or coalition of parties.

Union Territory of J&K

As I have argued in Chapter 3, it was wrong to downgrade J&K from a state to two union territories of J&K and Ladakh. Abrogation of Article 370 had nothing to do with this downgrading but the Central government perhaps felt that it would help in dealing with any agitation that may arise against the abrogation decision. Sufficient time having elapsed, Jammu and Kashmir regions should now be given statehood, as soon as possible. Upgrading it to statehood will create a congenial atmosphere for recommencement of the political process and will also mend the hurt feelings of the people of the area.

Union Territory of Ladakh

As brought out in Chapter 3, the people of Ladakh wanted it to be a union territory for a long time. In view of the Chinese aggression in East Ladakh in 2020, it will be advisable to keep it as a UT.

Union Territory of Andaman and Nicobar Islands

Due to its geographic and strategic location, the Andaman and Nicobar Islands should also continue to be a union territory.

Other Union Territories

There is no justification to retain the other UTs under the Central government administration and they should be merged with the adjacent states. Special reference may be made to Puducherry and Chandigarh.

Union Territory of Puducherry

Puducherry was a French colony and was made a UT to conserve its separate identity and culture. As in the case of NCR, the former Lt

Governor of Puducherry, Kiran Bedi, was having a tussle with her Chief Minister V. Narayanasamy for quite some time. The chief minister (who resigned on 21 February 2021 after losing the trust vote) had written to the President of India seeking her recall. Following the Supreme Court ruling in the case of Lt Governor of Delhi, referred to above, the Madras High Court held that the Lt Governor cannot interfere in the day-to-day affairs of running the administration of the territory. It was alleged before the court that Bedi was running a parallel government in Puducherry. The High Court said that the 'Central government as well as the Administrator should be true to the concept of democratic principles' (*The Indian Express*, 1 May 2019, p. 5), There is no justification to retain Puducherry as a UT any longer and it should be merged with Tamil Nadu. To retain its separate identity, it should be made a separate district in Tamil Nadu state.

Union Territory of Chandigarh

For years, the Chandigarh question has become linked in public discourse with the Fazilka-Abhor area. This is because of Indira Gandhi's insistence that Chandigarh could be given to Punjab only if Punjab agreed to give its Fazilka-Abhor area to Haryana, as compensation. Noorani, in his article 'A White Paper on a Black Record' reproduced by Patwant Singh et al. in their book, *Punjab –The Fatal Miscalculation,* has brought out some critical aspects of the problem which have very rarely come into public discussion, except among the few experts and knowledgeable persons who may have been closely involved with the subject:

i. *Fazilka-Abhor is not contiguous to Haryana.*
ii. *At least 60 of its115 villages are Punjabi-speaking.... According to one estimate, of the total population of 4,00,000 of Fazilka tehsil, 1,50,000 were Sikhs.*
iii. When linguistic states were created in 1956, only two states were excluded from it—namely, east Punjab and Bombay.
iv. When Punjabi Suba was conceded a decade later after much

violence, Chandigarh was denied to it.

v.   The terms of reference of the Boundary Commission, which was appointed on 23 April 1966, were loaded against Punjab. The commission was directed to apply the linguistic principle with due regard to the census figures of 1961 and other relevant considerations.... Everyone knew that the census figures of 1961 were unfair to Punjab for the simple reason that in the communally charged atmosphere, to which the Akalis had also contributed, large numbers of Punjabi-speaking Hindus claimed Hindi as their mother tongue. *The concern for the preservation of tehsils was indefensible.*

vi. Chandigarh was surrounded on three sides by the Punjabi region and on the remaining side it abutted the Hindi region. Even the highway which connected it with the Hindi region passed through the Punjabi area first.

vii. On 22 January 1984, some 150 eminent Punjabis highlighted that '*Chandigarh was built to compensate Punjab for the loss of its capital, Lahore.* There is no reason for that decision to be altered. Surely, the nation can afford to give Haryana the funds for its own capital'.

viii. Other disputed areas, like Fazilka and Abhor, should be settled on the basis of contiguity with village as a unit.

Noorani has rightly underlined that 'Mrs Gandhi's stand on Fazilka and Abhor alone was responsible for the deadlock: The country has been made to pay a heavy price for it' (Patwant Singh 1985, pp. 153-156, 160).

Ambedkar was fond of saying that boundary *marking* is the job of a surveyor; *boundary making* is the task of a statesman.

Noorani has drawn a parallel between the stand taken by the Central government in regard to Bombay (now Mumbai) and Chandigarh. So far as Nehru's stand against Bombay being given to Maharashtra was concerned, it was based on his sincere conviction that linguistic states were not in the interest of the country in the long term, and bilingual or multilingual states would be more suited to India. I fully shared Nehru's views. I had expounded on them in my book, *The God Who Failed: An Assessment of Jawaharlal Nehru's Leadership* (pp. 157-160). The fierce, and often narrow-minded regional, linguistic and cultural ethos evident in a number of states and the intense inter-state disputes and conflicts that have risen in recent years have shown how justified Nehru's concerns were. As seen in Chapter 4, the Congress Party had strongly advocated the concept of linguistic states right from the 1930s and it was unable to turn the tide of public opinion. Having conceded the principle of linguistic states all over the country, it was difficult to justify making an exception only in a few cases. As people of both Maharashtra and Gujarat were not prepared to live in a bilingual state, the only question which remained was that of the future of Mumbai city. Finally, after much violence and agitation, including the death of a number of agitators, Mumbai was reluctantly given to Maharashtra.

As I had argued in my book, *Indira Gandhi: An Era of Constitutional Dictatorship*, in the case of Chandigarh, at no time was the decision of the Centre to link it with Fazilka and Abhor justified. There was no justification whatsoever for making Chandigarh a union territory. A new capital could easily have been constructed for Haryana. The most recent example is that of Andhra Pradesh where Chandrababu Naidu, with his astute leadership and commendable statesmanship, decided to build a green-field capital for the state at Amaravati.[1] Even in this case, suggestions were made to declare Hyderabad as a union territory and, following the example of Chandigarh, to make it the capital of both Telangana and Andhra Pradesh. Fortunately, wiser counsel prevailed.

It is only due to Indira Gandhi's rigid stand that the Chandigarh question remained unresolved during her lifetime. If she had taken a reasonable position on the subject, and Chandigarh had been given to

---

1. The current YSRCP (Yuvajana Sramika Rythu Congress Party) government in AP has made a proposal to trifurcate the state capital. The matter is now pending before the high court.

Punjab, the whole Punjab agitation would have taken a different and more conciliatory turn. It is even possible that Operation 'Blue Star' might have been avoided.

It is unfortunate that even after Indira Gandhi's assassination, though almost all political parties have been in power at the Centre at one time or another, this issue has remained unaddressed. I strongly believe that a new beginning should be made by announcing the transfer of Chandigarh to Punjab and a decision announced to build a new capital for Haryana.

As for the future of other Punjabi and Hindi-speaking areas in dispute, a boundary commission may be appointed with a clear guideline that village should be adopted as the unit, subject to the other usual criteria such as contiguity, communications, cultural ties, etc. (Godbole 2018, pp. 61-65).

Setting up of a Constitutional Court

The Constitution of India has conferred wide powers on the Supreme Court under Articles 32 (remedies for enforcement of rights conferred by law) and 136 (special leave to appeal by the Supreme Court). They enable the Supreme Court, by eschewing all technicalities, to evolve suitable procedures to dispense justice. Article 143 gives power to the President of India to consult the Supreme Court on any question of law or fact of public importance. In addition, the Supreme Court has appellate jurisdiction in appeals from High Courts in certain cases under Article 132. The Supreme Court has appellate powers in civil matters under Article 133 and in criminal matters under Article 134. It has exclusive jurisdiction to decide on all doubts and disputes arising out of or in connection with the election of the President, the Vice President and the Prime Minister.

Former Chief Justice of India, Subba Rao, in his book, *Some Constitutional Problems*, has underlined that the judiciary under our Constitution is the greatest unifying and integrating force in the country. Its jurisdiction is very wide and is far more extensive than that of any other court of a similar nature in any part of the world. It has original jurisdiction in any dispute between the GOI and one or more states or between the GOI and any state or states on one side and one or more other states on the other, or between two or more states if and insofar as the dispute involves any question, whether of law or fact, on which the existence or extent of legal right depends (Subba Rao 1970, p. 171).

Justice B.N. Srikrishna has stated: 'Articles 32, 136 and 142 of the Constitution invest extraordinary powers in the Supreme Court. By abandoning the principle of *locus standi*, judges have now become roaming knights errant on white charges tilting at windmills of injustice to defend the honour of Dame Justice. Extraordinary powers must be reserved for use in extraordinary occasions' (Srikrishna 2012, p. 14). I hold a somewhat different view. Looking at the conditions in India, as discussed in my book, *The Judiciary and Governance in India* (2008), I am a supporter of the activist role of the Supreme Court. I have cited Justice Srikrishna only to show how diverse the demands on the Supreme Court have been.

Justice Subba Rao is of the view:

The system of posting important constitutional matters before a Division Bench itself is not really conducive to the development of Constitutional law.... The best solution to this problem is to post all important Constitutional law cases before the entire court or at any rate before nine judges, the other two taken out by the mechanical process of lottery[2].... *Such cases will not be more than two or three in a year....* The people can no longer have any apprehension, whether justified or not, that the court is packed. In important matters, which affect the future of the country, the view of the entire court will be reflected.... *The judgment of the majority of the full court would be more acceptable to the people than the judgments of the Division Bench of the court. There will be an organic growth of Constitutional law,* instead of the present conflict of decisions retarding its growth.

---

2. At the time when this was written, the strength of the Supreme Court was 14 judges.

(Subba Rao 1970, pp. 207-8)

In his letter dated 15 January 1980 to Indira Gandhi, on her taking over as the Prime Minister, Justice P.N. Bhagwati had lamented, 'I also wish to bring to your notice that the judicial system in our country is in a state of utter collapse.... *The Supreme Court is also reeling under the weight of arrears.... The position is almost desperate* and yet there does not seem to be any sense of urgency in the Court' (Shourie 1983, p. 304).

The Chief Justice of India, P. Sathasivam, in August 2013, had expressed concern about *the 'growing crisis' in the judiciary, manifested by ever-increasing pendency,* consequent delays in the justice delivery system and a steady decline in the reputation of the judiciary as also of the legal profession (*The Indian Express,* 18 August 2013).

Similar sentiments were expressed by CJI T.S. Thakur on demitting the office in 2017. He had, in fact, said that *he was unable to spare judges to sit on the Constitutional Benches as this would have further increased the arrears in the Court.*

Eminent jurist and senior advocate late Nani Palkhivala had rightly said, 'I am not aware of any country in the world where litigation goes on for as long a period as in India.... The law may or may not be an ass, but in India it is certainly a snail and our cases proceed at a pace which would be regarded unduly slow in a community of snails.'

One would have expected a high level commission like the NCRWC to go in-depth into the complex field of judicial administration in the country, particularly since a majority of its members were former judges of the superior courts and jurists. As I had discussed in my essay in *The Economic and Political Weekly,* the report of the NCRWC was very disappointing on this score (Godbole 2002, p. 4008). Subhash C. Kashyap, who was a member of the NCRWC and Chairman of its Drafting and Editorial Committee, in his note of dissent observed: 'The Chapter 7 of the report is titled "The Judiciary". This chapter particularly is seriously flawed and distorted. The much needed judicial reform issues have not even been touched or these got deleted in the final draft' (GOI 2002, p. 261).

As far back as 1984, the Tenth Law Commission of India in the 95th Report had recommended that 'the Supreme Court of India should consist of two Divisions, namely (a) Constitutional Division, and (b) Legal Division'. It had said its preference was that 'only matters of Constitutional law may be assigned to the proposed Constitutional Division'.

The Government, in a press release, said that representations have been received from time to time from various sources for establishment of benches of the Supreme Court in various parts of the country. The Law Commission in its 229th Report, in addition to its 95th Report, has recommended as under:

1. A Constitution Bench be set up at Delhi to deal with constitutional and other allied issues; and
2. Four Cassation (Zonal) Benches be set up in the Northern region/zone at Delhi; the Southern region/zone at Chennai/Hyderabad; the Eastern region/zone at Kolkata; and the Western region/zone at Mumbai to deal with all appellate work arising out of the orders/judgments of the High Courts of the particular region.

Giving information in a written reply to a question in the Lok Sabha, Salman Khurshid, Minister of Law & Justice, said that the opinion of the Attorney General was obtained and the matter was referred to the Chief Justice of India, who informed that after consideration of the matter, the Full Court, in its meeting held on 18 February 2010, unanimously resolved that the recommendations of the Law Commission cannot be accepted.

It appears that the decision of the court primarily related to setting up of zonal branches of the court. I share the anxiety of the court on this score. But, I believe there should be no objection to the setting up of a division of the court to deal with constitutional matters, as proposed by the Tenth Law Commission as far back as 1984.

The Constitution has given appellate jurisdiction to the Supreme Court under Articles 132, 133 and 134. The Supreme Court is swamped with appeals from the decisions of the High Courts. The Founding Fathers of the Constitution did not visualise a situation in which the original jurisdiction and constitutional cases would be relegated to the back-burner. The question of whether a particular case needs to be referred to the Constitution bench is a matter of discretion of the CJI and at times has become controversial. It would have been best if the Constitution had itself segregated the constitution court from the appellate court. It is time this question is addressed urgently.

The Law Commission, in its 229th report, has highlighted:

> As constitutional adjudication occupies a place of its own, it always merits consideration as to whether there should be a separate constitutional court, as is the position in about 55 countries of the world (Austria established the world's first separate constitutional court in 1920), or at least the Supreme Court should have a Constitutional Division. Many continental countries have constitutional courts as well as final courts of appeal.

The Congress Party manifesto for the 2019 Lok Sabha elections had proposed to 'make the Supreme Court a Constitutional Court' and to 'establish a Court of Appeal' which would speed up resolution of pressing Constitutional issues and ease the SC's caseload. It was proposed that the Congress Party would introduce a bill in Parliament to amend the Constitution to make the Supreme Court a Constitutional Court that would hear and decide cases involving the interpretation of the Constitution and other cases of legal significance or national importance. It was also proposed that the party would introduce a bill to amend the Constitution to establish a Court of Appeal to hear appeals from judgments and orders of High Courts. The Court of Appeal would sit in multiple Benches of three judges each in six locations. But since the Congress Party lost in the elections, these commitments remained on paper.

Timely decisions of the Supreme Court on crucial constitutional questions are imperative for the proper functioning of the country as envisaged by the Constitution. Illustratively, reference may be made to some major pending cases.

Some election petitions were dismissed by the Supreme Court on the tenuous distinction between the Hindu religion and Hindutva. In *Manohar Joshi v. Nitin Bhaurao Patil and another* (AIR 1996 SC 796), the Court held: '*The word "Hindutva" by itself does not invariably mean Hindu religion* and it is the context and the manner of its use which is material for deciding the meaning of the word 'Hindutva' in a particular text. *It cannot be held that in the abstract the mere word "Hindutva" by itself invariably means Hindu religion.*' In *Dr Ramesh Yeshwant Prabhoo v. Prabhakar Kashinath Kunte* (AIR 1996 SC 1113), the Court held:

No precise meaning can be ascribed to the terms 'Hindu', 'Hindutva' and 'Hinduism'; and no meaning in the abstract can confine it to the narrow limits of religion alone, excluding the content of Indian culture and heritage. *The term 'Hindutva' is related more to the way of life of the people in the subcontinent.* It is difficult to say that the term 'Hindutva' or 'Hinduism' *per se*, in the abstract, can be assumed to mean and be equated with narrow fundamentalist Hindu religious bigotry, or be construed to fall within the prohibition in sub-section (3) and/or (3A) of section. Ordinarily 'Hindutva' is understood as a way of life or a state of mind and it is not to be equated with or understood as religious Hindu fundamentalism. *The word 'Hindutva' is used and understood as a synonym of 'Indianisation', i.e., development of uniform culture by obliterating the differences between all the cultures co-existing in the country.* Considering the terms 'Hinduism' or 'Hindutva' *per se* as depicting hostility, enmity or intolerance towards other religious faiths or professing communalism, proceeds

from an improper appreciation and perception of the true meaning
of these expressions.

Needless to say, such a philosophical discourse is hardly relevant in
the emotionally charged atmosphere during electioneering. Muslims and
persons of other religious denominations of minorities are unlikely to
subscribe or take kindly to the above interpretation. It might also evoke
fears of obliterating the religious and cultural identities of the minorities
in the country. Former CJI M.N. Venkatachaliah had observed: 'The
purpose of law in plural societies is not the progressive assimilation of
the minorities which make the society but to devise political, social and
legal means of preventing them from falling apart and so destroying the
plural society of which they are members.... *In a pluralist, secular polity,
law is perhaps the greatest integrating force*' (Shourie 1995, p. 36). Equally
difficult to understand is the logic of the court in its assertion that, 'A mere
statement that the first Hindu state will be established in Maharashtra
is by itself not an appeal for votes on the ground of his religion but the
expression, at best, of such a hope.'

The fact that all these election petitions were based on speeches made
by the leaders of the Shiv Sena and the BJP, whose political ideology
is based on the furtherance of Hindu religion at any cost, also has an
important bearing on the issues at hand. It is unfortunate that the tenets
on which these judgments of the Supreme Court were based and which
have such an important bearing on secularism have not been reviewed by
a larger Constitution bench so far. Revision petitions filed in these cases
have been pending for over two decades.

The petition challenging the Jammu and Kashmir Resettlement Act is
also pending in the Supreme Court for over two decades. The bill was
passed by the state legislature even after serious objections were raised by
the then Governor of J&K, B.K. Nehru. But when the legislature passed
the bill again without making any changes, the Governor had no choice
but to give his assent on 6 October 1982. The President of India sought an

advisory opinion of the Supreme Court but it was returned 'respectfully unanswered' on 8 November 2000. The petition challenging the Act was filed on 27 November 2001 (*India Legal*, 24 December 2018, pp. 40-2). The Act has serious security implications but the case is still pending in the Court.

The Citizenship Amendment Act 2019 has been challenged in the Supreme Court. It raises important constitutional issues but is yet to be heard by the court.

In an interview with Karan Thapar, A.P. Shah, former Chief Justice of Delhi High Court, said he was

> deeply disappointed by the way the Supreme Court was prioritising cases in front of them. Habeas corpus and other fundamental rights cases were being pushed back. Consequently, the Supreme Court had abdicated its duty to defend civil rights. The court was behaving like an executive court that defends the government and not like a rights court. The court should be the *sentinel on the qui vive* but it was not performing that duty.... He hoped that the court would assert itself but if it did not, the future was "dim, dark, dismal and bleak". (Thapar 2020, pp. 19-21)

Venkatasubramanian, in his article 'Lessons to be Learnt', states:

> Each CJI brings to the office a temperament and philosophy of his own and an approach to administer the affairs of the Court within the limited time in office. Take, for instance, the setting up of constitution benches to hear and settle important issues. The CJI, as master of the roster, has a huge responsibility to decide which issue should get priority and which should be referred to a constitution bench. On this there have been certain disappointments. (*India Legal*, 1 October 2018, pp. 16-18)

Venkatasubramanian has given instances of how important cases such as Right to Privacy and Aadhaar were delayed inordinately due to the reluctance of the CJIs to constitute large constitution benches for the purpose. In fact this analysis raises some important questions. Should it be a matter of discretion of the CJI to decide whether a case needs to be referred to a constitution bench? Can guidelines not be laid down for the purpose?

Abrogation of Article 370 has raised important constitutional questions. There are 23 petitions in the Supreme Court challenging this decision. Though over a year has elapsed, the case is still pending in the Court.

Normally, it is expected that *habeas corpus* petitions should be heard without any loss of time. But the cases filed regarding the detention of several political leaders in J&K are yet to be taken up for hearing though over a year has elapsed. In the meanwhile, most of them have been released from detention.

The case filed by the Government of Maharashtra against the inclusion of Belgaum, Karwar and other Marathi-speaking areas in Karnataka has been pending since 2004.

The *demonetisation* decision of the Central government on 8 November 2016 was challenged in several high courts. On 16 December 2016, a bench of three judges of the Supreme Court admitted the writ petitions, framed nine questions, withdrew all similar cases pending in the high courts to itself, and referred the case to a five-member constitution bench which is pending.

During the hearing of a review petition, the nine-member constitution bench decided to refer the *Sabarimala* decision to a larger constitution bench. One wonders how many years it would take before it comes up for hearing.

As Faizan Mustafa, Vice-Chancellor of the NALSAR [National Academy of Legal Studies and Research] University of Law, Hyderabad, has rightly underlined: 'For comparison, the British Supreme Court was widely appreciated for its prompt ruling against Prime Minister Boris

Johnson's decision to prorogue Parliament. One hopes our judges too will stand up to the new challenges and, through their judgments, put to rest all apprehensions about their independence. After all, they have taken oaths (sic) to adjudicate without fear or favour' (*India Today*, 21 October 2019, p. 18).

In a hard-hitting article, rights activist Usha Ramanathan has lamented: 'It is a well-worn saying that the Supreme Court is not final because it is infallible, but infallible because it is final. Reopening questions decided by constitutional benches, as happened in *Sabarimala* and *Puttaswamy II* (the UID/Aadhaar money bill case), in a little over a year, tempts the cynic to say *the Supreme Court is neither infallible nor final*' (*India Today*, 23 December 2019, p. 42).

Delhi-based lawyer Pranjal Kishore in the article, 'Uncertain Justice', writes:

> The Court's 40-day 'daily hearing' commitment in the Babri Masjid-Ram Janmabhoomi case was cited as a reason for its inability to deal with other important issues that came up before it. Foremost among these were the petitions challenging the communications lockdown in Kashmir and the effective repeal of Article 370. When these matters came up for hearing before the Court in August [2019], it pointed out, on multiple occasions, that it did not have time to hear the petitions. The delays *even prompted the United Nations High Commissioner for Human Rights to issue a statement criticising the Supreme Court*.... The Court's handling of the Kashmir petitions and the electoral bonds issue is an illustration of what lawyer Gautam Bhatia describes as *the "doctrine of judicial evasion"*. Faced with a dispute between individuals and the state over exercise of civil and constitutional rights, the court's response is often not to decide it one way or another but to simply refuse to hear the case.... In 2020, the court finds itself at a crossroads: it may continue to be, as Lord Atkins said in a famous dissent in *Liversidge v Anderson, "more Executive-*

minded than the Executive". (*India Today,* 6 January 2020, pp. 32-37)

The Indian Constitution has been acclaimed for entrusting the Supreme Court with the responsibility of enforcing the fundamental rights under Article 32. Speaking in the Constituent Assembly, Ambedkar had called this Article the very heart and soul of the Constitution. However, in the recent past, the Supreme Court was trying to 'discourage' recourse to this Article, which is the fundamental right to constitutional remedies. The Supreme Court is also seen to be asking the applicants to approach the high courts in the first instance. This is highly disturbing. Partly, this could be due to the large pendency of cases but it cannot be the reason for diluting its original jurisdiction. Ways must be found to safeguard the important fundamental right under Article 32.

The question of the huge backlog of court cases has continued to be neglected irrespective of which political party is in power. This is primarily because millions of harassed and dejected litigants are effectively faceless and unorganised, and do not count as a vote bank. For the first time in the history of India, former Chief Justice of India, T.S. Thakur, was moved to tears, more than once, showing his utter helplessness in dealing with the problem. India must be the only democracy which saw such a shocking spectacle.

Unfortunately, so far, the question of setting up a constitutional court has been linked with the question of setting up of regional branches of the Supreme Court. Understandably, the latter has met with considerable resistance, particularly from the Delhi Bar. These two issues need to be separated. Setting up a constitutional court needs to be given highest priority. Selection of judges for the Constitutional Court should be on the basis of their specialised knowledge, expertise and inclination to deal with constitutional issues.

It is time to divide the Supreme Court into two divisions—appellate and constitutional—with the Chief Justice of India heading the court, as at present. For assessing the work of the Supreme Court, a distinction has to be made between the original and constitutional jurisdiction, and appellate jurisdiction of the Court. Both are important. But, due to sheer workload, currently, appellate work seems to get excessive attention in the disposal of cases. Due to the limited strength of the Supreme Court judges, it is difficult to spare judges for the larger constitutional benches. Article 145 (3) of the Constitution has laid down that the minimum strength of a constitution bench should be five judges. In exceptional cases, it can be as large as nine or eleven or even thirteen judges. In this light, I would suggest that, to begin with, the constitutional division of the Supreme Court should have a strength of nine full-time judges who can sit as a full court. Considering the present total strength of the Court (34), this is reasonable. With the experience of its working, the number can be increased later, if necessary. When the court has to sit as an 11 or a 13-member bench, the required additional judges can be drawn from the appellate division of the court.

Apprehensions have often been expressed from time to time regarding the manner in which benches are designated for hearing important and sensitive cases. In the news conference held by the four judges of the Supreme Court—J. Chelameswar, Ranjan Gogoi, Madan Lokur and Kurian Joseph—in January 2018, they had, inter alia, stated: 'There have been instances where case(s) having far-reaching consequences for the nation and the institution had been assigned by the Chief Justices of this court selectively to the benches "of their preference" without any rational basis for such assignment.'

To address the apprehensions of 'bench-fixing', it is suggested that cases coming up for hearing before the constitutional court should be heard by the full court. This will increase the acceptability of the court's decisions and also help in developing credible constitutional law.

This is a long-overdue reform. In fact, such a division of responsibilities should have been made when the Constitution was framed. Setting up a constitutional division of the court will go a long way in further increasing the public esteem for the court, enabling building up of formidable constitutional law, imparting strength to India's federalism, and expeditiously translating the lofty constitutional dictums into a reality on a continuous basis.

Establishing a Trade and Commerce Authority of India

Article 301 of the Constitution unambiguously declares that 'Subject to the other provisions of this Part, *trade, commerce and intercourse throughout the territory of India shall be free.*' But, this is considerably watered down by the other provisions. Article 302 empowers Parliament to impose restrictions on trade, commerce and intercourse. Article 304 permits the legislature of a state to impose such *reasonable* restrictions on the freedom of trade, commerce or intercourse with or within that state as may be required in the public interest. However, it states that no bill or amendment for the purpose shall be introduced or moved in the legislature of a state without the previous sanction of the President. Under these provisions, the Centre had permitted the states to levy a tax on inter-state sale subject to a ceiling of 4 per cent. Effectively this converted the sales tax into an origin-based tax.

Article 286 lays down that 'No law of state shall impose, or authorise the imposition of a tax on the sale or purchase of goods where the sale or purchase takes place – (a) outside the state; or (b) in the course of the import of the goods into, or export of the goods out of, the territory of India. Entry 52 of the State List empowers the states to levy tax on the entry of goods into a local area for consumption, use or sale. In many states, this tax was assigned to urban local bodies and larger village panchayats and was called octroi or entry tax. I have brought out separately how difficult it was to abolish the octroi in Maharashtra and Gujarat and to replace it by accounts-based entry tax. Fortunately, all these taxes have now been subsumed in the GST.

Arvind Subramanian paints a rather glowing picture of the state of internal trade in India. According to him:

The first-ever estimates of inter-state flows indicate a trade to GDP ratio of about 54 per cent, a number that is almost comparable to other larger jurisdictions, and that contradicts the caricature of India as a barrier-riddled economy; the ratio of India's internal and international trade compares favourably with others. De facto, at least, India seems well integrated internally. A more technical analysis confirms this: trade costs reduce trade roughly by the same extent in India as in other countries. So, both India's international trade to GDP ratio (now greater than China's) and India's internal trade ratio appear quite robust. There is a surprisingly large ratio (68%) of intra-firm trade across states to inter-firm trade (or arms-length sales); intra-firm trade also faces more trading frictions than inter-firm trade...at least within India, we are making borders more and more porous to allow more goods and more Indians to flow through them. Long live internal integration. (Subramanian 2018, pp. 50-2)

It is reassuring to see this picture but as for India's internal trade to GDP ratio (54 per cent), there is quite some way to go when compared with China (74 per cent), Brazil (76 per cent) and USA (78 per cent).

The Economic Survey 2016-17 recognizes that: 'The analysis does leave open the possibility that some proportion of India's internal trade could be a consequence of current tax distortions, which are likely to be normalised under the GST. One market and greater tax policy integration but less actual trade is an intriguing future prospect.'

The Survey suggests:

Interestingly, the freedom to the states in Article 304 (b) is only different from that provided to Parliament in Article 302 in that states have to impose 'reasonable restrictions' whereas Parliament may impose 'restrictions'. Of course, states can only impose restrictions in areas that are either on the State or Concurrent List. *The gist of these provisions is that both the Centre and the States have considerable freedom to restrict trade and commerce that hinder the creation of one India. Moreover, the jurisprudence has unsurprisingly come down in favour of even more permissiveness.* Evidently, while the purpose of Part XIII [of the Constitution—Trade, Commerce and Intercourse within the Territory of India] was to ensure free trade in the entire territory of India, this is far from how its practical operation has panned out. Financial levies as well as non-financial barriers imposed by the States have become a major impediment to a common market. Levies in the nature of motor vehicles taxes, taxes at the point of entry of goods into specified local areas, sales tax on manufacturers of goods from outside a particular State, have always existed between States. *At the same time, many of such levies are constitutionally valid and have been upheld, in principle, by the Supreme Court....* At the same time, the notification increased the tax to be paid by the manufacturers of edible oil from other States from 4 per cent to 8 per cent. When challenged, the Supreme Court refused to quash this notification on the ground that it was necessary to protect the edible oil industry in the State of Jammu and Kashmir and was an adequate measure under the scheme of Part XIII of the Constitution. In several cases where entry taxes have been challenged, the Supreme Court has upheld their validity on the ground that these taxes are 'compensatory' in nature.

In the eyes of the Constitution, the taxes on goods are used for facilitating trade in the charging state. This was not entirely unexpected— in looking to achieve free trade while protecting the sovereignty of states to raise revenue would always have led to trade-offs. *With nearly 70 years of experience, it is clear that the trade-offs have been such that any hopes of a common market have been effectively crippled.* In 2016, even though the Supreme Court has rejected the compensatory tax theory, it has upheld the right of states to levy entry taxes. It is submitted that this view of the Court is entirely consonant with *the constitutional scheme of Part XIII, which when read as a whole, seeks economic integration while ensuring considerable leeway for states to differentiate their own products from those from other states.*

The evidence of this chapter and a review of Indian history suggest that *on the question of creating one economic India, technology, economics, and politics have been surging ahead. Perhaps, it is time for the Constitution to catch up to further facilitate this surging internal integration* (GOI 2017, pp. 244-245, 248).

This is further corroborated by the Economic Survey 2019-20 which states:

> The Indian economy is replete with examples where Government intervenes even if there is no risk of market failure, and in fact, in some instances its intervention has *created* market failures. This may be partly due to the legacy of post-Independence economic policies which the country followed. However, as the role of markets has been recognised globally, it is only natural that markets are allowed to work to enable quick wealth creation and thereby economic growth. (GOI 2020, vol. 1, pp. 71-72)

The Survey brings out the effects of government interventions in agricultural commodities, drugs, grain markets and loan waivers. The Survey makes a strong case that each department and ministry in the government must systematically examine areas where the government needlessly intervenes and undermines markets...interventions that were apt in a different economic setting may have lost their relevance in a transformed economy. Eliminating such instances will enable competitive markets and thereby spur investments and economic growth (GOI 2020, vol. 1, p. 98).

[As an example], the regulation of drug prices through the Drug Price Control Order (DPCO) 2013, has led to an increase in the price of a regulated pharmaceutical drug vis-à-vis that of a similar drug whose price is not regulated. Our analysis shows that the increase in prices was witnessed for more expensive formulations than for cheaper ones and those sold in hospitals rather than retail shops, reinforcing that the outcome is opposite to what DPCO aims to do—making drugs affordable. The evidence across different commodities (pulses, sugar, onions and drugs)—not just onions or sugar where cartelisation is often suspected—and episodes spanning different time periods (2006-19) suggest that the ineffectiveness of the Essential Commodities Act (ECA) stems from unnecessary government intervention that undermines markets (GOI 2020, vol. 1, p. 67).

Though India has made significant progress in enhancing economic freedom for firms and its citizens, it still counts among the shackled economies in the world. In the global indices of economic freedom, India ranks in the bottom half. The Index of Economic Freedom, which is brought out by the Heritage Foundation, and the Global Economic Freedom Index, which is brought out by the Fraser Institute, measure economic freedom as the freedom of choice enjoyed by individuals in acquiring and using economic goods and resources. In the Index of Economic Freedom, India was categorized as 'mostly unfree' with a score of 55.2 in 2019 ranking the Indian economy 129th among 186 countries, i.e., in the bottom 30 per cent of countries. In the component pertaining to 'investment freedom', which measures the ease of flow of investment capital both internally and across the country's borders, India scores a low 40.0 on a scale of 0-100 against the world average of 58.5. In the Index of Global Economic Freedom too, India ranks 79th among 162 countries with 108th rank in business regulation (GOI 2020, vol. 1, p. 68). The Economic Surveys thus show how much remains to be done towards creating a common, integrated market.

Govinda Rao and Nirvikar Singh have pointed out how several regulatory policies violated the principle of a common market. While many of the regulations restricting the free flow of goods and factors of production have been removed, the consequences of past policies continue to distort resources as the investment decisions once made cannot be reversed. The policy of freight equalisation is a case in point[3] (Rao and Singh 2005, p. 57).

A.T. Markose, in the Second Bhulabhai Desai Memorial Lecture on 'Inter State Commerce and the Indian Constitution', held under the auspices of the Institute of Constitutional and Parliamentary Studies, observed:

> The granting of regulatory powers over interstate commerce to the states by the Union Parliament *reflects politically centrifugal tendencies*. A strong judiciary imbued with the sanctity of the commerce clause can alone counter disintegrative forces. Further this increased delegation of the power to the states, which in the Constitution has been deemed improper, indicates a serious aberration.... Indeed what has taken place in India is sad. Under the guise of [the] Defence of India Act and thereafter the Essential Commodities Act (ECA), state legislatures and state executives were given unrestricted powers over interstate commerce.... *Of course, the real disability of the Union government in India is the absence of federal instrumentalities spreading all over the country to implement federal policies.* Unless this vital weakness of the Centre is remedied, Constitution cannot be obeyed properly. (*JILI* 1980, pp.124-5)

I agree with the broad thrust of Markose's argument. However, P. Chidambaram in his article, 'Coercive federalism on display' (*The Indian Express*, 13 September 2020, p. 7), takes the opposite view. He has argued that through the recent Ordinance [Farmers Produce, Trade and Commerce (Promotion and Facilitation) Ordinance, 2020, promulgated

---

3. Freight equalisation policy was introduced in 1952 by the Centre to facilitate equal growth of industry across the country. This essentially meant a factory could be set up anywhere in India and the long-distance transportation of minerals would be subsidized by the Central government. The policy was scrapped after adoption of economic liberalisation policies in the 1990s.

by the President on June 5], the Centre has curtailed the powers of the state governments to 'regulate' and to 'fix stock limits' and once the Ordinance is converted into an Act, the hoarders will celebrate. Chidambaram believes that 'One Nation, One Everything' [policy] will eventually destroy 'One Nation'. I, however, believe that it is this kind of socialist mindset which has held back the country's progress so far.

The National Commission to Review the Working of the Constitution (NCRWC), under the chairmanship of former CJI Venkatachaliah, has emphasised that in order that the country's competitiveness in trade, commerce and industry is enabled to respond to the increasing pressures of globalisation, it is necessary that barriers to inter-state trade and commerce, particularly, the free movement of goods on inter-state routes, should be progressively reduced with a view to their final elimination. *A statutory authority contemplated under Article 307 of the Constitution requires to be set up. As the effects of such an authority could as well go beyond the purposes of Article 307, the legislation could be comprehensive, drawing on Entry 42 of List I [inter-state trade and commerce] and, if necessary, Entry 97 [any other matter not enumerated in List II or List III, including any tax not mentioned in either of those Lists]....* For carrying out the objectives of Articles 301, 302, 303 and 304 [trade, commerce and intercourse within the territory of India], and other purposes relating to the needs and requirements of inter-state trade and commerce and for purposes of eliminating barriers to inter-state trade and commerce, *Parliament should by law establish an authority called the 'Inter-State Trade and Commerce Commission'* under the Ministry of Industry and Commerce under Article 307 read with Entry 42 of List I (GOI 2002, vol. I, p. 159).

The Farmers (Empowerment and Protection) Agreement on Price Assurance and Farm Services Act, 2020, seeks to facilitate contract farming agreements between primary producers and agri-business firms, processors, wholesalers, exporters or large retailers. This and other related reforms were long overdue to put agriculture on a viable basis. The initiative for reform of agricultural produce market committees should have, in fact, come from the states themselves. Instead, Congress-ruled states (and states ruled by parties opposed to the Centre) are stoutly opposing the reforms introduced by the Modi government, when the Congress Party itself had promised to bring forth these changes in its election manifesto in 2019. Bihar has been doing without the APMCs (Agricultural Produce Market Committees) for quite some time. Punjab and Chhattisgarh Legislative Assemblies have passed bills to counter the Central government's farm laws. Rajasthan is expected to follow suit soon. The minimum support price scheme has been in operation for decades but to insist that it be made applicable to sales of foodgrains anywhere in the state and to make it mandatory does not make sense. Such pointless opposition to long overdue reforms is clearly against national interest. According to one estimate, in Punjab, the government fears it will lose over Rs 3,000 crore it earns annually from the Food Corporation of India for wheat and paddy procurement, while middlemen in the state fear they will lose over Rs 1,200 crore a year (*India Today*, 9 November 2020, p. 3). The resistance of vested interests will have to be fought in the larger interest of the farming community.

Balveer Arora [Founder-Chairman, Centre for Multilevel Federalism (CMF) at the Institute of Social Sciences, New Delhi] writes in the *Outlook*: 'One nation, one market' is no doubt a laudable objective, but it rides roughshod over the principles of federal power sharing while making inter-state movements of goods easier and minimising internal tax barriers (2 July 2018, p. 51). Such misconceived notions of federalism are hindering much needed initiatives and all-round development.

However, the decision of the Central government in September 2020 to ban the export of onions following the increase in domestic prices comes as a surprise. Such ad hoc decisions have made a mockery of the proclaimed liberalisation policies. If Indian agriculture is to be made export-oriented, such interference is clearly counterproductive. Union Finance Minister Nirmala Sitharaman had announced on 15 May 2020 that steps such as clamping of stock limits will be taken only under 'very exceptional circumstances' like natural calamities and famines which cause a 'surge in prices' (*The Indian Express*, 16 May 2020, p. 1). This makes a mockery of ushering in of 'a 1991 moment for Indian agriculture' announced by the government.

A few years ago, the Central government, in relaxation of the policy of reserving the sector for public sector investment, permitted petroleum refineries approved in the private sector as 100 per cent exporting units to sell their products domestically! It made no difference which political party was in power at the given time for such ad hoc decisions.

The Economic Survey 2019-20 states: …India is still stuck with several forms of government intervention that are anachronistic with today's economy. In several spheres of the economy, India has traversed the transition from a command and control economy to a market-driven economy.… However, as highlighted in previous sections, several areas of unnecessary and inefficient government intervention still remain (GOI 2020, p. 93). *The Survey summarizes some key Acts, as low-hanging fruits to begin with, which have outlived their use and need to be repealed by one 'stroke-of-the-pen' as was done post-1990s or amended to enable functioning of competitive markets.*

These legislative constraints are compounded by the disturbing trends in the rise of sub-nationalism. Against this background, I am convinced that, more than mere constitutional safeguards, it is the greater economic, commercial and trade integration that will strengthen India's federalism. Unfortunately, in spite of the clear enabling provision in Article 307 of the Constitution, no action has been taken by the government during the last 70 years to appoint an authority for carrying out the purposes of the relevant Articles pertaining to trade, commerce and intercourse within the territory of India. Very early steps should now be taken for establishing a *constitutional,* and not just statutory, Trade and Commerce Authority of India to ensure that all states fall in line with the primary mandate given by the Constitution in Article 301. Early steps also need to be taken to review the provisions of several legislations and the Constitution.

Goods and Services Tax – A Giant Step Forward

France was the first country to adopt Goods and Services Tax (GST) way back in 1954. Since then, it has been adopted by more than 160 countries, with Malaysia being the latest to adopt it in 2015. GST rates vary across countries, with the lowest rate being in Malaysia (6 per cent) and the highest in Hungary (27 per cent). The OECD (Organisation for Economic Co-operation and Development) average GST rate is around 19 per cent, with most GST rates in most countries being in the range of 18 to 22 per cent. While each country of the European Union has the right to decide the GST rate, there is a directive that the rate cannot be less than 15 per cent. Some of the key principles of GST the world over are a wide tax base, limited exemptions and, over a period of time, moderate rates. Wider tax base and limited exemptions ensure higher tax revenues whereas full availability of tax credits ensures improved compliance (Dalvi and Venkatasubramanian 2016, pp. 6, 10, 19).

India has set an outstanding example of cooperative federalism by enacting the Goods and Services Tax (GST). Various facets of the problem were under discussion since 2000. An Empowered Committee of State Finance Ministers was set up on 10 May 2007. Since then, all political parties have come together to achieve this. Finally, an announcement was made by the then Union Finance Minister P. Chidambaram in his budget speech of 2007-2008 that GST would be introduced from 1 April 2010. Though the UPA government, led by the Congress, had taken the initiative in the matter, GST is now being unfairly derided by Rahul Gandhi, the former Congress president, as a Gabber Singh Tax. This is ridiculous, to put it mildly. 'If you have multiple rates then don't call it GST, call it by some other name...call it the RSS tax,' said Chidambaram (*The Indian Express*, 2 July 2018, p. 5). The world looks different when one is in power and when one is out of it!

Arvind Subramanian, who was the Chief Economic Advisor to the

GOI during the decision-making period, has explained in detail the complexities of the process of setting up of GST. It would have been unthinkable a few years ago to even imagine the states ever agreeing to give up their main source of revenue—namely, sales tax and more importantly, to surrender their powers in this regard to the Centre.

Having worked as the Principal Finance Secretary of the Government of Maharashtra (GOM) from 1986 to 1990, I was privy to the thinking of the state governments on the subject, as evident in the inter-state deliberations and the discussions pertaining to the Finance Commission. Reference may also be made to the two initiatives taken by the GOM at the time for abolition of octroi, and to increase sales tax on the leasing of films. Income from octroi was the highest in Maharashtra as compared to other states. A proposal was made to replace it with the levy of an entry tax, as recommended by the committee under the chairmanship of former Finance Secretary of the GOM, P.D. Kasbekar. This met with stiff resistance from trade and industry as they did not want their account books to be scrutinised by the sales tax authorities, among other arguments. The experience was the same in Gujarat. The other initiative of levy of sales tax on the leasing of films met with a 31-day strike by the film industry in October-November 1986, which was called off after a committee under my chairmanship suggested a way out (Godbole 1996, pp. 173-80; 196-198). I am citing these instances to underline how replacement of sales tax and other Central and state taxes by a unified GST was so crucial for the country.

The mechanism of an empowered group of state finance ministers was a novel idea to make the states accept the ownership of the GST initiative. The GST Council, on which the GOI and the states are represented, is the ideal mechanism in which decisions are arrived at with consensus.

Revenue neutrality was one of the prime objectives of the exercise to ensure that the states did not feel uneasy about entrusting their fortunes to the GOI. The Central government was equally anxious that it should not be burdened too much for compensating the states for reduction in the revenues. By and large, the GST revenue collection was satisfactory till the Covid-19 catastrophe struck. As *The Hindu* noted editorially (3 July 2018), there was a clear buoyancy in revenue after a wobbly initial trend. The government was eyeing a little over Rs 90,000 crore a month to make up for the revenues earned under the earlier regime and to compensate the states for any losses due to the GST. Finance Minister Piyush Goyal was confident that the average monthly collections in the year 2018-19 could touch Rs 110,000 crore. It was expected that this surge would allay the fiscal concerns of the Centre and the states, and nudge policymakers towards further rationalising the GST structure.

Unveiling a mini-Budget of sorts in the middle of 2018, the GST Council announced a reduction in the tax rates for over 85 goods. But the members of the GST Council, for the first time, questioned its functioning and alleged that not all of the changes and rate cuts were placed on the agenda. For a tricky tax that is still a work in progress, distrust between the Centre and the states would make further rationalisation difficult. Such friction must be avoided in a system in which the states have so far worked in tandem with the Centre.

Surjit S. Bhalla, in his article 'The fake news on GST', states: 'The striking good news is that despite the tax cuts, the GST tax revenues are very much on track and that instead of a deficit, the nation is looking at saving, at a minimum, all the compensation cess budgeted, that is at least Rs 90,000 crore, or 0.5 per cent of the GDP' (*The Indian Express*, 4 August 2018, p. 9). GST collection crossed Rs 1 lakh crore in October 2018. This trend continued and in January 2019 once again the GST revenue collection crossed Rs 1 lakh crore. Pratik Jain of PricewaterhouseCoopers (PwC), India, said: 'This again underlines that collections are increasing steadily as compliance is getting simplified, rates are getting reduced and administration is getting sharper' (*The Indian Express*, 1 February 2019, p. 14). With this upswing in revenue collections, suggestions were being made for rationalisation of rates, and to address the concerns of exporters about delays in getting refunds.

Initially, the industry had anxieties about the multiple tax rates, ranging from 0 to 28 per cent, with a cess on demerit goods. But gradually, the number of goods under the 28 per cent bracket has been brought down to 50 from around 200. A unique component envisaged in India's GST regime, matching of invoices for granting tax credits, has been kept on hold for fear of adding to taxpayers' transition pains. Despite its glitches and snarls, the new tax has taken firm root and is altering the economic landscape positively. The strongest sign of this was the entry of over 4.5 million entities in the country's tax net, many of which would have so far been part of the cash-driven, informal economy. This expansion of the tax net will also help increase direct tax collections (*The Hindu*, 3 July 2018).

The GST had, within one year of its launch, led to an over 70 per cent jump in indirect taxpayer base, done away with checkposts and merged 17 taxes and 23 cesses into one single tax. One year after its implementation, the GST system was perceived to be functioning well and had resulted in increased tax compliance across the country, according to officials in the GST Network and tax analysts. 'We are happy to state that the GST system is functioning well with around a crore returns being filed seamlessly every month,' A.B. Pandey, the then Chairman of the GST Network, had said in a note. GST has clocked an average revenue collection of approximately Rs 90,000 crore a month in the first year (FY18), with the same crossing Rs 1 lakh crore in April (2018). As many as 12 crore returns have been filed till date and 380 crore invoices processed. The taxpayer is now better informed and the errors in filing have also reduced substantially, he said. A total of 1,12,15,693 taxpayers have so far registered with the GST system, of which 48,38,726 are new entrants into the tax net, Pandey added.

In a comprehensive essay, Govinda Rao, former Director of the National Institute of Public Finance and Policy (NIPFP) and member of the Fourteenth Finance Commission, has written about the experience of implementation of GST till end 2019:

Almost all the 166 countries that have implemented GST in one form or the other have taken considerable time to stabilize the value-added tax that has been seen as a money machine and an appropriate instrument to offset revenue losses from reducing tariffs.... There is no 'one size fits all' GST; each country has had to adopt the system that it finds feasible.... Since the roll-out of the tax, there have been 42 meetings of the GST Council addressing changes in the structure and operations.

The overall experience shows that GST is here to stay and it will continue to evolve as the governments gain in confidence. The experience has also led to a moderation in expectations. It is now clear that significant additional reforms are needed to ensure better compliance and to minimize economic distortions.

The most important gain is from the abolition of inter-state checkposts erected to enforce taxes on cross-border transactions. This has reduced the impediments to the inter-state movement of goods, and helped to create a national common market. It is estimated that the long-distance travel time for goods transportation has reduced by almost 20 per cent.

The reform has also improved supply chain management and it is no longer necessary to create branch offices merely to avoid inter-state sales tax. The abolition of inter-state sales tax has made the tax destination-based and reduced inequitable inter-state tax exportation. Equally important is the compliance gain due to linkage and exchange of information between income tax and GST departments.

The creation of the GST Council is an important innovation in cooperative federalism. This has helped to minimize the transaction cost of reforming the calibration of domestic consumption taxes of the Centre and the states. However, it remains to be seen how the institution will eventually shape up.

While these gains are real, the full potential of reforms will depend upon further simplification and rationalization. The most important constraint, however, is stagnant revenues and unless immediate measures are taken to raise revenue productivity, the euphoria will wane.

By excluding petroleum products, real estate and electricity, 40 per cent of the internal indirect taxes at the Centre as well as states are not in the net. In addition, large-scale exemptions and the low-compliance composition scheme up to Rs 1.5 crore turnover has added to the cascading.

A major reform needed is to include petroleum products and electricity in the GST base. Petroleum products contribute about 42 per cent of the revenue from domestic indirect taxes and in the interest of ensuring competitiveness, their inclusion in the tax base is essential. However, given the large contribution to revenues, this becomes feasible only when the revenue from the tax stabilizes. All these reforms should be sequenced and calibrated over a period of two-three years.

It is important to have a strong technical secretariat comprising administrators, economists, accountants and lawyers to advise the GST Council based on rigorous research. The team should have the capability to estimate the effects of changes in the base and rates, administrative and legal implications of various measures, and present the options to the GST Council to take informed decisions.

Equally important is the need to make all data, which is not sensitive to enforcement, available in the public domain. Reluctance to share the data is a major constraint for undertaking independent research.... When a constitutional body like CAG (Comptroller and Auditor General) itself has difficulties, it is not surprising that independent researchers find it impossible to get the data to undertake quality analysis. Hopefully, the GST Council will facilitate independent research; it does not help to shoot the messenger when the objective is to improve the tax system (*Livemint*, 19 November 2019).

After the massive floods of 2018, Kerala had proposed that it should be permitted to levy a cess on state GST (SGST) in cases of *intra-state supply* of goods and services. Sumit Majumdar has argued that in the spirit of 'cooperative federalism', which is the hallmark of the Indian GST, Kerala may be allowed to levy an additional amount of SGST for a specified period for the exclusive purpose of utilizing the additional revenue in rebuilding itself (*India Legal*, 10 September 2018, pp. 46-7). I agree with the thrust of this argument. Such flexibility will go a long way in making the GST more acceptable to the states.

The controversy about the rate structure raised by some Opposition parties is difficult to understand. The move towards a single rate or two rates will have to be gradual after the revenue from the existing rates stabilises. The income tax and other Central taxes, which have been in operation for years together, have still not been able to reach the ideal rate structure. Taxation laws have to evolve in keeping with the developing situation, nationally as also internationally. To say that a multiple rate GST is not the GST is absurd.

What remains to be done with the GST is formidable. As Subramanian has emphasised, 'if land and real estate (LARE) could be brought into the GST, a key channel of black money creation could be tracked and eventually blocked.' He has tried to correct some major misconceptions among those opposing the extension of GST to LARE—namely, that stamp duties will be brought into the GST; agricultural land will be taxed; low-cost housing will be taxed and made unaffordable, and the tax burden will increase and hence the prices of land and real estate will go up. He has shown how these concerns are misplaced. The sale of land for non-agricultural purposes must itself be taxable. He has rightly stressed that *bringing LARE into the GST is a litmus test of whether state governments are serious in their efforts to address the scourge of black money* (Subramanian 2018, pp. 106, 123-4, 127). But for the same reasons, it will be resisted by all political parties, unless major electoral reforms to curtail the influence of black money on elections are undertaken.

Subramanian has shown how bringing electricity into the GST is important. Having worked in and being associated with the power sector reforms for a number of years, I am fully convinced of the arguments. The issues need to be considered by the states with an open mind, as otherwise the question of ever-increasing losses of the distribution companies will be a death knell not just for the power sector and the state budgets, but also the commercial banks which are faced with the insurmountable problem of non-performing assets (NPAs) due to large loan defaults by power generation and distribution companies.

Subramanian has rightly emphasised that by insisting on one market ('stick'), the Centre can nudge the states away from competitive populism; by providing a forum for regulators, it can build capacity and opportunities for mutual learning; by providing a political forum, it can foster policies in the collective interests, and by highlighting and rewarding best practices, it can incentivise competitive reforms. What the Centre did for the GST in creating the GST Council can be done for the power sector as well. *Experience of the GST can be the harbinger in which lies India's future* (Subramanian 2018, pp. 192-3).

Subramanian has also expounded on wrong policies followed on taxing of gold: more than 80-90 per cent of the gold is consumed by the richest segment of the population. And gold expenditure was a much higher fraction of the total expenditure for the richest than for the poorest, 3.5 per cent compared to 0.03 per cent.

The compensation formula for safeguarding the minimum 14 per cent annual growth in state revenues is unworkable in the situation following the Covid-19 pandemic. Actual collections fell short and compensation was paid only up to November 2019. This was a clear breach of the agreement.

Reference may be made to the decision of the Centre to permit additional borrowings by the states subject to certain conditionalities. The states have been allowed to increase their borrowing from 3 per cent to 3.5 per cent of GDP without any conditions. But they can borrow an additional 1 per cent of GDP only by fulfilling four reform conditions— meeting each condition will allow the states to borrow an additional 0.25 per cent of GDP per reform. The four reforms are:

1. Introduction of the 'One nation, one ration card' scheme for

all, which will require linking Aadhaar with ration cards and installing point of sale (PoS) machines in all fair price shops;

2. Improvement in ease of doing business, which requires (i) district-level assessment of ease of doing business according to the Department of Promotion for Industry and Internal Trade (DPIIT) norms, (ii) automatic renewal of state industrial and commercial licences to businesses, and (iii) making randomised inspections with prior notice and full transparency;

3. Implementation of power sector reforms, which would entail reducing aggregate technical and commercial losses, direct benefit transfers to farmers instead of charging them lower power tariffs, and reducing the gap between average cost and average revenues; and

4. Urban local body reforms requiring the states to notify property tax floor rates according to circle property values and to notify water and sewage charges.

Finally, if at least three of the above four reform conditions are satisfied, the states can borrow another 0.5 per cent of GDP as well, with the new ceiling yielding a total of an additional 2 per cent of GDP (Govinda Rao in *The India Forum*, 1 June 2020).

Rao is very critical of the conditions imposed by the Centre. He has argued that the Centre does not abide by any financial discipline and it has no right to lay down such precepts for the states. But, I hold a different view. There are not many leverages left with the Centre to further economic reforms and to reduce the ill effects of competitive populism, where the states are concerned. India has been a 'soft state' for too long. The Fifteenth Finance Commission has also recommended that 'Extra annual borrowing worth 0.5 per cent of GSDP will be allowed to the states during first four years (2021-25) upon undertaking power sector reforms including: (i) reduction in operational losses, (ii) reduction in revenue gap, (iii) reduction in payment of cash subsidy by adopting direct benefit transfer, and (iv) reduction in tariff subsidy as a percentage of revenue.'

Sushil Kumar Modi, Deputy Chief Minister of Bihar, who was the chairman of the Empowered Committee of Finance Ministers for quite some time, has rightly observed: '*GST faces its toughest test as it enters its fourth year.* The upcoming challenge to GST, however, does not stem from its design or structure or the way it has been run. It is up against a pandemic that has wreaked havoc on the global economy and India is no exception' (*The Indian Express*, 1 July 2020, p. 9). I agree with this assessment. Starting with October 2020, the GST monthly collections have exceeded Rs 1 lakh crore and reached an all-time high of Rs 1,19,847 crore in January 2021, with a growth rate of 8.1 per cent, the highest since July 2017. This trend has continued in February 2021.

But, the Centre must not be seen to be defaulting on its commitment to compensate the states for loss of revenue. The then Union Finance Minister, Arun Jaitley, had assured the GST Council:

> Compensation to the states shall be paid for five years in full within the stipulated period of five years and, in case the amount of the GST compensation fund falls short of the compensation payable in any bimonthly period, the GST Council shall decide the mode of raising additional resources *including borrowing from the market* which could be repaid by collection of cess in the sixth year or further subsequent years. (*The Indian Express*, 12 October 2020, p. 9)

What is at stake is not just the future of the GST but the very future of co-operative federalism in the country. As it is, with its high-handed dealings with the states over the years, the Centre has earned a very bad name for itself and there is an ever widening credibility gap, as seen from the resistance of the states to a number of initiatives of the Centre brought out in Chapter 1. Seen in this light, the initial stand of the GOI to leave it to the states to borrow through the RBI made no sense to me. The argument of the adverse implications of the Centre borrowing the sums also did not appear to be convincing. The Centre should have provided for this contingency.

At last, sense has prevailed and the Centre has, on 15 October 2020, reversed its earlier decision and has decided to borrow the required sum of Rs 1.1 lakh crore itself, rather than asking the states to do so. The reasoning which is alleged to have prevailed on the Centre to change its stance is hardly convincing. The back-to-back lending arrangement which is proposed to be adopted is not new and has been in vogue for years together. Clearly, what was lacking was the understanding of the larger issues at stake. This showed the Ministry of Finance in a very poor light. This has large implications for India's federal structure. Cooperative federalism will not be a reality without a change in the mindset of the Centre.

The present crisis in the management of GST due to the Covid-19 pandemic must be accepted as an act of God. The long-term objective of stabilising and improving the GST must not be permitted to be compromised. Much remains to be done in terms of extending the GST to excluded items such as land and real estate, electricity, petroleum products, alcohol, etc. Cooperation of the states will be necessary for the purpose. Creating a credibility gap about the Centre is not going to make this task easy. The C&AG report has brought out that the Centre violated the GST law by retaining Rs 47,272 crore of GST compensation cess in the Consolidated Fund of India during 2017-18 and 2018-19, and used the money for other purpose (*The Indian Express*, 25 September 2020, p. 1). The explanation adduced by the Central government for its actions is hardly convincing. Importantly, by such actions, hopes of replicating the experience of GST Council in other sectors will be ruined.

Inter-State Council – A Failure

Nehru had consciously set up a number of bodies for consultations with the chief ministers. This was particularly important since India had emerged as a democratically-ruled nation for the first time. The National

Development Council (NDC) was one of them. Several politically complex and troubling questions were discussed and settled in the NDC. Partly, it was because a single political party (the Congress) was in power at the Centre and in almost all the states at the time.

Nehru's fortnightly letters to the chief ministers was another unique innovation. The series of letters ran continuously from October 1947 to December 1963.[4] As Ramachandra Guha has written, 'They cover an astonishing range of subjects. Economic development, linguistic and religious politics, the ethics of governance, the Cold War, the passing [away] of literary giants—Nehru writes about all these, and more, in a tone that is alternately reflective and exhortative' (Guha 2010, p. 328). Its most important contribution was to make the chief ministers aware of the national (and even international) problems and broaden their outlook in the initial years after Independence. It made them feel a part of the decision-making process at the national level.

Under the States Reorganisation Act, 1956, five zonal councils were set up. The North Eastern Council was set up under the North-Eastern Council Act in 1971. The Zonal Council meetings are chaired by the Union Home Minister. The chief ministers and two ministers from member states are the members in each Zonal Council. There are two members from each UT. Each Zonal Council has set up a Standing Committee consisting of Chief Secretaries of the member states of the respective Zonal Councils. The Standing Committees meet from time to time to resolve the issues or to do necessary ground work for further meetings of the Zonal Councils. Senior officers from NITI Aayog, Central ministries and state governments are associated with the meetings, where necessary. The Zonal Councils have, so far, met 123 times since their inception. Sixty-one meetings of the Standing Committees have also been held. However, there is hardly anything to write about the impact of these fora.

Alice Jacob has argued that 'even the limited success the zonal councils

---

4. These were published in 1980s in five volumes, each exceeding 500 pages.

have achieved has been due to the Congress Party being in power both at the Centre and in the states. Nevertheless, these councils may be of use where different parties are in power at the state and national levels' (Jacob 1968, p. 613). Over the years since the time Jacob wrote this, there has been no evidence of it and it will be best to abolish them.

The study team of the First Administrative Reforms Commission (ARC), headed by eminent jurist M.C. Setalvad, had recommended establishing a body that would be 'wide-embracing and will provide a standing machinery for effecting consultations between the Centre and the states...on all issues of national importance'. The members were to be the Prime Minister and the Finance and Home Ministers, the Leader of the Opposition, and a representative of each of the zonal councils. The proceedings were to be secret. The study team had strongly suggested that the ISC should be kept away from inter-state disputes as it may divert the energies of the ISC from discussing Centre-state issues. It also apprehended that giving such powers to the ISC would result in opening a floodgate of such disputes. The study team had also excluded the role of ISC in appointments of constitutional functionaries. B.N. Rau, Constitutional Advisor, had also made such a proposal in the first draft of the Constitution but it was not pursued in the revised draft. Earlier, Ambedkar too had sought to revive the idea but it was turned down. To me, all this looks highly theoretical and far-fetched as no Central government would even contemplate giving such wide powers to the ISC.

As for the composition of the Council, the study team had proposed it as under: Prime Minister as chairman, and Union ministers of finance, home, labour, food and other subjects in the State and the Concurrent Lists, and the chief ministers or their nominees as members. This would be too lopsided with dozens of Central ministers as members and would not be acceptable to the states.

The ARC, however, took a more cautious line and recommended that the ISC should be set up for an initial two-year period and be limited to an advisory capacity as laid down in Article 263. The Law Ministry memorandum suggested that Article 263 did not envisage the ISC probing widely into Centre-state relations.

Setting up of the ISC became a rallying point for the Opposition parties. Several state governments in their memoranda to the Sarkaria Commission continued to advocate early setting up of the ISC. The Government of Andhra Pradesh proposed that the ISC could provide 'a very healthy way out of all delicate problems' and that far-reaching constitutional amendments should be placed before the ISC. The West Bengal government wanted the ISC to become the pivotal element in the structure of Centre-state relations and wanted it to meet four times annually, with the Prime Minister as chairman and the vice-chairmanship rotating among the chief ministers. The UP government, in its memorandum to the Sarkaria Commission, broke ranks with other Congress governments by suggesting that the ISC could serve a 'useful purpose' in sorting out differences, although it should not be a permanent body, but summoned only when necessary. Other Congress chief ministers formally opposed the setting up of the ISC, but several told Justice Sarkaria 'confidentially' that it was 'vital' that the ISC be established as soon as possible. They dared not advocate this openly because they had no firm base in their own legislature parties with which to fend off Central retaliation, should they be seen to be deviating from the party line.

Reflecting the Central government's position, the All India Congress Committee (Indira) [AICC(I)] claimed that in the ISC, the states would blow up their differences with the Centre 'out of all proportions'. Were the Centre to be outvoted in the ISC, it would be 'embarrassed' and the ISC would become 'a body more powerful than the Union Cabinet without responsibility to Parliament or the people'. The issues could be settled by dialogue and the Prime Minister will always be willing to hear the state authorities, the AICC(I) said (Austin 1999, pp. 625-7). There was quite some force in the above arguments of the Congress Party. A fine balance would have to be maintained in the ISC. As a result, successive Central governments avoided setting up the ISC.

L.M. Singhvi, senior advocate and MP, in his essay, 'Cooperative Federalism: A Case for the Establishment of an Inter-State Council', had advocated setting up a permanent Finance Commission and a permanent ISC as the principal forums for inter-state and Union-state consultations.

Singhvi believed that the Vice President of India ought to be the chairman and the ISC could also consist of a few others such as the CJI, former Attorney General and a few eminent scholars and statesmen (Grover 1997, pp. 666-68). To me, this does not make sense. Such a composition of the ISC will make it unworkable. The CJI should never be involved in such executive and policy bodies as it might lead to conflict of interest and would also be against the division of powers, which is a part of the basic structure of the Constitution.

The Rajamannar Committee had recommended that the ISC should be consulted on all matters of 'national importance' or which affect one or more states. It should also be empowered to discuss every bill of national importance or which is likely to affect the interest of one or more states and its views on such draft bills should be placed before Parliament at the introduction of the bill. It had also suggested that the recommendations of the ISC should be 'ordinarily binding' on both the states and the Centre. The ISC should consist of the Prime Minister as chairman and the chief ministers or their nominees as members. No other Minister of the Union Cabinet should be a member of the ISC. These suggestions were also unlikely to be acceptable to any Central government and therefore remained on paper.

The ISC was finally established by the V.P. Singh government in 1990 but Singh resigned soon thereafter and no action was taken thereon for several years. The ISC met for the first time only in 1996. The Standing Committee of the ISC was constituted in 1996 for continuous consultation and processing of matters for the consideration of the Council. The Union Home Minister is the Chairman of the Standing Committee, which has four Union Cabinet Ministers and seven chief ministers as members.

The Congress Party did not believe in institutionalising the Centre-state dialogue. As a result, as the Annual Report (2018-19) of the Ministry of Home Affairs shows, *since its inception in 1990, only 11 meetings of the ISC were held till March 2019.* The 11th meeting was held on 16 July 2016 after a gap of 10 years.

As decided in the 11th meeting of the ISC, the Punchhi Commission Report on Centre-state relations has been considered by the Standing Committee. The Punchhi report was submitted to the government in 2010 when the UPA was in power. Only after the NDA came to power in 2014 that it was referred to the ISC which in turn remitted it to its standing committee. The deliberations of the standing committee were completed in May 2018. The recommendations will now be placed before the ISC. Thus, though over a decade has elapsed since the submission of this report, its processing is still in progress! This is an eloquent commentary on the utility of the ISC.

Reference may be made to the proposal approved by the then BJP government in 2001 (Chapter 1) of enacting a law under Article 355 to enable the Central government to intervene by deployment of Central forces in the states, unilaterally. This proposal was to be placed before the ISC but has still not been done. This conveys a lot as both the UPA and the NDA governments were in power in the intervening period.

Power under Article 263 was also used to set up other coordinating bodies such as the Central Council of Health, the Central Council of Local Self-Government, and the four Regional Sales Tax Councils. But, their impact as coordinating bodies has not been perceptible.

The NCRWC has observed that Article 263 has vast potential but the same has not been fully utilised for resolving various problems concerning more than one state. The NCRWC, while endorsing the recommendations of the Sarkaria Commission, has recommended that in resolving problems and coordinating policy and action, the Union as well as the states should more effectively utilize the forum of the ISC. This will be in tune with the spirit of cooperative federalism requiring proper understanding and mutual confidence and resolution of problems of common interest, expeditiously (GOI, vol. I, 2002, p. 164).

The NCRWC has noted that Article 246 (1) read with Entry 14 of List I—Union List—empowers Parliament to make laws with respect to 'entering into treaties and agreements with foreign countries and implementing of treaties, agreements and conventions with foreign countries'. Article 253 [legislation for giving effect to international agreements] overrides the distribution of legislative powers provided for by Article 246 read with the three Lists in the Seventh Schedule. However, the NCRWC has recommended that for reducing tension or friction between the states and the Union and for expeditious decision-making on important issues involving the states, the desirability of prior consultation by the Union government with the ISC may be considered, before signing any treaty affecting the interests of the states regarding matters in the State List (GOI 2002, vol. I, p. 164-5).

The Second Administrative Reforms Commission has suggested, in its 7th report submitted in 2008, that the conflict resolution role envisaged for the ISC under Article 263 (a) of the Constitution should be effectively utilised to find solutions to disputes among the states or between all or some of the states and the Union. But its other recommendations, as under, are not workable:

(i) The ISC may not exist as a permanent body. As and when a specific need arises, a suitable Presidential order may be issued constituting and convening the Council. The body may cease to function once the purpose for which it was constituted is complete.

(ii) The composition of the ISC may be flexible to suit the exigencies of the matter referred to it.

(iii) If necessary, more than one ISC could be in existence at the same time with different terms of reference and composition as warranted for each ISC (GOI 2008, p. 221).

E.M.S. Namboodiripad, former Marxist Chief Minister of Kerala, in his article 'Centre-State Relations to the Fore', had emphasised that coordinating bodies like the NIC [National Integration Council] for the country as a whole, and similar bodies for the major subjects which are allotted to the states should be formed...while the Centre consults and takes advice of state governments, the latter facilitate concerted action by the Centre. Such cooperation between the Centre and the states alone will make it possible that, while more and more powers are transferred from the Centre to the states, there are constant efforts to bring about a national coordination of activities in the areas left to the state governments (Namboodiripad 2010, p. 176).

The ambit of the ISC as envisaged by AP, Tamil Nadu and West Bengal states, the Rajamannar Committee, and Namboodiripad had no relation to the scheme of the ISC as envisioned in the Constitution. It was also in conflict with the division of responsibilities between the Centre and the states laid down in the Constitution. It was contemplated in these suggestions that the states should be consulted and have a say in the national policies, and policies on subjects in the Union List. No political party in power at the Centre can be expected to agree to this scheme of things. For the same reasons the suggestion of the NCRWC that the Centre should consult the ISC before entering into any international treaties is also not likely to be acceptable to the Central government.

It is significant to note that, in spite of repeated demands, the ISC was not established for the first 40 years after the adoption of the Constitution. In fact, it was the fear of these demands which was uppermost in the cautious approach of the UPA to the ISC. Though after coming to power, the BJP has held some meetings of the ISC, its red line would be no different than that of the UPA. There are also fears of the states opposed to the Centre at any given time ganging up against the Centre. This was repeatedly seen in recent years on matters such as the Citizenship Amendment Act, the National Population Register, and even holding of the JEE (Joint Entrance Examination) and NEET (National Eligibility cum Entrance Test). Earlier, during the UPA rule, it was evident in the opposition of the states to the Communal Violence Bill. With complete polarisation of polity in the country, there are serious limitations on the ISC emerging as an effective instrument for Centre-state consultations in a non-partisan manner. It would therefore be best to accept that the idea of the ISC is not workable.

Instead, it might be better to follow the model of the GST Council, with its empowered group of ministers, for each of the major initiatives on which action is to be undertaken, such as the second generation economic reforms (and that too reform-wise), removing restrictions on inter-state trade, curtailing populist policies such as free power and loan waivers, pursuing the objective of 'one nation, one market', and rationalising state domiciliary policies. Such interactions will be well-defined with narrow, focused terms of reference, and more apolitical, business-like, and productive. Convergence of views is more likely in such deliberations.

The Way Forward

The discussion so far shows that although a way forward has to be found, it is not going to be easy for several reasons. *First*, the scheme of the Constitution is not really meant for a functioning, multi-party democracy. The Constitution was framed when the Congress Party had a hegemony and it was not visualised that this position will not continue for ever. The founding fathers had failed to see India becoming a highly polarised, multi-party democracy, with regional parties having ever-increasing say. *Second*, the cycle of unsynchronised elections to state legislative assemblies and Parliament keeps the country in continuous election mode. The level of debate in the elections has deteriorated and become highly acrimonious. Personal attacks on leaders of political parties have increased animosities which then persist till the next round of electioneering begins. *Third*, these differences are carried forward in all fora such as the National Integration Council, the National Development Council, the Inter-State

Council and even the National Institution for Transforming India (NITI). There is no forum left where issues can be discussed apolitically, in the larger interest of the country. Each participant carrying his own agenda to these consultative fora makes the exercise meaningless. **Fourth,** the states, opposed to the Centre, ganging up on issues, even on matters which are in the Central field, has become far too common and has increased the divide between the Centre and the states.

The issues pertaining to federalism have been examined by several high-level commissions. No other subject has had this distinction. There has been a broad consensus among these commissions in their approach to the issues, but these recommendations have mostly remained on paper. Almost all national and regional parties have been in power at the Centre during this period but the fact that none of them has taken a stand in the matter speaks volumes. Irrespective of what they say when in power only in the states, when in power at the Centre, they are not prepared to review and dilute the provisions of the Constitution providing for a strong Centre. Whatever their political rhetoric when not in power, the two main national parties—namely, the BJP and the Congress, have traditionally been and continue to be in favour of a strong Centre.

As can be seen from Appendix 1, the Constitution is largely a replica of the Government of India Act, 1935. *In fact, one inevitably comes to the disturbing conclusion that except for the Preamble and Parts I to IVA of the Constitution dealing with the territory of India, citizenship, fundamental rights, directive principles of state policy, fundamental duties, and some features such as the official language, the entire structure of governance has remained the same as in the colonial period.* As can be expected, several provisions of the Constitution have become controversial, particularly those with respect to Centre-state relations. A strong plea has been made for a review of this position.

Two of the most prominent irritants are the institution of the state Governor and the power of the Centre to impose President's Rule in a state. As for the latter, the Supreme Court has by its decisions reasserted the original objective underlying Article 356, which is a part of the 'emergency provisions', to make it a 'dead letter', except during exceptional circumstances. Now that the decision of the Centre to impose President's Rule is justiciable by the Supreme Court, its misuse has more or less stopped completely.

But, it is the failure of the Centre to act and impose President's Rule in extraordinary situations that has raised serious concerns. Two such instances when the imposition of President's Rule was warranted, were *before* the demolition of the Babri Masjid in 1992 in UP, and *after* the Godhra riots in Gujarat in 2002. Significantly, in the first case it was the Congress Party which was in power at the Centre and in the second, it was the BJP. Such an important provision of the Constitution must not be permitted to be left unused for the sake of safeguarding the fortunes of the ruling party. But, this was a failure of the political leadership and not of the Constitution. What kind of checks and balances should be provided to avoid such situations in the future is a challenge which must be addressed.

The institution of state Governor is clearly a vestige of the past and is anachronistic in the present conditions. None of the very salutary recommendations made by the Sarkaria Commission, the National Commission to Review the Working of the Constitution, the Administrative Reforms Commission, and the Punchhi Commission have been acted upon by any government. Neither have the salutary principles laid down by the Supreme Court been taken notice of by the Central government. The party in power at the Centre finds the awarding of governorships a useful device for accommodating its elder leaders in these positions. Over time, the actions of many Governors, irrespective of their background, had become highly controversial. It is high time the institution is abolished. This will remove a major irritant in Centre-state relations.

India fulfils an important requirement of federalism by providing for distribution of legislative powers between the Centre and the states. The three Lists—Union List, State List and Concurrent List—are drawn from the GOI Act, 1935, with the enlargement of the Union and Concurrent Lists in keeping with the ideology of providing for a strong Centre. There is certainly a case for revising these Lists but while doing so, rather than pandering to the rhetoric of federalism, the larger interest of the country, the need to have all-India policies on some subjects, promoting good governance and the compulsions of globalisation, will have to be borne in mind. This will be the real test of the statesmanship of the political leadership in the country.

Nehru and Patel were acutely aware of the dangers of linguistic sub-nationalism but the demands for linguistic states were so strong that they had to finally concede. No other subject, except the Chinese attack in 1962, had engaged the attention of Parliament as much as the linguistic reorganisation of the states. The alternative to linguistic reorganisation of states was to divide the country into administrative units, as in the British times. This was clearly not suitable, if administration was to be taken closer to the people. The States Reorganisation Commission was also aware of the dangers of riding the tiger of linguistic states and had made some rather superficial recommendations to get over them. Only one of its recommendations was likely to serve any purpose but it was precisely this suggestion which the Centre consciously kept aside, in spite of the acclaimed national leadership of Nehru and the hegemony of the Congress Party. This recommendation pertained to enacting a law under Article 16(3) of the Constitution to ensure equality of opportunity in matters of public employment. Such a law could have been easily passed at that time as a *quid pro quo* for linguistic reorganisation of states. Very early action now needs to be taken to enact such a law.

There is an unholy competition among states to restrict employment opportunities in the government and also the private sector to those domiciled in the state. The larger question of whether there should be only one national domicile or whether state domiciles should be continued to be recognised as at present needs to be seriously debated.

At one time, the Supreme Court itself had expressed a view in support of the former but a later ruling had overridden it. Even if state domicile is considered inescapable, its ambit needs to be restricted to ensure that the fundamental rights given by the Constitution in Articles 15 (the state shall not discriminate against any citizen on grounds of religion, race, caste, sex, place of birth or any of them), 16 (equality of opportunity in matters of public employment), 19 (d) (to move freely throughout the territory of India), and 19 (e) (to reside and settle in any part of the territory of India), are safeguarded. Early steps need to be taken to carry out suitable amendments to the Constitution.

The question of portability of benefits is being addressed, to some extent, by operationalising the 'One Nation, One Ration Card' scheme.

The question of permitting the persons belonging to SC and ST categories to avail of these benefits anywhere in the country needs to be pursued without loss of time.

In view of the rise of provincialism, it is also imperative to amend Article 15 of the Constitution to specifically bar discrimination based on language.

The creation of Telangana state, primarily on the basis of cultural differences with Andhra, has added a new dimension to the problem of linguistic states. In view of the large cultural and other diversities in the country, conceding such demands will lead to fragmentation of the country.

Yet another disturbing development is the creation of smaller states which is the ideology of the BJP. This policy has large implications for India's federalism and needs to be reconsidered.

Official language continues to be a divisive issue though, with globalisation, its intensity has considerably reduced with the spread of English even in the rural and semi-urban areas in the Hindi belt. It is hoped that the southern states will also adopt a less strident position and leave the decision of learning Hindi to the younger generation, rather than making it a political issue. It is time English language is included in the Eighth Schedule of the Constitution.

In a multi-religious, multi-racial, multi-ethnic country like India, the importance of secularism need not be overemphasized. The Constitution has made explicit provisions for the right to freedom of religion, and cultural and educational rights of minorities. The Supreme Court has declared secularism as a part of the basic structure of the Constitution. But, with the emergence of the BJP at the national level, particularly since 2014, and its strident advocacy of a Hindu *Rashtra* (nation) as its ultimate objective, for the first time since the adoption of the Constitution, secularism is under serious threat. In such a situation, separating religion from politics has assumed new urgency but with the opposition of the BJP, the Shiv Sena, the Shiromani Akali Dal, and other religion-based political parties, and more importantly, the weakening of the national secular parties, it looks like a lost cause. This fault line is likely to pose a serious danger in the future.

I have highlighted the ramifications of the Kashmir fault line. Kashmir has been a permanent item on the agenda of unfinished tasks since Independence. The Kashmir problem had become acute due to the litany of blunders by the Central government. Abrogation of Article 370 was long overdue and should have been done years ago to set the record straight on the status of J&K. As seen from the speeches of Nehru and other leaders like Gulzarilal Nanda and M.C. Chagla, though the Congress Party was convinced of the need to abolish Article 370, it did not have the political courage to do it. Now in the Opposition, the Congress Party is leading the charge of the brigade opposing the abrogation. Looking apolitically and dispassionately at the history of the Article, it is imperative that all political parties come together and take a united stand in support of the abrogation. Constitutionally, though the integration of Kashmir is complete now, it must be accepted that much remains to be done for the closer emotional bonding of the Kashmir valley with India. Concerted efforts made over the years to solve the Kashmir problem, reduce the alienation in the Kashmir valley and bring about its emotional integration with the rest of India, had failed. I have suggested a 12-point programme for bringing about normalisation of the situation. As a part of this process, very early steps need to be taken to restore the statehood of the Kashmir valley and the Jammu region to create a congenial atmosphere for the recommencement of the political process, and to assuage the feeling of hurt among the people.

At present, there are eight union territories. The justification for the continuance of union territories has never been examined so far. It is proposed that the status of Delhi should be continued as it is, Chandigarh should be given to Punjab, and Andaman & Nicobar, and Ladakh should continue as UTs. The Kashmir valley and the Jammu region, which were converted into a union territory in 2019, should be upgraded and given a statehood as soon as possible. The remaining UTs should be merged with the adjoining states. In view of its history as a French colony, Puducherry should be made a separate district of Tamil Nadu to maintain its identity.

If federalism is to be strengthened, the Rajya Sabha will have to be the representative of the states in the real sense of the term. This will call for amendment of the Constitution to make residence in the state for a minimum period a prerequisite for election to the Rajya Sabha.

Cordiality in Centre-state relations is a litmus test of the success of a federal structure. On this criterion, there is cause for serious concern. As compared to the early years after Independence, there is increasing stridency and bitterness in Centre-state relations. This was also true in Indira Gandhi's term as prime minister. But, for the first time, the states are challenging actions of the Centre, not just politically but also in the courts, even in respect of subjects which constitutionally fall in the Centre's sphere. There is an increasing tendency among the states to take a united stand against the Centre. All these are disquieting trends and have increased the distrust between the Centre and the states. The root cause of it is the breakdown of communication at the political level.

The question of creation of All India Services was discussed in detail in the Premiers' [of Provinces] Conferences on 21 and 22 October 1946 by Sardar Patel (GOI 1967, pp. 135-8). The Commission on Centre-State Relations had in its report [para 8.19.01 (i)] recommended that the All India Services are as much necessary today as they were when the Constitution was framed and continue to be one of the premier institutions for maintaining the unity of the country. (GOI 1988) The role of the All India Services, which were expected to act as the bridge between the Centre and the states, has fallen short of expectations. The underlying issues require urgent attention.

It is time to open a new chapter on India's federalism by pursuing the objective of cooperative federalism, which has remained on paper so far except in the solitary case of GST. This is not going to be an easy task and will require a complete change in the mindset of the Centre and the states. This will help India achieve real integration and fulfil the goal of 'One India One Market'. Ways need to be explored for strengthening India's quasi-federal structure.

With all its shortcomings, the GST has helped India take giant strides towards the objective of cooperative federalism. The problems created by Covid-19 epidemic must be treated as an 'act of God'. The basic thrust of achieving full potential of GST must be pursued. There is a long way to go which will call for concerted efforts on the part of the Centre and the states.

India is still riddled with a number of hurdles and restrictions on free trade and commerce in the country. The objective laid down in Article 301 of the Constitution of ensuring free trade, commerce and intercourse throughout the territory of India has been overtaken by the other provisions of the Constitution which have given considerable latitude to the Centre and the states to impose restrictions on trade, moving and stocking of goods, etc. Though 70 years have elapsed since the adoption of the Constitution, and in spite of the globalisation and economic liberalisation policies adopted from 1990-91, a Trade and Commerce Authority of India has still not been set up, as contemplated in Article 307. Action on this needs to be expedited.

The Indian Supreme Court has been given an exceptionally wide jurisdiction, as compared to any other country. However, the Court is swamped with appellate work. As a result, cases falling under its original jurisdiction and constitutional matters are being given secondary treatment and have been languishing for years together. Over 55 countries have established separate constitutional courts. A strong plea has been made for creating a separate constitutional division of the Supreme Court consisting of nine full-time judges. It is proposed that both the constitutional and the appellate divisions should function under the Chief Justice of India.

The Inter-State Council has been ineffective so far. It is clearly unworkable for various reasons. At the same time, a federal structure cannot work without viable mechanisms for Centre-state and inter-state consultations. It is time alternate mechanisms are adopted. Some suggestions have been made for the purpose.

Appendix I

I. COMPARATIVE TABLES.

Of the articles of the Constitution of India
and
the sections of the Government of India Act, 1935.

COMPARATIVE TABLE No. 1

Constitution of India. Articles.	Government of India Act, 1935. Sections.
Part I: The Union and its territories.	
1	...
2, 3	290
4	...
Part II : Citizenship	
5	...
6	...
7	...
8	...
9	...
10	...
11	...
12	...
13	...
14	...
15	298
16	275, 298
17	...
18	...
19(f), (g)	298(1)(2)
20	...
21	...
22	...
23	...
24	...
25	...
26	...
27	...
28	...
29	...
30	...
31(1)	299(1)
32	...
33	...
34	...
35	...
Part IV : Directive Principles of State Policy.	
36	...
37	...
38	...
39	...
40	...
41	...
42	...
43	...

Constitution of India. Articles.	Government of India Act, 1935. Sections.
44	...
45	...
46	...
47	...
48	...
49	...
50	...
51	...
Part V : The Union.	
52	...
53(1)	7(1)
53(2)	...
54	...
55	...
56	...
57	...
58	...
59	...
60	...
61	...
62	...
63	...
64	...
65	...
66	...
67	...
68	...
69	...
70	...
71	...
72	295
73	8
74(1)	9
74(2)	10(4)
75(2)	10(1)
76	16
77	17
78	17(4)
79	18(1)
80	...
81	18(2) (3)
82	...
83	18(4) (8)
84	...
85	19
86	20
87	...
88	21
89	22(1)

4148   COMPARATIVE TABLE NO. 1

Constitution of India.	Government of India Act, 1935	Constitution of India.	Government of India Act, 1935.
Articles.	Sections.	Articles	Sections.
90	22(2)	Part VI: The States in Part A of the First Schedule	
91	22(3)	152	46
92	...	153	...
93	22(1)&(5)	154	49(1)
94	33(1)&(5)	155	48(1)
95	22	156	...
96	...	157	...
97	22(4)&(5)	158	...
98	...	159	...
99	24	160	...
100	23	161	...
101	25	162	49
102	26	163	50 (1) & (3) 51 (4)
103	...	164	51 (1) (2) & (3)
104	27	165	55(1) (2) & (3)
105	28(1)(2)&(5)	166	59(1) (2) & (3)
106	29	167	59(4)
107	30	168	60
108	31	169	...
109	37	170	...
110	37	171	...
111	32	172	61(2) (3)
112	33(1)(2)(3)	173	Sch. V, para 1.
113	34	174	62 (1) (2)
114	...	175	63
115	36	176	...
116	...	177	64
117	37	178	65(1)
118	38(1)	179	65 (2)
119	...	180	65 (3)
120	39	181	...
121	40(1)	182	65(1) & (5)
122	41	183	65(2) & (5)
123	43	184	65(3) & (5)
124	200	185	...
125	201	186	65(4) (5)
126	202	187	...
127	202(2)(3)	188	67
128	...	189	66
129	203	190	68
130	203	191	69
131	204(1)	192	...
132	205	193	70
133 } 134	...	194	71
135	...	195	72
136	...	196	73, 74(1)
137	...	197	...
138	...	198	82(1) (2)
139	..	199	82
140	215	200	75
141	212	201	76 (1)
142	210(2)	202	78
143	213(1)	203	79
144	210	204	...
145	214	205	81
146	216(1)	206	...
147	...	207	82
148	166(1) (2) & (4)	208	84
149	166		
150	168		
151	169		

COMPARATIVE TABLE NO. 1   4149

Constitution of India.	Government of India Act, 1935	Constitution of India.	Government of India Act, 1935
Articles.	Sections.	Articles.	Sections.
209	...	255	106(2)
210	85	256	122
211	86(1)	257	126
212	87	258	124
213	88	259	...
214	219	260	...
215	220(1)	261	...
216	220(1)	262	130-133
217	220(2) (3)	263	135
218	...	Part XII : Finance, Property, Contracts and Suits.	
219	220(4)		
220	...	264	...
221	221	265	...
222	...	266	136
223	223(1)	267	...
224	...	268	...
225	223	269	137
225 Prov.	226(1)	270	138
227	224	271—137 Pro.	138 Pro. (b)
228	226(1)	272	140(1)
229	242(4)	273	140(2)
230	230(1) & (2)	274	141(1) & (3)
231	230 (3)	275	142 Para 1
232	231(3)	276	142A.
233	254(1) (2)	277	143(2)
234	255(1) (2)	278	...
235	255(3)	279	144
236	254 (3), 255 (1) Para 2	280	...
237	...	281	...
Part VII : The States in Part B of the First Schedule.		282	150 (2)
		283	151
238	...	284	...
Part VIII : The States in Part C of the First Schedule.		285	154
		286	297
239	94(3)	287	154A
242	97	288	...
Part IX : The Territories in Part D, etc.		289	155(1)
		290	156
243	96	291	...
Part X : The Scheduled and Tribal Areas.		292	163
		293	163(1),(2),(3)&(4)
244	...	294	172(1)-173(1)to(3)
Part XI : Relations between the Union and the States.		295	...
		296	174
245	99(1)	297	...
246	100	298(1)	175(1)
247	...	298(2)	175(2)
248	104	299(1)	175(3)
249	...	299(2)	175(4)
250	102(1), (4)	300	176
251	102(2)	Part XIII : Trade, Commerce and Intercourse.	
252	103	301-307	...
253	106	303	297(1) (2)
254	107(1), (2)	Part XIV : Services under the Union and the States.	
		308	...
		309	241(1) (2)

4150   COMPARATIVE TABLE NO. 1

Constitution of India.	Government of India Act, 1935
Articles.	Sections.
310	240(1) (2) (4)
311	240(2), (3)
312	...
313	276
314	Cf. 247-249
316	265(1)
318	265(2)
319	265(3)
320	266
321	267
322	268
323	...
Part XV : Elections	
324	...
325	...
326	...
327	291
328	...
329	...
Part XVI : Special Provisions re. certain classes.	
330	...
331	...
332	...
333	...
334	...
335	...
336	...
337	...
338	...
339	...
340	...
341	...
342	...
Part XVII : Official Language.	
343	...
344	...
345	...
346	...
347	...
348	214 (5), 227
349	...
350	...
351	...
Part XVIII: Emergency Provisions.	
352	102 (1) (3)
353(b)	...
354	...

Constitution of India.	Government of India Act, 1935
Articles.	Sections.
355	...
356 } Also see } 365 }	...
357	...
358	...
359	...
360	...
Part XIX : Miscellaneous.	
361	306
362	...
363	...
364	...
365	...
366	311
367	311
Part XX : Amendment of the Constitution.	
368	...
Part XXI : Temporary and Transitional Provisions.	
369	...
370	...
371	...
372	292 & 293
373	...
374	...
375	...
376	...
377	...
378	...
379	...
380	...
381	...
382	...
383	...
384	...
385	...
386	...
387	...
388	...
389	...
390	...
391	...
392	...
393	...
394	...
395	...

SCH. VII—LIST 1.—UNION LIST.

Constitution of India.	Government of India Act, 1935	Constitution of India.	Government of India Act, 1935
Entries	Items	Entries	Items
1	...	5	29, 30
2	1	6	...
3	2	7	...
4	3	8	1

COMPARATIVE TABLE NO. 1

4151

Constitution of India.	Government of India Act, 1935	Constitution of India.	Government of India Act, 1935
Entries	Items	Entries	Items
9	1	53	33
10	3	54	36
11	...	55	35
12	...	56	...
13	...	57	23
14	3	58	47
15	...	59	31
16	...	60	List III, 33
17	49	61	...
18	3	62	11
19	17	63	13
20	17	64	...
21	...	65	12
22	20	66	12
23	...	67	15
24 } 25 }	21	68	14
26	25	69	16
27	22	70	8
28	18	71	9
29	24	72	40
30	26	73	41
31	7	74	41
32	10	75	41
33	. List II, 9	76	...
34	...	77	53
35	6	78	...
36	5	79	...
37	...	80	39
38	...	81	50
39	7	82	54
40	48	83	44
41	19	84	45
42	...	85	46
43 } 44 }	33	86	55
45	28	87	56A
46	28	88	56
47	37	89	58
48	...	90	...
49	27	91	57
50	51	92	List II, 43
51	...	93	42
52	34	94	...
		95	21, 53
		96	59
		97	...

Sch. VII, Li   II. — State List.

Constitution of India.	Government of India Act, 1935	Constitution of India.	Government of India Act, 1935
Entries	Items	Entries	Items
1	1	11	17
2	3	12	10
3	1 and 2	13	18
4	4	14	20
5	13	15	20
6	14	16	20
7	15	17	19
8	31	18	21
9	32	19	22
10	16	20	25

4152   COMPARATIVE TABLE NO. 1

Constitution of India.	Government of India Act, 1935	Constitution of India.	Government of India Act, 1935
Entries	Items	Entries	Items
21	24	44	21
22	21	45	39
23	23	46	41
24	29	47	43
25	26	48	43A
26	27	49	42
27	29	50	44
28	27	51	40
29	30	52	49
30	27	53	48B
31	28	54	48
32	33	55	48
33	35	56	52
34	36	57	48A
35	8	58	47
36	9	59	53
37	11	60	46
38	12	61	45
39	12	62	50
40	12	63	51
41	6	64	37
42	7	65	2
43	5	66	54

SCH. VII, LIST III — CONCURRENT LIST.

Constitution of India.	Government of India Act, 1935	Constitution of India.	Government of India Act, 1935
Entries	Items	Entries	Items
1	1	24	27
2	2	25	...
3	cf. List I, 1 & II, 1	26	16
4	3	27	...
5	6, 7	28	List II, 34
6	8	29	30
7	10	30	List II, 14
8	14	31	List II, 18
9	12	32	32
10	9	33	...
11	12	34	...
12	5	35	20
13	4	36	26
14	...	37	21
15	23	38	31
16	18	39	17
17	22	40	cf. List I, 15
18	List II 30	41	...
19	19	42	...
20	...	43	4
21	...	44	13
22	29	45	24
23	28	46	List III, 15
		47	35, 36

COMPARATIVE TABLE No. 2.

Government of India Act, 1935	Constitution of India.	Government of India Act, 1935	Constitution of India.
Sections.	Articles.	Sections.	Articles.
3	54	9	74 (1)
7 (1)	53 (1)	10 (1)	75 (2)
8	73	10 (4)	74 (3)

COMPARATIVE TABLE NO. 2   4153

Government of India Act, 1935	Constitution of India.	Government of India Act, 1935	Constitution of India.
Sections.	Articles.	Sections.	Articles.
16	76	81	205
17	77	82 (1) (2)	198, 199
17 (4)	78	82	207
18 (1)	79	83	...
18 (2) (3)	81	84	208
18 (4)	83	85	210
19	85	86 (1)	211
20	86	87	212
21	88	88	213
22 (1) (2) (5)	89, 90, 93, 94, 95	93	
22 (3)	91	94 (3)	239, 242
22 (4) & (5)	97	96	243
23	100	99 (1)	245
24	99	100	246
25	101	102 (1) (3) (4)	250, 352
26	102	102 (2)	251
27	104	102 (3)	353 (b)
28 (1) (2) & (5)	105	103	252
29	106	104	248
30	107	106	253
31	108	107 (1) & (2)	254
32	111	109 (2)	255
33 (1) (2) (3)	112	122	256
34	113	124	258
36	115	126	257
37	109, 110, 117	130—133	262
38 (1)	118	135	263
39	120	136	266
40 (1)	121	137	269
41	122	137 Prov & 138 Pr (b)	270, 271
42	123	140 (1)	272
45, 93	356	140 (2)	273
46	152	141 (1) & (3)	274
48 (1)	155	142 Para 1	275
49 (1)	154, 162	142-A	276
50 (1) & (3); S 51 (4)	163	143 (2)	277
51 (1) (2) & (3)	164	144	279
55 (1) (2) & (3)	165	150 (2)	282
59 (1) (2) & (3)	166	151	283
59 (4)	167	154	285
60	168	154-A	287
61 (2) (3)	172	355 (1)	289
62 (1) & (2)	174	156	290
63	175	162	292
64	177	163 (1) (2) & (3) (4)	293
65 (1) (2) (3) (4) (5)	178, 179, 180, 182, 183, 184, 186	166 (1) (2) & (4)	148, 149
66	189	168	150
67	188	169	151
68	190	172 (1)—173 (1) to (3)	294
69	191	173	...
70	193	174	296
71	194	175 (1)	298 (1)
72	195	175 (2)	298 (2)
73, 74 (1)	196	175 (3)	299 (1)
74	...	175 (4)	299 (2)
75	200	176	300
76 (1)	201	200	124
78	202	201	125
79	203	202	126
		202 (2) (3)	127
		203	129, 130
		204 (1)	131

4154   COMPARATIVE TABLE NO. 2

Government of India Act, 1935	Constitution of India	Government of India Act, 1935	Constitution of India
Sections.	Articles.	Sections.	Articles.
205	132	247, 249	314
205, 207	...	254 (1), (2)	233
206	138	254 (3), 255 (1) Pr 2	236
210 (2)	142, 144	255 (1) & (2)	234
212	141	255 (3)	235
213	143	256	...
214	145	265	316-319 { 316-265 (1), 318-265 (2), 319-265 (3) }
215	140	266	320
216 (1)	146	267	321
219	214	268	322
220 (1) (2) (3)	215, 216, 217	275, 298	16
220 (4)	219	276	313
221	221	290	2, 3
222 (1)	223	291	327
223	225	292 & 293	372
224	227	295	72
225	228	297	286
226	225 Prov. 226	297 (1) (2)	303
227, 214 (5)	348	298	15
230 (1) & (2)	230	296 (1)	19 (f) (g)
230 (3)	231	299 (1)	31 (1)
231 (2)	232	304	160
240 (1) (2) (4)	310	306	361
240 (2) (3)	311	311	366, 367
241 (1) (2)	309	320	...
243 (4)	239	Sch V Para 1	Art 173
244	...		

SCHEDULE VII LIST I.

Government of India Act, 1935	Constitution of India	Government of India Act, 1935	Constitution of India
Items	Entries	Items	Entries
1	1	24	29
1	8, 9	25	26
List I—1 & List II item 1:	List III item 3	26	30
2	2, 3, 4	27	49
3	10, 14, 18	28	46
5	36	29, 30	5
6	35	31	59
6	37	32	53
7	31, 39	33	43, 44
8	70	34	52
10	32	35	55
11	62	36	54
11, 12	64	37	47
12	65, 66	38	45
13	63	39	80
14	68	40	72
15	67	41	73, 74, 75
15	40	42	93
16	69	43 & List III 35 }	94
17	19, 20	43	List III 30
18	28	44	83
19	41	45	84
20	22	46	85
21	24, 25	47	58
22	27	48	40
23	57	49	17

COMPARATIVE TABLE NO. 2   4155

Government of India Act, 1935	Constitution of India	Government of India Act, 1935	Constitution of India
Items	Entries	Items	Entries
50	81	56	88
51	50	56A	87
53	77	57	91
54	82	58	89
55	86	59	96

Schedule VII List II

Government of India Act, 1935	Constitution of India	Government of India Act, 1935	Constitution of India
Items	Entries	Items	Entries
1	1, 3,	26	25
1	List I-78	27	26, 28, 30
1	3 List III	28	31
2	79 List I	29	24, 27
	3 } II		33 List III
	65 } II	30	29
	46 III		18 List III
3	2	31	8
4	4	32	9
5	43	33	32
6	41	34	28-List III
7	42	35	33
8	35	36	34
9	List I-33,	37	64
	List II 36	39	45
10	12	40	51
11	37	41	46
12	38, 39, 40	42	49
13	5	43	47
14	6	43A	48
15	7	44	50
16	10	45	61
17	11	46	60
18	13, 31	47	58
19	17	48	92 List I
20	14, 15, 16		54, 55 List II
21	18, 22, 44	48A	57
	List 2	48B	53
	34 List I	49	52
21, 18, 19	56 List I	50	62
22	19	51	63
23	23	52	56
24	21	53	59
25	20	54	66

Schedule VII List III

Government of India Act, 1935	Constitution of India	Government of India Act, 1935	Constitution of India
Items	Entries	Items	Entries
1	1	10	7
2	2	12	9, 11
3	4	13	44
4	13, 43	14	8
5	12	15	14
6	5	16	26
		17	39
8	6	18	16
9	10	19	19

4156   COMPARATIVE TABLE NO. 2

Government of India Act, 1935	Constitution of India	Government of India Act, 1935	Constitution of India
Items	Entries	Items	Entries
20	35	29	22
21	37	30	29
22	17	31	38
23	15	32	32
24	45	32	List I-24
26	36	33	60-List I
27	24	36	47
28	23	53, 21	95 List I

Source: Chitaley, V.V. and Rao, Appu S. *The Constitution of India,* vol. 5. Nagpur: All India Reporter, 1959.

Appendix 2
Article 370 – The Genesis

In the note by the Ministry of States explaining the decisions regarding the Indian States, submitted to the Drafting Committee of the Constitution in July 1949, it was recommended as under:

The Government of India have carefully considered the position of Jammu and Kashmir State in the context of their international commitments. *Ordinarily they would have liked to treat this State like other States in the category of Part III States. The main difficulty in adopting this procedure is that the Premier of this State has definitely expressed his inability to extend the content of the accession of the State till the Constituent Assembly of the State has taken a decision in the matter. Against the present background, he is most anxious that the accession of the State should continue in respect of the three subjects of Defence, Foreign Affairs and Communications only.* During the course of the discussion at the Drafting Committee meeting, it was pointed out that the scheme embodied in the Draft Constitution visualized that all States in Part III would accept List I [Union List] and List II [State List] and in addition accept all provisions relating to fundamental rights and the provisions relating to the High Courts and Supreme Court. *It was further pointed out that if the quantum of accession of Kashmir State was not extended, difficulties would arise in respect of the citizenship of the subjects* of Kashmir State as also in connection with the operation of the provisions regarding fundamental rights and Supreme Court in respect of this State. The government of India have considered the matter in its various aspects and are of the opinion that in view of the present peculiar situation in respect of Jammu and Kashmir State *it is desirable that the accession should be continued on the exiting basis till the State could be brought to the level of other States. A special provision has therefore to be made in respect of this State on the basis suggested above as a transitional arrangement.* It may be added that "naturalization" is already covered by the existing Instrument of Accession signed by the Ruler of the State and this may perhaps meet the requirements in respect of citizenship of the subjects of this State.

The Ministry of States suggest for the consideration of the Drafting Committee the following approach to this question:

(i) Jammu and Kashmir State may be treated as part of Indian territory and shown in States specified in Part III of Schedule I.

(ii) A special provision may be made in the Constitution to the effect that until Parliament provides by law that all the provisions of the Constitution applicable to the States specified in Part III will apply to this State, the power of Parliament to make laws for the State will be limited to the items specified in the Schedule to the Instrument of Accession governing the accession of this State to the Dominion of India or to the corresponding entries in List I of the new Constitution.

In his speech in the Constituent Assembly on 12 October 1949, Vallabhbhai Patel, inter alia, reiterated the above position and said:

In view of the special problems with which the Government of Jammu and Kashmir is faced, *we have made a special provision for the continuance of the constitutional relationship of the State with the Union on the existing basis.* In the case of Hyderabad State the acceptance of the Constitution will be subject to ratification by the people of the State.[1]

During the discussion in the Constituent Assembly, on account of the peculiar circumstances relating to the Jammu and Kashmir State, it was not considered appropriate at that stage that the provisions relating to the other Indian States should apply to that State; and, on 17 October 1949, Gopalaswami Ayyangar introduced a special Article (306-A) specifically governing the relation of the State with the Union of India. The State of Jammu and Kashmir had acceded to the Union of India on 26 October 1947; and, as in the case of the other Indian States, this accession had taken place by means of an Instrument of Accession executed by the Ruler of the State and accepted by the Governor-General of India. As Ayyangar explained, *the Instrument of Accession would in the case of all these States be a thing of the past in the new Constitution.*

The States have been integrated with the Federal Republic in such a manner that they do not have to accede or execute a document of accession for the purpose of becoming units of the Republic, but are mentioned in the Constitution itself; and in the case of practically all States other than the State of Jammu and Kashmir their constitutions have also been embodied in the Constitution for the whole of India. All those other States have agreed to integrate themselves in that way and accept the Constitution provided.

Ayyangar went on to explain the distinction made in the Constitution between these States and the State of Jammu and Kashmir. He said:

(i) In the first place, there has been a war going on within the limits of Jammu and Kashmir State.

(ii) There was a ceasefire agreed to at the beginning of this year and that ceasefire is still on. But the conditions in the State are still

---

1. B. Shiva Rao, ed., The Framing of India's Constitution – Select Documents, vol. IV (New Delhi: The Indian Institute of Public Administration, 1968), pp. 555-7.

unusual and abnormal. They have not settled down. It is therefore necessary that the administration of the State should be geared to these unusual conditions until normal life is restored as in the case of the other States.

(iii) Part of the State is still in the hands of rebels and enemies. *We are entangled with the United Nations* in regard to Jammu and Kashmir and it is not possible to say now when we shall be free from this entanglement.

It is in the light of these complicating factors that the new draft Article made provision for the State. In the first place, it was recognised that Jammu and Kashmir was an integral part of the Indian Union; and the Article unequivocally stated that Article I (which enunciated that India would be a Union of States and that the States and territories of the Union would be the States and their territories specified in Parts I, II, and III of the First Schedule) would apply to the Jammu and Kashmir State; the name of the State was also incorporated in Part III of the First Schedule (Subsequently altered to Part B).

The Article laid down that, unlike other States in this category, the Constitution would not for the time being seek to provide for the internal constitution of the State; and stated accordingly that Part VI-A of the Constitution would not apply to the State of Jammu and Kashmir.

The Article had, however, to deal with the status of Jammu and Kashmir State as a unit of the Indian Union, and to provide for the legislative authority of Parliament and the executive authority of the Union Government in relation to the State. Broadly, these powers were governed by the Instrument of Accession of the State and related to the three main subjects of defence, foreign affairs and communications. The Article therefore provided that the power of Parliament to make laws for the state would be limited to those matters in the Union List and the Concurrent List which, in consultation with the government of the state, are declared by the President to correspond to matters specified in the Instrument of

Accession governing the accession of the State to the Dominion of India as the matters with respect to which the Dominion Legislature may make laws for the State.

It was not the intention that the power of the Union Parliament should be 'frozen' in regard to the subjects mentioned in the Instrument of Accession, and there was a further clause in the Article which made the powers of the Union Legislature more flexible. This clause enabled Parliament to make laws for the State on other matters as well, but these matters had to be specified in an order to be made by the President with the concurrence of the Government of the State.

In the light of this delimitation of the powers of Parliament it was further provided that such of the provisions of the Constitution (other than Article I which applied automatically) would apply in relation to the State subject to such exceptions and modifications as the President might by order specify.

All these provisions were to be of a temporary character, and the Article contained a further clause that when the Constituent Assembly of the State had met and taken a decision, both on the constitution of the State and on the range of federal jurisdiction over the State, the President might on the recommendation of the Assembly issue an order that the whole of Article would cease to be operative, or would be operative subject to such exceptions and modifications as might be specified by the President in the order. *When this was done it was contemplated that the position of the Jammu and Kashmir State would also correspond as closely as possible to that of the other States in the Indian Union.*

After Ayyangar had explained the scope and purpose of the special Article on Kashmir, *it was adopted by the Assembly without much discussion;* and at the revision stage it was numbered 370.[2]

Note: Emphasis added.

---

2. Ibid., pp. 552-3.

Appendix 3
Draft Article 306A
(Proposed by Sheikh Abdullah Government)

Munshi Papers, Indian Constitutional Documents, vol. II, (Bombay: Bharatiya Vidya Bhavan, 1967), pp. 519-20.

Notwithstanding anything contained in this Constitution, until on the recommendation of the Constituent Assembly constituted for the purpose of framing the Constitution of the Jammu and Kashmir State (hereinafter referred to as the State in this Article), the President may, by public notification, alter, modify or amend this Article:

a. Only such provisions of this Constitution shall apply in relation to the State as are declared by the President, in consultation with the Government of the State, to relate directly to the matters specified in the Instrument of Accession governing the accession of the State to the Dominion of India;

b. The power of Parliament to make laws for the State shall be limited to:

   those matters in the Union List and the Concurrent List which are declared by the President, in consultation with the Government of the State, to correspond to matters specified in the Instrument of Accession governing the accession of the

State to the Dominion of India as the matters with respect to which the Dominion Legislature may make laws for the State.

Explanation

The Government of the State in this Article means the person for the time being recognised as the Maharaja of the State by the Union acting on the advice of the Council of Ministers *as at present constituted* and not acting in his discretion or in his individual judgment.

Source: Noorani, A.G. *Article 370: A Constitutional History of J&K*, pp. 52-3. New Delhi: OUP, 2011.

Abbreviations

AASU	All Assam Students Union
AIADMK	All India Anna Dravida Munnetra Kazagam
AICC	All India Congress Committee
AICC(I)	All India Congress Committee (Indira)
AIR	All India Reporter
AIS	All India Services
AP	Andhra Pradesh
APMC	Agricultural Produce Marketing Committee
ARC	Administrative Reforms Commission
BJP	Bharatiya Janata Party
CAA	Citizenship Amendment Act
C&AG	Comptroller and Auditor General
CBDT	Central Board of Direct Taxes
CBI	Central Bureau of Investigation
CBIC	Central Board of Indirect Taxes and Customs
CII	Confederation of Indian Industry
CJ	Chief Justice
CJI	Chief Justice of India
CM	Chief Minister
CPI (M)	Communist Party of India (Marxist)
CrPC	Criminal Procedure Code
DA	Dearness Allowance
DPCO	Drug Price Control Order
ECA	Essential Commodities Act
EPW	Economic and Political Weekly

FICCI	Federation of Indian Chambers of Commerce and Industry
FIR	First Information Report
FSME	Federation of Small & Medium Enterprises
Gen	General
GoC	General-officer-Commanding
GOJK	Government of Jammu and Kashmir
GOI	Government of India
GOM	Government of Maharashtra
GOTN	Government of Tamil Nadu
GST	Goods and Services Tax
HM	Home Minister
HMG	Her Majesty's Government
HP	Himachal Pradesh
I&B	Information and Broadcasting Ministry
ICS	Indian Civil Service
IIC	India International Centre
IGC	Inter-Governmental Council
IPC	Indian Penal Code
ISI	Inter-Services Intelligence (of Pakistan)
JILI	Journal of Indian Law Institute
JEE	Joint Entrance Examination
J&K	Jammu and Kashmir
JMM	Jharkhand Mukti Morcha
JNMF	Jawaharlal Nehru Memorial Fund
LARE	Land and Real Estate
LG	Lieutenant Governor
LOC	Line of Control
LSS	Lok Sabha Secretariat
Lt	Lieutenant
MEA	Ministry of External Affairs
MFN	Most Favoured Nation

MHA	Ministry of Home Affairs
MLA	Member of Legislative Assembly
MP	Member of Parliament
MP	Madhya Pradesh
NALSAR	National Academy of Legal Studies and Research
NC	National Conference
NCAER	National Council of Applied Economic Research
NCR	National Capital Region
NCRWC	National Commission to Review the Working of the Constitution
NDA	National Democratic Alliance
NEP	National Education Policy
NEET	National Eligibility Cum Entrance Test
NIPFP	National Institute of Public Finance and Policy
NITI	National Institution for Transforming India
NMML	Nehru Memorial Museum and Library
NPA	Non-Performing Asset
NRC	National Register of Citizens
NSCN	National Socialist Council of Nagaland
NSDP	Net State Domestic Product
NWFP	North West Frontier Province
OBC	Other Backward Caste
OUP	Oxford University Press
PDP	People's Democratic Party
PEPSU	Patiala and East Punjab States Union
PM	Prime Minister
PMO	Prime Minister's Office
PoK	Pakistan-occupied Kashmir
POW	Prisoner of War
PTI	Press Trust of India
RAW	Research and Analysis Wing
RBI	Reserve Bank of India

RPA	Representation of People Act
RSS	Rashtriya Swayamsevak Sangh
SARC	Second Administrative Reforms Commission
SC	Supreme Court
SC	Scheduled Caste
SCC	Supreme Court Cases
SEZ	Special Economic Zone
SRC	States Reorganisation Commission
ST	Scheduled Tribe
SYL	Sutlej Yamuna Link
TA	Travelling Allowance
TMC	Trinamool Congress
TOI	Times of India
TRS	Telangana Rashtra Samiti
UID	Unique Identification Data
UNCIP	United Nations Commission for India and Pakistan
UNO	United Nations Organisation
UP	Uttar Pradesh
UPA	United Progressive Alliance
UT	Union Territory
VC	Vice-Chancellor
VIP	Very Important Person
WTO	World Trade Organisation

Bibliography

Books

Abdullah, Sheikh. *Flames of the Chinar*. Translated by Khushwant Singh. New Delhi: Penguin Books, 1995.

Aggarwal, R.C., ed. *Constitution of India and Pendency of Court Cases*. New Delhi: Oxford Software Institute, 2016.

Akbar, M.J. *Kashmir: Behind the Vale*. New Delhi: Viking, 1991.

Alexandrowicz, Charles Henry. *Constitutional Developments in India*. Bombay: OUP, 1957.

Ambedkar, B.R. *Thoughts on Pakistan*. Bombay: Thacker and Company, 1941.

Apte, Bal, ed. *Supreme Court on Hindutva: Extracts and Comments*. New Delhi: India First Foundation, 2005.

Austin, Granville. *The Indian Constitution: Cornerstone of a Nation*. Bombay: Oxford University Press, 1966.

Austin, Granville. *Working a Democratic Constitution: The Indian Experience*. New Delhi: Oxford University Press, 1999.

Basant, Rakesh and Abusaleh Shariff, eds. *Oxford Handbook of Muslims in India: Empirical and Policy Perspectives*. New Delhi: Oxford University Press, 2010.

Banerjee, A.C. *The Constituent Assembly of India*. Calcutta: A. Mukherjee & Co., 1947.

Basu, Durga Das. *Comparative Federalism*, second edition (revised). Nagpur: Wadhwa and Company, 2008.

Basu, Narayani. *V.P. Menon: The Unsung Architect of Modern India*. New Delhi: Simon & Schuster, 2020.

Bhagyalakshmi, J., ed. *Capital Witness: Selected Writings of G.K. Reddy.* New Delhi: Allied Publishers, 1992.

Bhattacharjea, Ajit. *Sheikh Mohammad Abdullah: Tragic Hero of Kashmir,* New Delhi, Roli Books, 2008.

Baxi, Upendra, Alice Jacob, & Tarlok Singh, eds. *Reconstructing The Republic.* New Delhi: Har-Anand Publications, 1999.

Behera, Navnita Chadha, ed. *State, People and Security: The South Asian Context,* New Delhi, Har-Anand Publications, 2002.

Behera, Navnita Chadha. *Demystifying Kashmir.* Washington D.C.: Brookings Institute Press, 2006.

Bombwall, K.R., ed. *National Power and State Autonomy.* Meerut/New Delhi: Meenakhsi Prakashan, 1977.

Bhutto, Benazir. *Daughter of the East: An Autobiography.* London: A Mandarin Paperback, 1988.

Carter, Lionel. ed. *Mountbatten's Report on the Last Viceroyalty, 20 March-15 August 1947.* New Delhi: Manohar Publishers, 2003.

Chagla, M.C. *Roses in December: An Autobiography,* Eleventh Edition. Mumbai: Bharatiya Vidya Bhavan, 2000

Chatterjee, Partha, ed. *State and Politics in India.* New Delhi: OUP, 1997.

Chaube, Shubanikinkar. *Constituent Assembly of India: Springboard of Revolution.* New Delhi: Manohar, 2000.

Chitaley V.V. and S. Appu Rao. *The Constitution of India: With Exhaustive, Analytical and Critical Commentaries,* vol. 5. Nagpur: All India Reporter, 1959.

Chopra, Pran. *Centre-State Relations and Co-operative Federalism.* New Delhi: Deep & Deep Publications, 1985.

Chopra, Pran, ed. *The Supreme Court Versus the Constitution: A Challenge to Federalism.* New Delhi: Sage Publications, 2006.

Dalvi, Santosh and Krishnan Venkatasubramanian. *An Introduction to Goods and Services Tax: The Biggest Tax Reform in India.* Gurgaon: Wolters Kluwer, 2016.

Das, Durga. *India: From Curzon to Nehru & After,* London: Collins, 1969.

Das, Durga, ed. *Sardar Patel's Correspondence 1945-50*, vol. 1. Ahmedabad: Navajivan Publishing House, 1971.

Das, Durga, ed. *Sardar Patel's Correspondence 1945-50, vol. 1, New Light on Kashmir.* Ahmedabad: Navajivan Publishing House, 1971.

Das, Durga, ed. *Sardar Patel's Correspondence 1945-50*, vol. 6. Ahmedabad: Navajivan Publishing House, 1973.

Das, Durga, ed. *Sardar Patel's Correspondence 1945-50*, vol. 7. Ahmedabad: Navajivan Publishing House, 1973.

Das, Durga, ed. *Sardar Patel's Correspondence 1945-50*, vol. 9. Ahmedabad: Navajivan Publishing House, 1974.

Das, Durga, ed. *Sardar Patel's Correspondence 1945-50*, vol. 10. Ahmedabad: Navajivan Publishing House, 1974.

Democracy and Federalism. Secunderabad: Andhra Pradesh Judicial Academy, 1995.

Deshmukh, C.D. *The Course of My Life.* New Delhi: Orient Longman, 1974.

Deshmukh, B.G. *A Cabinet Secretary Looks Back: From Poona to the Prime Minister's Office.* New Delhi: HarperCollins Publishers India, 2004.

Devasher, Tilak. *Pakistan: Courting The Abyss.* New Delhi: HarperCollins Publishers India, 2016.

Dhar, P.N. *Indira Gandhi, the 'Emergency', and Indian Democracy.* New Delhi: OUP, 2000.

Dhavan, Rajeev and Thomas Paul, eds. *Nehru and the Constitution.* New Delhi: Indian Law Institute & N. M. Tripathi Pvt. Ltd, 1992.

Diwan, Paras. *Abrogation of Forty-second Amendment: Does Our Constitution Need a Second Look.* New Delhi: Sterling Publishers, 1978.

Dreze, Jean and Amartya Sen. *An Uncertain Glory: India and its Contradictions.* New Delhi: Allen Lane/Penguin Books, 2013.

Dua, B.D. and M.P. Singh, eds. *Indian Federalism in the New Millennium.* New Delhi: Manohar, 2003.

Dulat, A.S. with Aditya Sinha. *Kashmir: The Vajpayee Years.* Noida:

HarperCollins Publishers India, 2015.

Frank, Katherine. *Indira: The Life of Indira Nehru Gandhi.* London: HarperCollins Publishers, 2001.

Gajendragadkar, P.B. *Secularism and the Constitution of India.* Bombay: Kashinath Trimbak Telang Endowment Lectures, University of Bombay, 1971.

Gandhi, Rajmohan. *Patel: A Life.* Ahmedabad: Navajivan Publishing House, 1990.

Gill, S.S. *The Dynasty: A Political Biography of the Premier Ruling Family of Modern India.* New Delhi: HarperCollins Publishers India, 1996.

Godbole, Madhav. *Unfinished Innings: Recollections and Reflections of a Civil Servant.* New Delhi: Orient Longman, 1996.

Godbole, Madhav. *The Holocaust of Indian Partition.* New Delhi: Rupa & Co., 2006.

Godbole, Madhav. *The Judiciary and Governance in India.* New Delhi: Rupa & Co., 2008.

Godbole, Madhav. *India's Parliamentary Democracy on Trial.* New Delhi: Rupa & Co., 2011.

Godbole, Madhav. *The God Who Failed: An Assessment of Jawaharlal Nehru's Leadership.* New Delhi: Rupa & Co., 2014.

Godbole, Madhav. *Good Governance Never on India's Radar.* New Delhi: Rupa & Co., 2014.

Godbole, Madhav. *Indira Gandhi: An Era of Constitutional Dictatorship.* New Delhi: Manas Publications, 2018.

Godbole, Madhav. *India's Governance: An Incisive Commentary on Some Burning Issues.* New Delhi: Konark Publishers, 2020.

Gopal, S. *Jawaharlal Nehru: An Anthology.* New Delhi: OUP, 1980.

Gopal, Niraja and Pratap Bhanu Mehta, eds. *Politics in India: The Oxford Companion.* New Delhi: OUP, 2010.

Gopal, S. and Uma Iyengar, eds. *The Essential Writings of Jawaharlal Nehru*, vols. I & II. New Delhi: OUP, 2003.

Gopal, Sarvapalli and Srinath Raghavan, eds. *Imperialists, Nationalists,*

Democrats: The Collected Essays. Ranikhet: Permanent Black, 2013.

Government of Maharashtra. *Statement by B.R. Ambedkar in Parliament in Explanation of his Resignation from the Cabinet*. 10 October 1951.

Government of India. *Independence and After: A collection of the more important speeches of Jawaharlal Nehru from September 1946 to May 1949*. New Delhi, 1949.

Government of India. *Report of the States Reorganisation Commission*. 1955.

Government of Madhya Pradesh. *Report of the Christian Missionary Activities Enquiry Committee (Justice Niyogi Committee)*, vol. I. 1956.

Government of India, Publications Division. *Jawaharlal Nehru's Speeches*, vol. 1. 1949.

Government of India, Publications Division. *Jawaharlal Nehru's Speeches*, vol. 2. 1954.

Government of India. *H.V. Pataskar Report on the Border Dispute between the States of Andhra Pradesh and Madras*. 1957.

Government of India, Ministry of Home Affairs. *Report of the Committee on Prevention of Corruption*. 1963.

Government of India. *Report on the Boundary Dispute between U.P. and Bihar*, vol. I. 1964.

Government of India. *Punjab Boundary Commission Report*. 1966.

Government of India. Report of the Study Team of Centre-State Relations, vol. II, Appendices. September 1967.

Government of India. *Report on the Haryana and Uttar Pradesh Boundary Dispute*. 1975.

Government of India, Ministry of Information and Broadcasting, Publications Division. *Democracy and Discipline: Speeches of Shrimati Indira Gandhi*. New Delhi, 1975.

Government of India. *Eighth and Concluding Report of the National Police Commission*. 1981.

Government of India. *Commission on Centre-State Relations Report*, Part I. New Delhi, 1988.

Government of India. *Commission on Centre-State Relations Report,* Part II. New Delhi, 1987.

Government of J&K, Information Department Publication. *Jammu & Kashmir 50 Years.* Srinagar, 1998.

Government of J&K. *Report of the Committee on Economic Reforms for Jammu and Kashmir* (Madhav Godbole Committee). 1998.

Government of India. *Reforming the National Security System: Recommendations of the Group of Ministers.* New Delhi, 2001.

Government of India. *Report of the National Commission to Review the Working of the Constitution,* vol. I. New Delhi: Universal Law Publishing Company, 2002.

Government of India, Planning Commission. *India Vision 2020.* New Delhi: Academic Foundation, 2004.

Government of India, Cabinet Secretariat. *Social, Economic and Educational Status of the Muslim Community of India: A Report (Justice Rajinder Sachar Report).* New Delhi, 2006.

Government of India, Ministry of Minority Affairs. *Report of the National Commission for Religious and Linguistic Minorities.* New Delhi, 2007.

Government of India, Second Administrative Reforms Commission. *Ethics in Governance,* Fourth Report. 2007.

Government of India, Second Administrative Reforms Commission. *Public Order,* Fifth Report. 2007.

Government of India, Second Administrative Reforms Commission. *Capacity Building for Conflict Resolution: Friction to Fusion,* Seventh Report. 2008.

Government of India, Second Administrative Reforms Commission. *Refurbishing of Personnel Administration: Scaling New Heights,* Tenth Report. 2008.

Government of India, Second Administrative Reforms Commission. *State and District Administration,* Fifteenth Report. 2009.

Government of India. *Commission on Centre-State Relations Report, Volume I – Evolution of Centre-State Relations in India (Justice M.M.*

Punchhi Commission Report). New Delhi, 2010.

Government of India. *Committee for Consultations on the Situation in Andhra Pradesh Report*. New Delhi, 2010.

Government of India. *Economic Survey 2016-17*. 2017.

Government of India. *Economic Survey 2019-20*. 2020.

Government of Tamil Nadu. *Report of the Centre-State Relations Inquiry Committee*. Madras, 1971.

Government of India, Ministry of Information & Broadcasting, Publications Division. *Democracy and Discipline: Speeches of Shrimati Indira Gandhi*. New Delhi, 1975.

Grigg, John, ed. *Nehru Memorial Lectures 1966-1991*. New Delhi: OUP, 1992.

Group of Interlocutors for J&K. *A New Compact with the People of J&K*, Final Report. New Delhi, 2010.

Grover, Verinder and Ranjana Arora, eds. *India 50 Years of Independence: Towards Independence – The Pre-1947 Period*. New Delhi: Deep & Deep Publications, 1977.

Grover, Verinder and Ranjana Arora, eds., *India 50 Years of Independence: To Independence And Beyond 1947-97*. New Delhi: Deep & Deep Publications, 1977.

Grover, Verinder, ed. *Gandhi and Politics in India*. New Delhi: Deep & Deep Publications, 1987.

Grover, Verinder and Ranjana Arora, ed. *Development of Politics and Government in India*, vol. 3. New Delhi: Deep & Deep Publications, 1994.

Grover, Verinder and Ranjana Arora, eds. *Development of Politics and Government in India*, vol. 4. New Delhi: Deep & Deep Publications, 1994.

Grover, Verinder, ed. *Federal System, Centre-State Relations and State Autonomy*. New Delhi: Deep & Deep Publications, 1997.

Guha, Ramachandra. *Makers of Modern India*. New Delhi: Penguin/ Viking, 2010.

Gundevia, Y.D. *The Testament of Sheikh Abdullah*, New Delhi: Palit & Palit, 1974.

Gundevia, Y.D. *Outside the Archives*. New Delhi: Orient Blackswan, 1994, Kindle edition, 2013.

Gupta, Sisir. *Kashmir: A Study in India-Pakistan Relations*. Bombay: Asia Publishing House, 1996.

Hidayatullah, Justice M. *A Judge's Miscellany*. Bombay: N.M. Tripathi, 1979.

Hodson, H.V. *The Great Divide: Britain-India-Pakistan*. Hutchinson of London, 1969.

Jaffrelot, Christophe. *The Hindu Nationalist Movement in India*. New Delhi: Viking Penguin Books India, 1996.

Jagmohan. *My Frozen Turbulence in Kashmir*, New Delhi: Allied Publishers, 1991.

Jain, M.P. *Indian Constitutional Law*, sixth edition. Nagpur: LexisNexis Butterworth's Wadhwa, 2010.

Jammu and Kashmir 50 Years. Information Department publication. Srinagar, 1998.

Jawaharlal Nehru Memorial Fund. *Selected Works of Jawaharlal Nehru*, Second Series, vol.14, Part I. New Delhi, 1992.

Jawaharlal Nehru Memorial Fund. *Selected Works of Jawaharlal Nehru*, Second Series, vol. 14, Part II. New Delhi, 1993.

Jawaharlal Nehru Memorial Fund. *Selected Works of Jawaharlal Nehru*, Second Series, vol. 15, Part I. New Delhi, 1993.

Jawaharlal Nehru Memorial Fund. *Selected Works of Jawaharlal Nehru*, Second Series, vol. 16, Part I. New Delhi, 1994.

Jawaharlal Nehru Memorial Fund. *Selected Works of Jawaharlal Nehru*, Second Series, vol. 17. New Delhi, 1995.

Jawaharlal Nehru Memorial Fund. *Selected Works of Jawaharlal Nehru*, Second Series, vol. 18. New Delhi, 1996.

Jawaharlal Nehru Memorial Fund. *Selected Works of Jawaharlal Nehru*, Second Series, vol. 19. New Delhi, 1996.

Jawaharlal Nehru Memorial Fund. *Selected Works of Jawaharlal Nehru,* Second Series, vol. 29. New Delhi, 2001.

Jhingran, Saral. *Secularism in India: A Reappraisal.* New Delhi: Har-Anand Publications, 1995.

Kapoor, Coomi. *The Emergency: A Personal History.* New Delhi: Penguin/ Viking, 2015.

Kashyap, Subhash C. *The Political System and Institution Building under Jawaharlal Nehru.* New Delhi: National Publishing House, 1990.

Kashyap, Subhash C., ed. *Reforming the Constitution.* New Delhi: UBS Publishers' Distributors, 1992.

Kashyap, Subhash C. *Delinking Religion and Politics.* New Delhi: Vimot Publishers, 1993.

Kashyap, Subhash C. *Our Constitution.* New Delhi: National Book Trust India, 1994.

Kashyap, Subhash C. *100 Best Parliamentary Speeches 1947-1997.* New Delhi: HarperCollins Publishers India, 1998.

Kashyap, Subhash C. *History of the Parliament of India,* vol. 1, Third Impression. Delhi: Shipra Publications, 2000.

Kashyap, Subhash C. *History of the Parliament of India,* vol. 2. Delhi: Shipra Publications, 1995.

Kashyap, Subhash C. *History of the Parliament of India,* vol. 3. Delhi: Shipra Publications, 1996.

Kashyap, Subhash C. *History of the Parliament of India,* vol. 4. Delhi: Shipra Publications, 1997.

Kashyap, Subhash C. *History of the Parliament of India,* vol. 5. Delhi: Shipra Publications, 1998.

Kashyap, Subhash C. *History of the Parliament of India,* vol. 6. Delhi: Shipra Publications, 2000.

Kashyap, Subhash C. *Blueprint of Political Reforms.* Delhi: Shipra Publications, 2003.

Kaul, T.N. *A Diplomat's Diary 1947-1999 – China, India and USA: The Tantalising Triangle.* New Delhi: Macmillan India, 2000.

Khan, Mohamed Raza. *What Price Freedom*. Madras: The Nuri Press, 1969.

Khosla, Madhav. *India's Founding Moment: The Constitution of a Most Surprising Democracy*. London: Harvard University Press, 2020.

Kishore, Pran. *Radio Kashmir and My Days in Broadcasting*. Pune: Sarhad, 2018.

Kohli, Atul. *Democracy and Discontent: India's Growing Crisis of Governability*. New York: Cambridge University Press, 1991.

Kohli, Atul, ed. *The Success of India's Democracy*. New York: Cambridge University Press, 2001.

Koithara, Verghese. *Crafting Peace in Kashmir Through A Realist Lens*. New Delhi: Sage Publications, 2004.

Kripalani, J.B. *My Times: An Autobiography*. New Delhi: Rupa & Co., 2004.

Krishna, Balraj. *Sardar Vallabhbhai Patel: India's Iron Man*. New Delhi: Rupa & Co., 2005.

Laxminath, A. *Basic Structure and Constitutional Amendments: Limitations and Justiciability*. New Delhi: Deep & Deep Publications, 2002.

Limaye, Madhu. *Cabinet Government in India*. New Delhi: Radiant Publishers, 1989.

Lok Sabha Secretariat. *Constituent Assembly Debates Official Report*, vol. VII, Book 2. New Delhi.

Lok Sabha Secretariat. *Constituent Assembly Debates Official Report, 30-7-1949 to 18-9-1949*, vol. IX. New Delhi, 2009.

Lok Sabha Secretariat. *Constituent Assembly Debates Official Report, 30-7-1949 to 18-9-1949*, vol. X. New Delhi, 2009.

Lok Sabha Secretariat. *Constituent Assembly Debates Official Report*, vols. X- XII, Book 5. 2009.

Mahanta, Prafulla Kumar. *The Tussle Between the Citizens and Foreigners in Assam*. New Delhi: Vikas Publishing House, 1986.

Malhotra, Iqbal Chand, and Maroof Raza, *Kashmir's Untold Story: Declassified*. New Delhi: Bloomsbury, 2019.

Menon, Meena. *Riots and After in Mumbai: Chronicles of Truth and*

Reconciliation. New Delhi: Sage Publications, 2012.

Menon, V.P. *The Story of the Integration of the Indian States.* Bombay: Orient Longman, 1956.

Menon, V.P. *Integration of the Indian States.* New Delhi: Orient Blackswan, 2014 edition.

Moily, M. Veerappa. *Unleashing India: Quest for Governance.* New Delhi: Mohan Law House, 2019.

Moon, Penderel, ed. *Wavell: The Viceroy's Journal.* Bombay: OUP, 1973.

Mukherjee, Rudrangshu. *The Great Speeches of Modern India.* New Delhi: Random House, 2007.

Mullik, B.N. *My Years with Nehru – Kashmir.* Bombay: Allied Publishers, 1971.

Munshi, K.M. *Pilgrimage to Freedom (1902-1950),* Indian Constitutional Documents, vol. I, second edition. Mumbai: Bharatiya Vidya Bhavan, 2012.

Munshi, K.M. *Pilgrimage to Freedom,* Indian Constitutional Documents, vol. II. Mumbai: Bharatiya Vidya Bhavan, 2013.

Namboodiripad, E.M.S. *The Frontline Years: Selected Articles.* New Delhi: Leftword Books, 2010.

Narasimhan, V.K. *Democracy Redeemed.* New Delhi: S. Chand & Co., 1977.

Narayan, Sathya, ed. *Selected Works of S.P. Sathe – Judicial Power and Processes,* vol. 2. New Delhi: OUP, 2015.

Nehru, B.K. *Nice Guys Finish Second.* New Delhi: Viking, 1997.

Noorani, A.G. *Constitutional Questions in India.* New Delhi: Oxford University Press, 2000.

Noorani, A.G. *Citizens' Rights, Judges and State Accountability.* New Delhi: OUP, 2002.

Noorani, A.G. *Article 370: A Constitutional History of Jammu and Kashmir.* New Delhi: OUP, 2011.

Noorani, A.G. *Jinnah and Tilak – Comrades in the Freedom Struggle.* Karachi: OUP, 2010.

Owen, Bennett Jones. *Pakistan: Eye of the Storm*. New Haven/London: Yale University Press, 2002.

Pandit, C.S. *End of an Era: The Rise and Fall of Indira Gandhi*. New Delhi: Allied Publishers, 1977.

Pal, Chandra. *Centre-State Relations and Co-operative Federalism*. New Delhi: Deep & Deep Publications, 1985.

Palkhivala, Nani A. *We, the Nation: The Lost Decades*. New Delhi: UBS Publishers' Distributors, 1994.

Pande, Ira, ed. *A Tangled Web: Jammu and Kashmir*. New Delhi: IIC Quarterly, Winter 2010 - Spring, 2011.

Parthasarathi G., ed. *Jawaharlal Nehru: Letters to Chief Ministers 1947-1964*, vols. 1-5. New Delhi: Jawaharlal Nehru Memorial Fund, 1985-1989.

Puniyani, Ram. *Communal Politics: Facts versus Myths*. New Delhi: Sage Publications, 2003.

Prasad, Rajendra. *Autobiography*. New Delhi: Penguin Books, 2010.

Ramesh, Jairam and Muhammad Ali Khan. *Legislating for Justice: The Making of the 2013 Land Acquisition Law*. New Delhi: OUP, 2015.

Ramesh, Jairam. *Old History New Geography: Bifurcating Andhra Pradesh*. New Delhi: Rupa & Co., 2016.

Rangarajan, C. and D.K. Srivastava. *Federalism and Fiscal Transfers in India*. New Delhi: OUP, 2011.

Rao, B. Shiva. *The Framing of India's Constitution: A Study*. Bombay: N.M. Tripathi, 1968.

Rao, Govinda M., and Nirvikar Singh. *Political Economy of Federalism in India*. New Delhi: Oxford University Press, 2005.

Rao, Justice K. Subba. *Some Constitutional Problems*. Bombay: University of Bombay, 1970.

Rau, B.N. *India's Constitution in the Making*. New Delhi: Orient Longman, 1960.

Sachar, Justice Rajinder. *In Pursuit of Justice: An Autobiography*. New Delhi: Rupa Publications, 2020.

Sahni, Sati. *Kashmir Underground.* New Delhi: Har-Anand Publications, 1999.

SarDesai, D.R. and Anand Mohan, eds. *The Legacy of Nehru: A Centennial Assessment.* New Delhi: Premila & Co. Publishers, 1992.

Sarila, Narendra Singh. *The Shadow of the Great Game: The Untold Story of India's Partition.* New Delhi: HarperCollins, 2005.

Sarkar, Bidyut, ed. *P.N. Haksar: Our Times and the Man.* New Delhi: Allied Publishers, 1989.

Seervai, H.M. *The Emergency, Future Safeguards and the Habeas Corpus Case: A Criticism.* Bombay: N. M. Tripathi, 1978.

Seervai, H.M. *Constitutional Law of India: A Critical Commentary,* fourth edition, vol. I. New Delhi: Universal Law Publishing, 1991.

Seervai, H.M. *Constitutional Law of India: A Critical Commentary,* fourth edition, vol. II. New Delhi: Universal Law Publishing, 1993.

Seervai, H.M. *Constitutional Law of India: A Critical Commentary,* fourth edition, vol. III. New Delhi: Universal Law Publishing, 1996.

Sen, Amartya. *The Argumentative Indian.* London: Allen Lane, 2005.

Setalvad, M.C. *Secularism: Patel Memorial Lectures.* New Delhi: Publications Division, Ministry of I&B, Government of India, 1967.

Setalvad, M.C. *My Life: Law and Other Things.* Bombay: N.M. Tripathi, 1970.

Setalvad, M.C. India: *Union and State Relations under the Indian Constitution.* Calcutta: Eastern Law House, 1974.

Shaban, Abdul, ed. *Lives of Muslims in India: Politics, Exclusion and Violence.* London: Rutledge, 2012.

Shankar, Kalyani. *Nixon, Indira and India: Politics and Beyond.* New Delhi: MacMillan Publishers India, 2010.

Shankar, V., ed., *Sardar Patel: Select Correspondence 1945-1950,* vol. 1 & 2. Ahmedabad: Navajivan Publishing House, 1977.

Sharma, G.S., ed. *Secularism: Its Implications for Law and Life in India.* Bombay: N. M. Tripathi, 1966.

Sharma, A.P. *Prelude to Indian Federalism: A Study of Division of Powers under the Acts of 1919 and 1935*. New Delhi: Sterling Publishers, 1976.

Sharma, S.K. *The Constitution of Jammu & Kashmir*. New Delhi: Universal Law Publishing, 2011.

Shourie, Arun. *Mrs. Gandhi's Second Reign*. New Delhi: Vikas Publishing House, 1983.

Shourie, Arun. *Religion in Politics*. New Delhi: Roli Books International, 1987.

Shourie, Arun, Swapan Dasgupta, Arun Jaitley, et al. eds. *The Ayodhya Reference: Supreme Court Judgment and Comments*. New Delhi: Voice of India, 1995.

Shourie, Arun. *Worshipping False Gods: Ambedkar and the Facts Which Have been Erased*. New Delhi: ASA, 1997.

Srivastava, C.P. *Lal Bahadur Shastri: A Life of Truth in Politics*. Delhi: OUP, 1996.

Singh, Tavleen. *Kashmir: A Tragedy of Errors*. New Delhi: Penguin Books, 1996.

Singh, Shriprakash. *Dr. Ambedkar on Minorities*. New Delhi: India First Foundation, 2005.

Sinha, Aditya. *Farooq Abdullah: Kashmir's Prodigal Son, A Biography*. New Delhi: UBS Publishers' Distributors, 1996.

Sinha, V.K., ed. *Secularism in India*. Bombay: Lalvani Publishing House, 1968.

Singh, Bhim. *Flames in Kashmir*. New Delhi: Har-Anand Publications, 1998.

Smith, Donald Eugene. *India As A Secular State*. Bombay: Princeton University Press and OUP, 1963.

Sorabjee, Soli J. *The Governor: Sage or Saboteur*. New Delhi: Roli Books International, 1985.

Sorabjee, Soli J. 'Freedom of Expression and the Indian Constitution', in Venkat Iyer, ed. *Constitutional Perspectives: Essays in Honour and Memory of H.M. Seervai*. New Delhi: Universal Law Publishing Company, 2001.

Subramanian, Arvind. *Of Counsel: The Challenges of the Modi-Jaitley Economy.* Gurgaon: Penguin Random House India, 2018.

Swaran Singh Committee Report, 1976.

Tahmankar, D.V. *Sardar Patel.* London: George Allen and Unwin, 1970.

Taseer, C. Bilquees. *The Kashmir of Sheikh Abdullah.* Srinagar: Gulshan Books, 2005.

Tumbe, Chinmay. *India Moving: A History of Migration.* New Delhi: Penguin/Viking, 2018.

Tully, Mark, and Zareer Masani. *From Raj to Rajiv: Forty Years of Indian Independence.* London: BBC Books, 1988.

Tyson, Geoffrey. *Nehru: The Years of Power.* New Delhi: UBS Publishers' Distributors, 1966.

Upadhyay, Devendra, ed. *The Handbook of Centre-State Relations in India.* New Delhi: Integrity Media, 2019.

Vijapur, Abdulrahim P., ed. *Dimensions of Federal Nation Building: Essays in Memory of Rasheeduddin Khan.* New Delhi: Manak Publications, 1998.

Vira, Dharma. *Memoirs of a Civil Servant.* New Delhi: Vikas Publishing House. 1975.

Vohra, Ranbir. *The Making of India: A Historical Survey.* London: M.E. Sharpe, 1997.

Wheare, K.C. *Federal Government.* London: OUP, 1956.

Wilkinson, Steven I, ed. *Religious Politics and Communal Violence: Critical Issues in Indian Politics.* New Delhi: OUP, 2005.

Articles

Agrawala, S.K. 'Jawaharlal Nehru and the Language Problem'. *Journal of Indian Law Institute* vol. 19 (January-March 1977).

Aggarwal, Dr K.K. 'One India: One Health Policy? *India Legal* (24 December 2018): pp. 32-33.

Ahmad, Salik. 'Go South, Young Man'. *Outlook* (30 July 2018): pp. 44-45.

Anand, Adarsh Sein. 'Kashmir's Accession to India'. *Journal of Indian Law Institute* vol. 6 (1964).

Badhwar, Inderjit. 'Changing Times, Letter from the Editor'. *India Legal* (21 May 2018): p. 3.

Bakshi, P.M. 'Higher Education and States'. *Journal of Indian Law Institute*, vol. 29 (1987).

Banerjee, Vikramjit & Sumeet Malik. 'Changing Perceptions of Secularism'. *7 SCC* [jour] (1998): 3.

Baxi, Upendra. 'A Constitutional Renaissance'. *The Indian Express* (16 July 2018).

Bhalla, Surjit. 'The fake news on GST'. *The Indian Express* (4 August 2018): p. 9.

Bhan, Ashok. 'Kashmiri Pandits demand commission of inquiry headed by retired Supreme Court judge', Legally Speaking. *The Sunday Guardian* (19 September 2020).

Bharatiya, V.P. 'Propagation of Religion: *Stainislaus v. State of M.P.'. Journal of Indian Law Institute,* vol. 19 (1977).

Bezbaruah, M.P. 'Anatomy of an anxiety'. *The Indian Express* (22 May 2018): p. 9.

Bidwai, Praful. 'Combating Muslim Exclusion'. *Frontline* (1 December 2006): pp. 106-8.

Breyer, Stephen. 'Does Federalism Make a Difference?' *Public Law* (Winter 1999).

Chidambaram, P. 'Across the Aisle: Will government wreck federalism'. *The Sunday Express* (15 April 2018): p. 12

Chatterjee, Dilip K. 'President's Rule and Union-State Relations in India'. *Journal of Constitutional and Parliamentary Studies,* vol. 14 (1980).

Debroy, Bibek. 'The anatomy of equity'. *The Indian Express* (11 April 2018): p. 9.

Debroy, Bibek. 'A case for deletion'. *The Indian Express* (10 October 2019): p. 11.

Deka, Kaushik. 'The Nowhere People: Assam and the citizenship register'. *India Today* (6 August 2018).

Deka, Kaushik. 'Native *Versus* Alien: Assam's Identity Crisis'. *India Today* (21 January 2019): p. 9.

Desai, Darshan. 'Leave!, This Land Isn't Your Home'. *Outlook* (22 October 2018): pp. 16-17.

Devidas, T. 'Indian Federalism—Half a Century of Error'. *The Lawyers Collective* (November 1997).

Dhavan, Rajeev. 'Engrafting the Ombudsman Idea on a Parliamentary Democracy—A comment on the Lokpal Bill, 1977'. *Journal of Indian Law Institute,* vol. 19 (July-September 1977).

Dhote, Yashwant and Mihir Srivastava. 'A Khaki Office'. *Outlook* (16 March 2015): p. 20.

Drabu, Haseeb A. 'If Article 35A is expended it will impinge on basic tenets of constitutional interpretation'. *The Indian Express,* New Delhi (30 March 2019): p. 8.

Gandhi, Rajmohan. 'Way forward in Kashmir'. *The Indian Express,* New Delhi (10 June 2019): p. 10.

Gehlot, N.S. 'Indian Federalism and the Problem of Law and Order'. *Journal of Indian Law Institute,* vol. 14 (1980).

Gill, Manohar Singh. 'When hope runs dry'. *The Indian Express* (16 March 2016): p. 10.

Godbole, Madhav. 'Federal Relations: Waiting for Godot?' *Financial Express* (27 June 1995): p. 6.

Godbole, Madhav. 'Report of the Constitution Review Commission: Some Reflections'. *Economic and Political Weekly* (28 September 2002).

Gogoi, Tarun. 'NRC our (Congress) baby.... don't try to make it Hindu or Muslim or Christian'. *The Indian Express* (1 August 2018): p. 7.

Gulati, Ashok. 'From Plate to Plough: A 1991 moment for agriculture'. *The Indian Express* (18 May 2020): p. 9.

Hasan, Zoya. 'The Dissident Citizen'. *India Today* (20 August 2018): pp. 48-50.

Hazarika, Sanjoy. 'Albatross Beyond The Chicken's Neck'. *Outlook* (19 August 2019): pp. 46-47.

Hingorani, Dr Aman. 'Genesis of the Kashmir issue does not lie in Article 370; solution doesn't lie in (removing) it'. *The Indian Express* (1 September 2019): p. 11.

Hooda, D.S. 'New target in the Valley'. *The Indian Express* (4 September 2018): p. 8.

Jacob, Alice. 'Centre-State Governmental Relations in the Indian Federal System'. *Journal of Indian Law Institute,* vol. 10 (1968).

Jacob, Alice and Rajeev Dhavan. 'The Dissolution Case: Politics at the Bar of the Supreme Court'. *Journal of Indian Law Institute,* vol. 19 (October-December 1977).

Jahagirdar, Justice R. A. 'Secularism in India: The Road Behind and the Road Ahead'. *The Radical Humanist* (December 2005).

Jahagirdar, Justice R. A. 'Secularism Revisited'. *The Radical Humanist* (February 2015).

Jahagirdar, Justice R. A. 'Secularism in India: The Inconclusive Debate'. *The Radical Humanist* (February 2016).

Janyala, Sreenivas. 'Chandrababu Naidu *versus* K. Chandrasekar Rao: What one has, the other wants'. *The India Express* (26 August 2015): p. 10.

Jain, M.P. 'Federalism in India'. *Journal of Indian Law Institute,* vol. 6 (1964).

Jain, M.P. 'Nehru and the Indian Federalism'. *Journal of Indian Law Institute,* vol. 19 (October-December 1977).

Jaffrelot, Christophe, and Sharik Laliwala. 'A new Other'. *The Indian Express* (22 October 2018): p. 8.

Jha, Shefali. 'Secularism in the Constituent Assembly Debates, 1946-1950'. *Economic and Political Weekly* (27 July 2002): pp. 3175-3180.

Jha, Prem Shankar. 'Experiments in Democracy'. *Outlook* (22 December 2014): pp. 68-69.

Khanna, Justice H.R. 'Supreme Court Judgment on Article 356'. *AIR [Journal] (1994).*

Khurshid, Salman. 'The Absent Helmsman'. *Outlook* (17 February 2020): pp. 41-44.

Mahmood, Tahir. 'From William Hunter to Rajinder Sachar'. *The Sunday Express* (19 November 2006): p. 6.

Malhotra, Inder. 'How a book was banned'. *The Indian Express* (14 December 2015): p. 11.

Markose, A.T. 'The Second Bhulabhai Desai Memorial Lecture on Inter-State Commerce and the Indian Constitution'. *Journal of Indian Law Institute,* vol. 14 (1980).

McWhinney, Edward. 'The Utility and Limits of Federalism in Contemporary Constitution-Making'. *Journal of Indian Law Institute,* vol. 4 (1962).

Mehta, Pratap Bhanu. 'The nuances of 35A'. *The Indian Express* (9 August 2018): p. 10.

Mehta, Pratap Bhanu. 'A blasphemous law: Using state power to enforce the sacred, Punjab's sacrilege law defiles the sacred, messes with secular'. *The Indian Express* (25 August 2018): p. 8.

Mehta, Pratap Bhanu. 'Covid lockdown is seen as a cover for Jammu and Kashmir'. *The Indian Express* (16 May 2020): p. 6.

Mishra, Navank Shekhar. 'How Free Is Free Speech?' *India Legal* (15 April 2016): pp. 60-61.

Mustafa, Faizan. 'Delhi power tussle: between the Supreme Court's lines'. *The Indian Express* (5 July 2018): p. 9.

Mustafa, Faizan. 'The US Report on Religious Freedom in India calls for Reflection'. *The Indian Express* (1 June 2020): p. 11.

Narayan, Jayaprakash. 'A Challenge to Indian Federalism'. *The Hindu* (28 October 2013).

Naqvi, Saba. 'Jack in The Pack: The Shiv Sena wants Muslims disenfranchised, shouldn't they be instead?' *Outlook* (27 April 2015): pp. 32-33.

Naqvi, Sadiq. 'Complex Case Of Goriya, Moriya, Oxomiya: Assam Set To Separate Indigenous Muslims From Migrants'. *Outlook* (24 February 2020): p. 22.

Nayak, Sajeev Kumar. 'Odia Pride Rising, Odisha to Get Own Anthem Soon'. *The Sunday Guardian* (15-21 July 2018): p. 6.

Noorani, A.G. 'How and Why Nehru and Abdullah Fell Out: Selected

Works of Jawaharlal Nehru.' *Economic and Political Weekly* (30 January 1999): pp. 268-272.

Noorani, A.G. 'Protecting Minority Rights'. *Economic and Political Weekly* (18 March 2000).

Noorani, A.G. 'The Legacy of 1953'. *Frontline* (16-29 August 2008).

Noorani, A.G. 'The Plague of Sedition' *Frontline* (13 March 2020): pp. 105-9.

Noorani, A.G. 'Why do riots erupt?' *Frontline* (27 March 2020): pp. 46-48.

Noronha, Rahul and Uday Mahurkar. 'Madhya Pradesh – Gujarat Water Wars'. *India Today* (5 March 2018): p. 30.

Quraishi, S.Y. 'Karnataka leftovers'. *The Indian Express* (7 June 2018): p. 10.

Rajoura, Sanjay. 'The Right to Offend'. *India Today* (20 August 2018): pp. 99-101.

Ramakrishnan, Venkatesh. 'Community on the margins'. *Frontline* (2-15 December 2006).

Raman, Sunder. 'From 42nd to 44th Constitutional Amendments: A Critical Evaluation'. *Journal of Indian Law Institute,* vol. 14 (1980).

Rangan, Pavithra S. 'In Cold Blood'. *Outlook* (6 April 2015): pp. 28-36.

Rao, P.S.N. 'Model Building Byelaws: Reforms rolled out, over to states now'. *The Indian Express* (2 April 2016).

Rao, M. Govinda. 'What the new GST should look like'. *The Live Mint* (19 November 2019).

Rao, M. Govinda. 'States' Loss of Fiscal Autonomy in a Centralised Federal System'. *The India Forum* (5 June 2020).

Rego, Stephen. 'Banning of Organisations: A Colonial Legacy'. *The Lawyers Collective* (January 1997): pp. 21-23.

Sabharwal, Manish. 'How knowing English helps'. *The Indian Express* (28 May 2018): p. 7.

Salam, Ziya Us. 'Mosques as target'. *Frontline* (27 March 2020): pp. 37-39.

Saraf, Pushp. 'Territory First or People?' *India Legal* (24 December 2018): pp. 40-41.

Sarila, Narendra. 'Kashmir & the Great Game', edit page. *Times of India* (14 August 2000).

Shariff, Abusaleh. 'Myth of Muslim growth'. *The Indian Express* (2 September 2015): p. 8.

Shariff, Abusaleh, 'Quota will help only rich Muslims'. *Outlook* (4 December 2006): p. 38.

'Should States have their own flags', OPED. *The Hindu* (9 February 2018).

Shriram, Ajay S. 'Creating the right "market connect" for boosting farm income'. *The Indian Express* (4 July 2019): p. 9.

Shunmugasundaram, Manuraj. 'Towards a southern brotherhood'. *The Indian Express* (12 April 2018): p. 11.

Singh, Tavleen. 'Now, win the peace'. *The Indian Express* (8 August 2019): p. 10.

Srikrishna, Justice B.N. 'Judicial Activism'. Lalit Doshi Memorial Lecture (2012).

Srinivasan, K. 'Wanted: More SC Benches in the Country'. *Legal Notes* (August 2019): pp. 6-7.

'Status of Policing in India Report 2019'. *Common Cause* (July-September 2019).

Subbarao, Duvvuri. 'Over to the states'. *The Indian Express* (18 November 2019): p. 8.

Sukumaran, Ajay. 'Drink to My Song with a Sedition Case'. *Outlook* (16 November 2015).

Sukumaran, Ajay. 'Playing With Pride In Polls'. *Outlook* (26 March 2018): pp. 28-29.

Srikrishna, Justice B.N. 'Secularism Under Our Constitution', Second V.M. Tarkunde Memorial Lecture. *The Radical Humanist* (October 2007).

Thapar, Karan. 'CAA Violates Secularism, Basic Structure of Constitution: A.P. Shah', Interview. *The Radical Humanist* (March 2020).

Tillin, Louise. 'A Southern Revolt'. *India Today* (30 April 2018): p. 18.

Talukdar, Sushanta. 'Assam: Defining Issue'. *Frontline* (27 March 2020): pp. 103-4.

Tambi, Nidhi. 'Data Tells Us India's State Assemblies Are Simply Not Working'. *The Wire* (7 March 2020).

Thakkar, Himanshu. 'A River Runs Through It'. *India Today* (5 March 2018): pp. 6-8.

Varadarajan, Siddharth. 'Gogoi as MP: A Matter of Great Public Importance Touching Upon the Independence of the Judiciary'. *The Wire* (18 March 2020).

Verma, Justice J.S. 'CBI had full autonomy but little will to pursue Hawala case'. *The Indian Express*, New Delhi (7 May 2004): p. 9.

Venkataramani, M.S. 'An elusive military relationship', Part I. *Frontline* (9 April 1999): pp. 66-70.

Venkataramani, M.S. 'An elusive military relationship', Part II. *Frontline* (23 April 1999): pp. 63-66.

Venkataramani, M.S. 'A mission without success'. *Frontline* (21 May 1999): pp. 61-65.

Yadav, Puneet Nicholas. 'No One Killed 426 People In Anti-Sikh Riots'. *Outlook* (10 February 2020): pp. 50-51.

Cases Cited

Attorney General of Ontario v. Canada Temperance Federation, The Privy Council (1946) A.C. 193: III Olmsted 424.

A.K. Gopalan v. State of Madras, AIR 1950 SC 27.

AIR 1979, SC 709 dated 4 May 1979.

Prem Nath Kaul v. The State of J&K, AIR 1959 Supreme Court 749.

Radhabai v. Bombay, (1955) Bom. 1039, ('55) A. B. 439, 442, 57 Bom. L. R. 827.

D.P. Joshi v. the State of Madhya Bharat ([1955] 1 SCR 1215; AIR 1955 SC 334).

State v. Narayandas Mangilal, (1957) Bom. 880, (58) A.B. 68, 59 Bom. L.R. 901.

Sampat Prakash v. The State of Jammu and Kashmir and another, AIR 1970 Supreme Court 1118.

Mohd. Maqbool Damnoo v. The State of J&K, AIR 1972 Supreme Court 963.

Maneka Gandhi v. Union of India, AIR 1978 SC 597.

Ebrahim Sulaiman Sait v. M.C. Mohammed and another, AIR 1980 SC 354.

Mohd. Ahmed Khan v. Shah Bano Begum and Others, (1985) 2 SCC 556.

S.R. Bommai v. Union of India, (1994) 3 SCC I.

Dr Ramesh Yeshwant Prabhoo v. Prabhakar Kashinath Kunte, (1996) SCC 130.

Manohar Joshi v. Nitin Bhau Rao Patil, (1996) 1 SCC 169.

Ramchandra K. Kapse v. Haribansh R. Singh, (1996) 1 SCC, 206.

Vineet Narain & Others v. Union of India & Another, 1997 (7) SCALE.

Prakash Singh and others v. GOI and others, writ petition (civil) No. 310 of 1996

Government (NCT of Delhi) v. Union of India and Another, (2018) 8 Supreme Court Cases 501.

Kuldip Nayar v. Union of India & Others, AIR SCW, 17 September 2006.

Automobile Transport (Rajasthan) Ltd v. State of Rajasthan, AIR 1962 SC 1406.

Shree Mahavir Oil Mills v. State of Jammu and Kashmir.

Newspapers and Periodicals

- *The Indian Express*
- *The Sunday Guardian*
- *The Tribune*
- *The Times of India*
- *The Hindu*
- *The Wire*
- *Rediff.com*
- *India Legal*
- *India Today*
- *Frontline*
- *Outlook*
- *The Radical Humanist*
- *Sakal*
- *Loksatta*
- *Dialogue Quarterly*
- *Common Cause*
- *Journal of Indian Law Institute*
- *Economic and Political Weekly*